Labour Law and Industrial Relations in Germany

Labour Law and Industrial Relations in Germany

Fifth Edition

Manfred Weiss
Marlene Schmidt
Daniel Hlava

This book was originally published as a monograph in the International Encyclopaedia of Laws/Labour Law and Industrial Relations.

Founding Editor: Roger Blanpain
General Editor: Frank Hendrickx
Volume Editor: Frank Hendrickx

Wolters Kluwer

Published by:
Kluwer Law International B.V.
PO Box 316
2400 AH Alphen aan den Rijn
The Netherlands
E-mail: international-sales@wolterskluwer.com
Website: lrus.wolterskluwer.com

Sold and distributed in North, Central and South America by:
Wolters Kluwer Legal & Regulatory U.S.
7201 McKinney Circle
Frederick, MD 21704
United States of America
Email: customer.service@wolterskluwer.com

Sold and distributed in all other countries by:
Air Business Subscriptions
Rockwood House
Haywards Heath
West Sussex
RH16 3DH
United Kingdom
Email: international-customerservice@wolterskluwer.com

ISBN 978-94-035-2460-3

e-Book: ISBN 978-94-035-2461-0
web-PDF: ISBN 978-94-035-2462-7

The Authors

Manfred Weiss, born in 1940, worked as Full Professor for Labour Law and Civil Law 1974 to 2008 (first at the University of Hamburg, Germany and since 1977 at the Goethe University in Frankfurt). Professor emeritus since 2008. He was Visiting Professor in many universities all over the world. From 2000 to 2003 he was President of ILERA. From 1998 to 2002, he was Deputy President of German Lawyers' Association (DJT). For many years, he has been a Consultant to the International Labour Organisation since 1980 and to the Commission of the EU. He received Honorary Doctorates from universities in Budapest/Hungary (2005), Lima/Peru (2006), Bordeaux/France (2011) and Potchefstroom/South Africa (2015). Awardee of the Labour Law Research Network (LLRN) for outstanding contribution to Labour Law (2015).

Marlene Schmidt, born in 1965, received her PhD from the Law School of Goethe University Frankfurt/Main. From 1996 to 2007, she served as an assistant professor at the Goethe University. From 2005 to 2007, she was an acting professor at the Martin Luther University Halle/Saale and at Dresden University of Technology, since 2009 an extraordinary professor at the Goethe University. Since 2009, she has been the managing partner of the law firm APITZSCH SCHMIDT KLEBE Rechtsanwälte, Frankfurt. Since 2017 Deputy Chairperson of the Arbitration Tribunal of the German Trade Union Confederation. During 2010–2020 Co-founder and Co-Director of the Hugo Sinzheimer Institute for Labour Law (HSI) of the Hans Böckler Foundation of the German Trade Union Confederation. From 2001 to 2010 she served as Managing Co-Editor of *The International Journal of Comparative Labour Law and Industrial Relations*. From 2010 to 2014 she was a Member of the Journal's Editorial Board.

The Authors

Daniel Hlava, born in 1986, received his PhD from the University of Kassel, Germany. Since 2014 he has been the expert for Social Law and European Labour Law at the Hugo Sinzheimer Institute for Labour and Social Security Law of the Hans Böckler Foundation in Frankfurt. Since 2017, he has been a lecturer at the European Academy of Labour (*Europäische Akadmie der Arbeit* – EAdA) at the Goethe University Frankfurt. Since 2018 he has been a lecturer at the University of Applied Sciences Fulda. He is the co-editor of *HSI Report on European Labour and Social Security Law.*

Table of Contents

Table of Contents

List of Abbreviations

AAG — *Aufwendungsausgleichsgesetz* (Act on Reimbursement of Employers' Expenses)
ADGB — *Allgemeiner Deutscher Gewerkschaftsbund* (General Federation of the German Unions)
AEntG — *Arbeitnehmerentsendegesetz* (Act on Obligatory Working Conditions in the Event of Posting of Employees)
AFG — *Arbeitsförderungsgesetz* (Act on Employment Promotion)
AG — *Aktiengesellschaft* (Public Limited Company)
AGBG — *Gesetz über Allgemeine Geschäftsbedingungen* (Act on General Terms and Conditions)
AGG — *Allgemeines Gleichbehandlungsgesetz* (General Act on Equal Treatment) 2006
ArbG — *Arbeitsgericht* (Labour Court of First Instance)
ArbGG — *Arbeitsgerichtsgesetz* (Act on Court Procedure in Labour Law Matters)
ArbNErfG — *Arbeitnehmererfindungsgesetz* (Act on Employee Inventions)
ArbSchG — *Arbeitsschutzgesetz* (Act on Occupational Health and Safety)
ArbStättV — *Arbeitsstättenverordnung* (Workplace Ordinance)
ArbVG — *Arbeitsvertragsgesetz* (Employment Contract Act)
ArbZG — *Arbeitszeitgesetz* (Act on Working Time)
AtG — *Altersteilzeitgesetz* (Act on Part-Time Retirement)
AÜG — *Arbeitnehmerüberlassungsgesetz* (Act on Commercial Temporary Work)
AufenthG — *Aufenthaltsgesetz* (Act on Residence)
BaFöG — *Berufsausbildungsförderungesetz* (Act Promoting Vocational Training)

List of Abbreviations

BAG	*Bundesarbeitsgericht* (Federal Labour Court)
BBiG	*Berufsbildungsgesetz* (Act on Vocational Training)
BDA	*Bundesvereinigung der Deutschen Arbeitgeberverbände* (German Confederation of Employers' Associations)
BEEG	*Bundeselterngeld- und Elternzeitgesetz* (Act on Parental Benefit and Parental Time)
BEM	*Betriebliches Eingliederungsmanagement* (Company Integration Management)
BErzGG	*Bundeserziehungsgeldgesetz* (Act on Benefits and Leave for Child Care)
BeschFG	*Beschäftigungsförderungsgesetz* (Act on the Improvement of Employment Opportunities) 1985
BetrAVG	*Gesetz zur Verbesserung der betrieblichen Altersversorgung* (Act on Occupational Pensions)
BetrVG	*Betriebsverfassungsgesetz* (Works Constitution Act) 1952 and 1972
BGB	*Bürgerliches Gesetzbuch* (Civil Code)
BGH	*Bundesgerichtshof* (Federal Court of Justice)
BPersVG	*Bundespersonalvertretungsgesetz* (Federal Act on Staff Representation) 1974
BRG	*Betriebsrätegesetz* (Works Councils' Act) 1920
BUrlG	*Bundesurlaubsgesetz* (Federal Act on Holidays)
CGB	*Christlicher Gewerkschaftsbund* (Federation of Christian Unions)
CDU	*Christlich-Demokratische Union* (Christian Democratic Union)
CJEU	Court of Justice of the European Union
CSU	*Christlich-Soziale Union* (Christian Social Union)
DAG	*Deutsche Angestellten-Gewerkschaft* (White-Collar Workers' Union)
Dbb	*Deutscher Beamtenbund* (German Federation of Career Public Servants)
DGB	*Deutscher Gewerkschaftsbund* (German Federation of Trade Unions)
DPG	*Deutsche Postgewerkschaft* (German Union of Post Employees)
DrittelbG	*Drittelbeteiligungsgesetz* (Act on One-third Participation)
EC	European Community
ECJ	European Court of Justice

EFZG	*Entgeltfortzahlungsgesetz* (Act on Continued Payment of Remuneration on Holidays and in Case of Sickness)
EU	European Union
FDP	*Freie Demokratische Partei* (Free Democratic Party)
FRG	Federal Republic of Germany
GdP	*Gewerkschaft der Polizei* (Police Union)
GDR	German Democratic Republic
GEW	*Gewerkschaft Erziehung und Wissenschaft* (Union of Education and Science)
GewO	*Gewerbeordnung* (Trade Act)
GG	*Grundgesetz* (Basic Law = Constitution)
GKG	*Gerichtskostengesetz* (Act on Court Fees)
HAG	*Heimarbeitsgesetz* (Act on Homework)
HBV	*Gewerkschaft Handel, Banken und Versicherungen* (Union of Trade, Banking, and Insurance)
HGB	*Handelsgesetzbuch* (Commercial Code)
IG	*Industriegewerkschaft* (Industrial Trade Union)
JArbSchG	*Jugendarbeitsschutzgesetz* (Act on Protection of Youth Employment)
KSchG	*Kündigungsschutzgesetz* (Act on Dismissal Protection)
KRG	*Kontrollratsgesetz* (Allied Control Council Act)
KUG	*Kurzarbeitergeld* (Short-Time Benefits)
LAG	*Landesarbeitsgericht* (*Land* Labour Court)
MiLoG	*Mindestlohngesetz* (Minimum Wage Act)
MindArbBedG	*Gesetz über Mindestarbeitsbedingungen* (Act on Minimum Working Conditions)
MitbestG	*Mitbestimmungsgesetz* (Co-Determination Act) 1976
Montan-MitbestG	*Montan-Mitbestimmungsgesetz* (Act on Co-Determination in the Mining, Iron and Steel Industry)
MuSchG	*Mutterschutzgesetz* (Act on Maternity Protection)
NachwG	*Nachweisgesetz* (Act on the Documentation of Employment Conditions)
NATO	North Atlantic Treaty Organization
ÖTV	*Gewerkschaft Öffentliche Dienste, Transport und Verkehr* (Union of Public Services, Transport, and Traffic)
SCE	European Cooperative Society
SE	*Societas Europaea* (European Society)

SchwbG	*Schwerbehindertengesetz* (Act on Disabled Persons)
SGB	*Sozialgesetzbuch* (Social Security Code)
SPD	*Sozialdemokratische Partei Deutschlands* (Social Democratic Party)
TDL	*Tarifgemeinschaft Deutscher Länder* (Association of German *Länder*)
TVG	*Tarifvertragsgesetz* (Act on Collective Agreements)
TV-L	*Tarifvertrag für den öffentlichen Dienst der Länder* (Collective Agreement for the Public Sector of the *Länder*)
TVöD	*Tarifvertrag für den öffentlichen Dienst* (Collective Agreement for the Public Sector)
TzBfG	*Gesetz über Teilzeitarbeit und befristete Arbeitsverträge* (Act on Part-Time Work and Fixed-Term Contracts)
UFO	*Unabhängige Flugbegleiterorganisation* (Independent Organization of Flight Attendants)
ULA	*Deutscher Führungskräfteverband* (Association of Executive Staff)
ver.di	*Vereinigte Dienstleistungsgewerkschaft* (United Union for Services)
VKA	*Verband kommunaler Arbeitgeber* (Association of Municipal Employers)
WRV	*Weimarer Reichsverfassung* (Weimar Constitution)

General Introduction

Chapter 1. General Background

§1. Geography

1. The Federal Republic of Germany (hereinafter Germany) covers an area of about 358,000 square kilometres.[1] Before the unification of 3 October 1990, the country was separated into the Federal Republic of Germany (FRG), covering an area of 248,630 square kilometres, and the German Democratic Republic (GDR), covering an area of 108,215 square kilometres. Germany is situated in central Europe. In the east and south-east the country borders on Poland and the newly formed Czech Republic; in the south its neighbours are Austria and Switzerland; in the west it borders on France, Belgium, Luxembourg and Netherlands, in the north on Denmark, the North Sea and the Baltic Sea.

2. Germany is a federal state. It now consists of sixteen *Länder* (states): Baden-Württemberg, Bavaria (Bayern), Berlin, Brandenburg, Bremen, Hamburg, Hesse (Hessen), Mecklenburg-Western Pomerania Mecklenburg-Vorpommern), Lower Saxony (Niedersachsen), North Rhine-Westphalia (Nordrhein-Westfalen), Rhineland-Palatinate (Rheinland-Pfalz), Saarland, Saxony (Sachsen), Saxony-Anhalt (Sachsen-Anhalt), Schleswig-Holstein and Thuringia (Thüringen). The *Länder*, whose present structure can only be explained historically, differ very much in size, Bavaria with 70,551 square kilometres being the largest, and Bremen with 404 square kilometres being the smallest.

§2. Population

3. When Germany was unified on 3 October 1990, it had a population of 79.67 million as a whole: 63.56 million in the old FRG and 16.11 million in the former GDR. In the meantime, the population has increased to more than 80 million. At the end of 2017 Germany had 82.79 million inhabitants.[2] The increase is almost exclusively due to continuing migration into the country. After a peak in the immigration surplus amounting to over a million persons in 1990 (1991: 602,523, 1992: 782,071), and due to further legal restrictions put in place in 1992, the number has

1. Statistisches Bundesamt (ed.), *Statistisches Jahrbuch 2019* (Wiesbaden), tab. 2.1.1.
2. *Ibid.*, tab. 2.1.1.

been dramatically decreasing ever since. In 2005 the immigration surplus amounted to only 72,963 persons.[3] In spite of the cut in immigration, the population has been slowly but steadily increasing for quite a while: from 80,974,000 in 1992 to 82,440,000 in 2001. Since then, however, the population stayed more or less the same. In 2005 it amounted to 82,437,000 persons and in 2017 to 82,792,000 persons.[4] There were about 42 million females and 40.8 male inhabitants.

4. Population density differs considerably across the country, the highest being in and around large cities. This explains why the size of the population in the different *Länder* does not necessarily correspond with the size of the respective areas. To quote a few examples: Bavaria with its 70,551 square kilometres has a population of only approx. 13 million whereas Berlin with only 881 square kilometres has a population of 3.61 million almost a quarter of the population of Bavaria; Mecklenburg-Western Pomerania with its 23,170 square kilometres has a population of only 1.61 million whereas the Saarland with only 2,570 square kilometres has a population of approximately 1 million, more than half of the number of people living in Mecklenburg-Western Pomerania. Population density is the highest in some urban areas in North Rhine-Westphalia. But there are also areas with an extremely low density.[5]

5. While the vast majority of the 'indigenous' population, is, linguistically speaking, German, small Danish and Frisian minorities can be found in the north; Sorbian, a Slavic language, is spoken by approximately 100,000 citizens in the east. Far more important for the cultural composition of the population than these minorities is, however, the already mentioned immigration into Germany. An important aspect of immigration in recent years, as it will continue to be in the future, has been the 'return' of millions of ethnic Germans from Eastern Europe, mainly from the former Soviet Union and Romania, whose forefathers emigrated there a very long time ago. These people are not affected by the new restrictive immigration laws. In 2018 among the 'foreigners', in a strict sense, the following were the most prominent national groups: 1,476,410 Turkish nationals, 860,145 Polish nationals, 745,645 nationals from Syria, 696,275 Romania nationals and 643,530 Italian nationals.[6]

§3. Political System

6. In 1871 the German Reich was founded as a constitutional monarchy. This political system lasted until the end of the First World War. Later the first democratic and parliamentary republic was established, the Weimar Republic, named

3. Statistisches Bundesamt (ed.), *Statistisches Jahrbuch 2007,* tab. 2.36.
4. Statistisches Bundesamt (ed.), *Statistisches Jahrbuch 2019*, tab. 2.1.2.
5. *Ibid.*, tab. 2.1.4.
6. *Ibid.*, tab. 2.3.4.

after the city where the assembly which was to draft the Constitution met. Democratic developments were interrupted in 1933 by the Nazi state which was overthrown in 1945. Germany lost large territories – mainly in the east to Poland and the former Soviet Union – and the remainder was divided by the allies into an American, a British, a French and a Soviet zone of occupation, in which the occupying powers exercised governmental authority.

7. In 1949, the three western zones were joined to form the FRG, a parliamentary, federal, republican democracy. In the eastern zone the former Soviet Union established the GDR, a communist totalitarian state. Over the years, the division of Germany became more and more intense. The border between the two German states was one of the most heavily guarded borders in the world. Attempts to cross it legally were extremely difficult from west to east and almost impossible in the other direction. This explains why the population in the two states did not have access to substantial information regarding the real situation in the other part.

8. At the beginning of the 1970s, the relations between the two German states as well as the situation of GDR citizens was considerably improved by the new *Ostpolitik* instituted by Chancellor Willy Brandt. Nevertheless, nobody believed that these extremely different political, social and economic systems would converge within the century. However, the total breakdown of the former Soviet bloc brought down the Berlin Wall and the German frontier as a whole. This led to the unification of the two German states on 3 October 1990, when the former GDR joined the FRG. The chance – if, indeed, it ever existed – to frame a new constitution which drew on the political and social experiences of both east and west, was not utilized. In the Unification Treaty of 31 August 1990, the GDR – with a few minor reservations – accepted the FRG's political, economic and legal system.

9. The capital of the old FRG was Bonn, while the capital of the former GDR was East Berlin. The capital of the new Germany is Berlin. In September 1999, the transfer of Parliament and of the government from Bonn to Berlin was accomplished.

10. According to the Basic Law-Constitution (*Grundgesetz*– GG) of 23 May 1949, the German constitutional system is characterized as follows. It is a democratic, parliamentary and Federal Republic, based on the rule of law and on the principle of welfare improvement (Article 20 GG). It is the latter principle especially which plays a significant role in the discussion of labour law and of social security law. It is important to the authorities of the federal state to safeguard the weaker groups by its policy. According to the GG, the sixteen *Länder* are in charge of all legislative and administrative matters not reserved for the Federal Republic. Since the powers expressly and implicitly granted by the GG are wide-ranging, the centre of power lies with the Federal Republic. Only in the areas of internal security, education, science and mass media, do the *Länder* retain decisive powers. In most other important areas they only have the duty to execute decisions and rules passed by the Federal Republic. This is especially true for labour law and social security law.

11. On a federal level, legislative power is primarily vested with the Federal Parliament (*Bundestag*). Its members are elected every four years. At the moment, the Federal Parliament has 709 members, but there are currently discussions to reduce the number of parliamentarians. There is a second legislative body representing the federal structure of the Federal Republic, the Federal Council (*Bundesrat*). It consists of the members of the governments of the different *Länder*, thereby representing their interests. Laws are passed by the Federal Parliament, but in matters in which the *Länder* have specific interests the consent of the Federal Council is required. Presently, the Federal Council consists of sixty-nine members, the four biggest *Länder* being represented by six members (Baden-Württemberg, Bavaria, Lower Saxony and North Rhine-Westphalia), the medium-sized *Länder* represented by five members (Hesse) or four members respectively (Berlin, Brandenburg, Rheinland-Palatinate, Saxony, Saxony-Anhalt, Schleswig-Holstein and Thuringia), and the small *Länder* only by three members (Bremen, Hamburg, Mecklenburg-Western Pomerania and Saarland). The decisive criterion for this distribution is not size of area but number of inhabitants.

12. The Federal Chancellor (*Bundeskanzler*) is elected by the Federal Parliament on proposal of the Federal President (*Bundespräsident*). Due to the experience gained of the Weimar Republic, the Constitution grants him or her a very strong position: the Chancellor chairs the government, and has the authority to set government policy. All ministers are bound by his or her decisions on broad, fundamental issues of policy, and s/he can also decide specific questions of particular importance. In addition, the Chancellor can only be removed from office by Parliament if, at the same time, a successor is elected. Hence, it is not enough that a majority wants him or her to leave office; there also has to be a majority for a new Chancellor.

13. The Federal President (*Bundespräsident*) has mainly representative functions. S/he is elected for five years by a separate body, called the Federal Assembly (*Bundesversammlung*), which consists of the members of the Federal Parliament and an equal number of members elected by the parliaments of the different *Länder*. The members of this second category are thus not necessarily members of the legislature. The Federal President can be re-elected only once. Since the beginning of 1994, the Federal President has been based in Berlin.

14. The Federal Constitutional Court (*Bundesverfassungsgericht*), seated in Karlsruhe, has the competence to verify the compatibility of legislative acts as well as the compatibility of court decisions of other courts with the Constitution. It is also the controlling body in cases where one body of the constitutional power structure violates its competences *vis-à-vis* another. The Federal Constitutional Court consists of two chambers (Senate), each composed of eight judges. Half of the judges of the Federal Constitutional Court are elected by the Federal Parliament, half are elected by the Federal Council. Their term of office is twelve years; re-election is not possible.

15. In order to be represented in the Federal Parliament a political party must obtain in an election at least 5% of the votes. This hurdle again is a consequence of experience in the Weimar Republic, when too many small parties made it difficult to obtain an effective majority in Parliament. Presently, six parties are represented in the Federal Parliament. The result of the last election in 2017 was as follows: Christian Democratic Union (*Christlich-Demokratische Union* – CDU) and its Bavarian sister party, Christian Social Union (*Christlich-Soziale Union* – CSU), forming a joint parliamentary group with 246 parliamentarians (33%), the Social Democratic Party (*Sozialdemokratische Partei Deutschlands* – SPD) with 152 parliamentarians (20.5%), the Alternative for Germany (AfD) with 94 parliamentarians (12.6%), the Free Democratic Party (*Freie Demokratische Partei* – FDP) with 80 parliamentarians (10.7%), Die Linke with 69 parliamentarians (9.2%) and Federation 90/The Greens having 67 parliamentarians (8.9%). There are presently six Members of Parliament belonging to none of the parliamentary groups. Since September 2005–2009 and since 2013 again Germany has been governed by a so-called big coalition between the three largest parties CDU/CSU and SPD under Chancellor Angela Merkel. The big coalition succeeded a coalition of SPD and Federation 90/The Greens led by Gerhard Schröder (1998–2005) and a government coalition of CDU/CSU and FDP under Chancellor Helmuth Kohl (1982–1996). From 2009 to 2013 Chancellor Merkel also led a coalition of CDU/CSU and FDP.

16. The judiciary is independent of the legislature and the administrative branches of government. Separation of state powers is a basic principle of the Federal Constitution. The vast majority of cases are handled by the *Land* courts. Federal courts are only courts of last resort.

17. Germany is a member of many supranational organizations, such as the European Union (EU), the European Council, the United Nations (UN), the International Labour Organization, the Organization for Economic Cooperation and Development and the North Atlantic Treaty Organization (NATO).

§4. Economy and Labour Market

18. The basic feature of the German economy is still the contrast between the economy of the 'old' FRG and the economy in the territory of the former GDR, the so-called new *Länder*. The old FRG, sponsored by the Western allies, grew into one of the economically most prosperous Western democracies. On the contrary, the former GDR followed a system of a strict centrally planned economy. After the fall of the Berlin Wall and the introduction of a free market economy almost overnight, the former GDR, whose economy had already been on a much lower level than that of the old FRG, suffered severe economic setbacks. The process of transforming the planned economy into a functioning market economy has proved to be a big challenge.

19. Privatization of the East German economy was more difficult than expected.[7] First, there was uncertainty as to whether, and to what extent, existing companies could be rescued and privatized, or whether they had to be closed down. In order to decide this crucial question, a huge bureaucratic body, the so-called *Treuhandanstalt* (privatization agency), was established (*see* paragraph 65). As of 1 July 1990, the day of the currency change, all state-owned enterprises were converted into private limited companies and stock companies, the shares of which were held by the Trust Agency. Its most important task was to privatize the assigned enterprises. Before privatization could take place, however, each industrial unit had to be evaluated and the necessary rescue measures had to be determined. This bureaucratic process was, by its very nature, extremely complicated. As a consequence, it led to significant delays in restructuring.

20. Furthermore, there were serious obstacles to effective investment in the economy of the former GDR. First, its infrastructure was in a desperate shape. The transport system did not meet the needs of a modern economy. The telecommunication system was functioning only to a marginal extent. The energy supply system had to be totally reorganized. Air pollution as well as land contamination had to be dramatically reduced. However, due to very significant support mainly stemming from the federal budget, much progress in improving this infrastructure has been made. A second obstacle to quick investment was the unclear legal position concerning property. The Unification Treaty entitled former owners to claim ownership if they could provide evidence that they were expropriated in an unjustified way in the territory of the former GDR after 1949. More than one million such claims were filed. They had to be handled by an administration which itself was in the process of reorganization, thus functioning under great difficulties. Sporadic records of property transactions thus exacerbated the problems. In view of the uncertainty of the question of ownership, investors, of course, were hesitant. The principle that expropriated owners should be given back their former property has therefore been modified by several legislative acts, making it easier for investors to acquire a secure property position. At the present time, these obstacles to the flow of investment have been more or less overcome and play only a marginal role.

21. The main feature of the German economy is its strong export position. At the same time, however, many goods are imported, among which are a high quantity of raw materials, because Germany lacks many essential natural resources. While in 1950 in the old FRG imports still exceeded exports (DM 11,374 billion compared to 8.326 billion DM), the relationship was already reversed by 1960 (DM 47,946 billion exports and only DM 42,723 billion imports). This relationship has remained more or less stable after unification. In 2018 Germany exported goods and services for EUR 1,318 billion, whereas imports amounted to EUR 1,090 billion, leaving a difference of EUR 228 billion.[8]

---

7. *Cf. also* M. Schmidt, *Legal Aspects of Privatisation in Germany: The Determinants of a Decision to Privatise under Constitutional Law and EC Law and the Problems Arising from Privatisation for Labour Law*, J. S. Afr. L., 478–500 (2002).
8. *Statistisches Jahrbuch 2019*, tab. 16.1.

22. Agriculture, forestry and fishing play only a marginal role in today's Germany. Whereas once in the old FRG 24.1% of the working population were employed in this primary sector, the figure is now only more or less 1% to 2%. The more important trend, however, is the shift from manufacturing to services. For a long time the big majority of the working population was employed in manufacturing, and now the majority is employed in services. The trend can be shown by taking the figures for 1991 and 2018:[9]

Sector of economy	1991	2018
Primary sector (million)	1,174	617
Manufacturing (million)	13,856	10,875
Service (million)	23,760	33,349

23. In the former territory of the FRG, the workforce increased from 25.5 million in 1985 to about 29.5 million in 1992. In the same period the rate of unemployment fell from 9.3% to 6.6%. In the meantime, the size of the workforce in Western Germany – 2018: 36,818 million – has significantly increased and the rate of unemployment decreases permanently (from 9.1% in 2006 to 4.8% in 2018).[10] In the territory of the former GDR, the size of the original workforce of about 9.8 million has been drastically reduced. In 1992, the workforce amounted to only a little more than 5 million and the unemployment rate officially ranged around 17%. Six years later, the workforce has increased again to 6.54 million, and the unemployment rate has risen to 19.5%. In 2018 the same figures in Eastern Germany amount to 8,021 million and 6.9% (2006: 17.3%).[11] In 2018, in Germany as a whole 2,340 million people were unemployed (unemployment rate 5.2%) – 1,759 million in the territory of the old FRG, and 581 million in the territory of the former GDR.[12] In addition, 26.8% of the workforce were employed on short-time work.[13]

24. The composition of the unemployed indicates the trends much better than the absolute figures. In 2018, 83.3% of unemployed were Germans and 26.7% were foreigners,[14] which implies an over-representation of foreigners. Only 9% of the unemployed are below 25 years of age.[15] The biggest age group is between 25 and 49 (about 57.3%). The proportion of those above the age of 50 still hovers at about 33.7%, although this figure is very misleading: many who had to leave work in this age group are in pre-retirement schemes and therefore do not show up as unemployed.

9. *Ibid.*, tab. 13.2.
10. Bundesagentur für Arbeit, *Der Arbeitsmarkt in Deutschland 2018* (Nuremberg), tab. IV.A.1.
11. *Ibid.*, tab. IV.A.1.
12. *Ibid.*, tab. IV.A.1.
13. *Ibid.*, tab. IV.B.9b.
14. *Ibid.*, tab. IV.C.1a.
15. *Ibid.*, tab. IV.G.18.

25. In 1950, in the old FRG about 15% of the working population were self-employed and another 15% were participating family members. Both figures fell drastically. In 2006, both groups together amounted to slightly above 9.4% (2018: 9.22% in the old FRG, 10.26% in the former GDR). That means that approx. 90.6% of the working population are employees (inclusive 4.48% civil servants).[16] In 1992, about 6.7 million people were employed in the public sector. Since that time, however, many privatizations have taken place. Consequently, the number of persons employed in the public sector has decreased to 4,802.9 million by 2018.[17]

26. In the old FRG the share of men between 15 and 65 years of age who were gainfully employed was always significantly higher than the share of women (in 1990 83% of men compared to 59% of women). This was different in the former GDR: there, about 82% of the women and 90% of men of active working age were employed. In the meantime, the trend in the former GDR is the same as it always was in the old FRG: the level of female employment in the territory of the former GDR has dramatically decreased. In 2018 in Germany as a whole 82.9% of the men and 74.3% of women between 15 and 65 years of age were gainfully employed.[18]

27. The formal qualification of the working population in both parts of Germany always was and still is quite high. However, it has to be stressed that the qualifications acquired in the former GDR can only be used to a limited extent in the context of the restructured economy and administration.

28. Even though the gap of working conditions between west and east is decreasing, it is still significant. For example, in 2018 in the territory of the old FRG the average monthly gross wage of all employees employed in manufacturing industries (including mining and construction) and trade, credit and insurance industries was EUR 3,994 (4,205 for men and 3,495 for women). At the same time, the same figure amounted to EUR 3,150 (3,187 for men and 3,081 for women) in the territory of the former GDR.[19] Sixteen years after reunification wages in the former GDR still amount only to 78.8% of wages in the old FRG.

16. Own calculations based on Bundesagentur für Arbeit, *Der Arbeitsmarkt in Deutschland 2018*, tab. IV.B.1.
17. *Statistisches Jahrbuch 2019,* tab. 13.4.
18. Bundesagentur für Arbeit, *Der Arbeitsmarkt in Deutschland 2018*, tab. IV.A.5.
19. *Statistisches Jahrbuch 2019,* tab. 14.1.2.

Chapter 2. Definitions and Notions

§1. Labour Law

29. In Germany labour law is understood to be the rules which are applicable to the employment relationship and which structure the collective relationship between capital and labour. As far as the employment relationship is concerned, labour law is only applicable to relationships based on private contract. Thus, an important group of the workforce is excluded from labour law, e.g., the career public servants in the strict sense of this notion (*Beamte*). The relationship between career public servants and the state is not a private contractual relationship but is defined by, and based on, public law. This is why the law of career public servants (*Beamtenrecht*) is considered to be a special section of public law. Their rights and duties as well as their working conditions are not determined by individual or by collective agreements but by acts passed by the legislative bodies of the Federal Republic and of the *Länder*. Disputes concerning career public servants are not settled by labour courts but by administrative courts. The exclusion of career public servants from labour law, however, does not mean that labour law does not cover the public service as a whole. There are not only career public servants, but also blue- and white-collar workers employed in public service. These public employees are ordinary employees with a normal contractual employment relationship and are therefore covered by labour law.

§2. Individual Labour Law

30. Individual labour law is focused on the individual employment relationship. It covers the rules on how a labour contract is concluded, what rights and duties the parties have in such a contractual relationship, how far the parties can dispose of these rights and duties by negotiating alternative clauses and, finally, how a labour contract can be terminated. In addition, it covers all the laws protecting individual employees, thereby setting minimum standards, which the parties to the individual contract cannot fall below. It is a significant feature of labour law that the legal protection of individual employees by minimum laws is very elaborate.

§3. Collective Labour Law

31. Collective labour law is focused on the structures of industrial relations. It defines and regulates who can be an actor on this scene, these actors' rights and duties, and how their activities and agreements affect the individual employment relationship. Collective labour law is thus composed of four main parts: the law on collective bargaining, including the law on trade unions and employers' associations; the law on industrial conflict; the law on employee representation by works councils; and the law on employee representation on the supervisory board of large companies. As far as the law on employee representation by works councils is concerned it should be pointed out that in this area there is the most significant difference between collective labour law in the private sector and collective labour law in the public sector. Whereas in the private sector the applicable law is the Works Constitution Act (*Betriebsverfassungsgesetz* – BetrVG) of 1952, fundamentally amended in 1972, the public sector is covered by the Federal Staff Representation Act (*Bundespersonalvertretungsgesetz* – BPersVG) of 1955, amended in 1974 and by the different and differing *Land* Staff Representation Acts. It is necessary to mention that career public servants, who are generally excluded from labour law, nevertheless play a certain role in the structure of the different BPersVG.

§4. Relationship Between Individual and Collective Labour Law

32. It would be a misconception to treat individual labour law and collective labour law as separate entities as they are closely related. What the working conditions in an individual employment relationship really are can only be evaluated if both collective and individual labour law are taken into consideration at the same time. The individual contract, the protective laws, the collective agreement, the works agreement concluded between works council and employer cannot be seen as isolated factors but must be seen as parts of a whole. Since in German labour law the powers of the individual parties to the labour contract are in many ways limited and shaped by the involvement of works council, it is obvious that individual labour law cannot even be described without taking into account the role of the works council. This is why in the section on individual labour law reference will quite often be made to the works council whose structure will be explained later in the part on collective labour law. Thus, some repetition will be inevitable. Since the area left to individual labour law can only be evaluated in view of the scope of collective labour law it would, at least from the point of view of German labour law, have been more appropriate to start with the latter instead of the former. Nevertheless, in order not to disturb the homogeneous structure of the *Encyclopaedia*, the suggested sequence of subjects is followed – but the reader is urged to keep in mind at all times the indicated relationship.

§5. Social Security Law

33. The main sections of German social security law are the acts dealing with social insurance, codified in the Social Security Code (*Sozialgesetzbuch* – SGB). The law on social insurance covers five important systems: health insurance (*Krankenversicherung* – SGB V), long-term care insurance (*Pflegeversicherung* – SGB XI), work accident insurance (*Unfallversicherung* – SGB VII), the statutory pension scheme (*Rentenversicherung* – SGB VI) including insurance for partial and full reduction in earning capacity and unemployment insurance (*Arbeitslosenversicherung* – SGB III). Most of these systems have a long tradition. The oldest system is health insurance. The Act on Health Insurance was first passed in 1883, followed by the Act on Work Accidents Insurance of 1884, and the Act on Retirement and Occupational Disability Insurance of 1889. All these acts were combined under one single Act in 1911. The statutory system of unemployment insurance was introduced in 1927. The most recent social security insurance system is long-term care insurance, which became effective in the beginning of 1995. In addition to this extensive statutory systems of social insurance means-tested unemployment benefits (*Grundsicherung für Arbeitsuchende – Arbeitslosengeld II*), regulated in SGB II, and social assistance (*Sozialhilfe*), formerly regulated by the Federal Act on Social Assistance, today integrated into the SGB as SGB XII, guarantee everybody living in Germany a minimum economic standard. The rehabilitation and participation of people with disabilities (*Rehabilitation und Teilhabe von Menschen mit Behinderungen*) is regulated in the SGB IX. Part 3 of the SGB IX also contains provisions for severely disabled persons that are relevant to employment relationships.

34. It is quite evident that social insurance law and labour law in particular are closely interrelated, and it is also evident that these parts of law are becoming increasingly important. The longer life expectancy grows, the more important the problems of the system of statutory retirement pension become. The higher the unemployment rate climbs, the more important the problem of unemployment insurance becomes.[20] In spite of this close interrelationship, social security law in Germany is strictly separated from labour law, and is understood to be a part of public law. Disputes arising in the field of social security are not settled by labour courts or administrative courts, but by special courts called social security courts (*Sozialgerichte*).

20. For more details on the relationship between labour and social law, *see* D. Hlava in Deinert, Heuschmid, Zwanziger (ed.), *Handbuch Arbeitsrecht*, 10th edition, Frankfurt/Main 2019, § 19 Verhältnis zwischen Arbeits- und Sozialrecht.

Chapter 3. Historical Background

§1. The Origins

35. The history of today's labour law can only be understood if the era before the founding of the German Reich in 1871 is included. It has to be considered that in Germany industrialization started much later than, for example, in Great Britain. In 1848 only 5.5% of the population above 14 years of age was working in factories and in mining industries, the remainder still working in agriculture or occupied in handicrafts. The prevailing rule at that time was individual freedom of contract. Nevertheless, in spite of the fact that workers lacked any organization and had no power whatsoever, there were already some signs of protective law in order to eliminate the worst abuses. Thus, by a law promulgated in Prussia in 1839, employment of children under 9 years of age was forbidden and employment of children between 9 and 16 years of age was restricted.

36. In spite of the fact that there was no freedom of association and that any association of workers without permission of the public authorities was subject to penal sanction, the origins of the German labour movement date back to the middle of the nineteenth century. After an initial period, between 1848 and 1854, the General German Workers' Association (*Allgemeiner Deutscher Arbeiterverein*) was founded in 1863. Its main goal was to promote workers' interests by giving everybody the right to vote. This clearly shows that this association, led by Lassalle, was in fact no trade union but a political party. In 1869, the second German Workers' Party was founded and led by Bebel and Liebknecht. In 1875 both parties were unified. This date is taken as the date of birth of the still existing Social Democratic Party (SPD). Even though these first organizations of workers were in fact political parties, they must be considered as the initial step to the most important trade union movement in German history, the so-called free unions or socialist unions. Free unions could not start their activities before 1869, when the Trade Act (*Gewerbeordnung* – GewO) for the Federation of Northern German Countries, eliminated, at least to a certain extent, the ban on freedom of association. In the same year another trade union movement was founded by Hirsch and Duncker. Unlike the socialist unions, these unions in principle accepted the capitalist structure of the economy and tried to strengthen workers' power by combining their force in the negotiation of working conditions. The ideological orientation of this movement was liberal. Thus, even before the German Reich was founded in 1871, two competing union movements already existed.

§2. Between Tolerance and Repression

37. While the liberal section of the labour movement was considered to integrate the workforce into society, the socialist unions were considered by the government to be a danger to the system. That is why, in 1878, an Act was promulgated strictly banning socialist trade unions (*Sozialistengesetz*). This Act, however, turned out to be an important element in strengthening the socialist labour movement. The socialist unions survived by clandestine activity and the Social Democratic Party became more successful from election to election. Therefore, this Act was repealed in 1890.

38. It was not on the initiative of the labour movement, but in order to restrain it, which between 1870 and 1890 in quite a few enterprises a kind of workers' representation was established voluntarily. These were rather powerless bodies, supposed to help to integrate the workers within the enterprise structure. In spite of the strong resistance of the socialist labour movement, these representative structures were recognized by law and thereby in fact ameliorated by the amendment to the GewO of 1891. Thus, the dualistic structure of German collective labour law, which involves a two-channel representation by unions on the one hand, and by works councils on the other, was already in being at that time. It should be added that the 1891 amendment to the GewO brought several improvements for the workforce, among which was the Sunday rest day, the ten-hour working day, the ban on night work for juveniles and females, etc.

39. The last decade of the nineteenth century was a time during which the labour movement was consolidated, and centralized organizational structures were developed. A third wing of unions, the Christian unions, were founded. At the turn of the century, the membership of the various unions was as follows: socialist unions 680,450, liberal unions 91,650 and Christian unions 76,744. These figures clearly show that the socialist unions were by far the most important group.

40. In the last decade of the nineteenth century the first signs of a change of strategy of the socialist labour movement could be discerned. Originally, the socialist unions had the goal of overthrowing the capitalist system by creating and strengthening a solidarity movement. The idea of concluding collective agreements was not at all compatible with this conception. Collective agreements were considered to be contracts with the class enemy; concluding such contracts would have meant accepting the legitimacy of their role. This conception was questioned in the so-called strategy debate within the socialist labour movement. This debate finally led to a shift from a revolutionary to a reforming strategy. Participation and democratization of all areas of society, including the economy, became the new key words of the socialist labour movement. This orientation not only led to a new attitude towards collective agreements, but also to a new understanding of the function and the necessity of workers' participation within the enterprise. This explains why the labour movement later on became more or less reconciled with the works council structure, which it had strongly opposed, when, in 1891, the GewO had been amended.

41. As a reaction to the strengthening of the labour movement, employers began to form employers' associations. Their original goal was not to conclude collective agreements; they were a long way from recognizing the socialist unions as legitimate spokesmen of the workers. Their primary aim was to diminish the socialist unions' influence on the workforce. The larger the company, the stronger was the resistance against union influence. Around 1905, the employers' associations already had a highly developed and centralized structure.

42. The basic factor which fundamentally changed the position of the socialist labour movement, and which led to its full recognition as legitimate representative of the workforce, was the cooperative attitude this movement demonstrated towards government activities in the First World War (so-called *Burgfriedenspolitik*).

§3. The Weimar Era

43. After the war, when the first German republic, the so-called Weimar Republic, was founded, the top organizations of employers' associations and trade unions formed the so-called Central Commission of Cooperation (*Zentralarbeitsgemeinschaft*). In the agreement, on which the Commission was based, the employers' associations guaranteed the trade unions full recognition, and both parties declared collective agreements to be the main instrument to regulate working conditions. In Section 159 of the Weimar Constitution (*Weimarer Reichsverfassung* – WRV), freedom of association was, for the first time in German history, guaranteed without any limitation.

44. The Weimar era was not only the time when the system of collective bargaining was growing rapidly, it was also the time when fundamental features of today's labour law were developed. Among these the most important were the Act on Works Councils (*Betriebsrätegesetz* – BRG) of 1920, the creation of a specific system of labour courts in 1926 and the establishment of a system of unemployment insurance and placement services in 1927. The General Federation of German Unions (*Allgemeiner Deutscher Gewerkschaftsbund* – ADGB) developed a concept of economic democracy which was meant to give workers influence on decision-making at all levels of the economic structure. This concept could not be realized in the Weimar era, and, from today's perspective, largely still remains a vision of the future.

45. In 1929 the economic world crisis struck Germany. It also led to a crisis in the developed system of industrial relations: union membership declined rapidly and unemployment grew to an enormous extent. The system of collective bargaining came under attack, and government intervention gained access to working conditions by so-called emergency decrees. As a consequence, the standard of working conditions decreased continually.

§4. The Nazi State

46. When the Nazis came to power in 1933, they dissolved trade unions as well as employers' associations. Instead they founded an organization which combined both, employers and workers, the so-called German Labour Front (*Deutsche Arbeitsfront*). This integrated organization was based on the idea of total harmony between all actors on the industrial scene, whether they were employers or workers. They all were supposed to have the same interest: the promotion of the Nazi state. It is unnecessary to mention that, in this concept, collective bargaining and industrial action were totally excluded. The function of collective bargaining was replaced by a state agency, the so-called Trustee of Work (*Treuhänder der Arbeit*). The basic features of the collective labour law structure as developed under the Weimar Republic were destroyed and replaced by the Act on the Order of Labour (*Arbeitsordnungsgesetz*) of 1934, the basic law for industrial relations under the Nazi state. The works council (*Betriebsrat*) was replaced by a so-called council of confidence (*Vertrauensrat*), whose main function was to improve the already existing harmony among the workforce and the 'leader' of the establishment. As far as individual labour law was concerned, the Nazis retained the legal structure developed during the Weimar Republic but turned it upside down by legal interpretation. The ideology of 'togetherness between the leader of the establishment and his workforce' (*Betriebsgemeinschaft*), the notion of a 'duty of loyalty' (*Treuepflicht*) that the worker owes to his employer, and the notion of a 'duty to give assistance' (*Fürsorgepflicht*) that the employer owes to the workers, became the decisive criteria of interpretation, allowing the Nazis to obtain the results they needed. It has to be pointed out that these notions were not invented by the Nazis – they had entered into the discussion on labour law concepts much earlier. However, the Nazis made use of them for their own ends by making them the pillars of the legal system.

§5. After the Second World War

47. After the downfall of the Nazis, the structures they had established were abolished. From the very beginning, however, reconstruction in the zone occupied by the Soviet Union took a different direction as compared with the zones occupied by the UK, France and the United States. Only in one respect, as a lesson from prewar history, was the same conclusion drawn: the labour movement tried to overcome ideological divisions. Therefore, in both parts of Germany trade unions were reorganized as unified organizations. Whereas, however, in the west this meant and still means that all ideological and political wings are covered under one umbrella, in the east it meant that only a trade union movement promoting the official ideology of the system was tolerated.

48. When in 1949 the FRG and the GDR were founded, the differences in the labour laws of the two systems were already remarkable and, from that time, they grew even further apart. Whereas in the FRG the features of collective labour law – with the exception of the already mentioned trade union structure – remained very much the same as they had been in Weimar, the GDR almost completely broke with this tradition. First the role of the trade union movement was a totally different one. Trade unions in the GDR were not primarily considered to be associations to represent employees' interests against employers. Their main task was to guarantee the performance of the economic plan and thereby to execute the Socialist Party's and the government's intentions. The link between party and trade unions was so close that it was difficult to draw a demarcation line. Since ideologically and by definition the interests of the party, of government, of the trade unions and of the workers were supposed to be identical, the multiple loyalty of trade unions was not considered to be a problem.

49. In the FRG the employers' associations were reorganized along the same pattern they had had before. In the GDR, however, employers' associations did not exist. Whereas in the FRG collective bargaining, including the possibility of putting pressure on the other side by means of industrial action was re-established, there was no similar pattern provided for in the GDR. So-called collective agreements concluded between trade unions on the one side, and government and single industrial units on the other, only had one thing in common with collective agreements in a western sense: the label. Their main function was not to fix minimum conditions for workers, but to specify the broad terms of the plan. They were not conceived as a compromise in collective conflict, but rather as a sort of additional legislation. Since the idea of conflict between collective actors was eliminated, mechanisms of conflict resolution never were developed. Strikes and lockouts were considered to be incompatible with such a system.

50. While in the FRG the system of labour courts was rebuilt, this special court system was abolished in the GDR. Labour matters were handled by ordinary courts. But the function of those courts again was different from that of ordinary courts in the FRG. They were not intended to be independent and neutral conflict-resolving bodies between individuals and management or government, but an instrument to promote the party's goals. The idea of separation of powers was unknown in the former GDR. Hence government, Parliament and the courts basically had the same function.

51. In the GDR labour law had mainly three functional goals: performance of the plan, full employment and workers' education in the spirit of 'socialist morality'. The right to work was guaranteed in the Constitution. Thereby each individual willing and capable to work was guaranteed a job. This led, on the one hand, to an enormous administrative effort to promote career planning and job distribution and, on the other hand, to extreme overstaffing, which could have been afforded only in an economy where market constraints had no role. The position of the individual worker did not compare to the position of workers employed in the FRG. Those in the FRG have always enjoyed individual rights. It always has been merely up to them whether or not they wanted to enforce them, if necessary with the aid of the courts. In the GDR, the main focus was on abuse of individual rights, thereby giving trade unions the power to decide whether or not it was suitable to insist on their protection. The educative effect for the collective of workers was the decisive criterion.

52. As in other communist countries, in the GDR the rules on labour law were codified and contained in a single comprehensive Labour Code (*Arbeitsgesetzbuch*), which was amended several times.

§6. UNIFICATION

53. On 2 March 1990 the Parliament of the GDR passed a resolution on 'basic traits of and perspectives for a social charter'. This resolution contained a programme for the development of a structure of social standards in a unified Germany according to which unification had to be achieved 'by way of a mutual reform of both systems of social protection in the two German states, integrating their positive elements'. For labour law this was supposed to mean that 'historically grown social standards in both German states are to be maintained, further developed and lifted to a higher level of social protection'. This strategy was considered to serve as a model 'for the economic, social and political integration of a unified Europe'. Labour law in a unified Germany was thus conceived as being a mixture of the better parts of both systems.

54. It soon became evident, however, that such a strategy would meet strong opposition in the FRG. In the process of unification, the FRG was interested in transferring its system, including labour law, to the territory of the former GDR. The first step in this direction was the Treaty on Monetary, Economic and Social Unification of 18 May 1990. This transferred the core elements of the FRG collective labour law to the GDR. At the same time, the GDR was supposed to abolish all legal provisions inconsistent with the treaty. This led to an amendment to the GDR Constitution on 17 June 1990, and to a total revision of the Labour Code on 22 June 1990. These attempts to adapt GDR law in order to integrate at least the rules of individual labour law into the future system of a unified Germany, however, were quickly overruled. In the negotiations on the Unification Treaty, the GDR delegation still tried to promote a position whereby, with reference to individual labour law, different standards would be maintained in the two territories. This attempt, however, remained unsuccessful. The FRG delegation's strategy, stressing the overarching need of having a homogeneous pattern throughout a unified Germany, was at the very end accepted.

55. According to Article 8 of the Unification Treaty, all law of the original FRG, including, of course, individual labour law, was extended to the territory of the former GDR. There were only a few exceptions according to which FRG provisions applied only in a modified version until a certain deadline, or GDR provisions remained temporarily valid. Since then even these differences have disappeared. To avoid depriving the GDR delegation of all hope, however, decisions regarding the character of individual labour law were not finalized in the treaty. According to Article 30, paragraph 1 of the treaty, the Parliament of unified Germany was supposed to codify as soon as possible, 'the law referring to the individual employment relationship as well as the protective standards referring to working time, work on Sundays and holidays and the specific protection of women'. Paragraph 2 of the same article extends this legislative programme to the codification of health and safety standards. In the meantime, the legislator has fulfilled its task with reference to working time and as regards health and safety. Whether or not an Act on the individual employment relationship will ever be subject of a codification, however, is still an open, extensively debated question.

56. Not only was the legal and institutional framework of the old FRG transferred to East Germany, but the actors of the industrial relations scene were also established. The trade unions of the former GDR were dissolved and the trade unions of the old FRG extended their scope of activity to the territory of the former GDR. The same happened with the employers' associations of the old FRG: now their scope of activity also includes the territory of the former GDR. In short, the factual conditions, which are necessary for the functioning of the law, were also exported to the territory of the former GDR.

Chapter 4. The Role of Government

§1. General Functions

57. In relation to those who are employed by the Federal Republic or the *Länder* on the basis of a private employment contract, the government has basically the same rights and duties as any other employer. In its proper role as government, intervention in the economy and in the labour market has become more and more important. There is such a large variety of instruments of intervention (ranging from indirect mechanisms as tax relief to more direct mechanisms such as subsidies) that it would be useless to list them all. One of the most important tools is certainly the channel of legislation. And here it is important to underline that it is not only labour law in a strict sense which is shaping the structure of the labour market and industrial relations; tax law, competition law, etc. are equally important.

58. In the 1960s, the so-called Concerted Action (*Konzertierte Aktion*) was established. This was a tripartite structure of more or less informal meetings of top representatives of the Federal Republic, the trade unions and the employers' associations. The purpose of these meetings was to reach a compromise on certain basic guidelines of economic and labour market policies. These guidelines were not legally binding, but in fact played an important role in public discussions, and thereby were shaping the activities of all actors involved. The trade unions left the Concerted Action to protest against the employers' associations' attitude towards the Co-Determination Act (*Mitbestimmungsgesetz* – MitbestG) of 1976. Although this Act, the content of which will be explained later (*see* paragraphs 668–681), had been passed by an overwhelming majority of the Federal Parliament it was attacked by the employers' associations as unconstitutional. When the employers' associations claimed the unconstitutionality of this Act before the Federal Constitutional Court,[21] the trade unions took this step as a reason to leave the Concerted Action. That was the end of this institution.

59. Nevertheless, formal as well as informal tripartite arrangements still play an important role. Particularly in the course of restructuring the economy and the labour market in the territory of the former GDR their function can hardly be overestimated. Since unemployment increased seriously after the unification in all parts of Germany several so-called pacts for employment (*Bündnisse für Arbeit*) have been established. The label 'pact for employment' is attributed to very heterogeneous forms of platforms on many different levels (establishment, enterprise, *Land*, federal level). The common denominator is the involvement of employee representatives, of one or more employer(s) or representatives, and the aim is to protect and, if possible, to create jobs. The government(s) is/are not necessarily involved in any case. However, on the *Land* as well as on the federal level there are also pacts of employment where the respective government participates. Among those, the most prominent is the pact of employment on federal level. The establishment of such a

21. BVerfG, dec. of 1 Mar. 1979, *BVerfGE*, vol. 50, p. 290.

pact on the federal level has been one of the most prominent campaign promises of Chancellor Schröder and was part of the agreement between the two parties to the governmental coalition. Under the Schröder government, the federal government, trade unions and employers' associations were in a constant process of communication to develop new ideas and strategies for the creation of new jobs.

60. According to the Act on the Promotion of Stability and Growth of the Economy (*Stabilitätsgesetz*) of 1967, the government presents at the beginning of every year a report explaining the economic and financial policy of the year. This report is based on a report from the so-called Council of Experts (*Sachverständigenrat*), a group of five scholars in the field of economics, who are recruited according to a formula laid down in an Act of 1963. The practical impact of this experts' report is far-reaching. It is important to know that this report deals with conditions which are important for maintaining or increasing economic prosperity. Thus, of course, the expenditure of enterprises plays an important role. This is why the experts' report always provides a margin for wage policy and other working conditions affecting the cost side. Even if these margins legally have no binding effect whatsoever, their practical implications cannot be overestimated. The authority of this scholarly analysis plays a dominant role and is used by all actors involved in determining working conditions as a strong argument in the bargaining situation.

§2. Specific Institutions

61. At federal as well as at *Land* level, there is a special department of labour and social security within government, being the top structure in charge of all activities dealing with this area of policy. The heads of these departments, the Ministers of Labour and Social Affairs, have important links with other institutions. They have in particular a certain influence on the recruitment of the judiciary in this field, a function which is very important in view of the decisive role that the labour courts play.

62. The Office of Labour Inspection (*Gewerbeaufsicht*) is established in every *Land* on three hierarchical levels. This office has the task of supervising and controlling the performance of a whole range of protective rules, mainly those which have to do with safety risks, working time, protection of motherhood, and of juveniles. The Office of Labour Inspection is not restricted to a controlling function, but is also supposed to take the initiative and advise employers how to carry out the protective regulations effectively. In some *Länder* the medical labour inspection is integrated into the Office of Labour Inspection, in others it is a separate institution.

63. There are special *Länder* agencies for specific groups which have controlling, advising and regulating functions. Among the most important are the Commissions for Homeworkers (*Heimarbeitsausschüsse*), the Agencies for Disabled Persons (*Integrationsämter*) and the Main Welfare Office for tasks within the framework of social compensation law (*Hauptfürsorgestellen*).

64. The most important agency in the field of labour administration is the Employment Agency (*Agentur für Arbeit*), until 2003 named the Employment Office. It is a combination of a *Land* agency and a tripartite organization. It is organized on three levels: at the top there is the Federal Employment Agency (*Bundesagentur für Arbeit*), in the middle the *Land* Employment Agencies (*Landesagenturen für Arbeit*) and at the lowest level the Local Employment Agencies (*Agenturen für Arbeit*). The Employment Agency not only administers the system of unemployment insurance, but has the task of actively intervening in the labour market. Although the monopoly of placement services, which had been held by the Employment Agency, was abolished in 1994, placement of labour is still one of the agency's main tasks. Furthermore, it organizes and finances training and retraining programmes, it can provide temporary employment for unemployed persons, and it can stimulate employment by providing subsidies to enterprises, etc. Finally, it has a research institute, called IAB, which continuously studies the problems of the labour market and develops strategies on how to manage the labour market in the future. Since the Employment Agency, in addition to all other functions already mentioned, has an advisory function for all the actors in the labour market, the practical importance of these research results is evident.

65. In the context of the change in structure of the economy and of the labour market in the former GDR, the so-called *Treuhandanstalt* (privatization agency) was set up in 1990. It was charged with the task of administrating, in the capacity of a trustee, the publicly owned property of the former GDR. Around 95% of all property was national property (so-called *Volkseigentum*). The task of the Treuhand Agency was essentially to carry out privatization (*see* paragraph 19). It had its headquarters in Berlin, plus fifteen branch offices. Because of the low level of competitiveness of most enterprises in Eastern Germany the process of privatization went rather slowly. In addition, the agency's costs far exceeded its revenue from selling of businesses. In 1994 several functions of the Trust Agency were transferred to the Federal Ministry of Finance. At the same time, the Trust Agency was renamed the 'Federal Agency for Special Tasks caused by the Unification' (*Bundesanstalt für vereinigungsbedingte Sonderaufgaben*). The major remaining tasks of this agency are control of concluded privatization contracts, reprivatization of enterprises, liquidation of establishments which have closed down, administration of capital of the political parties of the former GDR, and of organizations and legal entities closely related to them. These tasks are almost completely finished today.

Chapter 5. Sources of Labour Law

§1. Constitution

66. At the top of the hierarchy of sources of labour law is the Constitution (*Grundgesetz* – GG). It plays a dominant role in the field of labour law. This is especially true for collective labour law where legislation is very fragmented. Problems not regulated by the legislator have to be solved by recourse to the Constitution. Thus, for example, all rules on industrial conflict have been developed by interpretation of principles laid down in the Constitution. But the Constitution also plays an important role in individual labour law. It should be kept in mind that many legal provisions concerning the contractual relationship originate from the turn of the nineteenth century. They are embedded in the Civil Code (*Bürgerliches Gesetzbuch* – BGB), which was promulgated in 1900. Thus, many of those provisions are no longer compatible with basic principles laid down in the Constitution. This is why the Constitution, also in the area of individual labour law, to a great extent shapes the legal framework.[22] Since the principles laid down in the Constitution are very vague and unspecific, the leeway for interpretation is quite wide. It is evident that this recourse to the Constitution increases the powers of the interpreting agencies, particularly the powers of the Federal Constitutional Court.

§2. Ordinary Legislation

67. Notwithstanding what has been said about the dominant role of the Constitution, it should be pointed out that in Germany the level of protective legislation is comparatively high. Thus ordinary legislation is particularly important in so far as it sets minimum standards for all employees, whether or not they are union members. Since competence to legislate in the field of labour law is given to the federal legislator, it is almost exclusively federal legislation, which has to be taken into consideration. In spite of the federal structure of Germany this evidently leads to a homogeneous pattern of labour law in the different *Länder*. If constitutions of the *Länder* or ordinary laws contain provisions on labour law, they are only applicable in so far as they do not contradict federal law. Federal law always takes priority, even if the federal source has a much lower rank than the *Land* source. For example, ordinary federal legislation always takes priority over *Land* constitutions. There is one area where differences between the *Länder* play an important role, i.e., staff representation in the public sector. Here the BPersVG only sets a framework, which is interpreted differently by the acts on staff representation of the various *Länder*.

68. The problem is that the various legal provisions, quite often stemming from very different periods, are spread over so many specific acts that it is difficult, even for an expert, to get an overview of the whole structure. Therefore, several attempts were made to combine at least the principal rules of individual labour law into one

22. *See* M. Weiss, *The Interference Between Constitution and Labour Law in Germany* Comp. Lab. L. & Pol'y J. 181 et seq. (2005).

single code. All these attempts failed, among those attempts made in the 1970s. The previously mentioned clause in the Unification Treaty has revitalized the debate. In 1992 a group of labour law professors from east and west presented a draft for a code on employment contract law. Whether or not this will be a base for a bill to be presented to the Federal Parliament is still an open question. It is very unlikely that a comprehensive codification will be achieved. The mechanism of legislation, being constrained by diverging pressure groups, seems to have great difficulties in gaining the necessary majority for such an ambitious project. It is questionable whether, in view of European integration, it is desirable to increase the rigidity of the national law by such a codification.[23] Nevertheless, in 2005 the private Bertelsmann Foundation entrusted two distinguished German scholars with drafting an Employment Contract Act (*Arbeitsvertragsgesetz* – ArbVG). The Bertelsmann Foundation as well as the two drafters regard this project as a contribution of civil society to modern regulation. In 2006 a first draft was presented; in 2007 an amended draft was published.[24] Although both drafts have been discussed very openly and have found a lot of affirmation from German labour law scholars, the chances that the German Parliament will pass an ArbVG in the near future still seem rather small – even under the big coalition. Trade unions as well as employers' associations are much too afraid that the legal position of their respective constituencies would be worsened by the ArbVG.

69. The legislator, in many cases, delegates the power to regulate a specific matter to administrative agencies or other bodies. The Constitution requires that this delegation is precisely defined in order to eliminate the danger that of the respective agency or body playing a legislative role. For the same reason basic decisions cannot be delegated at all by the legislator.

§3. Court Decisions

70. As already indicated court decisions play a very important role in the field of labour law. This is not only true inasmuch as courts specify the general clauses and general terms of laws, but also inasmuch as they have to fill in the gaps left open by the legislator. According to the Act on Court Procedure in Labour Law Matters (*Arbeitsgerichtsgesetz* – ArbGG), the Federal Labour Court has the sole power to develop law further. In fact, in the field of labour law (especially collective labour law), the Federal Labour Court has become at least as important as the legislator.[25] Thus, it is not at all surprising that a wide discussion on the proper role of the labour

23. For an in-depth analysis of the problems going along with a codification *see* M. Weiss et al.: 'Welche wesentlichen Inhalte sollte ein nach Art. 30 des Einigungsvertrages zu schaffendes Arbeitsvertragsgesetz haben?' *Sitzungsbericht P zum 59. Deutschen Juristentag Hannover 1992* (Munich), pp. 8 et seq.
24. For more information *cf.* www.arbvg.de.
25. For more details *see* M. Weiss, *Judge Made Labour Law in Germany*, in *Labour Law into the Future: Essays in Honour of Darcy du Toit*, 122 et seq. (K. Malherbe & J. Sloth-Nielson eds, 2012).

courts, compared to that of the legislator, has been going on in Germany.[26] The question is to what extent the actual role of the courts, especially the role of the Federal Labour Court, is still in accordance with the principle of separation of legislative and judicial powers as laid down in the Constitution. But in view of the fact that the legislator is able to agree with its majority on specific issues in this contested area only in rare cases, the courts have no choice but to act on behalf of the legislator. The discussion thus remains more or less academic.

§4. Collective Agreements

71. The normative part of collective agreements (in contrast to the obligation part which deals with rights and duties between the contracting parties) directly affects the individual employment relationship. In other words, if rights laid down in normative clauses of collective agreements are violated, the individual employee and the employer to whom these clauses apply both have recourse to court assistance. But it should be kept in mind that, at least in principle, such clauses cover only union members employed by an employer who himself or herself is a member of the employers' association which signed the collective agreement (*see* paragraphs 463–464).

72. The relation between legislation and the normative part of collective agreements is rather complicated. If there is an Act stipulating a minimum standard, the collective agreement cannot fall below it but can only exceed this standard. But, as will be shown later, there are many exceptions where the legislator expressly allows a collective agreement to fall below the minimum standard. The reason for this legislative strategy is very simple: parties to a collective agreement are supposed to know better than the legislator what is appropriate from an overall and long-term perspective. If the law does not set a minimum standard but only provides a regulation for the use of the contracting parties, the collective agreement may disregard this regulation. The problem is that the legislator often does not expressly declare whether a law is setting a minimum standard or whether it is available to the contracting parties. This can only be determined by interpretation. Finally, the legal provision may be such that no deviation whatsoever is allowed whether for better or worse for the employee. Again, it has to be determined by interpretation whether a certain clause is compulsory.

73. The relation between collective agreements and court decisions is even more complicated. As long as the courts merely specify general clauses and general terms, however, no problem arises. They are supposed to interpret legal provisions, therefore it is evident that the relation is the same as the relation between legislation and court decisions. The real problem arises if the courts set standards that are not simply implied by existing legislation. This 'judge-made law' sets minimum standards

26. F. Gamillscheg, 'Die Grundrechte im Arbeitsrecht', *Archiv für civilistische Praxis*, vol. 164 (1964), pp. 388 et seq.; A. Soellner, 'Zur Verfassungs- und Gesetzestreue im Arbeitsrecht', *Recht der Arbeit*, 1985, pp. 328 et seq.

and thus, in principle, excludes clauses in collective agreements which fall below this standard. But this is not as inflexible as legislation. To describe the borderline generally is almost impossible; it can only be illustrated case by case. If, however, judge-made law is available to the contracting parties, it can certainly be put aside by collective agreements. The difficulty is to determine by interpretation whether this is the case.

§5. Works Agreements

74. As will be shown in detail later (*see* paragraphs 634–636), works councils and employers in the private sector (or the staff council and employer in the public sector) may sign works agreements containing normative clauses, having basically the same effect on the individual employment relationship as normative clauses of collective agreements. There is an important difference though: works agreements always cover the entire workforce, whether or not they are union members; collective agreements cover only those who are members of the union that signed the collective agreement. This basic disparity creates enormous problems of harmonization between the two sources of law. The relationship between collective agreements and works agreements is, for many reasons, one of the most difficult problems of labour law. This is why the question is left open here and will be explained later in the respective context (*see* paragraphs 637 et seq.).

§6. Individual Labour Contracts

75. The individual labour contract is still an important source of law even for those covered by protective laws, collective agreements and/or works agreements. The area dominated by the individual contract in these cases is above the minimum level already regulated. Thus, the function of the individual labour contract serves mainly to improve the individual working conditions already guaranteed by other sources.

§7. Custom

76. Custom may only be a source of law in favour of the employees. Under certain conditions, privileges voluntarily granted by the employer cannot simply be taken away. The mere fact that they were granted for a certain period may lead to employees being able to claim their continuation.[27] Such a claim is then treated as if it were based on individual contract.

---

27. K. Bepler, 'Betriebliche Übungen. Ein erweiterter Rechtsprechungsbericht', *Recht der Arbeit*, 2004, pp. 226 et seq.

§8. International Sources

77. As a Member State of the European Community (EC), of the EU, of the Council of Europe, of the UN and of the International Labour Organization, just to mention the most important organizations, Germany is not only subject to EU law, including the various directives, but it has also ratified most of the charters and conventions of the other organizations.[28] For a long time the consciousness of the relevance of international sources was rather underdeveloped in Germany, but it has fortunately grown over the last two decades. In some areas, the discrepancy between supranational law and national law has become an issue of public discussion. An important example was the compatibility of national law on the prohibition of sexual discrimination with the respective EC Directive. Another important example is the law on transfer of undertakings and, more recently, the case law on European annual vacation law. The decisions of the European Court received widespread attention in Germany and lead to increased sensitivity concerning the relevance of supranational sources in the field of labour law.

28. *Cf.* M. Weiss, *Fundamental Rights and German Labor Law*, in *Research Handbook on Labour, Business and Human Rights Law* 17 et seq. (J. Bellace & B. ter Haar eds, Elgar 2019).

Part I. The Individual Employment Relationship

Chapter 1. Definitions and Concepts

§1. The Definition of the Term 'Employee'

78. Until April 2017, when the legislator laid down a definition in Section 611a of the BGB, there was no statutory provision defining the notion of 'employee' as regards labour law. There is only a statutory definition of the term 'self-employed' in Section 84 paragraph 1 sentence 2 of the Commercial Code (*Handelsgesetzbuch* – HGB) that was used as a differentiation to the concept of employee. It reads: 'Anybody who essentially is free in organizing his work and in determining his working time is presumed to be self-employed.' Thus, personal freedom is the main characteristic of being self-employed.[29] This is why the traditional definition of 'employee' implies just the opposite of personal freedom, i.e., personal subordination. According to this still prevailing definition, an employee is a person who is obliged to work for somebody else on the basis of a private contract in a relationship of personal subordination.[30] The key element of this formula is personal subordination.[31] Another important element is the private contract, excluding on the one hand all relationships into which the individual did not voluntarily enter but in which he or she nevertheless is forced to work (e.g., a prisoner in prison), and on the other hand all relationships based on instruments of public law (e.g., career public servants or judges).

79. For a considerable time the notion of 'personal subordination' was accepted as a helpful and valid criterion to define the employment relationship. Personal subordination has always been understood to differ from mere economic dependency on the employer. Therefore, the question of whether or not a person is an employee has nothing to do with the salary the individual is earning. This difference between mere personal subordination and economic dependence is still valid, but meanwhile it has become highly contentious what personal subordination precisely means. The

29. *Cf.* B. Waas, *Employee and Self-employed under German Labour Law*, in *Labour Law and Flexibility in Europe* 203–216 (B. Caruso & M. Fuchs eds, 2005).
30. *Cf.* only Brox et al., *Arbeitsrecht,* 17th edn, pp. 14 et seq.; W. Dütz, *Arbeitsrecht,* 12th edn, pp. 20 et seq.
31. *Cf. also* Federal Labour Court, dec. of 26 Sep. 2002 – 5 AZB 19/01 with annotation by M. Schmidt, *International Labour Law Reports* 3–11 (2002).

traditional view of an individual simply obeying his or her employer's orders in determining the organization of his or her work or working time does not correspond with the fact that more and more highly skilled individuals enjoy more or less freedom in deciding how and when they carry out their work. In the early 1960s the problem arose whether a leading senior hospital physician-in-chief who personally decided what medical treatment was necessary, and how and when it had to be administered, could be regarded as being an employee. The Federal Labour Court had to choose whether to exclude such a physician-in-chief from labour law or to include him and to redefine the notion of personal subordination. Mainly due to the fact that the physician's capacity to work was almost totally absorbed by the hospital the court chose the latter option.[32] The relationship was therefore supposed to be a relationship of 'personal subordination'. This case not only demonstrated the inadequacy of the traditional notion but also provoked a big debate on the notion of 'employee' that is still continuing.

80. The above-mentioned debate has intensified and accelerated since the mid-1970s due to the several court procedures initiated by so-called free collaborators (*freie Mitarbeiter*) of the mass media. The plaintiffs had contracts with newspaper enterprises, radio stations, etc. to work for them as journalists, musicians and so on. According to the contracts on which these relationships were based, these individuals were expressly defined as being self-employed, i.e., independent contractors. When the economic crisis started to affect the budget of the mass media, these free collaborators thus had to face the fact that without the protection of labour law their position in the labour market was extremely precarious (especially in view of protection against dismissals). Many of them claimed that in fact they were employees and asked the labour courts to define their status. The labour court decisions showed a very important tendency with regard to the future of labour law. The notion of employee was extended in order to cover as many people as possible, thereby providing them with the protection established by labour law. The Federal Labour Court made perfectly clear that it was not up to the parties to the individual contract to define the legal character of their relationship.[33] Whether or not labour law is applicable depends only on the actual content of the relationship in practice. In other words, it is impossible to escape the constraints of labour law just by mutual agreement. This view evidently implies that the real content of such a relationship is evaluated. And here again the question arises of what 'personal subordination', as a criterion to distinguish an employee from a self-employed person, could possibly mean. It has to be admitted that there is still no clarity at all.

81. The Federal Labour Court has turned personal subordination into a very complex notion consisting of a wide range of elements that have to be combined and evaluated together. Thus, it is always up to the labour courts to determine whether or not in a particular case the combination of factors indicating the status

32. Federal Labour Court, 27 Jul. 1961 – 2 AZR 255/60, *Neue Juristische Wochenschrift*, 1961, pp. 2085 et seq.
33. Federal Labour Court, 13 Jan. 1983 – 5 AZR 14/82, *Arbeitsrechtliche Praxis*, No. 42 §611 BGB *Abhängigkeit*.

of an 'employee' is sufficient. The most important factors indicating the status of an 'employee' are: (1) the enterprise expects the individual to be always ready to accept new tasks; (2) the individual is not free to refuse tasks offered by the enterprise; (3) the individual is to a certain extent integrated into the organizational structure of the enterprise; (4) the time required by the individual for performing the tasks for an enterprise is quite long.[34] The underlying criterion of these factors is the following: to what extent can the situation of such an individual be compared with those whose status as an employee is not questioned? Thus, the really decisive criterion is no longer personal subordination but the generally accepted understanding of what an employee is. This understanding, however, is not defined. Since the factors indicating the status of an employee are numerous, it is in fact up to the courts to draw the new boundaries. And again it has to be stated that the courts tend to extend the scope of labour law as far as possible. This strategy of the labour courts, however, is opposed, mainly by the employers in the name of flexibility. Thus, the final outcome of the ongoing debate cannot be predicted.

82. In the meantime, the notion of employee respective of the employment contract is defined in Section 611a paragraph 1 BGB which came into force on 1 April 2017 and takes up the criteria developed by the case law of the labour courts. This was preceded by a major debate on what could be done to achieve greater legal certainty with regard to the concept of the employee, given the complexity and vagueness of the Federal Labour Court's approach and the wide discretionary scope of the courts. It is now defined as: 'Durch den Arbeitsvertrag wird der Arbeitnehmer im Dienste eines anderen zur Leistung weisungsgebundener, fremdbestimmter Arbeit in persönlicher Abhängigkeit verpflichtet', which means that an employment contract requires the provision of dependent services, whereby this dependence usually manifests itself in such a way that the employee is subjected to the instructions of another person.[35] Nevertheless, the judicial discretionary scope remains the same as before, even according to the legal definition. A higher degree of legal certainty has not been achieved with this provision. However, against the background of a variety of employment relationships and due to technological and organizational developments, a clearly defined concept of employee is not possible either, and a certain degree of judicial discretion is required.

83. According to case law and Section 611a paragraph 1 sentence 5 BGB the question, if someone could be classified as an employee or as a self-employed person, depends on an objective overall picture of the circumstances in the individual relationship. It depends on the degree of 'personal dependence', in which the extent of 'subservience to instructions' (e.g., in relation to how, when and where to perform work) plays a significant role. Another focus is on the question whether a person is integrated in the business of another, so-called organizational dependence.

34. Federal Labour Court, 9 Mar. 1977 – 5 AZR 110/76, *Arbeitsrechtliche Praxis*, No. 21 §611 BGB *Abhängigkeit*; 13 Jan. 1983 – 5 AZR 149/82, *Arbeitsrechtliche Praxis*, No. 42 §611 BGB *Abhängigkeit*.

35. Further *see* B. Waas in Waas *et. al.*, *Crowdwork – A Comparative Law Perspective,* 147 ((2017, Bund-Verlag).

However – as jurisdiction shows – working from one's home instead of working in the physical organization of an employer does not preclude the qualification of the relationship as employment. This is particularly important against the background of increasing mobile work and new forms of work like crowdwork. The State Labour Court of Hesse (*Landesarbeitsgericht Hessen*) qualified an IT programme developer as an employee, even though he worked from home and was not integrated in the (physical) premises of the employer's business.[36] The designation of the contractual relationship by the parties as an employment contract or something else is not decisive for the legal qualification. Indicators 'of the employment relationship can be drawn on, e.g., the obligation to exclusively provide services (exemption from performing work for others), the provision of work-related equipment by the contracting party, remuneration (single fee or monthly salary), the payment of taxes and social security contributions, request for an income tax card or granting of leave'.[37]

84. In addition, it should be noted that in social security law, compulsory social insurance in Germany primarily depends on 'insurable employment' of workers (sozialversicherungspflichtiges Beschäftigungsverhältnis), that is defined in Section 7 paragraph 1 sentence 1 SGB IV (Social Code IV) as 'Beschäftigung is non-self-employed work, especially under an employment relationship' ('Beschäftigung ist die nichtselbständige Arbeit, insbesondere in einem Arbeitsverhältnis'). The definition thus refers primarily to the existence of an employment relationship as mentioned above, but overall the definition in social security law has a slightly wider scope for other workers (e.g., it is possible to include some types of executive directors). Indicators for a 'Beschäftigung' are working under instructions and being integrated in the business of another.

§2. The 'Employee-Like' Person

85. The dichotomy between the self-employed, being excluded from labour law, and employees, being fully covered by labour law, has never been accepted as a satisfactory solution. This is why a third category was introduced to classify those who are self-employed but whose economic situation nevertheless resembles that of an employee much more than the situation of a self-employed person. Individuals in this group are supposed to be covered at least by some rules and principles of labour law. The criterion used to distinguish this group of self-employed from other self-employed is 'economic dependency'. The notion 'employee-like' person (*arbeitnehmerähnliche Person*), defining this group of individuals, has been initially developed by the courts. This initial definition was not very clear. The situation improved in 1974 when in Section 12a of the Act on Collective Agreements (*Tarifvertragsgesetz*– TVG) a statutory definition of 'employee-like' persons was

36. State Labour Court Hesse, 13 Mar. 2015 – 10 Sa 575/14, *LAGE § 611 BGB 2002 Arbeitnehmerbegriff No. 11*.
37. *See* B. Waas in Waas *et. al.*, *Crowdwork*, p. 149.

provided. Accordingly, individuals are economically dependent and need social protection comparable to that of an employee if they fulfil the following conditions: (1) they have to perform their contractual duties personally and essentially without the help of employees; (2) either the major part of their work is performed for one person or more than on average half of their income is paid by one person. It should be stressed that 'person' in this sense may also mean any institution, corporation or even a group of companies. Any individual working for different enterprises within a group is considered to work only for one institution in the sense of this definition. For artists, writers and journalists there is a specific definition provided for in Section 12 paragraph 3 TVG. For them it is sufficient that more than one-third of their income is paid by one person.

86. The following is not to be misunderstood: 'employee-like' persons are not covered by labour law as a whole, only by some specific sections of it. For example, they are not covered by the law protecting employees against dismissal (*see* paragraphs 291 et seq.). This is why so-called free collaborators in the mass media, who definitely were 'employee-like' persons, tried to obtain the status of employees. The main privileges 'employee-like' persons enjoy when compared to other self-employed individuals are the following: disputes between them and their contractual partners are to be settled by labour courts (Section 5 paragraph 1 sentence 2 ArbGG (*see* paragraphs 353 et seq.)); as far as minimum standards for annual holidays and public holidays are concerned, they are treated in the same way as employees (Section 2 sentence 2 Federal Act on Holidays (*Bundesurlaubsgesetz* – BUrlG) (*see* paragraphs 237 et seq.)); their working conditions can be regulated by collective agreements (Section 12a TVG (*see* paragraph 449); and finally they are entitled to non-discrimination on grounds of race or ethnic origin, sex, religion or belief, for being disabled, on grounds of age or sexual orientation (Section 6 paragraph 1 No. 3 General Act on Equal Treatment (*Allgemeines Gleichbehandlungsgesetz* – AGG) (*see* paragraphs 173–181, 208–215).

87. The first of the two categories of 'employee-like' persons that are treated separately by law is commercial agents (*Handelsvertreter*). There is a peculiar statutory definition of them being 'employee-like' persons provided for in Section 5 paragraph 3 ArbGG. The first precondition is that the commercial agent is either contractually prohibited from working for other enterprises or, in view of the kind and the volume of his work, is factually unable to work for other enterprises. The second precondition is low income: only if the income has not on average exceeded a EUR 1,000 during the last six months of the contractual relationship. Even if commercial agents are treated as 'employee-like' persons in terms of the ArbGG, unlike other categories of 'employee-like' persons they are explicitly excluded from Section 12a TVG and can hence not be covered by collective agreements.

88. The second category of 'employee-like' persons covered by specific statutory regulation is homeworkers (*Heimarbeiter*). The first Act on Homework (*Heimarbeitsgesetz*– HAG) dates from 1911; the actual statutory regulation originates from 1951 and has been amended several times since, most recently in 2019. According to Section 2 paragraph 1 of the HAG, a homeworker is anybody who works, either alone or with the help of family members, for another person or institution at a place of his or her own choosing, whether it is an apartment, a house, or any other place, and who leaves the utilization of the work results to the person or institution he is working for. A similar definition of homeworker exists for social security law in Section 12 paragraph 2 SGB IV. The HAG also applies to individuals who are, in a place of their choice, with at most two persons (non-family members) helping them, working for another person or institution leaving the utilization of the result of their work to that other person or institution, no matter whether or not the raw materials are provided. The first category of homeworkers mentioned are always supposed to be 'employee-like' persons by definition. In the case of the second category, i.e., those who rely on the help of more than two persons (non-family members) or who delegate the work they have to do for a person or an institution to homeworkers, it is necessary to determine whether or not they need social protection, which again leads to the question of whether they are economically dependent. An indication as to whether or not this question has to be answered in the affirmative is the number of people assisting, the dependency on one or more persons or institutions, the possibility of direct access to the sellers' market, the amount and kind of investment, as well as the turnover. These persons can only be included in the statutory regulation by a specific decree of the homework committee (*Heimarbeitsausschuss*), an institution established by the HAG.

89. The HAG mainly provides wage protection, working time protection, safety regulations and a very fragmentary protective regulation in the case of dismissal. As far as wages and other working conditions are concerned, collective agreements would theoretically be possible, but in practice do not play any role. The homework committee is composed of three representatives of homeworkers, three representatives of the individuals and institutions contracting with homeworkers and a chairman nominated by the supreme labour authority of the *Land* in question. Its main task is to determine minimum wages and working conditions in this area. In addition, it should be pointed out that in quite a few acts in the field of labour law the persons covered by the HAG are treated as if they were employees. In short, it can be said that among all the different groups of 'employee-like' persons the homeworkers are the group which is closest to employees. Nevertheless, in view of the total lack of organization of homeworkers, and in view of their isolation, there are many doubts as to the efficiency of the regulations concerning them.

90. For a rather long time the number of homeworkers decreased. In 1970 in the FRG there were 221,802 registered, in 1981 the minimum was reached with only 138,227. In 1983 the figure increased to 159,662 and climbed up to 166,947 in 1991 (in the territory of the old FRG, statistics for the former GDR are not available), which corresponds to an increase of 12.5% from 1983 to 1991. Since then, the numbers have dramatically decreased again. In 1998, only 96,882 homeworkers were registered in the whole FRG (including the former GDR). Almost half of the homeworkers are registered in two *Länder*: in Bayern (27,927) and North Rhine-Westphalia (24,663). As far as branches of industry are concerned, the most important branch is the metal and electric industries (25,009), followed by the chemical and plastics industries (15,061), the textile industries (12,081) and the paper manufacturing industries (11,213). At the end of 2018, there were only approximately around 24,000 homeworkers in Germany.[38] This does not include the significantly larger number of employees who, in agreement with their employer, work wholly or partly mobile or from home. Almost a third of the companies offer employees the opportunity to work from home. At over 50%, this proportion is higher among large companies with over 500 employees than in smaller companies.[39]

91. Although the HAG has little practical relevance today, it could become more relevant again in the future with regard to new forms of work. It is being discussed to what extent the law can provide a basis for better social protection of crowdworkers.[40]

§3. Different Categories of Employee

I. Manual Workers and White-Collar Workers

92. Although some acts still explicitly address manual workers (*Arbeiter*) and white-collar workers (*Angestellte*) these subcategories of employees are – as a result of a decision of the Federal Constitutional Court of 1990,[41] holding shorter periods of notice for manual workers and white-collar workers incompatible with the general principle of equal treatment as laid down in Article 3 paragraph 1 GG – no longer treated differently, either in individual or in collective statutory labour law.[42] Both groups are more and more often covered by uniform collective agreements. Even the two different statutory pension systems have been merged since 1 October 2005.

II. Executive Staff

93. That executive staff (*leitende Angestellte*) are treated as a separate category of employees is a more recent development. It is based on the assumption that the problems and interests of this group are in many ways not comparable with those of normal employees. Moreover, due to their very function, they are in a position of being opponents of employees. The practical importance of this group is much higher than its small proportion of the workforce (about 1.5%) suggests. There are

38. For further information *see* www.bmas.de.
39. D. Arnold, S. Steffes & S. Wolter, Mobiles und entgrenztes Arbeiten, *BMAS-Forschungsbericht 460*, 2015, p. 5.
40. *Cf.* B. Waas in Waas *et. al.*, *Crowdwork*, pp. 163–171; W. Däubler & T. Klebe, Crowdwork: Die neue Form der Arbeit – Arbeitgeber auf der Flucht, *Neue Zeitschrift für Arbeitsrecht (NZA) 17/2015*, pp. 1032, 1036.
41. 30 May 1990 – 1 BvL 2/83, BVerfGE, vol. 82, pp. 126–156.
42. For more details *see* M. Weiss, *Equalizing 'Blue Collar' and 'White Collar' in Germany – The Result of a Long Fight*, in *Steve Adler Book* 483 et seq (D. Lupo et al. eds, 2016).

also separate trade unions for executive staff, which are amalgamated in one umbrella organization, the Union of Executive Staff (*Union Leitender Angestellter*).

94. There are different definitions of 'executive staff' in different legal context. The notion of 'executive staff' in terms of the Act on Dismissal Protection (*Kündigungsschutzgesetz–* KSchG) is different from the notion used in the BetrVG. These differences are partly due to the functional necessity of treating executive staff in a way which may vary in different fields of labour law. But it also has to do with the debates on the role of executive staff in view of the regulations in a particular Act. For example, when the BetrVG was amended in 1972, there was a big disagreement between unions on the one side and employers' associations and organizations of executive staff on the other side. While the unions were asking for a definition keeping the number of executive staff to a minimum, the latter groups were in favour of a definition increasing the group of executive staff. The definition finally agreed upon in the BetrVG can only be understood as an attempt to compromise. As will be shown later (*see* paragraphs 587–591), the definition adopted has not solved the problem; it was finally left to the Federal Labour Court to fulfil this task. Only when the case law had become too complex did the legislator intervene. The latest amendment, effective since the beginning of 1989, clarified the definition of executive staff. But of course, many problems of interpretation were still left to the courts. At the same time, an Act was passed providing for a specific representation body for executive staff.

§4. Freedom of Contract as the Basic Principle of the Employment Relationship

95. Freedom of contract has always been the basis of the employment relationship. Originally, however, it was completely up to the parties to decide whether, with whom, and under what conditions they concluded an employment contract. From the perspective of the liberal philosophy of the nineteenth century, this was understood to be an important improvement in comparison with the constraints of the feudal state preceding this system. Total freedom of contract, however, turned out to be inadequate as a decisive instrument of labour market regulation. The competition among employees for jobs resulted in a deterioration of working conditions. Freedom of contract turned out to be nothing more than a legal disguise for unilateral powers of regulation on the employers' side. This basic insight has become the main stimulus for the development of labour law. In this view, the history of labour law can be seen as an evergrowing attempt to overcome the defects of the concept of freedom of contract. This has led to constraints on the conclusion of the employment contract, on the content of the contract and on its termination.

96. Nevertheless, it should be pointed out that freedom of contract has survived as one of the main principles of labour law. Freedom of contract as such has never been questioned in German labour law. It is understood to be a concept required and backed by the Constitution. In Article 2 GG, the right to free development of one's personality is guaranteed. This constitutional guarantee is taken as granting *inter alia* freedom of contract. In this way, the legitimacy of the concept of freedom of contract has evidently been increased. The concept of freedom of contract plays an important role in discussions in Germany and is mainly understood as guaranteeing the employer's freedom to decide whether, and with whom, he is contracting, as well as his freedom to terminate a contractual relationship. Whenever the question arose as to whether a specific group should be given a privileged position in entering the labour market, whether they were disabled persons or whether they were females, freedom of contract was used to justify minimizing such privileges.

97. The utilization of freedom of contract as a strategic argument has led to the invention of a strategic counterclaim: the so-called right to work. This notion claims that everybody should be given the opportunity to obtain work, and that it is not the employer's prerogative to decide on such opportunities. The so-called right to work is thus mainly a political term to urge the government to strive for full employment. It is meant to declare full employment to be the primary aim of government's policy. The source of the so-called right to work is considered to be derived from the Constitution, namely from the principle of welfare improvement as laid down in Article 20 GG. This principle, however, is very vague and unspecific.

98. Due to the fact that in the former GDR the right to work played an important role, the discussion on this right was revitalized after unification. There was a heated debate whether or not such a right should be integrated as a specific article into the GG. From the very beginning it was clear that it would only be meant as a constitutional policy goal, but not as an individual right to get a job. In order to avoid the generation of expectations among the population, and in order to avoid providing the courts with an opportunity to turn such a policy goal into a sort of individual right, the idea of amending the GG was finally given up. It should, however, be stressed that in some constitutions of the new *Länder* a right to work understood as a policy goal has been included. Whether or not it will have any effect in reality still remains an open question.

§5. Different Kinds of Individual Labour Contract

I. The Normal Case: The Full-Time Contract for an Indefinite Period

99. In Germany, a full-time contract for an indefinite period has always been and still is the usual case. In spite of recent changes, German labour law as a whole strongly favours this type of employment contract. It should be stressed that this legal development is due to a general understanding in German society that employees should be in a position to develop a lifetime perspective by having the possibility of being employed for an indefinite period. This attitude, which is very different from the job mentality existing, for example, in the USA, certainly influences legal developments.

II. The Contract for a Definite Period

100. Since January 2001 contracts for a definite period, i.e., fixed-term contracts (*befristete Arbeitsverhältnisse*)[43] have been regulated by the Act on Part-Time Work and Fixed-Term Contracts (*Gesetz über Teilzeitarbeit und befristete Arbeitsverträge–* TzBfG), implementing Directive 99/70/EC on Fixed-Term Contracts. Before the coming into force of the TzBfG, there were mainly two provisions regulating fixed-term contracts: Section 620 paragraph 1 BGB and Section 1 of the 1985 Act on the Improvement of Employment Opportunities (*Beschäftigungsförderungsgesetz 1985–* BeschFG 1985). Section 620 paragraph 1 BGB, dating back to 1900, stipulates that every employment contract ends after the expiry of the agreed period. Obviously in 1900 the legislator regarded the conclusion of employment contracts for a definite period as the usual case. However, since a fixed-term contract ends automatically when the fixed period ceases, the conclusion of fixed-term contracts is, from an employer's point of view, a comfortable strategy to avoid the problems and costs incidental to dismissal protection (*see* paragraphs 291 et seq.). In order to prevent this circumvention of the rules on dismissal protection German courts developed, soon after first protective measures of dismissal protection had been enacted by the BRG 1920, limitations on the conclusion of fixed-term contracts.[44] According to this well-established case law, in principle still applicable today, a contract for a definite period is lawful only on condition that there is an objective reason justifying the time limit.[45]

101. In the mid-1980s, in view of increasing unemployment, these restrictions on fixed-term contracts were questioned. After a remarkably heated debate, the BeschFG was passed in 1985. The main target of criticism[46] was Section 1 BeschFG, explicitly allowing the conclusion of fixed-term contracts for a maximum duration of eighteen months without being subject to a justification requirement. However, Section 1 BeschFG 1985 was only applicable to new employees and trainees immediately after the end of vocational training. Newly established enterprises and employer employing twenty or fewer employees were even entitled to conclude fixed-term contracts for up to twenty-four months. The legislator hoped that the possibility of concluding fixed-term contracts would be used frequently, and that previously unemployed persons and apprentices would find fixed-term employment that, once established, would later be converted into permanent employment. The passing of Section 1 BeschFG had been so controversial that the then parliamentary

---

43. For more details *see* M. Weiss, *Germany*, in *Fixed-Term Employment Contracts – A Comparative Study* (R. Blanpain & C. Grant eds, 2009) 185 et seq.
44. Fundamentally Reich Labour Court (*Reichsarbeitsgericht* – RAG), 19 May 1928, *RAGE*, vol. 1, pp. 361, 363; confirmed 28 Nov. 1930, *RAGE*, vol. 7, 93, 96. These decisions, however, dealt with consecutive fixed-term contracts. Unlike today, the Reich Labour Court moreover required the employer's intention to circumvent dismissal protection.
45. Fundamentally Federal Labour Court (Large Senate – *see* para. 362), dec. of 12 Oct. 1960, *Arbeitsrechtliche Praxis*, No. 16 §620 BGB *Befristeter Arbeitsvertrag*; more recently 21 Feb. 2001, *Arbeitsrechtliche Praxis*, No. 226 §620 BGB *Befristeter Arbeitsvertrag.*
46. *See* e.g., O. Kempen, 'Arbeitnehmerschutz, Tarifverträge und Beschäftigungsförderungsgesetz', *Arbeit und Recht*, 1985, pp. 374 et seq.; U. Mückenberger, 'Der verfassungsrechtliche Schutz des Dauerarbeitsverhältnisses', *Neue Zeitschrift für Arbeitsrecht*, 1985, pp. 518 et seq.

majority of CDU/CSU and FDP limited its effectiveness to a period of five years; after these five years Section 1 BeschFG was twice extended for another five years, finally until 31 December 2000. In 1996, the BeschFG was once again amended.[47] Since 1 May 2000, Section 623 BGB has constituted a formal, but important requirement for a valid limitation as to time (*Befristungsabrede*): while employment contracts can generally be concluded either orally or in writing, a limitation as to time of an employment contract is, according to Section 14 paragraph 4 TzBfG, valid only if it is laid down in writing.

102. Trade unions and social democrats have always disapproved of Section 1 BeschFG because, while its unemployment reducing effects were uncertain, it invited employers to extend the time of probation (*see* paragraph 301) to up to twenty-four months. It was therefore apparent that, after a new parliamentary majority of SPD and Federation 90/The Greens had entered into power in September 1998, the BeschFG would have to be amended in 2000 in any case. In addition, Germany was obliged to implement the Part-time Directive 97/81/EC by 20 February 2000, and Directive 1999/70/EC on Fixed-term Contracts by 10 July 2001. The bill proposing to replace the BeschFG by the TzBfG evoked protests from trade unions and employers likewise. While the employers strictly opposed the bill because, above all, it proposed a right to reduce the individual working time (*see* paragraphs 118 et seq.), trade unions were disappointed because they had expected that Section 1 BeschFG 1985 would simply be abolished. The legislator, however, decided not only to codify the case law of the Federal Labour Court concerning fixed-term contracts in Section 14 paragraph 1 TzBfG but also to retain Section 1 BeschFG 1985 in principle as Section 14 paragraphs 2 and 3 TzBfG.

103. According to the legal definition laid down in Section 3 paragraph 1 TzBfG, a fixed-term contract is given if either its date of expiry is determined by a specific date (*zeitbefristeter Arbeitsvertrag*) or if its date of expiry follows from the kind, purpose, or nature of the work (*zweckbefristeter Arbeitsvertrag*). Employment contracts concluded under a dissolving condition (*auflösend bedingter Arbeitsvertrag*) are not covered by this definition. However, Section 4 paragraph 2, Section 5, Section 14 paragraphs 1 and 4, Section 15 paragraphs 2, 3 and 5 as well as Sections 16–20 TzBfG apply to them, according to Section 21 TzBfG, *mutatis mutandis*.

A. *The Principal Requirement of a Justifying Reason*

104. As regards the substantial requirements for a valid limitation as to time, the principal rule is laid down in Section 14 paragraph 1 TzBfG. Accordingly, the conclusion of a fixed-term contract is valid only if there is a justifying reason. Examples of such reasons are given in Section 14 paragraph 1 Nos 1–8 TzBfG. Accordingly, a justifying reason is particularly given if:

47. For details *cf.* M. Schmidt: *News of Atypical Work in Germany: Recent Developments as to Fixed-Term Contracts, Temporary and Part-Time Work,* 3 German L. J. (2002).

- there is only temporary internal company demand for work (No. 1);
- the limitation as to time takes place subsequent to training or studies in order to smooth the employee's transfer into further employment (No. 2);
- the employee is employed in order to replace another employee (No. 3);
- peculiarities of the work justify the limitation as to time (No. 4);
- the limitation as to time takes place in order to test the employee (No. 5);
- there are reasons in the employee justifying the limitation as to time (No. 6);
- the employee is paid from budgetary funds which are, according to budgetary law, intended for fixed-term employment, and if he or she is employed accordingly (No. 7); or
- the limitation as to time is based on a settlement in court (No. 8).

Except for Section 14 paragraph 1 No. 2 TzBfG these examples mainly correspond to the case law of the Federal Labour Court developed in the context of Section 620 BGB. Before the coming into effect of the TzBfG, the requirement of a justifying reason, however, was applicable only to employment contracts concluded for a duration of more than six months by an employer employing more than five employees. For only then did the KSchG apply (*see* paragraph 301). Nevertheless, Section 14 paragraph 1 TzBfG applies to any fixed-term employment contract, whether or not they are concluded for more than six months or a shorter period, whether or not the employer employs a number of employees exceeding the application threshold of the KSchG.

B. Exceptions

105. There are three exceptions to the rule that a limitation as to time of an employment contract is valid only if there is an objective reason justifying the time limit. The first exception is provided for in Section 14 paragraph 2 TzBfG, perpetuating Section 1 BeschFG: a contract for a definite period may, without any justifying reason, be concluded for a maximum duration of two years; a contract for a shorter period may be prolonged up to three times up to the same maximum duration. Unlike Section 1 BeschFG, however, the conclusion of a fixed-term contract on the basis of Section 14 paragraph 2 TzBfG is invalid if an employment relationship with the same employer, albeit of limited or of unlimited duration, has ever existed before. According to the wording this means that it is completely irrelevant how much time has passed since the first employment relationship. This highly disputed provision is an important amendment to the former situation under the BeschFG, severely restricting the lawfulness of fixed-term contracts without a justifying reason. The Federal Labour Court had previously understood the regulation in this sense.[48] In recent years, however, it had changed its case law to the effect that a fixed-term contract of two years without an objective reason is possible if the end of the previous employment relationship was more than three years ago. The court justified this view by stating that a lifelong prohibition of a former employment relationship was not necessary in order to achieve the purpose of the regulation, namely

48. Federal Labour Court, 6 Nov. 2003 – 2 AZR 690/02, BAGE 108, 269.

to avoid chains of fixed-term contracts.[49] This highly controversial interpretation of Section 14 paragraph 2 TzBfG was reversed by the Federal Constitutional Court in 2018. A general limitation of the pre-employment ban to three years is not compatible with the Constitution.[50] However, the court also stated that if a pre-employment was very long ago, of a completely different nature or of very short duration (e.g., in the case of minor employment during school and study or family time), a fixed-term contract is possible. Subsequently, in another case, the Federal Labour Court (*Bundesarbeitsgericht* – BAG) determined that after the expiry of twenty-two years since the termination of an employment relationship, a fixed-term contract without an objective reason, when the employee is hired again with the same employer, is permitted.[51]

106. In collective agreements, the number of prolongations or the maximum duration of the fixed-term contract can be determined differently to Section 14 paragraph 2 TzBfG. Employers and employees falling under the scope but nevertheless not bound by such a collective agreement (*see* paragraph 461) may agree that the provisions of the collective agreement should be applicable.

107. The second exception refers to start-ups. In the first four years after the establishment of a company, an employment contract may be limited in time without an objective reason up to a duration of four years according to Section 14 paragraph 2a TzBfG. Up to this total duration of four years, multiple extensions of the fixed-term contract are also permissible. Excluded from the scope of Section 14 paragraph 2a TzBfG are start-ups in connection with the legal restructuring of companies and groups.

108. The third exception is intended to promote the employment of older workers. According to Section 14 paragraph 3 TzBfG as passed in 2000, the conclusion of a fixed-term contract neither requires a justifying reason nor is the fixed-term contract subject to any maximum duration if the employee was 58 (now 52) years of age or older. A limitation as to time, however, is invalid if there is a close objective link with a preceding employment contract of unlimited duration with the same employer. Such a close objective connection is in particular to be assumed if, at the time when the fixed-term contract is concluded, less than six months have passed since the termination of the employment contract of unlimited duration. For a limited period that ended in December 2006, the age threshold had even been reduced from 58 to 52 years. As expected by many, the Court of Justice of the European Union (CJEU) in its contentious decision in *Mangold*[52] found that a provision such as Section 14 paragraph 3 TzBfG, though motivated by a legitimate aim, violates

49. Federal Labour Court, 6 Apr. 2011 – 7 AZR 716/09, BAGE 137, 275.
50. Federal Constitutional Court, 6 Jun. 2018 – 1 BvL 7/14, 1 BvR 1375/14, BVerfGE 149, 126.
51. Federal Labour Court, 21 Aug. 2019 – 7 AZR 452/17, NZA 2020, 40.
52. CJEU, 22 Nov. 2005 – C-144/05, ECLI:EU:C:2005:709; *Cf.* only U. Preis, 'Verbot der Altersdiskriminierung als Gemeinschaftsgrundrecht, Der Fall "Mangold" und die Folgen', *Neue Zeitschrift für Arbeitsrecht*, 2006, pp. 401 et seq.; M. Schmidt: *The Principle of Non-discrimination in Respect of Age. Dimensions of the ECJ's Mangold Decision*, German L. J. 505 et seq. (2006); both with many

the principle of proportionality and hence cannot be justified under Article 6 paragraph 1 of Directive 2000/78/EC. As a consequence, Section 14 paragraph 3 TzBfG has been amended. Since 1 May 2007 the conclusion of employment contracts for a definite period of up to five years has been lawful without any objective reason justifying the time limit, provided that at the beginning of the employment relationship the employee is at least 52 years old and provided that he or she has been without employment within the meaning of Section 138 paragraph 1 SGB III for at least four months. Up to a maximum duration of five years the employment contract may be prolonged repeatedly. Even though Section 14 paragraph 3 TzBfG as amended explicitly refers to prior unemployment, it is still debatable whether or not it is compatible with the ban of age discrimination in terms of Directive 2000/78/EC.[53] On the one hand, the necessary duration of prior unemployment is rather short with the consequence that only those persons are covered who immediately after the termination of an employment relationship find a new one. On the other hand, the reference to Section 138 SGB III means that persons without employment but not being unemployed are also covered.

109. Outside the TzBfG, the Scientific Term Contract Act (*Wissenschaftszeitvertragsgesetz* – WissZeitVG) contains further regulations for scientific employees (with the exception of professors). According to Section 2 WissZeitVG, employees who do not hold a doctorate can be employed on fixed-term contracts for up to six years without any material reason. After completion of the doctorate, temporary employment for a further six years, in the field of medicine up to nine years, is permissible if the temporary employment is for the purpose of promoting the employee's own scientific or artistic qualifications.

C. Consequences of an Invalid Limitation as to Time

110. The consequences of an invalid limitation as to time, as developed by case law, are now laid down in Section 16 TzBfG. Accordingly, the fixed-term employment contract is regarded as being concluded for an indefinite period of time if the limitation is invalid; the employer can terminate it by way of ordinary dismissal at the agreed time of expiry at the earliest, unless ordinary dismissal (with notice) has been agreed in accordance with Section 15 paragraph 3 TzBfG. However, if the limitation is invalid only due to a lack of writing, the employment contract can be terminated even before the agreed time of expiry. If an employee wants to claim that the limitation as to time of his or her employment contract is invalid, he or she has to bring an action before the Labour Court of First Instance within three weeks after the agreed expiry of the employment contract, claiming the court's statement that the employment relationship has not been terminated due to the limitation as to

further proofs. *Cf. also* D. Schiek, *The ECJ Decision in Mangold: A Further Twist on Effects of Directives and Constitutional Relevance of Community Equality Legislation* Indus. L. J. 329–345 (2006).

53. *Cf.* F. Bayreuther, 'Die Neufassung des §14 Abs. 3 TzBfG. Diesmal europarechtskonform?', *Betriebs-Berater*, 2007, pp. 1113 et seq.

time. This follows from Section 17 TzBfG. If no such claim is lodged within the three-week period, the limitation is statutorily deemed to be valid since Sections 4–7 KSchG (*see* paragraph 298) apply *mutatis mutandis*. If the employment relationship is continued after the agreed date of expiry the three-week period starts upon receipt of the employer's written announcement that the employment contract is terminated due to the limitation as to time.

D. The Principle of Equal Treatment

111. If the limitation as to time of an employment contract is valid, an employee employed on the basis of a fixed-term contract must, on account of the limitation as to time of his or her employment contract, not be treated in a less favourable manner than a comparable employee working on the basis of an employment contract of unlimited duration, unless there are objective reasons justifying unequal treatment. Comparable is, according to Section 3 paragraph 2 TzBfG, any employee of the same establishment, working on the basis of an employment contract unlimited as to time, employed in the same or a similar activity. If there is no comparable employee in the establishment working on the basis of an employment contract unlimited as to time, the comparable employee has to be determined with the help of the applicable collective agreement; in all other cases it has to be taken into account who is usually regarded as a comparable employee working on the basis of an employment contract unlimited as to time in the respective branch of economy. An employee working on the basis of a fixed-term contract is entitled to pay and other fungible monetary benefits which are granted for a specific calculation period, at least to an extent corresponding to the share of the duration of the employment in the calculation period. If the entitlement to certain working conditions depends on the duration of the employment relationship in the same establishment or enterprise the same periods have to be considered for employees working on the basis of fixed-term contracts as for employees working on the basis of permanent employment contracts, unless there are objective reasons justifying unequal treatment. Before the coming into effect of the TzBfG, the principle of equal treatment of employees with a fixed-term contract and employees with an open-ended contract, as today laid down in Section 4 paragraph 2 TzBfG, had not been acknowledged in German labour law. Its introduction was necessary in order to implement Directive 1999/70/EC.

E. Termination of a Fixed-Term Contract

112. If the duration of a fixed-term contract is determined by way of the calendar the employee knows exactly in advance when his or her contract will expire: by the end of the agreed period (Section 15 paragraph 1 TzBfG). If the duration of a fixed-term contract follows from the kind, purpose, or nature of the work, however, the date of expiry is not always foreseeable for the employee. Hence, Section 15 paragraph 2 TzBfG stipulates that the contract expires on reaching the purpose of the contract, at the earliest two weeks after receipt of the written information of the employee by the employer about the date when the purpose will be attained. A fixed-term contract is, in accordance with Section 15 paragraph 4 TzBfG, regarded as being continued for an undetermined period of time if it is, with the employer's knowledge, continued at expiration of the contract, unless the employer immediately objects to the continuation or immediately informs the employee that the purpose of the contract has been attained.

113. By means of ordinary dismissal (with notice) a fixed-term contract can be terminated only provided that the right to ordinary dismissal has been agreed upon, either individually or in the applicable collective agreement (Section 15 paragraph 3 TzBfG). If the employment contract has been concluded for the lifetime of a person or for a period longer than five years the employee is entitled to give notice of termination after five years. The notice period is then six months.

F. Rights to Information

114. In order to ensure that fixed-term employees have the same opportunity to secure permanent positions, Section 18 paragraph 1 TzBfG obliges the employer to inform employees with fixed-term contracts about vacancies in the enterprise or in the plant. The information can be given by way of general announcement in a suitable place in the establishment and the enterprise accessible to employees. Furthermore, the employer, according to Section 19 TzBfG, has to ensure that employees with a fixed-term employment contract can participate in vocational and occupational training aiming at the promotion of occupational development and mobility, unless urgent internal company reasons or the wishes of other full-time or part-time employees concerning vocational or occupational training are an obstacle. Section 19 TzBfG does not establish a genuine entitlement to vocational or occupational training. If the employer, however, decides to offer such training to permanent employees, employees working on the basis of a fixed-term contract are to be treated equally. Section 19 TzBfG hence concretizes the right to equal treatment as laid down in Section 4 paragraph 2 TzBfG. Last but not least, the employer has to inform the employee representatives of the number of employees working on the basis of fixed-term contracts and their share in the total number of employees of the establishment and the enterprise. This follows from Section 20 TzBfG.

III. Part-Time Work

115. Although full-time employment is still the prevailing pattern, part-time work (*Teilzeitarbeit*) has become more and more important. One reason for the growing importance of part-time work is the increasing participation of women in gainful employment; another reason is the fact that part-time employment offers greater flexibility, and flexibility is regarded by many as a necessary condition to overcome the difficulties of the economic crisis and to cope with the economic challenges of the future. Since 2001, part-time work has been regulated in the TzBfG (*see* paragraph 100). The statutory definition of part-time work under the TzBfG is similar to the definition of part-time work under the former BeschFG.[54] According to Section 2 paragraph 1 sentence 1 TzBfG, any employee whose regular weekly working time is shorter than that of a comparable full-time employee is working part-time. Comparable are, according to Section 2 paragraph 1 sentences 3 and 4 TzBfG, any full-time employees of the same establishment in the same kind of employment relationship employed in the same or a similar activity. If there is no comparable full-time employee in the establishment the comparable full-time employee has to be determined by recourse to the applicable collective agreement which usually determines the regular working time of full-time employees. If there is no applicable collective agreement or if the applicable collective agreement does not determine the regular working time it has to be taken into account who is usually regarded as a comparable full-time employee in the appropriate branch of the economy. Hence, part-time work can be anything between 36 or 35 hours, depending on the branch, and 1 hour per week. If a regular weekly working time has not been agreed upon an employee is nevertheless working part-time as long as his or her regular working time during a given period of up to one year is on average shorter than the working time of a comparable full-time employee (Section 4 paragraph 1 sentence 2 TzBfG). The TzBfG is also applicable to marginal part-time workers excluded from the statutory systems of social security. This follows from the definition in Section 2 paragraph 1 TzBfG and is explicitly confirmed in Section 2 paragraph 2 TzBfG.

116. The law on statutory social insurance for marginal part-time work has been amended several times recently.[55] Today, German law on statutory social insurance differentiates two kinds of marginal part-time work: if the monthly remuneration for any employment is less than EUR 450 (Section 8 paragraph 1 number 1 SGB IV), the job is a so-called mini job, a monthly income between EUR 450 and EUR 1,300 makes a so-called midi-job. Persons employed in a mini job are, according to Section 27 paragraph 2 SGB III, Section 7 SGB V, Section 6 paragraph 1b SGB VI, Section 20 SGB XI excluded from the statutory systems of social security, irrespective of the number of weekly hours worked. Nevertheless, the employer has to pay social security contributions for any mini-jobber amounting to 31.15% of the remuneration (15% statutory pension insurance, 13% statutory health insurance, 1.09% share in the costs of the employer's benefits in case of sickness and pregnancy) plus flat-rate taxes of 2%. For mini-jobbers employed in private households, the rates of contribution are at 14.69% considerably lower. The employee performing a mini job is in principle obliged to pay neither statutory social security contributions nor taxes for income resulting from the mini job. He or she is not entitled to benefits from the statutory systems of social security. For the pension insurance, however, the legislator made a change in 2013 towards an opt-out regulation. According to this system, mini-jobbers are generally subject to compulsory insurance as employees, but can be exempted from this on application under Section 6 paragraph 1b SGB VI.

54. For more information on part-time work under the BeschFG 1985 *cf.* M. Weiss & M. Schmidt, *Labour Law and Industrial Relations in Germany*, paras. 104–109 (3rd ed. 2000).

55. For details *see* M. Schmidt, *Part-Time Work in Germany*, in *Labour Law and Flexibility in Europe* 77 et seq. (B. Caruso & M. Fuchs eds. 2004).

Unlike mini jobs so-called midi jobs are covered by statutory social security systems. However, in order to avoid any disincentives for employees to earn more than EUR 450, the full rate of employees' social security contributions applies only from EUR 1,300 upwards. This regulation in Section 20 paragraph 2 SGB IV came into force on 1 July 2019 and has replaced the previous 'sliding zone' (formerly EUR 450 to EUR 850) with a 'transition zone'. Between EUR 450 and EUR 1,300 a month, a special contribution calculation is made for the benefit of employees. The lower employee contribution in the transition zone results from a calculated reduction in income. In contrast, the employer pays the contributions from the actual gross wage. In 2018, the number of part-time employees covered by the statutory social security system amounted to 9.26 million, a number which corresponds to 28.2% of all employees covered by the statutory social security system (in 1998 the percentage was still 13.9 and in 2008 19.2%).[56] In addition, for 4.74 million marginal part-time workers the mini job was their only job, while 2.83 million performed a mini job in addition to another job covered by the statutory social security system.[57]

A. *The Principle of Equal Treatment*

117. According to Section 4 paragraph 1 TzBfG, a part-time worker may not, because of the part-time work, be treated in a less favourable manner than a comparable full-time employee, unless there are objective reasons justifying unequal treatment; a part-time employee is moreover explicitly entitled to pay or other fungible monetary benefits at least in an extent corresponding to the share of his or her working time in the working time of a comparable full-time employee. The standards of this test as elaborated by the Federal Labour Court are so strict that reasons justifying differential treatment of full-time and part-time employees are accepted in exceptional cases only.

B. *The Right to Part-Time Work*

118. One of the most disputed provisions of the TzBfG is Section 8, granting employees the right to reduce the agreed working time, the so-called right to part-time work.[58] Modelled upon the Dutch example,[59] the right to part-time work was introduced to promote job creation and to contribute to equal employment opportunities for men and women. The right to part-time work applies only if two conditions are fulfilled. An employee must have been continuously employed for more than six months (Section 8 paragraph 1 TzBfG) by an employer employing more

56. Bundesagentur für Arbeit, *Der Arbeitsmarkt in Deutschland 2018*, p. 12.
57. *Ibid.*, p. 12.
58. As to details *cf.* M. Schmidt, *The Right to Part-Time Work under German Law: Progress in or a Boomerang for Equal Employment Opportunities?* Indus. L. J. 335– 351 (2001).
59. *Cf.* A. Jacobs & M. Schmidt, *The Right to Part-Time Work: The Netherlands and Germany Compared*, The Int'l J. Comp. Lab. L. & Indus. Rel. 371 et seq. (2001).

than fifteen employees (Section 8 paragraph 7 TzBfG). Small employers are released from organizational and administrative burdens resulting from the right to part-time work. The right to part-time work is applicable to employees of any category, be they full-time, part-time, temporary or fixed-term employees. The right to part-time work also applies to employees in managerial positions.

119. According to Section 8 paragraph 2 TzBfG the employee has to request the reduction of his or her agreed working time and to specify the volume of the reduction at least three months in advance. Reasons for the request do not have to be given. The three-month period gives the employer sufficient time to make organizational arrangements, for instance to hire an additional employee. Voluntary agreements to reduce working time can, of course, still be concluded at any time. Section 8 paragraph 2 TzBfG furthermore stipulates that the employee must, together with the request to reduce the working time, inform his or her employer of the requested distribution of the reduced working time, i.e., from when to when the employee would like to work. Section 8 paragraph 3 TzBfG obliges the employer to discuss the requested reduction of working time with the employee, explicitly with the aim of reaching an agreement. Employee and employer must furthermore reach an agreement about the distribution of the working time. Section 8 paragraph 3 TzBfG demonstrates the legislator's hope that the parties to the employment contract will usually voluntarily agree to reduce the working time. If such an agreement is reached, the employment contract changes accordingly. If no agreement can be achieved, working time may nevertheless be reduced, provided that following further requirements are met.

120. The employer has to grant the requested reduction of working time and to determine the distribution of working time in accordance with the employee's wishes, provided that no 'operational reasons' (*betriebliche Gründe*) are conflicting. The crucial question is, of course, what kind of reasons can be regarded to be 'operational reasons' within the meaning of Section 8 paragraph 4 TzBfG. The answer to that question is one of the most important and therefore most contested aspects of the right to part-time work. Section 8 paragraph 4 explicitly states that operational reasons may in particular be found if the reduction in working time interferes significantly with the organization, the course of work or the safety in the establishment, or if the reduction of working time causes disproportionate costs. What that means in detail is highly disputed. Only two points seem to be clear: the additional administrative and organizational burdens resulting from the employment of part-time workers as such cannot be regarded as operational reasons excluding the right to part-time work, otherwise the statutory right would be led *ad absurdum*. Likewise, the employer's objection that he or she was not able to find a suitable additional employee does not constitute an operational reason, unless he or she can prove that no such employee is available on the labour market. According to the case law established in the meantime of the Federal Labour Court,[60] the existence of 'operational reasons' has to be tested in three steps: (1) first of all the organizational concept, developed and executed by the employer, and underlying the regulation of working time regarded as operational necessary has to be identified; (2) then it has to be verified whether the regulation of working time resulting from the organizational concept in fact conflicts with the reduction of working time desired by the employer; (3) finally it has to be examined whether the conflicting operational reasons are so grave that the implementation of the employee's desire to change the working time would considerably interfere with the organization, the course of work or safety in the establishment, or if the reduction of working time would cause disproportionate costs.

121. Legitimate reasons for rejection can be specified in collective agreements (Section 8 paragraph 4 TzBfG). According to Section 22 paragraph 1 TzBfG, however, collective agreements are not allowed to deviate from Section 8 TzBfG to the employee's disadvantage. As a consequence the reasons laid down in collective agreements have to be at least 'operational reasons' within the meaning of Section 8 paragraph 4 TzBfG. Employers and employees who fall within the scope of a collective agreement defining operational reasons but who are not bound by it can individually agree that the provisions of the collective agreement on legitimate rejection reasons shall be applied to the respective individual employment relationship (Section 8 paragraph 4 TzBfG).

122. If the employer agrees to the requested reduction of working time and its distribution, the working hours and their distribution change accordingly. If the employer denies the request he or she, according to Section 8 paragraph 5 TzBfG, has to inform the employee about his or her decision on the reduction of working time and the distribution of the reduced working time at least one month before the reduction of working time should, according to the employee's request, become effective. The employer's decision must be given in writing; but he or she is not required to give any reasons for his decision. On condition that the employer's decision is submitted in time and observes the correct form, the employee's request to work part-time has been effectively rejected; the working time is not reduced. The employee may later on request again a reduction of working time, but he or she is not allowed to do so before two years have passed (Section 8 paragraph 6 TzBfG). If the employee does not want to accept the employer's refusal his or her only option is to seek redress in court. The labour courts then have to decide whether there have been operational reasons conflicting with the employee's request to work part-time. If the labour court finds that there are no operational reasons the court decision replaces the employer's consent to change the employment contract in accordance with the employee's wishes. As soon as this decision has become non-appealable, the employment contract changes accordingly.

60. Fundamentally Federal Labour Court, dec. of 18 Feb. 2003 – 9 AZR 164/02, *Arbeitsrechtliche Praxis*, No. 2 §8 TzBfG.

123. If the working time has been reduced and distributed in accordance with the employee's request, either by agreement between employer and employee or automatically, the employer is, according to Section 8 paragraph 5 TzBfG, entitled to change the distribution of working time if the interests of the establishment outweigh the employee's interests in maintaining the distribution of working time; the employer is only obliged to announce such a change one month in advance.

124. Although the public debate focuses on the right to part-time work, the TzBfG also grants part-time employees a right to claim an extension of their working time to a larger part-time volume or to the regular working time of full-time employees, whether or not the part-time agreement is based on a voluntary agreement with the employer or has been enforced upon the employer automatically in accordance with Section 8 paragraph 5 TzBfG. The right to request an extension of working time follows procedural and material rules which are less complex than those applicable to the right to part-time work. If an employee has informed the employer of his or her request to extend working time the employer has, according to Section 9 TzBfG, 'to give preference' to this request, unless this would conflict with urgent operational reasons or the requests of other part-time employees. Although the wording is vague the duty to 'give preference' has to be interpreted as a duty to grant the request provided that the conditions are met. Contrary to the right to part-time work granted under Section 8 TzBfG, neither thresholds nor time limits apply to Section 9 TzBfG. Hence from the very first day of employment every part-time employee in every enterprise is entitled to claim an extension of his or her working time, as long as there are no 'urgent operational reasons' or conflicting requests of other employees.

C. Employment on Call and Job-Sharing

125. The BeschFG provided a few minimum regulations for two specific forms of part-time work. These have been taken over by the TzBfG, only minor amendments being made. According to Section 12 TzBfG, employer and employee can agree that work is to be performed in accordance with the work accumulation. The agreement of such 'employment on call' (*Abrufarbeit*) has to specify the duration of the weekly and daily working time. If a specification of the weekly working time is lacking a weekly working time of twenty hours is implied by law. This minimum time was increased in 2019 and was previously ten hours. If the daily working time is not specified the employer is obliged to employ the employee for a minimum duration of three hours at a time. The employee is obliged to work only on condition that he or she has been informed at least four days in advance. In a collective agreement, these provisions can be altered, even to the employee's disadvantage, as long as the weekly and daily working time are specified and a period of advanced notice provided for (Section 12 paragraph 3 TzBfG). Employees and employers falling under the scope of such a collective agreement but not bound by it can, according to Section 12 paragraph 3 sentence 2 TzBfG, agree to apply the collectively agreed provisions on employment on call.

126. Part-time work in the form of job-sharing is explicitly permitted in Section 13 paragraph 1 TzBfG: employer and employee may agree that several employees share the working time at one workplace (*Arbeitsplatzteilung*). If one of the job-sharers is unable to work the other job-sharer(s) are, in accordance with Section 13 paragraph 1 sentence 2 TzBfG, only obliged to replace him or her if they have agreed to do so in every individual case or if the employment contract provides for a replacement obligation in cases of urgent operational reasons and if this can reasonably be expected in every individual case. Moreover, Section 13 paragraph 2 TzBfG states that the mere termination of the employment contract of one job-sharer never justifies the dismissal of other employee(s) involved in the job-sharing relationship; the employer's rights to pronounce a dismissal to change working conditions (*Änderungskündigung*) (*see* paragraphs 344–348) on this occasion or to dismiss due to other reasons remains unaffected. This very strict limitation of a replacing obligation of job-sharers is deemed to be the main reason why job-sharing is hardly ever practised in Germany. According to Section 13 paragraph 3 TzBfG, Section 13 paragraphs 1 and 2 apply *mutatis mutandis* if groups of employees work alternately on particular work places in determined periods, without there being job-sharing within the meaning of Section 13 paragraph 1. In a collective agreement Section 13 paragraphs 1 and 3 TzBfG can be altered, even to the employee's disadvantage, as long as the collective agreement contains provisions on the replacement of job-sharers. Employees and employers falling under the scope of such a collective agreement but not bound by it can, according to Section 13 paragraph 4 sentence 2 TzBfG agree to apply the collectively agreed provisions on employment on call.

D. Rights to Information

127. The employer is obliged to advertise vacancies also as part-time jobs provided that a certain job which the employer intends to advertise either in public or within the establishment is suitable for part-time work (Section 7 paragraph 1 TzBfG). Furthermore, the employer has to inform employees who have informed him or her of their wish to change the duration or the distribution of their working time about corresponding vacancies in the enterprise or in the plant (Section 7 paragraph 2 TzBfG). In addition, the employer has to inform the employee representatives about part-time work in the establishment or the company, in particular about existing or planned part-time jobs and about the transformation of part-time jobs into full-time jobs or vice versa. At the request of the employee representatives the necessary documents have to be put at their disposal (Section 7 paragraph 3 TzBfG).

128. The employer is moreover obliged to ensure that part-time employees can participate in vocational training and occupational training aiming at the promotion of occupational development and mobility unless urgent internal company reasons or wishes of other full-time or part-time employees concerning vocational or occupational training are an obstacle (Section 10 TzBfG).

E. Dismissal Protection

129. Last but not least, Section 11 TzBfG prohibits the termination of an employment relationship because of an employee's refusal to change from a full-time employment relationship to a part-time relationship or vice versa. Such a dismissal is invalid. Section 11 TzBfG does explicitly not affect the employer's right to terminate the employment relationship for other reasons.

IV. Temporary Work

130. Under the Act on Commercial Temporary Work (*Arbeitnehmerüberlassungsgesetz–* AÜG), commercial temporary employment (*gewerbliche Arbeitnehmerüberlassung/unechte Leiharbeit*, also called *Zeitarbeit*) is structured as follows: the temporary employee has a normal contractual relationship with an employer (hirer-out – *Verleiher*), usually a so-called temporary Employment Agency. The hirer-out assumes any of the usual employer's duties. Unlike in a normal employee/employer relationship, both parties agree that the employee will be regularly hired out to a third party (hirer – *Entleiher*), where he or she is to perform work. There are contractual relationships between hirer-out and hirer on the one hand, and between hirer-out and temporary employee on the other hand, but there is no contractual relation between temporary employee and the hirer for whom the employee is working. Hence, the temporary employee receives his or her wages from the hirer-out. Nevertheless, certain duties as regards work performance are incumbent on the temporary employee towards the hirer; the hirer also has specific rights and duties in respect of the temporary employee. The AÜG aims at an effective control of the operation of temporary work and, at the same time, at a minimum protection of the temporary employees as to employment conditions and social security. While the conditions of administrative permission are in detail regulated in Sections 2–8 AÜG, the AÜG does not provide comprehensive regulation as to employment protection and social security. Only the specific peculiarities resulting from the splitting of the employer's functions between hirer-out and hirer are regulated in Sections 9–14 AÜG. Since 1994, the AÜG has been deregulated step by step.

131. In a very important branch of economy, in the building industry, commercial temporary work had been totally banned since 1982. This ban, provided for in Section 1b AÜG, was a reaction to the ever-increasing abuses of temporary work and to the inefficiency of administrative control in this specific industry. In 1994, the ban on commercial temporary work in the building industry was relaxed. Since that time, commercial temporary work between establishments of the building industry has been admissible if either the same framework of collective agreements and social fund collective agreements or an order imposing extension of these collective agreements is applicable to the establishments (Section 1b paragraph 1 sentence 2 AÜG).

132. Due to the high rate of unemployment and the step-by-step deregulation of the AÜG, the number of temporary employment contracts had continuously been increasing up to their interim peak in November 2017 with 1.08 million temporary workers (in 1990 the 100,000 mark was exceeded for the first time). Thereafter, the number of temporary workers declined slightly, which can be attributed to better regulation and the economic upswing. In June 2019, the average annual temporary employment was around 948,000.[61] About 71% of them were male, only 29% female. Approximately 54% were employed with unskilled labour. The figures show that mainly younger people are temporarily employed: 49% were younger than 35 years (overall, this age group accounted for only 33% of total employment at that time). Comparatively many temporary workers have a foreign nationality (35% compared to 12% of all employees).[62] Most of the temporary workers are employed in production jobs (40%) and every third worker worked in an economic service occupation, e.g., in security or cleaning jobs. About 14% were employed in personal service occupations (e.g., hospitality and health care occupations) and 11% in commercial occupations (commerce or business management).[63] Of the new temporary employment contracts concluded in the first half of 2019, 65% were unemployed immediately before, including 18% who have been unemployed for more than one year.[64]

A. *Requirement of Permission*

133. In order to ensure the effective control of the operation of temporary work, commercial temporary work is subject to administrative permission. Any enterprise commercially hiring out employees requires a special licence. The conditions to be fulfilled in order to get a licence, the measures of administrative control and the factors which can lead to a withdrawal of the licence are regulated comprehensively in Sections 2–8 AÜG. If the hirer-out has no licence or if he or she has lost his or her licence, his contractual relationship with the employee is or becomes void. Instead the hirer is, according to Section 10 paragraph 1 AÜG, statutorily assumed to be the contractual partner of the employee for the time the employee has worked for him or her. The content and duration of the contract implied in law depend on the provisions applicable to the hirer's establishment (Section 10 paragraph 1 sentence 4 AÜG). The temporary worker is entitled to at least the wages agreed upon with the hirer-out.[65]

---

61. Bundesagentur für Arbeit, *Aktuelle Entwicklungen in der Zeitarbeit*, January 2020, p. 6.
62. *Ibid.*, p. 10.
63. *Ibid.*, p. 9.
64. *Ibid.*, p. 13.
65. For more details *see* M. Weiss, *Regulating Temporary Work in Germany*, in *Temporary Agency Work in The European Union and the United States* 113 et seq (R. Blanpain ed. 2013).

B. Formalities of the Temporary Employment Contract

134. When concluding the temporary employment contract the hirer-out is obliged to fulfil certain requirements in order to guarantee efficient control and in order to increase the employee's protection. In particular, in addition to the obligations in terms of the NachweisG (*see* paragraph 170), the hirer-out has to issue a document containing the company's name, its address, the authority which has issued the licence of the hirer-out, place and date of conferral, the kind and amount of benefits for times during which the temporary employee will not be hired out to any hirer (Section 11 paragraph 1 AÜG).

135. Until 1997 a temporary Employment Agency was, according to Section 3 Nos 3–6 AÜG, not allowed to conclude employment contracts of limited duration unless the temporary employee himself justified the limitation (No. 3), or to conclude unlimited employed contracts but to dismiss and re-engage the temporary employee within three months after the termination of the employment relationship (No. 4), or to limit the duration of the employment relationship to the period of the first assignment to a hirer (No. 5), or to hire a temporary employee out to a hirer for a period longer than six consecutive months (No. 6). In this way, the legislator wanted to prevent hirers from appointing temporary workers to permanent jobs.[66] Faced with increasing unemployment, all these restrictions have been step by step relaxed since 1997 until they were finally abolished by the beginning of 2004.[67] For statistics show that temporary work can help to bring formerly unemployed persons back into work.[68]

C. Principle of Equal Treatment

136. Very often temporary employees earn less than comparable employees employed by the user undertaking. Irrespective of their occupational qualification, the wages of temporary employees have generally been significantly lower. In 1996, temporary workers earned 40.3% less and temporary skilled workers earned 28.6% less than the average remuneration of all employees in the national economy. Until recently, this was lawful since the general principle of equal treatment (*see* paragraph 209) applies only to employees of the same employer. Between the user

66. As regards the situation prior to 1997 *cf.* M. Weiss & M. Schmidt, *Temporary Work and Labour Law in Germany*, in *Temporary Work and Labour Law of the European Community and Member States* 121–161 (R. Blanpain ed. 1993).
67. As to these reforms *cf.* D. Schiek, *Agency Work – From Marginalisation Towards Acceptance? Agency Work in EU Social and Employment Policy and the "Implementation" of the draft Directive on Agency Work in German Law*, German L. J., 1233–1257 (2004); *cf. also* B. Waas, *Temporary Agency Work in Germany: Reflections on Recent Developments,* The Int'l J. Comp. Lab. L. & Indus. Rel. 387–404 (2003).
68. For details *see* M. Weiss, *Germany*, in *Temporary Work and the Information Society* 127 et seq (R. Blanpain & R. Graham eds. 2004); *Bundesagentur für Arbeit,* Aktuelle Entwicklungen in der Zeitarbeit, January 2020, p. 13.

undertaking and the temporary employee, however, there is no contractual relationship (*see* paragraph 130). In 2001, Section 10 paragraph 5 AÜG became effective, obliging the temporary agency to grant temporary employees the same working conditions, including pay, that are applicable to comparable employees in the establishment of the user undertaking. This principle of equal treatment was, however, initially applicable only when the temporary employee had been posted for more than twelve months to the same user undertaking. Since 1 January 2004 Section 10 paragraph 5 AÜG has been repealed. Today, the principle of equal treatment is granted in Section 8 AÜG to which Section 3 paragraph 1 No. 3, Section 9 paragraph 1 No. 2 AÜG refer since 2017. According to Section 8 AÜG, 'the hirer-out has to grant temporary employees hired out to a hirer for the time of hiring the same essential working conditions, including wages, as granted to a comparable employee employed in the hirer's establishment (principle of equal treatment). If the temporary employee receives the collectively agreed remuneration owed for a comparable employee of the user in the user undertaking or, in the absence of such remuneration, a remuneration under the collective agreement applicable to comparable employees in the assignment industry, it is presumed that the temporary employee is treated equally with regard to remuneration within the meaning of the first sentence. If remuneration in kind is granted in the hirer's business, a value adjustment in euros may be made.'

137. The principle of equal treatment is sheltered rather strongly: if the principle of equal treatment, including wage, is infringed, the licence of the hirer-out may not be prolonged or even withdrawn (Section 3 No. 3 and Sections 4 and 5 AÜG). Furthermore, any agreements providing worse working conditions than granted in the establishment of the hirer during the period of hiring out are, according to Section 9 paragraph 1 No. 2 AÜG, null and void. The temporary employee is, according to Section 10 AÜG, entitled to claim the better working conditions from the hirer. In this context, the activity which the hirer has expressly or impliedly assigned to the temporary worker by approval or acquiescence and which is not formally regulated in the temporary employment contract is decisive for determining the settlement remuneration.[69] In order to enable the hirer-out to fulfil his or her obligations resulting from the principle of equal pay, Section 12 paragraph 1 AÜG obliges the hirer to provide the hirer-out with the required information in the written contract between hirer and hirer-out. In order to enable the temporary employee to control the working conditions Section 13 AÜG grants him or her a right of information concerning the essential working conditions, including wages, of any hirer.

138. Nevertheless, the principle of equal treatment as provided for in Section 8 AÜG is still mere theory for the first nine to a maximum of fifteen months of a hiring-out. For the legislator has allowed any parties to a collective agreement to provide for 'differing', i.e., worse conditions. Such a deviating collective agreement

69. Federal Labour Court, 23 Nov. 2016 – 5 AZR 53/16, *BAGE 157*, 213; *cf.* D. Hlava, Equal Pay: Higher Value Work Entails Higher Payment, International Labor Rights Case Law (ILaRC) Vol. 4 (2018), pp. 83-88.

may not, however, fall below the lower wage limit laid down by statutory order pursuant to Section 3a paragraph 2 AÜG. In 2020, the regulation on the minimum wage limit expired. Since then, the statutory minimum wage is currently considered the lower limit. For the protection of temporary employees, a deviating collective agreement provision does not apply if the temporary worker was employed by the hirer in the last six months prior to the hiring-out. According to Section 8 AÜG, the principle of equal pay can only be deviated from for the first nine months of a transfer. A longer deviation by collective agreement is only permissible up to a duration of fifteen months, whereby after a training period of six weeks at the most, a gradual approach to this comparable remuneration must take place.

139. However, hardly any temporary employees are trade union members. This is why the legislator explicitly allowed employers and employees, who are, by their lack of membership in the associations that are parties to a collective agreement (*see* paragraph 463), not automatically bound by such an agreement, to agree individually that the applicable collective agreement deviating from the principle of equal pay should apply. A statutory clause granting a maximum (i.e., equal treatment) and allowing the parties to a collective agreement to agree only on worse conditions is a unique feature in German labour law. It was hence very much contested. The Federal Constitutional Court, however, did not find that formerly Section 3 No. 3, Section 9 No. 2 AÜG (now Section 8 AÜG) infringed the collective freedom of association as granted in Article 9 paragraph 3 GG (*see* paragraphs 407 et seq.).[70]

140. For a long time, German trade unions regarded temporary employment primarily as an instrument for rationalization with negative implications for the labour market. They hence on principle refused to contribute to an improvement of the working conditions of temporary employees by concluding collective agreements. Only in 1999 was the first collective agreement between a German trade union, the IGM and a temporary Employment Agency concluded, regulating the working conditions of 7,000 temporary employees. The Metal Workers' Union regards this agreement as an important step from the trade union side to a more positive attitude towards the branch of temporary work. The 2004 amendment of the AÜG, however, has led to the conclusion of several collective agreements in terms of Sections 8 AÜG between the Federal Association of Temporary Employment Agencies (*Bundesverband Zeitarbeit*) and all eight member unions of the German Federation of Trade Unions (*Deutscher Gewerkschaftsbund* – DGB), providing for remuneration for different wage groups. According to the current wage tables for temporary work, hourly wages in April 2020 in the old FRG range from EUR 10.15 in wage group 1 to EUR 22.12 in wage group 9 and in the former GDR area from EUR 9.88 to EUR 20.79.[71]

70. BVerfG, 29 Dec. 2004, *Neue Zeitschrift für Arbeitsrecht*, 2005, 153.
71. DGB (ed.), *Tarifrunde Leiharbeit 2019/2020*, https://www.dgb.de/themen/++co++972724c0-217c-11ea-bd05-52540088cada.

V. Telework and Mobile Work

141. In 1983, the German Metal Workers' Trade Union was claiming that telework (*Telearbeit*) should be forbidden by law.[72] Social isolation, technological possibilities of monitoring the teleworkers' performance and behaviour, monotony of work content, poor career outlooks, destruction of the traditional separation of the spheres of work and family, overburdening of women with family obligations, danger of self-exploitation and low job security were considered to be factors characterizing telework and thereby endangering all the achievements of the labour movement. This fundamental opposition was soon given up. Telework nowadays is accepted in principle and has grown significantly in the last twenty years. Studies show that almost one-third of the companies offer their employees the opportunity to work from home. At over 50%, this proportion is higher among large companies with over 500 employees than in smaller companies.[73] There are still quite a few barriers for further growth of telework. Employers in particular are afraid that the cost/benefit calculation is a negative one for them, that teleworkers cannot be controlled adequately and that the problems of data protection cannot be resolved properly.[74] The driving force in promoting telework is nowadays rather employees than the employers. Increase in work autonomy and better compatibility of work and family obligations[75] are the most important incentives.

142. The predominant pattern of telework in Germany is rotating telework. This means that work is performed partly in the company and partly at the teleworkplace. The latter may be either in a private home or a satellite office of the company. This type of telework has the advantage that the integration into the workforce of the establishment is maintained to a certain extent. The second pattern is mobile telework, a subcategory of rotating telework where work is partly performed in different locations outside the enterprise. The third pattern is called pure telework where work is fully externalized (be it in the private home or elsewhere). According to a study in the late 1990s, about 95% of the teleworkers belonged to the rotating model, more than half of them to the subcategory of mobile telework.[76] Only 2.5% worked exclusively at home. This shows clearly that the vast majority are somehow integrated into the workforce of the company. There is no indication that this has changed in the meantime, which is also indicated by more recent studies.[77] Almost

---

72. *Cf.* 14th ordinary trade union conference of IG Metall in 1983, summarized in the magazine metallzeitung no. 21, 21. Oct. 1983, p. 21.
73. D. Arnold, S. Steffes & S. Wolter, Mobiles und entgrenztes Arbeiten, *BMAS-Forschungsbericht 460*, 2015, p. 5.
74. L. Kamp, *Betriebs- und Dienstvereinbarungen 'Telearbeit' – Analyse und Handlungsempfehlungen* (2000), p. 7.
75. For general information on the German regulations on work-life balance *see* M. Weiss, *Work-Life Balance: The German Experience*, in *Work-Life Balance and the Economic Crisis* 59 et seq (L. Mella Méndez & Lavinia Serrani eds. 2015).
76. For all these figures *see* H. Freudenreich, B. Klein & P. Wedde, *Entwicklungen der Telearbeit. Arbeitsrechtliche Rahmenbedingungen*, Forschungsbericht im Auftrag des BMA, 1997.
77. *Cf.* Eurofound and ILO (ed.), *Working Anytime, Anywhere: The Effects on the World of Work*, Luxemburg und Genf 2017.

all teleworkers, be they in a rotating scheme or fully externalized, have an employment contract. Thereby they enjoy the full protection of labour law. According to the already mentioned study more than 75% of them were not hired as teleworkers but had worked as employees already before in the company. They voluntarily changed to telework by mutual agreement. Unlike the pattern elsewhere in Europe self-employed teleworkers only play a very marginal role. The study also reveals the high level of education of the big majority of teleworkers in Germany. Only in exceptional cases is teleworking a low-skill job. Recent studies such as the working time survey conducted by the Federal Institute for Occupational Safety and Health (*BAuA*)[78] have shown that in 2017, 12% of employees have teleworking contracts (in 2015 this figure was still 9%). 8% of employees work at least one day a week in telework. Even without an agreement, people work from home, at least occasionally, which applies to about a third of all employees. Telework is more common in primarily intellectual work, office work and work requiring a high level of qualification. Moreover, telework is more common among full-time employees than among part-time employees. During the global COVID-19 pandemic, working from home increased significantly in 2020. It can be assumed that teleworking and other mobile working will also receive a significant boost in the post-crisis period and that noticeably more people will work partially in the home office than was previously the case. This will also be favoured by the advancing digitalization and the better technical possibilities for teleworking or mobile work associated with it.

143. Since the late 1980s, there has been a discussion about whether special legislation for telework is needed. Several drafts have been elaborated. In the meantime, it seemed as though this idea had been abandoned. The German legislation only rarely refers to telework. The 2002 amendment to the BetrVG specifies that teleworkers are employees in the sense of this act, thereby entitled to vote for the works council and/or to be elected (*see* paragraphs 575 et seq.). This, however, is merely a clarification. For a long time, only a few acts have regulating equal opportunities in employment relationships in the public sector, the Act for the Federal Administration and the Federal Courts (*Gleichstellungsdurchsetzungsgesetz*) of 2001 and the Act for the Public Service of the State of Baden-Württemberg (*Gesetz zur Verwirklichung der Chancengleichheit von Frauen und Männern im öffentlichen Dienst des Landes Baden-Württemberg*) of 2005, contain norms according to which telework is to be offered to employees with family obligations if this is possible in the context. The provisions also give preference to employees with family obligation if employees for telework are to be chosen. And they expressly state that teleworkers must have the same career opportunities (promotion, training, etc.) as other employees. Finally telework cannot be used as an instrument to give teleworkers work of lower value. It is, however, doubtful whether these provisions have much impact on actual practice. In recent years, the discussions about a legal framework for teleworking have again increased significantly. For example, some parties are calling for a right to mobile work and politicians are discussing the introduction of a right to work from home.

78. BAuA (ed.), *BAuA-Arbeitszeitbefragung: Telearbeit in Deutschland*, 2nd edn, 2020, https://www.baua.de/DE/Angebote/Publikationen/Bericht-kompakt/Telearbeit-2.html.

144. It is not only labour law that protects teleworkers. The very elaborate legislation on data protection also covers telework.[79] If exceptionally teleworkers are not employees but self-employed they may be covered by the HAG (*see* paragraphs 88 et seq.) which was established long ago for traditional homework. Since the amendment of the Workplace Ordinance (*Arbeitsstättenverordnung* – ArbStättV) in 2016, the term telework has been legally defined for the first time and has been taken into account in teleworking workplaces in the protection regulations for workplace equipment. According to Section 2 paragraph 7 ArbStättV:

> telework stations are monitor-based workplaces permanently installed by the employer in the private sphere of the employees, for which the employer has specified a weekly working time agreed with the employees and the duration of the installation. A teleworking workstation is only set up by the employer when the employer and employees have laid down the conditions of teleworking in an employment contract or within the framework of an agreement and the necessary equipment for the teleworking workstation with furniture, work equipment including communication facilities has been provided and installed by the employer or a person commissioned by the employer in the private sphere of the employee.

As employees, teleworkers are also covered by social insurance, although there are some special features regarding accident insurance cover.

145. Since telework is not yet a significant feature of the German labour market, only a few, but more and more collective agreements taking into account the specific problems of telework have been concluded. Moreover, trade unions in Germany do have a macro-perspective, focusing on the branch of activity as a whole rather than on specific conditions of individual enterprises (*see* paragraphs 444 et seq.). This explains why collective agreement regulations on telework are still rare. Even the European Framework Agreement on Telework at least so far has remained without any significant follow-up in Germany. In 2018, IG Metall Baden-Württemberg concluded an overarching sectoral collective agreement on mobile working which, among other things, includes a right to the employee not being available outside the agreed working hours and leaves many other detailed regulations to the company partners (employer and works council). In general, the shape of telework is considered to be essentially and first of all a task for the regulation by work agreement concluded between employer and works council. Since the works council has a powerful position in this context, there is no danger that telework could be abused to deprive teleworkers of protection. The rules on telework are to be developed and adapted according to the needs of the individual companies. These needs as well as the potential of the respective companies are well known by the works councils. They, therefore, are the ideal actors to cooperate in this respect with

79. *See*, for example, Section 26 Federal Act on Data Protection (*Bundesdatenschutzgesetz*).

the employer.[80] Examples of work agreements on mobile working can be found in the large companies in the automotive industry, among others.[81] Daimler's overall works agreement includes a right to be unavailable and a basic right to work mobile, provided this is compatible with the respective work task. At VW, there is a stricter regulation on the use of smartphones: according to this, no e-mails can be received via business smartphones for half an hour after the end and before the start of the daily flexitime framework and on weekends. This is intended to counteract the blurring of boundaries between work and private life, although this regulation is sometimes seen as patronizing.[82]

§6. Special Groups of Employed Persons

I. Apprentices

146. The system of vocational training is highly developed in Germany. The difference between skilled and unskilled workers has always played an important role. The high standard of apprenticeship training is due to the system through which those skills are acquired. The notion of the skilled worker is not primarily related to actual skills but to the successful conclusion of a period of apprenticeship, and admission is by examination only. The structure of the apprenticeship is regulated by the Act on Vocational Training (*Berufsbildungsgesetz* – BBiG) of 1969. According to this Act apprenticeship is organized as a dual system, training in the enterprise combined with education in special schools for vocational training. The enterprise, and the persons responsible for the training, have to be specially qualified. This qualification is subject to state control. Apprenticeship is only possible for a listed number of occupations recognized as trades by the federal government. The government is also empowered to regulate the structure and the requirements of the training for a specific trade (especially the skills to be acquired and the sequence of the training programme). Depending on the trade, the length of the apprenticeship varies between two and three years. Special examining committees are set up; from the viewpoint of the enterprise they are external institutions. Details of the examinations are regulated by statute. The procedure of the examination is very elaborate and, due to the homogeneous structure of these examinations all over Germany, the standard of vocational training remains, at least in principle, equal no matter where the apprenticeship takes place. This is the main reason for the high esteem this highly formalized system of training still enjoys.

---

80. For more information *cf.* M. Weiss, *Germany*, in *European Framework Agreement and Telework. Law and Practice. A European Comparative Study* (R. Blanpain ed.) Bull. Comp. Lab. Rel. 171 et seq. (2007); L. Kamp, *Telearbeit- Betriebs- und Dienstvereinbarungen*, 2000, Der Setzkasten.
81. *Cf.* J. Heuschmid in Deinert, Heuschmid, Zwanziger (ed.), *Handbuch Areitsrecht*, § 118 Telearbeit und Mobilarbeit, para. 74; for an overview of further regulations *see* BMAS (ed.), *Zeit- und ortsflexibles Arbeiten in Betrieben, Sammlung betrieblicher Gestaltungsbeispiele*, Berlin 2015.
82. *Cf.* J. Heuschmid in Deinert, Heuschmid, Zwanziger (ed.), *Handbuch Areitsrecht*, § 118 Telearbeit und Mobilarbeit, para. 74.

147. Technically speaking, the contract between an apprentice and an employer is not a labour contract. But according to Section 10 paragraph 2 BBiG, the rules and principles governing the labour contract are to be applied, except in cases where the BBiG expressly states an exception or where the application of labour law would not be compatible with the nature and the aim of the apprenticeship. This latter exception evidently creates many problems of interpretation. A contract of apprenticeship is, by statutory definition in Section 21 BBiG, always concluded for a definite period; the contract automatically ends with the apprenticeship. If the apprentice does not pass the examination, the contract is automatically extended until the next examination, which may be repeated only once.

148. Several legislative measures were taken to further promote this pattern of vocational training. In 1976, the Act on Promoting Offers for Apprenticeship (*Berufsausbildungsförderungsgesetz* – BaFöG) initiated special measures to stimulate and to support the increase of the number of places for apprenticeship. The 1981 Act on Promotion of Vocational Training by Planning and Research (*Berufsbildungsförderungsgesetz*) introduced instruments to ensure that the development of vocational training is in line with the technological and economic needs of the society. A special institution, the Federal Institute for Vocational Training (*Bundesinstitut für Berufsbildung* – www.bibb.de) has been established. Its main tasks are to prepare the annual report delivered by the ministry, to assist the government in promoting vocational training and to carry out research in the field. In 2019 about 525,100 new contracts of apprencticeship were concluded in Germany.[83]

149. In the former GDR, the pattern of vocational training was very similar to that in the FRG. The dual system survived in both systems in spite of the ideological differences. However, the function of the schools of vocational training was very different. Instead of providing skills to be used in a market economy, they offered mainly ideological training in socialism. Hence, after unification these schools had to be totally restructured, mainly by replacement of a large number of the teaching personnel. Practical training was mainly concentrated in the big state enterprises, many of which had to close in the course of restructuring. Hence, substitute possibilities for vocational training had to be established in the territory of the former GDR. In this context mainly two strategies became important: first, the establishment of so-called training centres for a whole range of small and medium-sized enterprises within a region, and second, subsidies to companies offering places for apprenticeship. The financial means mainly come from the Federal Republic, but, to a certain extent, also from the new *Länder* in the territory of the former GDR. The result of all these – and some other – instruments was that, at least since 1996, almost all applicants leaving school and searching for an apprenticeship in the former GDR have been offered a job. In 2018, 57,700 apprencticeship places remained unfilled throughout Germany. This was the highest figure since 1994.[84]

83. B. Milde, et al, *Die Entwicklung des Ausbildungsmarktes 2019*, p. 27.
84. *Ibid.*, p. 15.

II. Children and Juveniles

150. As already mentioned in the introduction (*see* paragraph 35), the history of origins of the protection of juveniles dates back to 1839. The actual Act on Protection of Youth Employment (*Jugendarbeitsschutzgesetz* – JArbSchG) was passed in 1976 and amended comprehensively in order to implement Directive 94/33/EC in 1998. According to Section 1 JArbSchG, the Act covers all employed persons under 18 years of age. The employment of persons under 15 years of age (children) is, at least in principle, prohibited. This follows from Section 5 JArbSchG. The same applies, according to Section 2 paragraph 3 JArbSchG, to persons under 18 but no longer under 15 years of age (juveniles) who are subject to full-time compulsory education. The prohibition of child work does not, however, apply to the employment of children for the purpose of employment and work therapy, to the employment of children in the course of a works traineeship, and to the employment of children in implementation of a judicial order. The prohibition of child work is furthermore not applicable to the employment of children of 13 years of age and older, if the person having parental custody has given his consent and if the employment is 'easy and suitable for children'. Employment is supposed to be 'easy' if, due to its character and the particular conditions under which it is to be performed, it adversely affects neither children's safety, health and development nor their school attendance, nor their participation in measures of apprenticeship, nor their ability to attend school lessons to their benefit. Different kinds of employment permissible for children are specified in a governmental decree (*Kinderarbeitsschutzverordnung*) promulgated in 1998. If an employment is easy and suitable for children, a child may be employed for a daily maximum duration of two hours – in family farms up to three hours – but not between 6 pm and 8 am, not before and not during school lessons. The general ban on child work is finally not applicable to the employment of juveniles during school holidays for a maximum duration of four weeks per year.

151. The main parts of the JArbSchG deal with the employment of juveniles. They refer to working time regulations, to occupations that are forbidden for juveniles, to safety measures to be taken in order to protect juveniles and to the extensive measures of health control that are a condition of youth employment.

152. To conclude an employment contract, minors under 18 years of age need the permission of the person having parental custody. Once this permission is issued, they are legally responsible for all matters connected with the employment relationship as provided for in Section 113 BGB.

III. Disabled Persons

153. The problem of integrating disabled persons into the labour market was regulated for the first time in 1923. The first legal regulation in the FRG, the Act on Disabled Persons of 1953, only covered persons whose handicap originated from a specific cause (war, work accidents, etc.). This restriction to specific causes was abandoned in the new Act on Disabled Persons (*Schwerbehindertengesetz* –

SchwbG) of 1974, last amended in 1986 and integrated into the Social Security Code as Book IX (SGB IX) in 2001, which was fundamentally revised by the Federal Participation Act (*Bundesteilhabegesetz*) at the end of 2016. Since 1986 the German law on disabled persons has no longer focused on the cause but merely on the degree of the handicap. In practice, this means that many more people are covered by the law. The main goals of the SGB IX are the integration of disabled persons in employment relationships, special assistance during employment and special protection against dismissals. The integration offices (*Integrationsämter*) control the application of the law and execute certain functions in case of dismissal. In 2009, Germany ratified the UN Convention on the Rights of Persons with Disabilities, which has also provided an impetus for the further development of the rights of persons with disabilities (e.g., greater recognition that failure to provide reasonable accommodation is a form of discrimination and that more efforts must be made to improve accessibility for disabled persons).

154. As follows from Section 154 SGB IX, employers in both the private and public sector providing on yearly average at least twenty jobs per month are obliged to employ severely disabled persons in at least 5% of these jobs. Anybody who, according to Section 2 paragraph 2 SGB IX, has a degree of handicap of at least 50% is severely disabled; disabled persons whose degree of handicap is between 30% and 50% may apply for equal treatment (Section 2 paragraph 3 SGB IX). Whether this rather narrow concept of disability is compatible with Directive 2000/78/EC, however, remains to be seen. Employers with fewer than forty jobs only have to employ one disabled person; employers providing fewer than sixty jobs have to employ two disabled persons. When this obligation is not fulfilled the employer has to pay between EUR 125 and EUR 320 per year, depending on the level of his annual employment quota, to the administrative agency previously mentioned. This money has to be spent exclusively on supporting the situation of disabled persons. This mechanism has led to the fact that many employers prefer to pay the comparatively low sum of money rather than fulfil the obligation of employing disabled persons. Consequently, the rate of unemployment among disabled employees, especially with a severe disability, is significantly higher than the average: in 2017, the employment rate of severely disabled people between the ages of 15 and 65 was only 49%, compared to 78.2% for the overall population.[85] In 2014 in the private sector only 4.1% of jobs were performed by severely disabled persons. In the public sector the share of disabled employees was considerably higher: the quota amounted to 6.6% and hence exceeded the statutory quota of 5%.[86]

155. In addition to the above-mentioned obligation to employ (severely) disabled persons, Part 3 of SGB IX obliges the employer to further the employment and integration of (severely) disabled persons in other ways. For example, Section 164 SGB IX obliges the employer to examine whether persons with severe disabilities or persons of equal status could be employed when vacancies are to be filled.

---

85. Bundesagentur für Arbeit, *Situation schwerbehinderter Menschen*, April 2019, p. 7.
86. *Zweiter Teilhabebericht der Bundesregierung über die Lebenslagen von Menschen mit Beeinträchtigungen*, 2016, p. 177.

The same provision grants disabled employees the right to be accommodated by employment in such a way that they are able to fully develop and use their knowledge and skills, privileged provision for in-plant measures of vocational training in order to further their professional advancement, facilitated participation in external measures of vocational training and the equipping of workplaces with the requisite technical equipment. Moreover, specific representation for disabled employees (*Schwerbehindertenvertretung*) and specific dismissal protection is provided for. Last but not least, the provisions of the AGG (*see* paragraphs 172–180, 207–214) apply.

IV. Foreign Employees

156. In June 2018 about 3,848 million foreign employees subject to statutory social insurance contribution were employed in Germany, including 2,116 million from EU Member States.[87] The unemployment rate of foreign employees is significantly higher than the employment rate of German nationals. In 2018, when the overall unemployment rate in Germany was 4.9%, the unemployment rate for foreigners amounted to 12.6%.[88] This means that 11.7% of all unemployed persons were foreigners.[89]

157. Foreigners who are citizens of a country belonging to the EU – so-called EU nationals – enjoy freedom of movement as granted in Article 45 TFEU. Their entry and residence in Germany is regulated by the Act on Freedom of Movement/EU (*Freizügigkeitsgesetz/EU* – FreizügG/EU) of 2004. They neither need a visa nor a residence permit (*Aufenthaltstitel*) or a work permit (*Arbeitserlaubnis*). Their spouses and children who are non-EU nationals also have free access to the German labour market provided that they live in the same household as the EU national. These rules also apply to EEA nationals (Norwegians, Icelanders, Liechtensteiners) and Swiss.

158. Non-EU nationals, however, require a residence permit explicitly allowing them to work in terms of Section 18 of the Act on Residence (*Aufenthaltsgesetz*– AufenthG) of 2004. The question of whether or not a foreigner is allowed to stay in Germany (whether for a limited or for an unlimited period) is determined by the aliens office (*Ausländerbehörde*); if he or she applies for a residence permit allowing him or her to work the Federal Agency of Employment has to give its consent in accordance with Section 39 AufenthG. The consent may (only) be given if this is provided for in any intergovernmental agreement, any statutory law or decree, as e.g., the decrees issued by the Federal Minister of Labour and Social Affairs on the basis of Section 288 SGB III. Generally speaking, the question whether or not the consent will be given primarily depends on two factors: (1) that there is no preferential employee available for the job and (2) that the terms of employment are not

87. Bundesagentur für Arbeit, *Der Arbeitsmarkt in Deutschland 2018*, Tab IV.B.2a.
88. *Ibid.*, Tab IV.G.17.
89. *Ibid.*, Tab IV.G.16.

worse than those of comparable German employees. However, there are some exceptions and, in particular in recent years, the right to immigrate, especially for skilled workers, has been and is being reformed repeatedly. In many cases, the residence permit can also be issued without the consent of the Federal Agency of Employment. Employees who are EU nationals or equitable are preferential. This shows that the labour market perspective is not regulated in the AufenthG itself but is left to government discretion. In other words, the AufenthG provides a mechanism allowing government to react in a flexible way to the economic and labour market situation.

159. In principle, foreign employees have the same rights and duties as German employees.[90] This, of course, does not say anything about the implementation of those rights and duties. There are indications that there are discrepancies. For example, since 1972 foreign employees have been able to be elected as members of works councils. The number of foreign employees among works council members, however, has always remained and still remains significantly lower than their share of the workforce. This indicates a misrepresentation. On the contrary, the number of union members among foreign employees is significantly higher than the number among German employees. The unions have special departments to deal with the problems of foreign employees. Thus, it may be expected that foreign employees will receive support from this quarter.

V. Posted Employees

160. Employment contracts concluded between an employer, seated in Germany, and an employee performing his or her work in Germany, are generally subject to German law, regardless of the employee's nationality or the employer's nationality. To employment contracts falling under a foreign legal system, the appropriate foreign laws and collective agreements apply. Thus, different working conditions are applicable to employment contracts concluded in accordance with different legal systems. According to the rules of international private law, however, the applicability of a foreign legal regime is not set aside if the employee is being temporarily posted to another state. Consequently, different working conditions may apply to employees temporarily posted to Germany and to employees working on the basis of an employment contract under German law, even if they are equally performing the same work.

161. At the beginning of the 1990s, the posting of employees to Germany dramatically increased, primarily in particular branches such as e.g., the building and construction industries. In 1994, 122,000 employees of the building and construction industry were unemployed, while about 150,000 posted workers from other EC Member States were working in the German building and construction industry. In

90. More detailed information on the special labour law features of the employment of foreign workers *see* D. Hlava, in Deinert, Heuschmid, Zwanziger (ed.), *Handbuch Arbeitsrecht*, § 107 Ausländische AN.

1996, the number of unemployed employees in that branch ranged between 300,000 and 180,000, while, at the same time, there were 200,000 foreign posted workers employed on German construction sites. In other EC Member States, similar developments could be observed. Nevertheless, attempts to define an EC wide core of national rights applicable to workers posted to another EC Member State failed. This is why Germany, as well as Austria, Belgium and France, adapted a national Act on Obligatory Working Conditions in the Event of Posting of Employees (*Arbeitnehmer-Entsendegesetz* – AEntG). The original version of the AEntG, in force since March 1996, was applicable only to employees in the building and construction industry. In December 1996, Directive 96/71/EC concerning the posting of workers in the framework of the provision of services has finally been adopted. Its personal scope of application is, unlike the personal scope of application of the 1996 AEntG, not limited to employees of one branch but includes employees of all branches. Therefore, already soon after its enactment, the 1996 AEntG had to be amended in order to implement Directive 96/71/EC. In December 1998, the freshly elected legislator took this chance to adapt several further modifications aiming at improving the effectiveness of the 1996 AEntG.[91]

162. The main provision of the 1998 amendment, bringing the AEntG in line with the former Directive 96/71/EC, is Section 7 AEntG, stipulating that legislative and administrative provisions concerning the following working conditions are applicable to any employment relationship between an employer seated abroad and his or her employee performing his or her work in Germany: maximum working time and minimum rest periods, paid annual holiday, minimum wages including overtime pay, conditions for hiring-out of employees, in particular by temporary work agencies, occupational health and safety and workplace hygiene, protective measures in connection with working and employment conditions of pregnant women and women in childbirth, of children and juveniles, and equal treatment of men and women and other bans on discrimination. As far as posted workers perform their work in the territorial scope of application of a collective agreement which has been extended (*see* paragraphs 472–475), the provisions of the collective agreement concerning the above-mentioned topics – except minimum annual holiday and minimum wages – also apply. Actions for working conditions granted under the AEntG may be brought before German labour courts. This is clarified by Section 8 AEntG, incorporated by the 1998 amendment.

163. In the past, minimum paid annual holiday, and minimum wages including overtime pay, provided for in an extended German collective agreement were applicable to posted employees of only one branch: to employees of the building and construction industries. The reason why posted workers in the building and construction industries were treated differently from employees of other branches posted to Germany is that in that branch the competitive problems arising from employees posted to Germany seemed to be particularly urgent, the most urgent

91. For this development *see* M. Weiss, *The Implication of the Service Directive on Labour Law in a German Perspective*, in *Freedom of Services in the European Union* 77 et seq (R. Blanpain ed. 2005).

problem being the differences as to pay in its broadest sense between posted workers and workers employed in accordance with German working conditions. To date remuneration is, however, not fixed by the German legislator but the essential matter to be negotiated between the parties to a collective agreement. This is why the 1996 AEntG was originally restricted to remuneration in its broadest sense, guaranteed in extended collective agreements for the building and construction industries. Directive 96/71/EC, however, primarily provides for the applicability of working conditions guaranteed in legislative and administrative provisions to posted workers. The extension of working conditions provided for in collective agreements to posted workers of the building and construction branch has been a mere concession to the fact that the German AEntG had been already adopted when the directive passed the Council of Ministers.

164. According to Section 1 of the 1996 AEntG, as amended in 1998, the normative provisions (*see* paragraphs 461 et seq.) of an extended collective agreement (*see* paragraphs 472–475) of the building and construction industries concerning minimum wages including overtime pay, duration of annual holiday, holiday pay or an additional holiday allowance, were also applicable to an employment relationship between an employer seated abroad, and an employee performing work in the territorial scope of application of the respective collective agreement, provided that the establishment were predominantly producing building or construction work, and on condition that employers seated in Germany were also obliged to grant employees who were performing work in the territorial scope of the collective agreement the working conditions as provided for in the collective agreement. The same applied, according to the former Section 1 paragraph 2a, to temporary workers performing work in the territorial scope of application of an extended collective agreement. Compliance with these rules must be achieved by a multitude of control measures and severe sanctions: before commencing any building or construction work, an employer intending to post employees to Germany was obliged to notify the former *Land* Employment Agency competent for the area where the work is to be performed in writing about the most important particulars (surname, name and date of birth of the employees to be posted to Germany, start and termination of employment, place of employment, surname, name, date of birth of the responsible person in Germany, etc.). Furthermore, the employer had to add an affirmation that he or she will grant the working conditions provided for in Section 1 AEntG. In addition, the employer was obliged to record information concerning the employment of the posted workers. He or she had to document start and termination as well as duration of the employee's daily working time, and was obliged to keep records for two years. The competence to control working conditions rests with the principal customs office.

165. Of course, as a consequence of the extension of any collective agreement in terms of Section 1 AEntG not only employees posted to Germany but also those regularly employed by an employer seated in Germany are covered. Any other solution would infringe the Community freedom of services under Article 49 TFEU. This is why the AEntG has been discovered as a tool to bring about general minimum wages for certain branches as construction, building cleaning, mail services, security services, mining, laundry services, waste management, education and training services for the unemployed and meat processing. In addition, the possibility of extending nationwide collective agreements to all sectors was extended in 2014 (*see* paragraph 255).

166. An employer who does not comply with the rules established by the AEntG, has to face severe sanctions: apart from administration fines of up to EUR 500,000 he or she may temporarily be excluded from a competition for public authority orders. In addition, an entrepreneur who entrusts another entrepreneur with work or services is liable for the obligations of the charged entrepreneur and for the obligations of any entrepreneur further charged as to minimum wages, etc. arising from Section 3 AEntG.

167. In 2018, the EU adopted Directive (EU) 2018/957 to amend the Posting of Workers Directive, which had to be implemented in national law by July 2020. This resulted in the need to reform the AEntG. According to the directive, posting companies have to be bound by all remuneration regulations in force in the host country for the remuneration of their posted employees. From day one, posted workers must receive the same standard wage as their colleagues in the host country. In addition to the basic salary, posted workers are explicitly entitled to all other remuneration components such as bonuses or allowances (including Christmas bonus, holiday pay, mobility allowances, bad weather allowances), provided that these are laid down by law or in generally binding collective agreements (equal pay principle). Employers are also obliged under the reform to bear the travel, board and lodging costs of posted employees. This is intended to counteract the current practice of deducting any costs from the employees' wages. In addition, postings are limited to twelve months. As an exception, an extension to eighteen months is permissible.[92]

168. However, the current reform of the AEntG does not meet these requirements of the Posting of Workers Directive in every respect. For example, the extension of collective agreements is to differentiate between 'minimum rates of pay' and 'components of pay exceeding these rates', whereas the directive, however, covers the entire pay. Furthermore, not the entire pay scale is to be included, but only a few pay scales. Furthermore, there is a differentiation in the application of nationwide collective agreements and regional generally binding collective agreements. It remains to be seen whether the final reform does sufficiently implement the requirements of Union law. The CJEU will have the last word on this issue.

92. *Cf.* Änderungen in der EU-Entsenderichtlinie: Aufwändige Regeln für wenig mehr Gerechtigkeit, in: *Legal Tribune Online*, 19 Jul. 2019, https://www.lto.de/persistent/a_id/36585/.

Chapter 2. Conclusion of the Individual Labour Contract

§1. Restrictions on the Freedom of Contract

169. As already mentioned, freedom of contract is still the guiding principle of German labour law. This implies that each individual is free to choose the occupation and employment he or she desires. This freedom is guaranteed under Article 12 GG and also implies the prohibition of forced labour, warranted in Article 12 paragraphs 2 and 3 GG. According to these provisions, no person may be required to perform work of a particular kind except within the framework of a traditional duty of community service that applies generally and equally to everybody. Forced labour may be imposed only on persons deprived of their liberty by court decision.

170. The principle of freedom of contract implies that no special formalities are required. An oral agreement suffices. Nevertheless the Act on the Documentation of Employment Conditions (*Nachweisgesetz*– NachwG), enacted in 1995 in order to implement Directive 91/533/EEC into German law, obliges every employer to hand out to his or her employees a document containing the main terms of the employment contract. This, however, does not mean that observance of written form is required to conclude a valid employment contract.

171. Freedom of contract finally implies that the employer is free to choose with whom he or she wants to conclude a contract. However, this freedom is to a certain extent restricted.

I. Principles of Equal Treatment

A. The Principle of Equal Treatment as Granted in Article 33 GG

172. Until very recently, as to restrictions of the freedom to choose with whom to conclude an employment contract, a distinction had be drawn between employment in the private sector and employment in the public service. Under the German GG, applicants applying for a job in the public service have always enjoyed the right to equal treatment as guaranteed in Article 33 GG. According to that provision, 'personal aptitude, the qualifications and professional achievements' of the applicant are the legally accepted criteria on which the decision of whom to hire has to be based. In fact, however, this restriction should not be overestimated as these criteria leave a very wide leeway for selection. Only in very rare cases can the applicant derive a right to be employed from this constitutional provision, i.e., in a situation where it is evident that he or she is the only person fulfilling these criteria.

B. The Principle of Equal Treatment Granted under the AGG

173. On 18 August 2006 eventually the AGG, implementing Directives 2000/43/EC, 2000/78/EC, 2002/73/EG and 2004/113/EC into German law, became effective. At this time, the Commission had already executed two 'successful' infringement proceedings against Germany for reasons of non-implementation.[93] The four years' delay in implementation was due to strong political opposition to any kind of anti-discrimination law and, consequently, against any transposition exceeding the minimum required by the anti-discrimination directives. The criticisms mainly referred to the government's intention to implement Directive 2000/78/EC by going beyond what was required, i.e., to ban discrimination on the grounds of religion and belief, disability, age and sexual orientation also in respect of access to and supply of goods and services which are available to the public within the meaning of Article 3h of Directive 2000/43/EC. The finally adopted AGG is largely identical with the ADG Bill passed in the summer of 2005, drafted under the former red-green coalition. According to Sections 7, 1 AGG employed persons may not be discriminated against on any of the grounds mentioned in Section 1 AGG, i.e., race or ethnic origin, sex, religion or belief, disability, age or sexual orientation.

174. In personal respects, the AGG is applicable to employed persons (*Beschäftigte*) as defined in Section 6 AGG. The notion 'employed person', within the meaning of Section 6 paragraph 3 AGG, comprises employees, apprentices (*Auszubildende*) and persons who are, due to their economic dependency, regarded as employee-like persons (*arbeitnehmerähnliche Personen*). In addition, applicants for a job and persons formerly employed within the meaning of Section 6 paragraph 1 AGG are regarded as 'employed persons' in terms of Section 6 paragraph 1 AGG. The legal term 'employed person' (*Beschäftigte*) in Section 6 paragraph 1 AGG is hence far wider than the term 'employee' (*Arbeitnehmer*). In material respects, Section 2 No. 1 AGG applies. Accordingly, discrimination on any of the grounds mentioned in Section 1 AGG is illegal in relation to conditions for access to employment, to self-employment or to occupation, including selection criteria and recruitment conditions, whatever the branch of activity and at all levels of the professional hierarchy, including promotion.

175. The term 'discrimination' is defined in Section 3 AGG and distinguishes between direct discrimination, indirect discrimination, harassment and instructions to discriminate. Again, the legislator simply copied the definitions from the anti-discrimination directives. According to Section 3 paragraph 1 AGG, direct discrimination is taken to occur where one person is treated less favourably on any of the grounds mentioned in Section 1 than another is, has been or would be treated in a comparable situation. Indirect discrimination is defined in Section 3 paragraph 2 AGG. It is to be taken to occur where an apparently neutral provision, criterion or practice would put persons, due to any of the grounds mentioned in Section 1 AGG,

93. Judgments of 28 Apr. 2005, case C-329/04 (*Commission v. Germany*), OJ 2005, C 143/13 (Directive 2000/43/EC), and of 23 Feb. 2006, case C-43/05 (*Commission v. Germany*), OJ 2006, C 131/23.

at a particular disadvantage compared with other persons, unless that provision, criterion or practice is objectively justified by a legitimate aim and the means of achieving that aim are appropriate and necessary. Furthermore, an instruction to discriminate against persons on any of the grounds mentioned in Section 1 shall be deemed to be discrimination (Section 3 paragraph 5 AGG). In the employment context, such an instruction will be deemed to be particularly clear if somebody persuades another person to act in a discriminatory manner or in a way that discriminates against an employed person. Multiple discrimination is sanctioned in Section 4 AGG. Accordingly, discrimination on several of the grounds mentioned in Section 1 AGG can only be justified in terms of Sections 8–10 AGG if the justifications cover all of these grounds. With regard to the ground of disability, an interpretation of the AGG in line with international law, Union law and constitutional law recognizes a further form of discrimination if the provision of reasonable accommodation for people with disabilities is denied.[94] According to Section 2 of the Convention on the Rights of Persons with Disabilities 'Reasonable accommodation' 'means necessary and appropriate modification and adjustments not imposing a disproportionate or undue burden, where needed in a particular case, to ensure to persons with disabilities the enjoyment or exercise on an equal basis with others of all human rights and fundamental freedoms'.

176. Under the AGG there are two general exceptions to the rule that unequal treatment on any of the grounds mentioned in Section 1 AGG is illegal: positive action in terms of Section 5 AGG on the one hand,[95] and genuine and determining occupational requirements in accordance with Section 8 AGG on the other. Since indirect discrimination is already *per definitionem* not given if there is a legitimate aim justifying the provision, criterion or practice, Sections 5 and 8 AGG mainly apply to direct discrimination. According to Section 5 AGG, notwithstanding the reasons mentioned in Sections 8–10 AGG, a difference of treatment will be lawful if disadvantages linked to any of the grounds mentioned in Section 1 AGG are prevented or compensated by appropriate and proportionate measures (so-called positive action). Accordingly, with a view to ensuring full equality in practice, the principle of equal treatment should not prevent any Member State from maintaining or adopting specific measures to prevent or compensate for disadvantages linked to race or ethnic origin, religion or belief, age, disability, sexual orientation. Section 8 AGG stipulates that differences of treatment based on a criterion related to any of the grounds referred to in Section 1 AGG shall not constitute discrimination where, by reason of the nature of the particular occupational activities concerned or of the context in which they are carried out, the criterion constitutes a genuine and determining occupational requirement, provided that the objective is legitimate and that the requirement is proportionate.

---

94. *See* E. Eichenhofer, *Angemessene Vorkehrungen als Diskriminierungsdimension im Recht*, 2018; F. Welti, A. Frankenstein & D. Hlava, *Angemessene Vorkehrungen und Sozialrecht*, Berlin 2018.

95. As regards the European concepts of positive action *cf.* D. Schiek, *Positive Action Before the European Court of Justice: New Conceptions of Equality in Community Law?*, Int'l J. Comp. Lab. L. & Indus. Relations 178–199 (2000).

177. As Section 8 paragraph 2 AGG clarifies, the fact that particular protective provisions apply to one age is no legitimate reason justifying the agreement of a reduced remuneration for equal work or work of equal value. Section 8 paragraph 2 AGG hence reformulates and extends the principle of equal pay for equal work and work of equal value that had been hitherto guaranteed in Section 612 paragraph 3 BGB.

178. Regardless of Section 8, unequal treatment on grounds of religion or belief is also permissible if, in respect of employment by religious communities, by any institution assigned to them irrespective of its legal form or by associations having made the collective ministration of religion or belief their task, a certain religion or belief constitutes a justified occupational requirement, taking into account either the self-conception of the respective religious community or association or the kind of activity to be performed. This follows from Section 9 paragraph 1 AGG. The ban of discrimination on grounds of religion and belief furthermore does not, according to Section 9 paragraph 2 AGG, affect the right of any of those religious communities, of any institution assigned to them irrespective of their legal form or of any association having made the collective ministration of religion or belief their task referred to in paragraph 1 to ask for loyal and honest conduct within the meaning of their respective self-conception from their employees.

179. Sections 1–5, 6–8, 11–16 AGG apply to discrimination on any of the grounds mentioned in Section 1 AGG, i.e., also to age discrimination. In addition, however, the German legislator has used the options granted in Article 6 of Directive 2000/78/EC to approve further specific exceptions from the ban of age discrimination.[96] According to Section 10 AGG differences of treatment on grounds of age do not constitute discrimination if they are objectively and reasonably justified by a legitimate aim; the means of achieving that aim must be appropriate and necessary. Section 10 AGG applies to individual employment contracts as well as to collective agreements and the employer's unilateral measures or instructions.[97] As regards access to employment, Section 10 Nos 1–3 AGG apply. According to Section 10 No. 1 AGG, differences in treatment not constituting discrimination on the grounds of age may include the fixing of special conditions on access to employment and vocational training, employment and occupation, including dismissal and remuneration conditions, for young people, older workers and persons with caring responsibilities in order to promote their vocational integration or to ensure their protection may be compatible with the ban on age discrimination. Section 10 No. 2 AGG further allows the fixing of minimum conditions of age, professional experience or seniority in service for access to employment or to certain advantages linked to employment. Since Section 10 No. 2 AGG only denominates examples possibly compatible with the ban of age discrimination, any such measure still has to be in

---

96. As regards the German provisions implementing the ban on age discrimination *cf.* M. Schmidt, *Germany*, in *Age Discrimination in the EU* 29–54 (M. Sargeant ed. 2008).
97. M. Schmidt, in Dagmar Schiek (ed.), *Allgemeines Gleichbehandlungsgesetz (AGG). Ein Kommentar aus europäischer Perspektive* (2007), §10 para. 3.

pursuit of a legitimate aim and to comply with the principle of proportionality. Differences in treatment not constituting discrimination on grounds of age may, according to Section 10 No. 3 AGG, furthermore include the fixing of a maximum age for recruitment, which is based on the training requirements of the post in question or the need for a reasonable period of employment before retirement. What exactly constitutes a reasonable period of employment is highly problematic and will have to be defined by the CJEU.

180. The AGG is not restricted to material provisions but also contains procedural rules, *inter alia* indicating how employers may lawfully avoid becoming liable for age discrimination. First of all, Section 11 AGG prescribes that a vacancy may not be advertised contravening the ban on age or other grounds of discrimination. Like the former Section 611b BGB, however, Section 11 AGG does not explicitly provide for any sanction in case of non-compliance. It may, however, safely be assumed that the labour courts will interpret any violation of Section 11 AGG, as formerly any violation of Section 611b BGB, as an indication of discrimination in the course of hiring. Second, Section 12 paragraph 1 AGG obliges the employer to take such measures, including preventive measures, as protection against discrimination on any one of the grounds mentioned in Section 1 AGG. The employer must, in a proper kind and manner, particularly in the framework of vocational training and advanced vocational training, point out that discrimination is illegal and work towards ensuring that it does not happen. If the employer provides appropriate training of his or her employees in order to prevent discrimination, the employer will be deemed to have met his or her obligations under Section 12 paragraph 1 AGG. The problem is now, of course, what makes training 'appropriate' in terms of Section 12 paragraph 1 AGG. Furthermore, the text of the AGG and of Section 61b ArbGG as well as any information about the institution responsible for handling of grievances in accordance with Section 13 AGG, have to be published within the establishment. Publication may take place by displaying them at appropriate places or by use of the information and communication techniques usual at the establishment concerned.

181. Any provisions in agreements contravening the ban on discrimination guaranteed in Section 7 paragraph 1 AGG are null and void. In case of access to employment, the main sanction for discrimination in employment provided for by the AGG is compensation for material and non-material damages as laid down in Section 15 AGG.[98] Section 15 paragraph 1 AGG obliges the employee to compensate for any damages resulting from discrimination, unless he or she infringed his or her duties neither negligently nor deliberately. A right to be hired or promoted, however, is explicitly excluded in Section 15 paragraph 6 AGG, unless this right should result from other legal grounds. For non-material damages the employee may, according to Section 15 paragraph 2 AGG, furthermore claim adequate compensation. Contrary to Section 15 paragraph 1 AGG, the right to compensation in terms of Section 15 paragraph 2 AGG is generally not subject to the employer's fault. However, if

98. For more details *cf.* O. Deinert, 'Anwendungsprobleme der arbeitsrechtlichen Schadensersatzvorschriften im neuen AGG', *Der Betrieb*, 2007, p. 398.

discrimination results from the application of collective agreements, the employer is liable for compensation only if he or she has acted deliberately or been grossly negligent (Section 15 paragraph 3 AGG). In cases of discrimination in the course of the hiring process, compensation for non-material damage may not exceed three months' wages if, even in the case of a non-discriminatory hiring procedure, the applicant would not have been employed (Section 15 paragraph 2, sentence 2 AGG). According to Section 15 paragraph 4 AGG, a claim for compensation in terms of Section 15 paragraphs 1–3 AGG, however, should be claimed in writing within two months, unless the parties to a collective agreement applicable to the employment relationship have agreed otherwise. In cases of an application or a promotion the period begins to run at the time when the person to be employed or to be promoted receives the negative answer; in all other cases the period commences at the time when the employee notices the discrimination. The fact that liability under Section 15 paragraphs 1 and 3 AGG is subject to fault is quite amazing. After all, the CJEU has stated already several times that the employer's liability for sex discrimination may not be made subject to proof of fault.[99]

II. Limitations on the Employer's Right to Question Applicants

182. A further restriction refers to the employer's treatment of applicants. Initially, employers had been free to ask all the questions they wanted and to make applicants undergo all kinds of tests. However, under the GG the individual's right to privacy as guaranteed by Articles 1 and 2 GG is seen as an important restriction on such practices. Consequently only questions that are in the employer's rightful and provable interest and needing to be answered because of the employment relationship to be established may be asked. The employer's interest must actually be so strong that the employee's interest in protection of his or her personal rights and the inviolability of his or her privacy are considered less important. The applicant is not obliged to answer inadmissible questions. To prevent the employer from concluding from the employee's mere refusal to answer that something is worth hiding, the applicant is allowed to answer inadmissible questions with a lie. According to the consistent practice of the Federal Labour Court only a false answer to a rightfully asked question can be a lawful reason for dismissal or a fraudulent misrepresentation with the legal consequence that the employer may contest the contract of employment.[100] The general tendency, in view of the right to privacy, is to more and more restrict the employer's right to ask questions invading the private life of the applicant.

183. For example, the employer may only ask about previous convictions if the future work requires this. Thus, for example, an accountant or a cashier may be

99. Dec. of 8 Nov. 1990, case 177/88 (*Dekker*), *European Court Reports*, 1990, I-3941 (para. 25); dec. of 22 Apr. 1997, case C-180/95 (*Draempaehl*), *European Court Reports*, 1997, I-2195 (para. 18).

100. Federal Labour Court of 5 Dec. 1957 – 1 AZR 594/56, *Arbeitsrechtliche Praxis*, No. 2 §123 BGB; of 21 Feb. 1991 – 2 AZR 449/90, *Arbeitsrechtliche Praxis*, No. 35 §123 BGB; of 5 Oct. 1995 – 2 AZR 923/94, *Arbeitsrechtliche Praxis*, No. 40 §123 BGB.

questioned about his or her previous convictions for property offences, or a truck driver may be asked about his or her previous convictions for traffic offences.[101] The applicant, however, is not obliged to declare previous convictions or disclose the underlying facts of the conviction if the previous convictions are no longer registered in the Federal Central Register for Convictions (*Bundeszentralregister*) or if they need no longer be listed in the policy certificate of good conduct, i.e., not in cases of insignificant offences or offences committed more than five years previously.

184. The employer's right to ask female applicants whether they are pregnant, irrespective of the position to be filled, was uncontested for quite a long time. In 1961, the Federal Labour Council had justified this right referring to the employer's obligations deriving from statutory maternity protection.[102] According to the view of the court, an employee's maternity encumbered the employer not only with heavy financial burdens but also had the consequence that, due to prohibitions and restrictions of employment, internal company work routines were made more difficult. Therefore, the court acknowledged that the employer had a considerable legal and financial interest in finding out whether an applicant was pregnant. In 1986, however, when the Federal Labour Court had to decide on that question again, the position developed in 1961 could not be upheld.[103] For in the meantime Section 611a BGB had been passed in order to implement Directive 76/207/EEC. Whether the employer's question as to an existing pregnancy contravened that prohibition was highly controversial. It was perfectly clear that the employer's intention in asking that question was usually to avoid the employment of pregnant women. The crucial question was whether discrimination against pregnant women was also discrimination based on sex. The Federal Labour Court answered that question in a very unconvincing way. The court held the view that the question as to an existing pregnancy was to be regarded as discrimination on the grounds of sex only if there were male and female applicants competing. If only women had applied for the job, every applicant could be concerned, and therefore discrimination was not at issue. This decision has been heavily criticized and was superseded by a decision of the CJEU in 1990.[104] In a case referred to it by a Dutch court, the CJEU decided that if an employer refused to conclude an employment contract with a female applicant because he was afraid of the disadvantages which arise from the employment of a pregnant woman as a result of the applicable statutory regulation, this was a violation of the prohibition on discrimination based on sex under Directive 76/207/EWG. In 1992 the Federal Labour Court therefore renounced its view and concurred with the legal opinion of the CJEU.[105] It concluded that the question as to a pregnancy during recruitment negotiations was generally inadmissible as an infringement of Section 611a BGB.

101. Federal Labour Court of 5 Dec. 1957, *supra*; of 20 May 1999 – 2 AZR 320/98, *Arbeitsrechtliche Praxis*, No. 50 §611 BGB.
102. Federal Labour Court, 22 Jun. 1961 – 1 AZR 241/60, *Arbeitsrechtliche Praxis*, No. 15 §123 BGB.
103. Federal Labour Court, 20 Feb. 1986 – 2 AZR 244/85, *Arbeitsrechtliche Praxis*, No. 31 §123 BGB.
104. ECJ of 8 Nov. 1990, case 177/88 (*Dekker*), *European Court Reports*, 1990, I-3941.
105. Federal Labour Court, 15 Oct. 1992 – 2 AZR 227/92, *Arbeitsrechtliche Praxis*, No. 8 §611a BGB.

185. Since the problems of handicapped persons in finding employment are similar to those of pregnant women, the question of whether or not the employer is generally entitled to ask applicants about any handicaps has been highly contested. Even though Article 3 paragraph 3 GG has been amended by the sentence 'no one may be disadvantaged because of his handicap' in 1994, the Federal Labour Court has held the view that an incorrect answer to that question may justify the contract's voidability.[106] After the coming into effect of the AGG and also Section 164 paragraph 2 SGB IX this legal practice can hardly be upheld. The Federal Labour Court had left this question open in a decision from 2011.[107] The question of physical or mental abilities will at most only be admissible if they are an absolute prerequisite for the professional activity advertised. The same, of course, applies to any other of the reasons for discrimination mentioned in Section 1 AGG.

III. The Influence of the Works Council

186. If the employer uses written questionnaires the works council must agree on their content (Section 94 paragraph 1 BetrVG). If no agreement can be reached, it is again the arbitration committee (*see* paragraphs 611 et seq.) which determines the content. In the case of oral interviews, however, the works council has no right whatsoever. Even though this rule is felt to be inadequate, it nevertheless is the law. Tests (creativity, psychological, etc.) are only allowed if they are justified by the requirements of the specific occupation.[108] The employer also requires the applicant's agreement. It is up to the employer also to select the test and the person administering it, etc. It is also up to him to draw the conclusions and to lay down general criteria for the evaluation of the test results. But if the employer does so, he or she again needs the consent of the works council (Section 94 paragraph 2 BetrVG).

187. If, in enterprises employing regularly more than twenty employees, there is a works council the employer must go through certain procedures before the person he or she has selected can be employed (Section 99 BetrVG). First of all, the employer is obliged to inform the works council of the details of the envisaged employment relationship and to show the works council the application documents of all applicants. The works council has one week to react. If the works council agrees, the person selected by the employer can be employed. If the works council does not react at all its consent is implied to be given by law after one week. Within this week, the works council can refuse to give his consent in writing under the following (alternative) conditions:

---

106. Federal Labour Court, 13 Dec. 1998, 2 AZR 923/94, *Arbeitsrechtliche Praxis*, No. 40 §123 BGB.
107. Federal Labour Court, 7 Jul. 2011 – 2 AZR 396/10, *Arbeitsrechtliche Praxis*, No. 70 §123 BGB.
108. U. Preis, *Erfurter Kommentar zum Arbeitsrecht*, ed. R. Müller-Glöge et al, 2020, Verlag C.H. Beck, § 611a BGB paras. 303 et seq.

(1) The employment of the selected person violates a statutory Act, a decree, a collective agreement, a court decision or an administrative order. In short, the works council has to control the compatibility of the envisaged employment with the law.
(2) The employment of the selected person violates a guideline on selection in terms of Section 95 BetrVG. This, of course, is only relevant if such a guideline exists.
(3) The employment of the selected person implies the danger that another employee will be dismissed or will suffer disadvantages which are not justified by technical or personal reasons.
(4) The planned employment puts the employee concerned at a disadvantage without operational or personal reasons to justify this.
(5) In spite of the works council's request the vacancy has not been advertised in the establishment.
(6) Certain facts indicate that the person to be employed will disturb the peace within the establishment by unlawful behaviour or by violation of principles as laid down in the BetrVG.

If the works council refuses to give its approval for one of the above reasons the employer cannot employ this person. But he may appeal to the labour court, which will replace the works council's consent when it turns out that the refusal was unjustified.

188. In cases of urgency the employer is, according to Section 100 BetrVG, allowed to employ the selected person provisionally before the works council has reacted, even if the works council has refused to give its approval. In doing this, the employer must fulfil several requirements that makes such a provisional employment rather difficult and impractical.

189. The above-sketched restrictions on the employer's freedom of contract by the works council's participation only refer to the private sector. In the public sector, the comparable restrictions by staff council participation are even stronger. As federal law only provides the framework, the regulations differ in detail from *Land* to *Land*.

IV. Formal Restrictions by Collective Agreements

190. Further restrictions on the employer's freedom of contract are regulated by collective agreements. Thus, many collective agreements lay down that the labour contract must be in writing. As far as other provisions are concerned, there is no general pattern.

§2. General Terms and Conditions of Employment

191. When an employment contract is to be concluded, it is usually the employer who presents a draft contract, very often formulating general terms and conditions of employment drafted by a legal expert on behalf of the employer. Since the 1976 Act on General Terms and Conditions (*Gesetz zur Regelung des Rechts über Allgemeine Geschäftsbedingungen* – AGBG), later on also implementing the Unfair Contract Terms Directive 93/13/EEC, explicitly excluded employment contracts, such general terms and conditions of employment only had to comply with the general rules of contract law, particularly with the principle of bona fide as granted in Section 242 BGB. In 2002 however, when the German law of obligation was amended fundamentally and the AGBG was integrated into the BGB as Sections 305–310 BGB, the legislator found that the exclusion of employment contracts was no longer adequate. This is why Section 310 paragraph 4 sentence 2 BGB as amended provides that the law on general contract terms and conditions is applicable to employment contracts but that the peculiarities of labour law have to be taken into account adequately.

192. In order to find out whether an employment contract is compatible with the law on general terms and conditions of employment, the following questions have to be dealt with. First of all, the conditions and terms of employment at stake have to be general conditions and terms of employment within the meaning of Section 305 BGB. Accordingly, general conditions and terms are stock conditions formulated for a multitude of contracts, provided by one party to the contract to the other one when concluding the contract. General terms and conditions are not given if the terms and conditions have been negotiated in detail. According to Section 305b BGB, individual agreements always take priority over general terms and conditions. General terms and conditions that are, according to circumstances, in particular according to the appearance of the contract, so exceptional that the contracting party of the user does not have to anticipate them, do not become a component part of the contract (Section 305c BGB). Any doubts as regards the interpretation of the general conditions and terms are interpreted for the user's benefit. Whether or not a certain clause is valid has to be judged taking recourse to Sections 307–309 BGB. While Section 309 BGB contains a long list of clauses being automatically and in any case invalid, the clauses mentioned in Section 308 BGB are invalid only if the judge finds that a concrete clause is contravening the principle of bona fide, identified as the general principle of the law on general terms and conditions in Section 307 paragraph 1 BGB. Only if a clause neither contravenes Section 309 BGB nor Section 308 BGB, can Section 307 paragraph 1 BGB be applied directly. Accordingly, provisions in general terms and conditions are void if the contracting party of the user is, contrary to the principle of bona fide, unduly disadvantaged. Such a disadvantage can follow from the fact that a provision is not formulated clearly and understandably (Section 307 paragraph 1 sentence 2 BGB). According to Section 307 paragraph 2 BGB, an undue disadvantage is, when in doubt, furthermore to be assumed if a provision is either incompatible with the essential idea of the statutory provision from which it is departing or where fundamental rights or duties, following from the nature of the contract, are so restricted that the achievement of the contract's purpose is endangered.

193. Employment contracts are consumer contracts. This follows from the wide definition of the term 'consumer' in Section 13 BGB.[109] Contrary to the definitions used in EC consumer protection directives, a consumer in terms of Section 13 BGB is any natural person who is concluding legal transactions for purposes that can neither be attributed to his or her trade nor to his or her self-employed profession. As a consequence, Section 310 paragraph 3 BGB, comprising facilitations for consumer contracts, also applies to employment contracts. Accordingly, general terms and conditions of employment are to be regarded as being provided by the employer, unless they have been provided by the employee. Section 305c paragraphs 2 and 3, Sections 306 and 307–309 BGB apply, even though the general terms and conditions of employment are meant for unique usage and the employee, due to the fact that the general terms and conditions were drafted by the employer, is not able to influence their content. Last but not least, the circumstances of the conclusion of the contract have to be taken into account when judging whether or not the employee has been unduly disadvantaged.

194. If general terms and conditions of employment fully or partly have not become component part of the employment contract or if they are fully or partly invalid, the remainder of the contract continues to be valid. Inasmuch as the provisions have not become component part of the contract or are invalid, the content of the contract follows from the general statutory provisions replacing the invalid clause. This follows from Section 306 BGB.

195. The application of the law on general terms and conditions to employment contracts, brought about by the amendment 2002, has caused a flood of case law. During the years since 2002, the Federal Labour Court has had to decide more than a hundred cases dealing with Sections 305–310 BGB. Among the questions to be decided, the obligation to take into account adequately the characteristics of labour law in terms of Section 310 paragraph 4 BGB is the most delicate. An example of this characteristic can be found in the rule that an employee's obligation to perform work cannot be enforced, as follows from Section 888 paragraph 3 of the Code of Civil Procedure (*Zivilprozessordnung* – ZPO). As a consequence, unlike other obligees, the employer lacks any possibility of enforcing his or her contractual primary right, the performance of work. Hence, there is a need for instruments allowing the employer to urge the employee to fulfil his or her contractual main duty. In many cases, a contractual penalty constitutes the only effective possibility of achieving this. For although an employee who does not take employment or does not keep the agreed term of notice may often cause large losses, an employer's claim for damages will usually fail because the causality between the breach of duty and the loss or its amount cannot be proven. This is why the Federal Labour Court[110] found that,

109. Federal Labour Court, 27 Nov. 2003 – 2 AZR 135/03, *Arbeitsrechtliche Praxis*, No. 1 §312 BGB.
110. Federal Labour Court, 4 Mar. 2004 – 8 AZR 196/03, *Arbeitsrechtliche Praxis*, No. 3 §309 BGB.

although contract penalties in standard form contracts are, according to Section 309 No. 6 BGB, generally impermissible, they are permissible in standard form employment contracts. Of course, the amount of the contract penalty is still subject to the general principle of bona fide as substantiated in Section 307 BGB.

§3. Annulment of the Labour Contract and the Concept of the Factual Employment Relationship

196. The labour contract may be null from the very outset if binding legal rules are violated (Sections 134, 138 BGB), or it may be voided at a later date for specific reasons such as deceit or error (Sections 119, 123 BGB). According to the rules of ordinary civil law, the voiding of a contract renders it void from the very beginning. If a contract is null from the very outset, or if it is voided at a later stage, the question arises how to treat the employment relationship for the time it had existed before the reason for its nullity became known or before avoidance was declared. In view of the legal implications, the nullity of the employment contract would have for the employee, it is not considered practical to treat the relationship as if there was no contract to start with. This is why the conception of the so-called factual employment relationship has been developed. This means that for the time period from the establishing of the employment contract until the discovery of its nullity or its voiding, the relationship is treated as if there had been a valid contract.[111] Thus, the nullity of the employment contract only affects future employment (i.e., the nullity/voidance is effective *ex nunc* instead of *ex tunc*).

111. *Cf.* Brox, et al., *Arbeitsrecht,* 17th edn, pp. 62 et seq.

Chapter 3. Duties of the Parties in the Course of the Employment Relationship

197. The purpose of this chapter is not to describe in detail the rights and duties of the parties to an employment relationship. Some of these will be analysed separately later on. The intention here is to describe only the basic structure of the reciprocal rights and duties of the parties to an employment contract.

§1. Duties of the Employee

I. The Duty to Work

198. The employee's main duty is to carry out the work that employer and employee have agreed upon in the employment contract (Section 611 BGB). It is always the employee himself who has to fulfil this duty. He is not allowed to provide a substitute. This implies that the employee is not obliged to find a substitute if he or she is unable to fulfil his or her duty to work. Whereas place and kind of work can easily be derived from the contract, it is not so easy to define the amount of work the employee owes to the employer. According to the Federal Labour Court an employee owes an amount of work which on the one hand he or she is capable of doing, and on the other hand is limited by the necessity to preserve the employee's health.[112] The work duties may include activities that are related to work such as cleaning machines, fetching material, etc. If this is not specifically laid down in the contract, it depends on the practice in the specific branch and region which activities are included. In case of an emergency, the employee is obliged to temporarily carry out other and/or additional work. An emergency arises if, without the performance of other and/or additional work, irreparable damage would result. The employee is never obliged to carry out work that would violate the law.

199. The employee is obliged to work under the employer's command, authority and control. In other words, the employer has the right to specify the contractual obligations of the employee by giving him or her orders as granted in Section 106 GewO. The employer can delegate this power to supervising personnel within the organization of the establishment. The employee must obey these orders. The limitation of the power to give orders is laid down in the labour contract. This implies that the contractual duty to work cannot be changed by unilateral order, but only by mutual agreement or by a certain kind of dismissal (i.e., dismissal to change working conditions), which will be explained below (*see* paragraphs 344 et seq.). The problem is to determine whether a change of conditions requested by the employer is still within the limits of the contract or whether it goes beyond these limits and therefore has to be evaluated as a change of contract. A criterion, which helps to distinguish the two cases, is the fact that poorer working conditions (lower level of

112. Established case law, *cf.* Federal Labour Court, 11 Dec. 2003 – 2 AZR 677/02, *Arbeitsrechtliche Praxis*, No. 48 §1 KSchG 1969 *Verhaltensbedingte Kündigung*; 21 May 1992 – 2 AZR 551/91, *Arbeitsrechtliche Praxis*, No. 3 §1 KSchG 1969 *Verhaltensbedingte Kündigung*.

appreciation of work, lower wages, etc.) are never covered by the power to give unilateral orders, but are always understood to be a change of contract.[113] Difficulties arise especially if the contract is concluded for the whole enterprise and states that, under certain conditions, it is possible to transfer the employee from one establishment to another. Here the question arises whether such a contractual clause is valid at all. This depends very much on the employee's status and on the circumstances. In most cases, such a clause would be void. Difficulties also arise if an employee is transferred from one workplace to another within the same establishment. Here again it depends on the circumstances whether this is allowed by unilateral order or whether this has to be understood as a change of contract. It has to be stressed that, according to individual labour law, only a transfer which is considered to be a change of the labour contract is a transfer in the legal sense.

200. If an employee employed in an establishment of more than twenty employees is transferred, the consent of the works council is required (Section 99 BetrVG). The works council can refuse this consent under virtually the same conditions as previously explained for employment (*see* paragraphs 186 et seq.). In addition to the different reasons justifying the works council's refusal in the case of hiring, an alternative has to be mentioned: a refusal is also possible if the employee concerned would suffer disadvantages due to the transfer that are not justified by operational or personal reasons. The definition of transfer in the sense of individual labour law differs from the meaning of 'transfer' in terms of the BetrVG, which makes things extremely complicated. Transfer in the sense of individual labour law, as just explained, always implies a change of the labour contract. Transfer in terms of the BetrVG also covers cases that, from the perspective of individual labour law, would not be understood as being transfers. It also includes to a certain extent transfers that can, from the perspective of individual labour law, unilaterally be executed by order of the employer. In the context of the works' constitution, transfer covers, according to Section 95 paragraph 3 BetrVG, 'every change of work which is expected to last for more than one month, or which implies a considerable change of working conditions'. The idea is that the works council should also have the possibility of controlling movements within the establishment that are unilaterally admissible. This also explains why the works council should be involved in cases of transfer, regardless of whether the transfer implies better or worse working conditions or whether the employee agrees to the transfer. Even if the employee is transferred to a position with better conditions and even if the employee concerned has agreed, the works council has to be involved. This clearly shows that the works council's power is bestowed upon it not merely and mainly in the interest of the particular employee, but in the interest of the workforce as a whole.

201. But even if the employer's order to perform work remains within the contractual limits, it is important to stress that the employer's discretionary powers to

113. Federal Labour Court, 14 Jul. 1965 – 4 AZR 347/63, *Arbeitsrechtliche Praxis*, No. 19 §611 BGB *Direktionsrecht*; as regards the change of working conditions by collective agreements *see* Federal Labour Court, 22 May 1985 – 4 AZR 427/83, *Arbeitsrechtliche Praxis*, No. 7 §1 TVG *Tarifverträge: Bundesbahn*, with an annotation by M. Weiss.

give orders are limited by the employees' fundamental rights as derived from the Constitution. To give just one example: if the employee is asked to perform work which he or she considers to be incompatible with his or her conscience the employee is entitled to refuse the order since the Constitution guarantees freedom of conscience. The Federal Labour Court, based on rulings of the Federal Constitutional Court, has further developed and specified the employee's right in such a conflict.[114]

II. Ancillary Duties

202. It would be impossible to list exhaustively all the ancillary duties connected with the main duty to work. Thus, the employee is prohibited from disclosing secrets, from damaging the employer's property, from acting as a competitor when carrying out an additional job, etc. The ancillary duties depend very much on the circumstances of the specific case. The problem is not so much the existence of these duties but their legal foundation. It is still a subject of controversy whether the employment relationship should be treated as something more than just a contractual relationship, or whether the personal element should play a decisive role. The consequences of the latter view would be that the so-called duty of loyalty would still be an important source of other ancillary duties. However, the tendency is to reduce the relevance of the personal element more and more and consequently to reduce the relevance of the 'duty of loyalty'. This leads to the fact that the 'duty of loyalty' can no longer be taken as a justification for the existence of all ancillary duties, but that it is necessary to prove, as in other contractual relationships, that the contract can only be carried out if certain additional duties are accepted. There has to be a justification for each ancillary duty justified by the circumstances of the specific employment relationship.

203. The employee is also obliged to respect duties of behaviour which are not derived from the contractual obligation but which are established for the order of the establishment, e.g., the duty not to smoke, not to drink alcohol, to respect certain procedures of gate control, etc. Such duties of behaviour can only be imposed as far as they do not interfere in an unjustified way with the employee's right to privacy. Thus, for example, the duty to have a certain haircut, at least in general, cannot be imposed; there may, however, be exceptions in which the employee's appearance plays an important role. In any case the employer's interest in such duties on the one hand and the employee's right to privacy on the other must always be balanced. But it should be pointed out that in establishments where there is a works council, the employer needs the works council's consent to impose such duties (Section 87 paragraph 1 No. 1 BetrVG). If an agreement between employer and works council cannot be reached, it is again the arbitration committee, which may take the decision.

114. Federal Labour Court, 20 Dec. 1984 – 2 AZR 436/83, *Arbeitsrechtliche Praxis*, No. 27 §611 BGB *Direktionsrecht*; 24 May 1989 – 2 AZR 285/88, *Arbeitsrechtliche Praxis*, No. 1 §611 BGB *Gewissensfreiheit*.

204. If duties concerning the order of the establishment are imposed, the question arises of how far the employee has to face sanctions in the case of infringement. Where there is a works council, sanctions can only be imposed and executed with the works council's consent. Should the required consent not be obtained, the arbitration committee is again the deciding body. In addition, the Federal Labour Court has developed a whole range of limitations for the employer's disciplinary power.[115] First, sanctions are only justified if they are published in advance in writing, informing employees. Second, it should be specified exactly what kind of violation leads to what sanction. Third, before sanctioning there has to be a procedure in the course of which the employee has the right to be heard and has the right to legal assistance. Fourth, the works council also has to participate in this procedure and, finally, the sanction may not exceed a certain amount of money (not more than one day's salary). It should be pointed out, however, that nobody knows whether or not these limitations are in fact respected. Control turns out to be very ineffective. As long as the sanction imposed is not dismissal, employees avoid having recourse to the labour courts.

§2. Duties of the Employer

I. The Duty to Pay Remuneration

205. The employee's duty to work and the employer's duty to pay remuneration are the reciprocal main duties between the two parties according to Section 611 BGB. If the remuneration is neither specified in the contract nor based on collective agreement the remuneration usually paid for the specific work in the specific branch and region is due (Section 612 paragraph 2 BGB).

II. The Duty to Employ the Employee

206. Since the wording of Section 611 BGB does not mention the duty to employ the employee, the original view was that such a duty did not exist. The employer was considered to fulfil his or her contractual obligations by just paying the remuneration, no matter whether or not he or she employed the employee. This view has changed as this approach was more and more understood to be incompatible with basic principles as laid down in the Constitution, human dignity and the right to free development of one's personality. That is why the Federal Labour Court has elevated the duty to employ the employee to be the employer's second main duty.[116] At first, the duty to employ the employee was only accepted for certain occupations; now it is a general and uncontested rule. Under certain very restricted

115. Federal Labour Court, 5 Dec. 1975 – 1 AZR 94/74, *Arbeitsrechtliche Praxis*, No. 1 §87 BetrVG 1972 *Betriebsbuße*; 17 Oct. 1989 – 1 ABR 100/88, *Arbeitsrechtliche Praxis*, No. 12 §87 BetrVG *Betriebsbuße*.
116. Federal Labour Court, 11 Oct. 1955 – 2 AZR 591/54, *Arbeitsrechtliche Praxis*, No. 2 §611 BGB *Beschäftigungspflicht*; Large Senate (*see* para. 362), 2 Feb. 1985 – GS 1/84, *Arbeitsrechtliche Praxis*, No. 14 §611 BGB *Beschäftigungspflicht*.

conditions (e.g., if the employee is suspected of grave misconduct) the employer can unilaterally declare the suspension and thereby is freed from the duty to employ. But in such a case of unilateral suspension, the duty to pay remuneration still remains.

III. Ancillary Duties

207. The employer has numerous ancillary duties connected with the contractual obligation and imposed by many laws. The duty to protect employees' health and safety is generally stated in Section 618 BGB and is specified in many statutes and decrees, the most important being the Act on Occupational Health and Safety (*Arbeitsschutzgesetz* – ArbSchG), enacted in 1996 in order to implement Directives 89/391/EEC and 91/383/EEC, and the decrees based on that Act. According to Section 3 ArbSchG, the employer is obliged to take the measures necessary for the safety and health protection, taking into account the circumstances influencing employees' health and safety at work. He or she has to examine the measures as regards their effectiveness and, if necessary, to adjust them to changing circumstances, aiming at an improvement of safety and health protection of his or her employees. What this means in a particular case and how the employer has to proceed are further specified in the ArbSchG and the decrees based on it. Here, as well as on the employee's side, the question arises whether, and how far, the 'duty of loyalty' (which is called 'duty to give assistance') plays a role as an element from which ancillary duties may be derived. Overall, it may be stated that the tendency is the same as outlined previously when discussing the employee's 'duty of loyalty'.

IV. The Duty of Equal Treatment

208. Besides the ban on discrimination on grounds of trade union membership explicitly provided for in Article 9 paragraph 3 GG (*see* paragraph 404) and the ban on discrimination due to nationality as granted in Article 45 TFEU, of employees with fixed-term contracts (*see* paragraph 111), of part-time workers (*see* paragraph 117) and of temporary workers (*see* paragraph 136), the employer has to respect the general principle of equal treatment and the many different bans on discrimination provided by the AGG 2006.

A. The General Principle of Equal Treatment

209. Whereas the duty of equal treatment only plays a marginal role in the selection procedure before employment, it has become a decisive factor as far as the regulation of working conditions is concerned. It should be stressed from the very outset that the duty of equal treatment only applies to group-oriented regulations of working conditions. The principle of equal treatment, on the one hand, demands that every member within a group must be treated equally. It limits, on the other hand, the employer's freedom to divide the work force into different groups with different working conditions. The principle of equal treatment does not totally exclude different treatment. It prohibits arbitrary distinctions but allows differences, which are specifically justified. The requirements for such a justification become more and more onerous. The general principle of equal treatment is supplemented by specific bans of discrimination.

B. Equal Treatment in Terms of the AGG

210. Under the AGG 2006 any discrimination in respect of ethnic origin or race, on grounds of sex, religion or belief, disability, age or sexual identity is banned (*see* paragraphs 173–181). The AGG applies also to an existing employment relationship. According to Section 2 No. 2 AGG, discrimination on any of the grounds mentioned in Section 1 AGG is illegal in relation to employment and working conditions, including pay and dismissals, particularly in individual and collective agreements and measures concerning the performance and termination of an employment relationship and concerning professional advancement. In respect of the rights and duties following from an employment contract once established, the following provisions should be mentioned (in addition to those mentioned already in paragraphs 163–171).

211. Section 2 paragraph 2 AGG states that the Act on Occupational Pensions (*Betriebsrentengesetz* – BetrAVG) applies to occupational pensions (*see* paragraph 257). According to the explanatory memorandum,[117] Section 2 paragraph 2 AGG aims at guaranteeing that the bans on discrimination based on the BetrAVG apply. Furthermore, Directive 86/378/EEC on the implementation of the principle of equal treatment for men and women in occupational social security schemes as amended by Directive 96/97/EC is applicable. Since the BetrAVG does not stipulate any explicit ban on discrimination and in view of the legislator's unmistakable intention to ignore its obligation to implement the anti-discrimination directives in the area of occupational pension schemes, Section 2 paragraph 2 AGG seems to clearly contravene Directives 2000/43/EC, 2000/73/EC and 2002/73/EC. Of course, it is true that there is plenty of case law stating that the general principle of equal treatment in employment (*arbeitsrechtlicher Gleichbehandlungsgrundsatz*) (*see* paragraph 209) and the principle of equal treatment of men and women as guaranteed in Article 157 TFEU and in Directive 86/378/EC apply.[118] Theoretically the implementation of Directives 2000/43/EC, 2000/78/EC and 2002/73/EC could similarly be left to court interpretation. However, the labour courts' competence to ignore the legislator's (illegal) intention and interpret Section 2 paragraph 2 AGG in a manner compatible with the directives was highly contentious.[119] Nevertheless, only one year after the coming into effect of the AGG, the Federal Labour Court rightfully

117. *Bundesrats-Drucksache*, 329/06, p. 33.
118. Fundamentally as regards the general principle of equal treatment Federal Labour Court, 6 Jun. 1974 – 3 AZR 44/74, *BAGE*, vol. 26, p. 178.
119. P. Schrader & J. Schubert, in W. Däubler (ed.), *Handkommentar-AGG* (2007), §2 para. 139.

decided that the AGG also applied to occupational pension schemes.[120] The court regarded Section 2 paragraph 2 AGG as a rule of collision between the AGG and BetrAVG. Several provisions of the BetrAVG refer explicitly to attributes covered by the AGG such as, for example, age. According to the Federal Labour Court's view Section 2 paragraph 2 AGG has to be interpreted as stipulating that these provisions are not amended.

212. As Section 8 paragraph 2 AGG clarifies, the fact that particular protective provisions apply to one age group is no legitimate reason justifying the agreement of a reduced remuneration for equal work or work of equal value. Section 8 paragraph 2 AGG hence reformulates and extends the principle of equal pay for equal work and work of equal value, hitherto guaranteed for men and women in Section 612 paragraph 3 BGB.

213. Among the legitimate aims, an employer or parties to a collective agreement may pursue ranks of course the aim of rewarding professional experience (*Berufserfahrung*). However, it has to be taken into account that there are professions where, after a certain period of time, longer professional experience does not result in further qualification, while there are other professions where every extra day brings about additional insights and hence additional qualification. To what extent rewarding of professional experience in the first category of professions can still be regarded as legitimate – and not simply dressing up age as experience – will have to be judged in every single case. It is of course true that the CJEU assumes that length of service goes hand in hand with experience and that experience enables the worker to perform his or her duties better and hence accepts the length of service (*Dauer der Betriebszugehörigkeit*) as a generally legitimate criterion to determine wages.[121] Whether professional experience and length of service can be equated, seems very questionable. Furthermore, even the CJEU[122] admits that there may be situations in which recourse to the criterion of length of service must be justified by the employer in detail. That is so, in particular, where the worker provides evidence capable of giving rise to serious doubts as to whether recourse to the length of service is, in the circumstances, appropriate to attain the mentioned objective. In such circumstances, it is for the employer to prove that what is true as a general rule, namely that length of service goes hand in hand with experience and that experience enables the worker to perform his or her duties better, is also true as regards the specific job in question.

214. If employees violate the ban on discrimination laid down in Section 7 AGG, the employer has to take appropriate, necessary and proportionate measures to eliminate the discrimination, as, for example, dissuasion, transfer, relocation or dismissal (Section 12 paragraph 3 AGG). If employees are discriminated against by a third party while performing their work, the employer is, according to Section 12

120. Dec. of 11 Dec. 2007 – 3 AZR 249/06, not yet published.
121. ECJ, 17 Oct. 1989, case 109/88 (*Danfoss*), *European Court Reports*, 1989, p. 3199, paras 24–25; 3 Oct. 2006, case C-17/05 (*Cadman*), *European Court Reports*, 2006, I-9583, paras 34–36.
122. Dec. of 3 Oct. 2006, case C-17/05 (*Cadman*) (*supra*), paras 37–39.

paragraph 4 AGG, responsible for taking the appropriate measures which are necessary and proportionate in respect of the individual case to protect his or her employees.

215. Besides the sanctions provided in Section 15 AGG (*see* paragraph 181) any provisions in agreements contravening the ban on discrimination guaranteed in Section 7 paragraph 1 AGG are null and void. This legal consequence already results from general rules of civil law, i.e., Section 134 BGB, and is simply put straight into Section 7 paragraph 2 AGG. Hence, not only contractual agreements of individual or collective nature but also any employer's unilateral measure such as any direction, dismissal etc. contravening Section 7 paragraph 1 AGG is automatically null and void. Moreover, Section 7 paragraph 3 AGG states that any discrimination within the meaning of Section 7 paragraph 1 AGG committed by the employer or by the employee shall be deemed to infringe their respective contractual obligations. Consequently, not only the employer but also a colleague discriminating against an employee may become liable to compensation for any material damages (*Schadensersatz*) in accordance with the general rules of contract law. These, however, require default. This is why further rights to compensation of immaterial damages not subject to default are laid down in Section 15 paragraph 2 AGG (*see* paragraph 181).

V. The Duty to Provide a Reference

216. At the end of an employment relationship, the employer is obliged to provide, at the employee's request, a reference. Section 109 GewO distinguishes two types of references, the non-qualified reference and the qualified one. The non-qualified reference only states how long and in what function the employee has been employed. The qualified reference evaluates the work performance as well as the employee's behaviour. The information given in a reference must be true. When the employee contests the truth of these facts, he may claim a reference at the Labour Court. It is up to the employee to request a qualified or a non-qualified reference.

Chapter 4. Working Time, Public Holidays and Annual Holidays

§1. Working Time

217. Working time refers to the period from the beginning to the end of daily work performance, breaks and periods of absence not included. But working time is not necessarily to be identified with actual work performance. If the employee, for example, is present in the establishment, waiting for the employer's orders, or waiting for new material, this waiting time would be included in the working time. The decisive criterion is presence at the workplace, whether it is inside or outside the establishment.

218. In 1994, a new Act on Working Time (*Arbeitszeitgesetz* – ArbZG) replaced the older Act on Working Time (*Arbeitszeitordnung*), originating from 1938. The ArbZG also implemented the Working Time Directive 93/104/EC. The ArbZG, as all its predecessors, only fixes the maximum amount of the regular daily working time. This has, in principle, not changed since the early 1920s when the eight-hour day was fixed as the normal pattern. According to Section 3 ArbZG, the regular daily working time is still eight hours a day. However, the ArbZG allows much more flexibility than its predecessors do. Without any further precondition, the daily working time may be extended up to ten hours provided that, within a period of six months or within twenty-four weeks, an average of eight daily hours is not exceeded.

219. Section 8 ArbZG entitles the federal government to further restrict the daily working time for specific work or for specific groups of employees if there are specific dangers for employees' health. However, the labour inspectorate may also allow a longer daily working time for work with continuous shifts (in order to reach additional free shifts) and for migrating maintenance employees (Section 15 ArbZG). Special allowances also can be given to seasonal enterprises. In case of emergency and in some other similar situations, extension is possible without any allowance (Section 14 ArbZG).[123] For some sectors, temporary derogations from the ArbZG were permitted for the period of the COVID-19 crisis.[124]

220. The working time of juveniles is regulated in the JArbSchG of 1976. Except for specific cases (*see* paragraph 149 above), employment of children under 15 years of age is forbidden (Section 5 JArbSchG). According to Section 8 JArbSchG, juveniles under 18 years of age may not be employed more than eight hours

123. For more details *cf.* B. Waas, 'Regulation of Working Time in Germany', in K. Boonstra, R. Knegt and M. Schaapmann (eds.), *Regels voor arbeids- en rusttijden in negen Europese landen* (2004), Amsterdam.

124. Deviations from the ArbZG were made in April 2020 by the COVID-19 Working Hours Ordinance (*COVID-19-Arbeitszeitverordnung*). According to this ordinance, working hours of up to twelve hours per day and a reduction of the daily rest periods to up to nine hours may be permissible for activities in numerous sectors, including the production and transport of goods for daily use and pharmaceuticals, in health services, public authorities and energy suppliers. It should also be possible to work on Sundays and public holidays.

a day and forty hours at five days a week. Except for certain branches (i.e., agriculture, restaurant business, in bakeries, etc.) juveniles may not be employed between 8 pm and 6 am (Section 14 JArbschG). The rules on maximum daily and weekly working time do not apply in cases of emergency, but only if adult employees are not available to fight the emergency situation (Section 21 JArbSchG).

221. The 1994 ArbZG does not specify the weekly working time. However, since it is based on the assumption of six working days a week, the maximum weekly working time an employee is allowed to work is 48 hours. This figure, however, is not to be equated with the number of working hours an employee is contractually obliged to work. The ArbZG does not specify contractual obligations but sets minimum standards in order to protect employees' health and safety. The number of weekly hours to be worked is subject to individual or collective agreement. In 1979, the forty-hour week was guaranteed by collective agreements for about 93% of the workforce. Since the mid-1980s working time reduction has accelerated dramatically. The forerunner in this respect was the metal industry where, according to an agreement of 1990, working time has been reduced step by step, to reach in 1995 the crucial figure of 35 hours a week. This collective agreement, however, still only applies to the territory of the old FRG. There, at the end of 2016, collective agreements provided for 37.6 hours weekly working time, ranging from 34 hours for Deutsche Telekom AG, 35 hours (in the wood and plastic processing industry, in the printing industry, the metal industry, in the iron and steel industry and in the paper processing industry) to 40 hours in agriculture, in the mining industry and in the main construction industry.[125] In the former GDR, the average working time provided for in collective agreements still amounted to 38.7 hours, i.e., about one hour more than in the old FRG.[126]

222. Since the mid-1980s the reduction of working time has always been linked to the maintenance of wage levels in West Germany, but combined with 'flexibilization'. This means that the weekly working time is merely to be understood as an average to be reached within a certain period. As far as the length of these periods is concerned, there is a broad range: from one year in agriculture and in the retail trade over six months in the chemical and metal industries, three months in insurance and two months in banking and in public service down to four weeks in coal mining.

223. In the 1994 bargaining round, due to the dramatic situation in many companies, however, new patterns were developed, combining reduction of working time with reduction of wages, and compensating the wage reduction with a job guarantee (*see* paragraphs 638–639). The forerunner in this context was the collective agreement for the Volkswagen Company where working time was reduced to 28.8 hours a week to be distributed over four days. This led to a wage reduction of about 10% to be compensated by a guarantee that no dismissals for economic reasons

125. R. Bispinck, T. Schulten & WSI-Tarifarchiv, *WSI Arbeitszeitkalender 2017*, Düsseldorf 2017, p. IV.
126. *Ibid.*

would take place during the next few years. According to the collective agreement in the metal industry, works councils and individual employers are entitled to deviate by works' agreement from the thirty-six-hour pattern as fixed in the collective agreement. Thus they may reduce the weekly working time down to a minimum of 30 hours, correspondingly reducing wages in a linear way, compensating for this wage loss by a job security guarantee. In short, this new tendency has decentralized the regulation of the weekly working time and, for the first time, has not compensated for the wage reduction resulting from working time reduction in order to decrease labour costs.

224. The daily distribution of working hours, as well as the distribution of breaks, can only be regulated with the works council's consent (Section 87 paragraph 1 No. 2 BetrVG). As far as breaks are concerned, their minimum frequency, and their minimum duration are regulated by law (Sections 4, 5 ArbZG). Special regulations for women have been abolished by the ArbZG. Frequency and duration of the breaks are often subject to collective agreement.

§2. Overtime and Short-Time Work

225. According to the flexible pattern of the 1994 ArbZG, overtime work may no longer seem to be a problem. This impression, however, is misleading. Collective agreements still provide for extra payment if regular working time is exceeded. In this context it has to be stressed that the notion 'overtime' as used in legislation, and as used in collective agreements, is to be distinguished. When used in collective agreements, the term 'overtime' (*Mehrarbeit* or *Überstunden*) refers to working time exceeding the regular daily or weekly working time as fixed in the respective collective agreement, e.g., 38 hours per week (*see* paragraph 220). As a consequence, overtime in this sense may remain even below the level of the working time allowed by the ArbZG.

226. In many collective agreements there are regulations fixing the admissible maximum of overtime. Different patterns are used. One directly limits the maximum number of overtime hours per year. Others use an indirect method by fixing an absolute daily or weekly time. A third method is the fixing of a maximum number of days in which overtime work may be performed. All those collective agreements provide for additional payment in case of overtime. These overtime premiums usually range around 25%.

227. Except for emergency cases, no employee is obliged to work overtime. The employer always requires the employee's consent. But even if the employee agrees, the works council can still prevent overtime since the employer also requires the works council's consent (Section 87 paragraph 1 No. 3 BetrVG (*see* paragraph 621). But in spite of the trade unions' policy of reducing overtime as far as possible in order to better distribute available work load and hence jobs, works councils in most cases agree to overtime for a very simple reason: their constituency is anxious to earn extra money and therefore pushes the works council to agree.

228. As an extremely important instrument in crisis management, short-time work plays a very significant role. As overtime work, short-time work can only be introduced with the works council's approval (Section 87 paragraph 1 No. 3 BetrVG). Under certain conditions the Employment Agency pays out short-time benefits (*Kurzarbeitergeld* – KUG) which are supposed to compensate, at least to a certain extent, for the reduction in wages the employees on short time are facing (Sections 95–109 SGB III). KUG is paid if there is a significant loss of work due to economic reasons or an unavoidable event, if it is temporary and unavoidable and if at least one-third of the employees employed in the company is affected by a loss of earnings of more than 10% each (Section 96 SGB III). Before the beginning of the COVID-19 crisis in 2020, the KUG was basically 60% (or 67% for employees with children) of the lump sum net remuneration lost as a result of short-time working, which was paid for a maximum of twelve months (Sections 104, 105 SGB III).[127] In addition, some collective agreements provide for an increase in short-time working compensation. Against the background of the technological change in the world of work and the associated requirement for a further qualification of the workforce in order to maintain jobs, trade unions and employers' associations, especially in the metal industry, have recently demanded the implementation of a transformation short-time work allowance (*Transformations-Kurzarbeitergeld*).

§3. Night Work and Shift Work

229. The Working Time Regulation (*Arbeitszeitordnung* – ArbZO) of 1938 did not place any restriction on night work for male employees. Female manual workers, however, could not be employed between 8 pm and 6 am, at least in principle. In a decision of 28 January 1992, the Federal Constitutional Court considered the exclusion of manual female workers from night work to be unconstitutional.[128] It was understood to be a violation of the constitutional guarantee of equal treatment of men and women as laid down in Article 3 paragraph 2 GG. At the same time, the court stressed that the Constitution also guaranteed health protection in Article 2 paragraph 2 GG. Therefore, the Federal Constitutional Court in its decision urged the legislator to pass a law not only allowing night work irrespective of sex but also containing a framework of regulation for night work to make sure as soon as possible that night workers were not exposed to intolerable risks endangering their health. According to the Federal Constitutional Court's decision there is no doubt

127. As a result of the new temporary legislation in the COVID-19 crisis, the maximum period of entitlement to KUG was increased to twenty-one months. In addition, from the fourth month on, the KUG will be increased to 70% (or 57% for workers with children) of the loss of earnings for employees who work at least 50% less than before, and to 80% (or 87%) of the loss of earnings from the seventh month of benefit. In addition, instead of one-third, only 10% of employees in the company must be affected by the loss of earnings. Employers will be reimbursed in full by the Federal Employment Agency for the social security contributions they have to pay for short-time work. The new regulations were initially limited until the end of 2020.

128. Federal Constitutional Court, 28 Jan. 1992 – 1 BvR 1025/82, 1 BvL 16/83 and 1 BvL 10/91, *Neue Zeitschrift für Arbeitsrecht*, 1992, p. 270.

that a mere permission for night work without further safeguards for night workers would be a violation of Article 2 paragraph 2 GG.

230. Implementing this decision, the 1994 ArbZG treats both sexes equally as far as night work is concerned. In Section 6 paragraph 1 ArbZG, regulating night work and shift work, special reference is made to the research results in ergonomics that have to be applied. Therefore, Section 6 paragraph 3 ArbZG grants night workers a medical check-up to be provided on the employer's expenses at least every third year. For employees of 50 years of age and older this check-up has to be provided every year. The daily working time for night workers – as for normal employees – is eight hours (Section 6 paragraph 2 ArbZG). Whereas normally an extension up to ten hours is possible if an average of eight hours is reached within six months, the reference period in the case of night work is limited to one month. In addition, Section 6 paragraph 4 ArbZG lists situations in which night workers are entitled to be transferred to day work as e.g., health reasons, a child under 12 years needing to be taken care of, a person in need of nursing dependent on the worker. If the employer cannot meet the request due to urgent reasons connected with the nature of the production, the services, or the organization of the respective establishment, the works council is to be involved as a mediator. The ArbZG only provides for a suitable number of free days or additional money for night work, leaving the specification up to parties to collective agreements.

231. Even if the ArbZG no longer distinguishes between male and female employees, this does not mean that women are not particularly protected during pregnancy and breastfeeding. The Maternity Protection Act (*Mutterschutzgesetz* – MuSchG) prohibits employers from employing a pregnant or breastfeeding woman between 8 pm and 6 am. The limit can be raised to 10 pm by means of an official exemption permit, for which the woman's consent is required, among other things (Section 5 MuSchG). In addition, the MuSchG contains further protective provisions, including those relating to working hours, in favour of a pregnant or nursing woman (e.g., a ban on overtime and special regulations on rest periods).

232. Collective agreements usually contain rules on additional payment for shift work, and – to a still marginal extent – on compensation for shift work with additional free time. It has to be stressed that, according to Section 87 paragraph 1 No. 2 BetrVG, the employer needs the works council's consent on whether there should be shifts at all and if so, from when to when they should take place. If they cannot reach an agreement, it is up to the arbitration committee to decide.

§4. Work on Sundays and Public Holidays

233. Since the 1891 amendment to the GewO, work on Sundays has been forbidden, at least in principle. Special rules are contained in specific acts for specific types of businesses (shops, bakeries and confectioners) and for specific groups of employees (pregnant or nursing women, juveniles). As far as the general rule is concerned, the rest time for each Sunday is at least 24 hours. The 1994 ArbZG does not change this pattern. According to Section 9 ArbZG, employees are still prohibited from working on Sundays in the period from midnight of Saturday to midnight of Sunday. In plants with regular day and night shifts, the beginning and the end of this rest may take place earlier or later up to six hours – if there is a rest of 24 hours after the beginning of this rest time.

234. Under the former law specific groups of employees and specific activities were not covered by the ban on Sunday work. These exemptions were extended by the 1994 ArbZG in Section 10 ArbZG in order to increase flexibility. At the same time, the ArbZG specified the situation of Sunday employees by stating that an employee who has to perform work on Sundays is entitled to another day of rest within a period of two weeks (Section 11 ArbZG). One Sunday per month, also for those employees, has to remain completely free of work. The parties to collective agreements, the federal government and the labour inspectorate are, under certain conditions, entitled to increase the possibility of Sunday work further. Among the labour inspectorate's powers one right is especially interesting to mention: the labour inspectorate may allow Sunday work if there is evidence that, due to longer working hours or to other working conditions, competitiveness with foreign countries is seriously endangered and has to be secured by Sunday work. This reflects the core of the political controversy on Sunday work. Whereas the trade unions want Sunday to remain free of work, employers want to include it as much as possible in order to maintain competitiveness.

235. The legal rules on Sunday work also apply to public holidays. Since in Germany the different *Länder* are competent to declare their own public holidays, the number of public holidays differs from *Land* to *Land*. The majority of public holidays have a religious origin. In some cases, it depends on the religious composition of the population in the respective region whether or not there is a holiday. However, there are three holidays, which have nothing to do with religion: 1 January, 1 May and 3 October. The number of holidays in the different *Länder* differs from nine to thirteen days. In the context of the establishment of long-term care insurance, the number of public holidays has partly been reduced. The new insurance, as most other elements of the social security system, is financed by contributions of employers and employees, each side paying half. When long-term care insurance was about to be introduced, employers asked for a compensation for the additional labour costs. The Act introducing long-term care insurance therefore provided that each *Land* should reduce the number of public holidays by one, turning it into a normal working day. It was up to each *Land* which holiday was to be chosen. The employees, in addition, may opt for an alternative: not to work on the respective day, thereby losing a day of holiday.

236. Remuneration on public holidays was originally guaranteed by the 1951 Act on Payment of Remuneration on Holidays (*Feiertagslohngesetz*). Since 1994 it is warranted by Section 2 of the Act on Continued Payment of Remuneration on Holidays and in Case of Sickness (*Entgeltfortzahlungsgesetz* – EFZG). According to this provision, the employee is entitled to the remuneration he would have earned if there had not been a holiday.

§5. Annual Holidays

237. The employee's right to annual holidays is guaranteed by the 1963 BUrlG. Originally, this Act provided for a minimum annual holiday of eighteen business days (*Werktage*), a 1994 amendment raised it to twenty-four business days. Business days, i.e., days which are neither Sundays nor public holidays are to be distinguished from working days (*Arbeitstage*), which are neither Saturdays nor Sundays nor public holidays. During annual holidays, average remuneration is guaranteed (Section 11 BUrlG). The point of reference for calculating the average is the average remuneration the employee received during the thirteen weeks preceding the beginning of the holidays. Section 19 JArbSchG provides for longer minimum annual holidays for young persons according to the following scale: employees younger than 16 years of age are entitled to a minimum of thirty business days, employees between 16 and 17 years of age are entitled to a minimum of twenty-seven business days, and employees between 17 and 18 years of age are entitled to a minimum of twenty-five business days. Section 208 SGB IX provides for an additional holiday of five working days for severely disabled employees.

238. The results of collective bargaining have exceeded by far the minimum guarantee as provided for by the BUrlG. In the territory of the old FRG for most branches annual holidays of thirty working days are guaranteed, which means that six weeks of annual holidays are given. In the new *Länder* the level is still a little lower. However, even there in the meantime thirty working days have been achieved in most branches. Only in a few branches (e.g., agriculture, hotel and restaurant industry) does the duration of paid annual holiday still range between twenty-three and thirty working days.[129]

239. Many collective agreements also provide for an additional holiday bonus. In the territory of the old FRG these bonuses range from 25% to 50% of the normal wage; in the territory of the former GDR they are still lower. Choice options are also possible: as a result of the 2018 collective bargaining round in the metal industry, employees with children, relatives to care for or working in shifts were given the opportunity to choose either a collectively agreed additional remuneration or eight additional days off per year.

§6. Special Leave

I. Parental Time

240. According to the Act on Maternity Protection (*Mutterschutzgesetz* – MuSchG) of 1968, as amended in 1997 and reformed in 2018, female employees who have given birth to a child may not be employed for a period of eight weeks after confinement (*see* paragraph 276). In addition to that period of maternity protection, so-called mother's leave was introduced in 1979. In 1985 mother's leave was

129. WSI-Tarifarchiv, *2019 Tarifpolitik, Statistisches Taschenbuch*, Düsseldorf 2019, Tab. 2.7.

replaced by 'parental leave', applying to mothers as well as to fathers, as guaranteed in the Act on Benefits and Leave for Child Care (*Bundeserziehungsgeldgesetz* – BErzGG), which has been amended several times since, *inter alia* to implement Directive 96/34/EC.[130] In 2006, the BErzGG has been replaced by the Act on Parental Benefit and Parental Time (*Bundeselterngeld- und Elternzeitgesetz* – BEEG), replacing childcare benefit by parental benefit and parental leave by parental time.[131]

241. Any employee residing in Germany, living together with a child and having the custody of that child, looking after and educating that child, is entitled to take parental time (*Elternzeit*) until the child is three years old (Section 15 BEEG). Since parental time can be taken for every child, Section 15 paragraph 2 Sentence 1 BEEG, parental time may add up to six to nine years or even a longer period, depending on the number of children. Any employee wishing to take parental time is supposed to apply for parental time with the employer in writing, at least seven weeks in advance (Section 16 BEEG). The application has to specify for which periods within two years parental time is requested.

242. The right to parental time is very flexible: parental time can be taken fully or in parts, i.e., for a few months, by either mother or father and even by both parents at the same time (Section 15 paragraph 3 BEEG). With the employer's approval up to twelve months of parental time can even be postponed to a later point of time before the child's eighth birthday (Section 15 paragraph 2 sentence 4 BEEG). Both parents can divide their entitlement to parental time into two periods and, with the employer's consent, into even more periods (Section 16 paragraph 1 sentence 5 BEEG).

243. For parents having been gainfully employed before, taking parental time means that the mutual main obligations resulting from an employment relationship are suspended. In other words, an employee taking parental time is not obliged to work but does not receive any remuneration either.

244. One of the reasons why more mothers than fathers take parental time is that the family cannot do without the income. In order to remove or at least attenuate this financial disincentive, the legislator decided to replace the former childcare benefit (*Erziehungsgeld*) by a so-called parental benefit (*Elterngeld*).[132] Modelled upon the Scandinavian example and unlike the former childcare benefit, parent benefit is designed as an income related benefit amounting to 67% of the former net income (maximum, EUR 1,800, minimum, EUR 300) (Section 2 paragraphs 1 and 4 BEEG); income thresholds do not apply. If the former net income was below EUR

---

130. *Cf.* D. Schiek, *From Parental Leave to Parental Time: Effects of Directive 96/34/EC on German Employment Law*, Indus. L. J. 353–361 (2002).
131. As to the current debate on compatibility of family and work life *cf.* M. Schmidt, *Employment, the Family and the Law: Current Problems in Germany*, Comp. Lab. L. & Pol'y J. 451–485 (2006).
132. *Cf.* the Bill of an Act introducing parental benefit, *Bundstags-Drucksache*, 16/1889.

1,000, the parental benefit increases to up to 100% of the former net income (Section 2 paragraph 2 BEEG). Parental benefit is then paid for up to twelve months (Section 2 paragraph 1 BEEG). The parents can freely decide if only one of them or if both reduce(s) his or her working time, whether consecutively or simultaneously. But only if also the respective other partner (in open words: mostly the father) reduces his working time, parental benefit is paid for two additional months, i.e., fourteen months altogether. This follows from Section 4 BEEG. The available data for the first half of 2015 show that 87.5% of women used parental benefit for twelve months, while fathers generally (78.7%) used only the two additional partner months and only one in five men, who used parental benefit, took three or more months of paid time off.[133]

245. As it has been already the case under the BErzGG, the continuation of the employment relationship is specifically safeguarded by Section 18 BEEG: from the time a parent has informed the employer that he or she intends to take parental time – however, at most eight weeks before parental time is due to begin – until the end of parental time the employer is not allowed to terminate the employment relationship. Only in very specific cases, a dismissal can be declared admissible, provided that the *Land* Office for Labour Inspection gives its consent. The dismissal protection provided for by Section 18 BErzGG is similarly strict to the one granted by Section 17 paragraph 2 MuSchG (*see* paragraph 321).

246. In order to avoid parental time working as a 'family trap' for parents taking parental time, the legislator allows them to continue working, albeit at a reduced level. According to Section 15 paragraph 4 BEEG both parents are entitled to work up to thirty hours per week, either for their old employer or for another company. In the latter case, however, the employee on parental time needs his or her old employer's consent. The same applies if the employee on parental time wants to work in a self-employed capacity. In case an employee on parental time prefers to perform his or her old job but would simply like to reduce the working time, he or she may request a reduction of his or her working time (*see* paragraphs 118 et seq.).

247. More than 1.8 million parents had taken advantage of parental benefits in 2018.[134] This is not surprising if one knows that, for children under three there are only very few childcare facilities available in the former FRG although there has been a legal entitlement since 2013 for children over the age of 1 to childcare in an institution. In a European comparison, the former FRG is one of the countries with a relatively low level of facilities for this age group.[135] In 2000 in the old FRG, only 6% of those aged under three spent part of their day in such facilities. In contrast, the new *Länder* had a particularly high number of childcare facilities, also when compared to other EU countries. In the year 2000, 35% of all children under three

133. *See* with further proofs WSI, *Dauer des Bezugs von Elterngeld 2007-2015*, https://www.boeckler.de/51835.htm.
134. Statistisches Bundesamt, *Öffentliche Sozialleistungen, Statistik zum Elterngeld 2018*, tab. 1.
135. H. Engstler & S. Menning, *Families in Germany: Facts and Figures*, (Federal Ministry for Family Affairs, Senior Citizens, Females and Youth ed. 2004), available at www.bmfsfj.de, p. 36; *Eurostat*, Pressemitteilung 94/2016.

were taken care of outside the home, although in 1995 the figure had been as high as 40%. This drop is probably the result of the reduced labour market participation by East German women with small children. In recent years, however, childcare has increased significantly. In 2006, the childcare rate for under-threes was 13.6% and by 2018, it was 33.6%.[136] One main reason for the negligible number of fathers taking parental time is the fact that taking parental time by fathers is accepted by law but still not enough by society,[137] and especially not by employers, so that male employees taking parental time fear disadvantages for their career development.[138] Slowly, however, a change seems to be taking place. Another important restraint is that, due to the fact that men on average still earn more than women, many families would simply rather do without the mother's than without the father's income.[139]

248. To an increasing extent collective agreements and works agreements provide for career break regulations. Works agreements in a rather significant number of big companies in the metal industry, in the chemical industry and in the service sector serve as trendsetters for collective agreements. The agreements are different in detail, but follow a general pattern. After termination of parental time either one of the parents is entitled to a career break of a certain duration, ranging between three and four years. During this period, the employment relationship is suspended. There is a guarantee of obtaining a job of equal quality in the same company. Of equal importance is the guarantee that financial disadvantages for the employee may not occur, including the companies' duty to offer opportunities to the parent to have further training in order to keep up with the skills progression the employees staying in the company enjoyed. It should be stressed that, even if some of those agreements treat both sexes equally, these career break rules in practice turn out to be rules for women. Moreover, it has to be pointed out that in the private sector they only apply to big companies.[140]

II. Leave for Employee Representatives

249. The 1972 BetrVG and the 1974 BPersVG contain rules for educational leave for members of the representative bodies established by these acts. According to Section 37 paragraph 6 BetrVG work council members are entitled to attend vocational training courses without loss of pay if the knowledge imparted is necessary for the proper execution of their activities. The period of this leave is not fixed, the frequency and duration depending on the particular circumstances of the

136. Bundesministerium für Familie, Senioren, Frauen und Jugend (BMFSFJ), *Kindertagesbetreuung kompakt, Ausbaustand und Bedarf 2018*, p. 10.
137. 25% hold fathers taking parental time for effeminate; *cf.* the survey by TNS Infratest for the *Spiegel* of 28–30 Mar. 2006, published in *Der Spiegel* 17/2006, p. 26.
138. 22% think that parental time is incompatible with a father's job; *cf.* TNS Infratest, *supra. Cf.* further R. Puchert, M. Gärtner & S. Hoeyng (eds), *Work Changes Gender, Men and Equality in the Transition of Labour Forms* (2006).
139. 48% are of the opinion that the family cannot do without the father's income. *Cf.* TNS Infratest, *supra.*
140. For more information *cf.* WSI (ed.), *Tarifhandbuch 2005*, pp. 49–60.

establishment. In addition to this training, each member of these bodies is entitled to paid leave of four weeks once during his or her term of office in order to attend a seminar to broaden his or her general knowledge. This four-week period, granted in Section 37 paragraph 7 BetrVG, only refers to newcomers in their first term of office. In subsequent terms, it is decreased to three weeks.

III. Miscellaneous

250. Special acts provide for educational leave for specific groups (company doctors, safety officers, disabled persons). In statutory acts of most German *Länder*– except Bavaria and Saxony – paid educational leave (*Bildungsurlaub*) is provided for all employees, at least in principle. The duration of such an educational leave ranges from five to ten days. In fact, however, only about 3% of entitled employees actually take educational leave. Finally, it should be mentioned that in all *Länder* employees who participate in youth training schemes are entitled to a special annual leave of twelve days without remuneration.

Chapter 5. Remuneration and Benefits

§1. The Notion of Remuneration

251. It is necessary to differentiate between a narrow and a wider notion of remuneration. Remuneration in its narrow sense is nothing more than basic pay, being compensation for the work performed. Remuneration in its wider sense includes all kinds of fringe benefits as well as payments made by an employer in addition to social insurance benefits. It is not just an academic exercise to include additional payments as bonuses, indemnities, premiums, family allowances, additional pensions, etc. in the concept of remuneration. The original idea was that payments of this kind were merely voluntary gifts provided by the employer, having nothing to do with the work carried out. The development of the concept of remuneration in a wider sense has gone beyond this original idea and includes all these additional payments in the context of the employment relationship. The practical implications of this new understanding have mainly two effects: first, the arbitrary handling of these payments is largely excluded by law and, second, the scope of the works council's powers is more and more extended to these additional payments.

252. If remuneration has to be paid for non-performance of work (e.g., in the case of annual holidays or sickness) or is the basis for deduction of taxes and social insurance contributions, the law concerned defines what is to be understood as 'remuneration' for the specific purpose.

§2. The Regulation of Remuneration

253. For a long time (until the end of 2014) there was no regulation providing for a statutory minimum wage for all branches of industry. This has to be stressed in spite of the fact that an Act with the misleading title of Act on Minimum Working Conditions (*Gesetz über Mindestarbeitsbedingungen* – MindArbBedG) had existed from 1952 to 2014. This Act only provided a mechanism to determine minimum working conditions in a situation in which the collective bargaining system would prove to be unable to provide such minimum conditions. This assumption so far remained merely theoretical. In other words, since its adoption in 1952 the MindArbBedG had played no role whatsoever. Minimum standards of wages and other parts of remuneration were only regulated in collective agreements. The main legal source for the real wages and additional payments, however, remains the labour contract. Since 2015, after heated debate, there has been a statutory cross-sector minimum wage for the first time, regulated by the Minimum Wage Act (*Mindestlohngesetz* – MiLoG)

254. The new statutory minimum wage is paid per working hour and has been EUR 9.35 per hour since 1 January 2020. It is adjusted every two years by a minimum wage commission and implemented in a binding manner by means of a statutory ordinance. The Commission consists of three representatives each from the employer side and the employee side, two scientific members and a chairperson.

The MiLoG contains various protective provisions designed to prevent an employee from not being paid the minimum wage, not being paid in full or being paid too late. If the employer does not comply with these regulations, he or she is threatened with sanctions in the form of fines and maybe exclusion from public contracts. In addition, general contractors of service or work contracts are liable for the payment of the minimum wage to employees in subcontractors. The statutory minimum wage applies only to employees. However, there are exceptions, which are regulated in Section 22 MiLoG. Under certain conditions trainees, children and young people without vocational training, apprentices, volunteers and the long-term unemployed in the first six months of employment are exempt from the entitlement to the statutory minimum wage. In addition to the exceptions, the appropriate level of the minimum wage is also criticized, as a minimum wage of currently EUR 9.35 is not sufficient to secure an adequate retirement pension even with uninterrupted full-time employment.

255. However, even collective agreements do not always guarantee a wage level high enough to earn one's living with full-time work. Moreover, collective agreement coverage has steadily been declining. This is why in 2018 there were nearly 800,000 persons working but earning less than necessary for a modest living and hence being entitled to additional social benefits (17.6% of them were in full-time employment subject to social insurance contributions).[141] Since the necessity, the benefits and the risks of a general statutory minimum wage were heavily disputed in Germany, the former legislator had decided to leave the decision on minimum wages to the trade unions and the employers' associations of the branches concerned. Should they be able to agree on a minimum wage for their members and provided of course that the other requirements of the AEntG are fulfilled, in a first step the AEntG will be amended to cover the branch. In a second step, the branch collective agreement on minimum wages will be extended by governmental decree. So far, the AEntG has been amended several times to cover more branches. Since 2014, the Act is no longer restricted to the sectors expressly mentioned in the AEntG, but is open to all sectors.

256. If the employer grants fringe or additional benefits or payments in addition to social insurance, and if these payments are not required by law, two questions arise: can the employees claim a right to get these benefits, and can the employer deny such a right by making the reservation that whatever he or she pays is merely voluntary and that he or she is not willing to be bound in any way?[142] As far as the first question is concerned, the employee acquires a right if the employer grants the benefits several times without declaring a reservation. The idea is that the employee's confidence in receiving the benefits in future has to be protected. Once such a right has been established it is treated as if it were included in the individual contract. As far as the second question is concerned, it has to be stated that, at least in principle, the employer can prevent an employee's right by declaring a reservation.

141. Bundesagentur für Arbeit, *Der Arbeitsmarkt in Deutschland 2018*, tab. IV.D.4b.
142. K. Bepler, 'Betriebliche Übungen. Ein erweiterter Rechtsprechungsbericht', *Recht der Arbeit*, 2004, pp. 226 et seq.

However, there are restrictions. If, for example, the employer promises an additional retirement pension he or she may declare that he or she wishes to remain free to revoke this promise at any time. Such a declaration would be treated as void in view of the fact that such an additional payment is understood to be part of the remuneration. Thus, the right to revoke is severely restricted, no matter what the employer declares when introducing the system.

257. As far as additional occupational pensions are concerned, it was originally quite often stipulated that a claim to occupational pension became extinct if the employee terminated employment before retirement age. When, from the perspective of a wide notion of 'remuneration', additional occupational pensions were understood as being a compensation for the work performed, such clauses were regarded as being unfair. This is why the Federal Labour Court decided that, after a certain length of service, claims to occupational pensions could not be revoked. Inspired by this decision, the legislator has passed the Act on the Improvement of Occupational Pension Schemes (*Gesetz zur Verbesserung der betrieblichen Altersversorgung* – BetrAVG) in 1974. According to Section 1b BetrAVG, claims to occupational pensions cannot be revoked if the employee is at least 21 years of age and if the pension commitment has existed for at least three years.

258. In the area of remuneration, the principle of equal treatment plays an important role. Thus Sections 7, 1 AGG outlaw discrimination on grounds of sex, race and ethnic origin, religion or belief, sexual orientation, age or disability (*see* paragraphs 173 et seq. and paragraphs 208 et seq.).

259. Nevertheless, there are problems of equal treatment. One of the problems has to do with job classification. The question arises of how far it is possible to classify work according to factors that may lead to discrimination against certain groups of employees, for example physical strength as a decisive criterion. Or is it possible to grant certain benefits on condition that the employee has been in service of the enterprise for a long time – knowing that there are usually more males than females who fulfil this condition? These cases of so-called indirect discrimination still occur. Their illegality depends on how easy or difficult it is to prove that sexual discrimination is the effect of using these factors as criteria. It, however, has to be repeated that due to the European Court of Justice's (ECJ's) input, the Federal Labour Court has a tendency to increase the requirements justifying indirect discrimination once it is proved. The Federal Labour Court has especially succeeded, through a number of decisions, in making differential treatment of manual workers and white-collar workers less easy.[143] Distinctions are only justified if they not only refer to the difference between the two groups but if the employer can prove that, in view of its function or status, one of the two groups needs or deserves the specific benefit more than the other group. This evaluation has to be made taking into account the specific purpose pursued by the benefit in question.

143. Federal Labour Court, 25 Jan. 1984 – 5 AZR 89/82, *Neue Zeitschrift für Arbeitsrecht*, 1984, pp. 326 et seq.; 12 Oct. 2005 – 10 AZR 640/04, *Neue Zeitschrift für Arbeitsrecht*, 2005, pp. 1418 et seq.

§3. PAY SYSTEMS

260. There are unlimited possibilities for determining the level of remuneration: according to time, according to results, piece rate, etc. (so-called principles of remuneration). The parties to the individual labour contract are free to select the system they prefer. However, with regard to the part of the remuneration in the amount of the statutory minimum wage, the provisions of the MiLoG on the due date and indispensability of the minimum wage must be observed.[144] It also should be pointed out that, in this area also, the works council has important powers of co-determination. According to Section 87 paragraph 1 Nos 10, 11 BetrVG all general regulations related to remuneration arrangements (choice between principles of remuneration, choice between methods of determining the remuneration based on a given principle, etc.), are subject to co-determination, i.e., the employer needs the works council's consent when making his or her choice and in developing the general structure of remuneration (*see* paragraphs 618, 621).

261. If payment according to results is chosen, the works council's position is the strongest. In this case, every single aspect of the wage system (what is normally expected from an average employee, how much is to be paid per piece or per time unit, which methods of determining the wage in single cases are to be used, how the application of these methods is to be carried out, etc.) needs the works council's approval. The reason for this different treatment of pay systems is very simple: payment by results is understood to be less transparent than payment according to time. Thus, the works council's controlling powers are more extensive.

262. If the employer is not obliged to pay certain elements of remuneration (fringe or additional benefits, additional social insurance payments, etc.) it is up to him whether he wants to grant such payments. This freedom is not restricted by the works council's participation. The employer is also free to determine the amount of money he or she wants to spend on additional payments. And, finally, he or she can decide whether or not the additional payments should be restricted to certain groups. Here, of course, the principle of equal treatment (*see* paragraph 209) has to be taken into account. The employer is entitled to make these decisions on his or her own. For all the remainder (how to distribute the additional payments, how to organize the payment system, etc.) the employer requires the works council's consent.

263. Time, place and other modalities of the payment of remuneration must be determined by the employer in cooperation with the works council; here again nothing can be done without the works council's approval.

144. *See* U. Preis & D. Ulber, *Ausschlussfristen und Mindestlohngesetz – Der Mindestlohn als unabdingbarer Sockelanspruch*, Frankfurt/Main 2014.

§4. Level of Remuneration

264. If the average gross wages of employees in 2015 are taken as reference point and evaluated as 100%, a steady wage increase until 108.1% in 2018 can be demonstrated.[145]

265. As already indicated above (*see* paragraph 28), the wage level in East Germany is still significantly lower than in West Germany. In 1991 and 1992, in order to overcome this gap, about fifty collective agreements were concluded, envisaging equalization step by step, reaching an equal standard at least of basic wage somewhere between 1994 and 1997. The forerunner in this respect was the collective agreement in the metal industry of March 1991, according to which equalization of wages had to be achieved until 1994. It soon, however, turned out that the increase as regulated in this agreement would overburden quite a few companies. Therefore, after a rather dramatic conflict the agreement was modified in 1993, postponing full equalization until 1996. This example shows the difficulties in trying to reach equal conditions in East and West Germany.

266. The gross wage indicates neither the employer's labour costs nor the employee's income correctly. In addition to the gross wage, the employer has to pay his share of statutory social security contributions. Employees, however, have to face wage deductions: their share of statutory social security contributions and taxes is deduced from the gross income. In 2020, employers' and employees' contributions amounted to respectively circa 20.4% of employees' gross income'.

§5. Remuneration in Case of Temporary Non-performance of Work

I. The Theory of Employer's Risk

267. Since remuneration is considered a quid pro quo for work performance, remuneration, in principle, has to be paid only if work has been performed: no work, no remuneration. One important exception to that rule has already been outlined: annual paid holiday and special leave for which statutorily continued payment of remuneration is guaranteed. Another important exception to the principle of 'no work, no pay' is laid down in Section 615 BGB. Accordingly, the employer is obliged to pay remuneration if the employee offers to work, but the employer does not accept this offer. This rule assumes that the employer is in a position to accept the employee's offer. Thus, the question arises of what should happen if the employer, due to reasons beyond his or her control, is unable to accept the employee's offer to work (e.g., the plant is destroyed by fire). There is no clear answer to that question provided by law. Hence, it was, as it often is, up to the labour courts to develop a solution. In the Weimar era, the courts developed the following solution which they thought to be adequate: the employer, who usually makes the profit,

145. Statistisches Bundesamt (ed.), *Statitisches Jahrbuch 2019, Verdienste und Arbeitskosten*, tab. 14.1.6.

was also supposed to bear the risk (*Betriebsrisikolehre*). As a consequence, remuneration has to be paid if the employer is, due to reasons beyond his or her control, unable to accept the employee's offer to work. The Federal Labour Court has always applied this theory. In 2002 the legislator indirectly codified it in Section 615 sentence 3 BGB.

268. There are two exceptions to this rule, developed by case law. The first, however, has turned out to exist only in theory. The obligation to pay remuneration although no work has been performed is reduced or eliminated if, due to the payment of remuneration, the existence of the establishment would be endangered. The second exception, however, has played a very important role from the 1920s until today. It refers to the case in which the cause of the employees' inability to work originates in industrial conflict. The original understanding, as developed in 1923, was that the employer does not have to pay wages if the cause of the inability to work is due to industrial action of the workers. If a strike was the cause for their inability to work wages never had to be paid, even if the particular workers themselves had nothing to do with the strike. All workers were understood to be united by the idea of solidarity. This so-called theory of spheres (*Sphärentheorie*), was initially adopted by the Federal Labour Court,[146] but became more and more contested. This is why, in a very important decision of 1980, the Federal Labour Court gave up this theory and replaced it by a model developed in accordance with the criteria structuring the law of industrial conflict.[147] Therefore, this new theory will be explained further in Part II, in the context of the law on industrial conflict (*see* paragraphs 559 et seq.).

II. The Employee's Absence of Short Duration for Personal Reasons

269. A third important exception to the principle 'no work, no pay' is guaranteed in Section 616 BGB. Accordingly, continued remuneration has to be paid if the employee is, due to personal reasons and only for a short period, absent from work. Personal reasons may be the death of a relative, the birth of a child, etc. The notion 'personal reasons' refers to situations in which the employee cannot be expected to perform work. It, however, does not cover reasons preventing employees from performing their work unrelated to circumstances of their personal life (weather conditions, traffic jams, etc.). The meaning of 'personal reasons' has been defined to a great extent by the fact that in collective agreements these reasons are specified in detail. The same goes for the term 'short period of time'. The general notion is, however, that, depending on the gravity of the personal reason, two or three days are about the maximum.

146. 8 Feb. 1957 – 1 AZR 338/55, *Arbeitsrechtliche Praxis*, No. 2 §615 BGB.

147. Decisions of 22 Dec. 1980 – 1 ABR 2/79 and 1 ABR 76/79, *Arbeitsrechtliche Praxis*, Nos 70 and 71, Art. 9 GG *Arbeitskampf*; critically M. Weiss, 'Die neue Arbeitskampfrechtsprechung des BAG', *Kritische Vierteljahresschrift für Gesetzgebung und Rechtswissenschaft*, 1986, pp. 366 et seq.

III. Sickness

270. A fourth important exception to the rule 'no work, no pay' is the principle of continued remuneration in cases of sickness. For a long time only white-collar workers were guaranteed continued remuneration in case of sickness. According to Section 616 paragraph 2 BGB, a provision originating from 1930, white-collar workers received normal remuneration for six weeks in the case of sickness. It was not until 1969 that the Act on Continued Payment of Remuneration (*Lohnfortzahlungsgesetz* – LFZG) was passed, and guaranteed manual workers basically the same rights. In spite of the fact that different legal sources applied, the rules for continued remuneration in case of sickness were more or less the same for white-collar and for manual workers. The maximum period of payment was, in both cases, six weeks. In the case of repeated sickness within a year, the total period of continued payment of remuneration remained six weeks, but if between the first and the second period of sickness there was a lapse of at least six months, the employee was again entitled to six weeks of continued payment of remuneration.

271. In 1994, the former acts were substituted by the already mentioned EFZG (*see* paragraph 236). The EFZG did not change the basic pattern of continued payment of remuneration in case of sickness but covers both groups of employees, manual workers and white-collar workers, in one and the same Act: no further distinction is made. At the same time, specific rules governing the situation in the territory of the former GDR were abolished. Major changes, however, were introduced only two years later. Concerned about increasing unemployment, the former coalition between CDU/CSU and FDP decided that, in order to give employers' incentives to employ more workers, labour costs should be reduced. To that aim, the 1996 Labour Law Act on the Improvement of Employment Opportunities (*Arbeitsrechtliches Beschäftigungsförderungsgesetz*) introduced several amendments to different acts. One of the most important and most disputed amendments was that concerning continued remuneration in case of sickness. Before 1996, employees had been entitled to continued payment of remuneration in case of sickness from the very first day of the employment relationship. Since the 1996 amendment, a claim to continued remuneration arises only after four weeks of employment. In addition, except for cases of work accidents or occupational diseases, the amount of continued remuneration was decreased from 100% to 80% of the normal remuneration. Only on condition that the employee decided to dispense with one day of paid annual holiday for five days of sickness, was full remuneration guaranteed for these five days, the annual claim to paid holiday being correspondingly reduced. The limit was the statutory minimum number of holidays (*see* paragraph 237). However, since continued remuneration in cases of sickness is one of the topics regulated in almost every collective agreement, deregulation was not as easy as expected. Due to the constitutional guarantee of autonomy in collective bargaining (*Tarifautonomie*) (*see* paragraph 408), the legislator was not able to restrict claims to continued remuneration in case of sickness established in collective agreements. In other words, the 1996 amendments were effective mainly for employees not covered by collective agreements. The rise of continued remuneration in case of sickness to 100% for all employees, effective since 1 January 1999, was one of the first legislative initiatives of the new coalition, which came into power in autumn 1998. The four-week waiting period, also introduced in 1996, was, however, left untouched.

272. Today, every employee, who has been employed continuously for more than four weeks and is unable to work due to sickness is, according to Section 3 EFZG, entitled to six weeks of continued remuneration in full. Should he or she become sick due to the same disease again, he or she is entitled to another six weeks of continued remuneration only if he or she has been able to work for at least six months before the renewed sickness or if twelve months have passed since being unable to work due to the same sickness. In any case, however, a claim to continued remuneration in case of sickness provides that the sickness is not the employee's fault. It is highly problematic what this notion really means. The formula developed by the courts defines 'fault' in this context as 'if the employee acts in a manner which is strongly opposed to what a reasonable person in his own interest would do'. This very vague formula certainly does not decide specific cases. This is why a tremendous number of court decisions exist.

273. Employers employing regularly not more than thirty employees are reimbursed 80% of their expenses for continued remuneration in case of sickness by the health insurance, Section 1 paragraph 1 of the Act on Reimbursement of Employers' Expenses (*Aufwendungsausgleichsgesetz* – AAG).

274. After six weeks of continued remuneration by the employer, an employee, who is still ill, can receive sickness benefit (*Krankengeld*) from his or her statutory health insurance fund (*see* Sections 44–51 SGB V). This amounts to 70% of the employee's regular pay. As a rule, there is no time limit for the sickness benefit. In the event of incapacity to work due to the same illness, however, it can be received for a maximum of seventy-eight weeks within a three-year period. If another illness occurs during the period of incapacity for work, the duration of benefits is not extended.

275. In order to reduce absenteeism due to sickness employers quite often use the instrument of a specific premium which is paid to its full extent (be it monthly or yearly) on condition that the employee has never been absent during the respective period. For each day of absence, a specific amount of money is deducted from the premium, no matter what the reason for the absence might be. There has always been a rather heated debate about whether such an instrument is lawful or whether it has to be considered to be an unlawful abuse of rights, deviating from the intention of the sickness payment system. In the 1980s, after initial reluctance, the Federal Labour Court considered these premiums to be unlawful.[148] In the 1990s,

148. Federal Labour Court, 19 May 1982 – 5 AZR 466/80, *Arbeitsrechtliche Praxis*, No. 12 §611 BGB *Anwesenheitsprämie*.

however, evidently as a sort of very peculiar attempt of crisis management, this premium was revitalized and considered to be lawful, at least under certain conditions.[149]

IV. Pregnancy and Maternity

276. According to the MuSchG 1952 (reformed in 2017), pregnant women are, under specific conditions, not permitted to perform work in order to avoid health risks. If such a prohibition of employment applies, Section 18 MuSchG obliges the employer to pay continued remuneration. According to Section 3 paragraph 1 MuSchG, expectant mothers are in any case strictly forbidden to work during the last six weeks before confinement. After confinement, a strict prohibition of employment applies for another eight weeks (Section 3 paragraph 2 MuSchG). If the child is born prematurely or if the mother has given birth to more than one child, this period is extended to twelve weeks. During that time women obtain, according to maternity allowance from the health insurance (Section 19 MuSchG). This amount, of course, is usually a lot lower than the woman's normal net income. The difference between net income and this amount is to be covered by the employer (Section 20 MuSchG). In the first few months after the period of general and strict prohibition of employment following a confinement, mothers may be employed only if their health permits employment. If employment is not permitted, full remuneration nevertheless has to be paid. In order to reduce disincentives to employ women, employers employing regularly not more than thirty employees are reimbursed payments in terms of Sections 18 and 20 MuSchG to their full extent by the health insurance (Section 1 paragraph 2 AAG).

V. Employee Representatives

277. For members of works councils, staff representative councils and other bodies of employee participation there are specific guarantees of continued payment of remuneration for periods when they fulfil their duties of office or when they participate in training programmes (*see* paragraphs 602–604). The structure of these regulations will be explained in Part II.

149. Federal Labour Court, 15 Feb. 1990 – 6 AZR 381/88, *Arbeitsrechtliche Praxis*, No. 15 §611 BGB *Anwesenheitsprämie*; confirmed in dec. of 26 Oct. 1994 – 10 AZR 482/93, *Arbeitsrechtliche Praxis*, No. 18 §611 BGB *Anwesenheitsprämie*.

Chapter 6. Employee Liability

278. According to the rules of ordinary civil law (Sections 280 et seq. and Sections 823 et seq. BGB) applied to the employment relationship, the employee is responsible for any damage caused in the course of work performance, whether the damage has been caused intentionally or by negligence. In the Weimar era, the courts had decided, however, that this civil law pattern was inadequate for an employment relationship.[150] There were mainly two reasons for developing a new solution: first, work in many cases increases the risk of causing damage, and second, the employee is economically not in a situation enabling him or her to compensate for such damage. Hence it was thought to be more appropriate to transfer the risk of having to compensate such damage to the employer.

279. In 1957, in a fundamental decision of the Large Senate (*see* paragraph 362), the Federal Labour Court generally accepted the idea that employee liability should be limited – provided that the inherent nature of the work to be performed involved a high probability that even the most careful employee would make occasional mistakes which, when considered separately, were avoidable (*gefahrgeneigte Tätigkeit*).[151] At the time when this distinction was launched, the most prominent example of work with such inherent dangers was professional driving. The liability was limited as follows. Employees performing work with such inherent dangers should only be liable for damages caused intentionally or by gross negligence.[152] The remaining 'normal' negligence was split into two further categories: light negligence and medium negligence. In case of light negligence, the employee should never be liable.[153] In case of medium negligence, the liability for damages was to be divided between employer and employee taking into account the circumstances of the specific situation.[154] In the course of many years of case law the courts, on the one hand, have developed a tendency to be very generous in assuming light negligence, thereby eliminating the employee's liability. On the other hand, only very grave faults were considered to be gross negligence.

280. The main problem referred to the question of whether or not it is possible at all to distinguish between work with an inherent danger of causing damage and other work. For a long time, the labour courts resisted giving up this distinction even though more and more occupations were considered to be work with such inherent dangers. In 1993, after a long and sophisticated debate, the Federal Labour Court finally abandoned the distinction.[155] Today the above-mentioned differentiation into

150. Reich Labour Court, ARS 30, p. 3; 37, p. 269.
151. Large Senate (*see* para. 362), 25 Sep. 1957 – GS 4/56, *Arbeitsrechtliche Praxis*, No. 4 §898 RVO.
152. Federal Labour Court, 29 Jun. 1964 – 1 AZR 434/63, *Arbeitsrechtliche Praxis*, No. 33 §611 BGB *Haftung des Arbeitnehmers*.
153. Federal Labour Court, 29 Jun. 1964, *supra*.
154. *Ibid.*
155. Large Senate (*see* para. 362), 12 Jun. 1992 – GS 1/89, *Arbeitsrechtliche Praxis*, No. 102 §611 BGB *Haftung des Arbeitnehmers*; 29 Sep. 1994 – GS 1/89 (A), *Arbeitsrechtliche Praxis*, No. 103 §611 BGB *Haftung des Arbeitnehmers*.

different levels of negligence, originally developed for work with the inherent danger of causing damage, is applicable to all kinds of work. As a result, the present situation is as follows. If an employee performs any kind of work, i.e., if he or she performs any activity that has been necessitated for operational reasons, and causes damage he or she is not liable at all provided that he or she has acted with merely light negligence. If the damage has been caused with medium negligence he or she is liable for only a part of the damage. Only in cases of gross negligence or intent is the employee liable for the whole damage. The same rules apply if it is a third party who has suffered the damage. The employer is obliged to indemnify the employee from his liability towards the third party if the employee is free of liability due to light or medium negligence.

281. Today, the limitation of the employee's liability is still more or less based on the same idea already developed in the 1930s: every employee, even the most conscientious, may make a mistake that inherently could have been avoided but usually leads to excessive financial demands. Moreover, the employee performs his or her work in an organization determined and organized by somebody else, i.e., the employer. Hence, the employee is unable to master the risk of becoming liable while the employer is very well able to influence the organizational and technical equipment. The latter can particularly change the workflow, provide better surveillance and safety devices, accumulate capital surplus, contract insurance. An employee's mistake in the course of time is an inevitable part of the employer's sphere of risks, likewise the casual breakdown of an engine.

282. In respect of damages to the employee's property caused by himself or herself, the labour courts, for a very long time, had refused to grant him or her a right to compensation. In the 1980s, however, the Federal Labour Court made the system of employee liability consistent by granting the employee such a right, at least under certain conditions.[156]

283. Nevertheless, the system of employee liability as developed by the labour courts is still insufficient. Even where the employee causes damage by gross negligence the question arises whether the amount of compensation should not be limited. So far the principle 'all or nothing', which is based on civil law, still applies. Further, it has turned out that liability may be used as a disciplinary measure to put pressure on the employee. That is why a discussion is continuing as to whether liability should be restricted even further.[157]

156. Dec. of 11 Aug. 1988 – 8 AZR 721/85, and of 4 Apr. 1989 – 8 AZR 632/87, *Arbeitsrechtliche Praxis*, Nos 7 and 9 §611 BGB *Gefährdungshaftung des Arbeitgebers*; *cf.* H. Reichold, *Münchener Handbuch zum Arbeitsrecht,* R. Richardi & O. Wlotzke ed., Verlag C.H. Beck, § 57.
157. *Cf.* H. Reichold, *Münchener Handbuch zum Arbeitsrecht, supra*, § 57, para. 58.

Chapter 7. Termination of the Individual Labour Contract

§1. Termination by Mutual Consent

284. It follows from the principle of freedom of contract that it is always possible to terminate a labour contract by mutual consent. Such a cancellation contract (*Aufhebungsvertrag*) can be concluded without any precondition except that, according to Section 623 BGB effective since May 2000, it has to be in writing. Not even the works council has a right to intervene. Only in the case of disabled employees under very strict conditions may the integration office in charge of severely or equally treated disabled persons exercise controlling powers (Section 168 SGB IX). Whether or not the freedom to terminate the employment contract mutually by cancellation of a contract should be upheld without any restriction has become a highly debated issue. Often employees are, without notice, put in a situation where they have virtually no choice but to agree to the termination of the employment contract. And quite often they are offered a financial compensation which at first glance leads them to sign an agreement but afterwards turns out not to pay off in view of the labour market situation and in view of the fact that such compensation is to a certain extent and under certain conditions deducted from unemployment benefits (*see* Sections 157 and 158 SGB III). All attempts to establish an employee's right to revoke the cancellation contract within a certain period or to submit the conclusion of a cancellation contract to the works council's control have failed so far. Temporary expectations that the courts would establish conditions limiting the freedom to conclude a contract terminating an employment contract have turned out to be futile. Previous attempts to convince the labour courts that a cancellation contract – usually concluded at the workplace – was a contract in terms of Section 312 BGB as amended 2002, granting the consumer a right of cancellation in respect of contracts negotiated in doorstep sale and similar situations, has not been crowned with success.[158] In literature, however, this was and is highly controversial for a long time. The new version of Section 312 BGB in June 2014 has given new upswing to the debate. However, the Federal Labour Court has continued to reject this in more recent times.[159]

§2. Retirement

285. Until 1991, the statutory retirement age was 65 years for men and 60 years for women in Germany. If certain conditions were fulfilled (35 years' membership in the statutory pension system, of which at least 180 months of membership were due to employment) it was possible for male employees to retire at an age of 63 and receive an old age pension from the statutory pension system. Specific groups of male employees (disabled persons and those who qualify for the social security system for those who are no longer capable of working, either generally or with reference to their respective job qualification) were even allowed to retire at an age of

158. Federal Labour Court, 27 Nov. 2003 – 2 AZR 135/03, *BAGE*, vol. 109, 32.
159. Federal Labour Court, 7 Feb. 2019 – 6 AZR 75/18, *BAGE* 165, 315.

60. Then in 1992, the statutory pension system was fundamentally reformed. *Inter alia* the age limits for men and women were equalized upwards step by step. Another fundamental reform took place in 2007, when, after several minor reforms of the statutory pension system had taken place, and in view of demographic developments – increasing life expectancy on the one hand, the low reproduction rate on the other – the legislator decided to raise the age limit for the ordinary statutory old age pension step by step from 65 to 67 years. Those born in 1964 and later will not receive the old age pension benefit before 67.

286. In 1992 an old age pension due to unemployment (*Altersrente wegen Arbeitslosigkeit*) was introduced in Section 38 SGB VI, allowing unemployed persons who had been unemployed for at least fifty-two weeks within the last eighteen months, who had paid contributions to the statutory old age insurance for at least eight years within the last ten years, and who had been members of the social insurance system for at least fifteen years to retire at the age of 60. In 2000, in view of demographic developments, the old age pension due to unemployment was limited to those born before 1952 (Section 237 SGB VI). Since 2006, the age limit of 60 for persons born between 1946 and 1948 has been increased step by step to 63. However, for persons born before 1952 protection of confidence has been provided: they are still entitled to the old age pension due to unemployment from 60 years on, however, with deductions of up to 18%.

287. Individual agreements according to which the employment relationship expires automatically at the time when the employee is entitled to the regular retirement pension – i.e., 65 or older – are very common. Quite often, such clauses are also contained in collective agreements and in works agreements. According to Section 41 SGB VI, as amended in 1992, however, such clauses were valid only on condition that they had been concluded within the last three years before attainment of retirement age or if they had been confirmed by the employee within that period. The idea was that the employee should be free to choose whether to stay or to leave when retirement age was close. According to a decision of the Federal Labour Court,[160] this provision was not only applicable to individual agreements, but also to collective agreements and works agreements. Consequently, the employee was in a good bargaining position: if the employer wanted to terminate the employment relationship upon the employee attaining retirement age the employee could make his or her consent conditional on adequate financial compensation. The Federal Labour Court's decision provoked a very fierce controversy about whether or not this amendment should be abolished again. Due to the employers' very strong opposition to the new regulation, the legislator amended Section 41 SGB VI in 1994. Since that time, clauses providing for an automatic termination at the time when the employee reaches the regular retirement age (i.e., 65 or older) have again complied with this provision. Whether or not such clauses are compatible with the ban of age discrimination as provided in Directive 2000/78/EC and Section 10 No. 5 AGG 2006 (*see* paragraphs 329 et seq.), however, has been a matter of controversy for a long time. In the Rosenbladt ruling in 2010, the CJEU also ruled that an age limit

160. Federal Labour Court, 11 Jun. 1997 – 7 AZR 186/96, *Arbeitsrechtliche Praxis*, No. 7 §41 SGB VI.

based on collective bargaining agreements is compatible with Union law.[161] In 2014, Section 41 SGB VI was supplemented by a third sentence. This provides that if a termination of the employment relationship is agreed upon when the standard age limit is reached, the parties to the employment contract may postpone the date of termination, if necessary, several times, by agreement during the employment relationship. This provision on temporary continued employment after reaching retirement age was also considered permissible by the CJEU.[162]

288. In the 1980s, steps were taken to promote early retirement in order to combat unemployment. According to the Act on Optional Early Retirement (*Vorruhestandsgesetz*) of 1984, employers who paid employees in early retirement (58 years and older) at least 65% of their former gross income and who employed a former unemployed person in the retiree's job were entitled to 35% reimbursement of their expenses. The conditions as fixed in the Act could be improved by collective agreements. That happened to a great extent. In 1989, the 1984 Act expired and was replaced by the Act on Part-time Retirement (*Altersteilzeitgesetz* – AtG).[163] This new Act gave up the rigid alternative between staying or leaving and provided a possibility for gradual entry into retirement. In 1992, the 1989 AtG was replaced by the already mentioned Act fundamentally reforming the system of statutory retirement insurance that, again, was replaced by a modified AtG in 1996. All these models have in common that part-time work for employees approaching retirement age, and hence part-time retirement, is a subsidized form of part-time work and therefore, from the employee's point of view, a lot more attractive than normal part-time work. However, it is important to note that the financial support for Part-time Retirement provided by the Federal Employment Agency expired at the end of 2009 and only benefits those employees who reduced their working hours before 1 January 2010. Since then, subsidies have only been available within the framework of regulations on part-time work for older employees in collective agreements, works agreements or agreements with the employer.

289. Under Sections 2 and 3 AtG 1996, the situation is as follows. If employees agree with their employer to reduce working time to half of the previous weekly working time, their pro rata payment from the part-time employment is – under certain further conditions – increased to at least 70% of the former full-time net income; social security contributions are calculated and paid on the basis of 90% of the former full-time income. Collective agreements usually provide for even higher net income and higher statutory pension contributions (*see* paragraph 266).[164] For a maximum period of six years the 20% pay increase and the additional contributions are reimbursed by the Federal Employment Agency (Section 4 AtG), when Part-time Retirement started before 2010. There is, however, one important additional condition for reimbursement as laid down in Section 3 paragraph 1 No. 2 AtG. For

---

161. CJEU, 12 Oct. 2010 – C-45/09, ECLI:EU:C:2010:601.
162. CJEU, 28 Feb. 2018 – C-46/17, ECLI:EU:C:2018:131.
163. M. Schmidt, *The Need for Modernising German Labour Law Arising from the Ban of Age Discrimination*, in *Modernisation of Labour Law and Industrial Relations, Liber Amicorum for Marco Biagi* 353 et seq (R. Blanpain & M. Weiss eds. 2003).
164. WSI (ed.), *Tarifhandbuch 2006, supra*, p. 268.

a post vacant due to old age part-time work or due to a shift of employees that has taken place in this context the employer has to employ either a formerly unemployed person or a person who has just completed vocational training. If the employer does not usually employ more than fifty employees it is also sufficient to hire an apprentice. Whether or not the AtG is compatible with the ban of age discrimination as provided for in Directive 2000/78/EC is highly debatable; employees younger than 55 may also be interested in reducing their working time from full-time to part-time. But since their employer is not entitled to reimbursement of any costs, they will hardly receive more than pro rata payment. Besides, no legitimate reason justifying this discrimination against younger employees can be found. The AtG has in fact proved to be inappropriate to promote a smooth transition into retirement. Section 2 paragraph 2 AtG allows a flexible distribution of the reduced working time over rather long equalization periods of up to ten years, provided that within six years of the overall equalization period the weekly working time does not exceed half of the regular weekly working time. Old age part-time work can hence be organized in long periods of full-time employment, followed by an equally long period of non-employment. Due to the fact that neither employers nor employees are interested in a smooth transition more than 90% of cases are performed in the form of this so-called block model.[165]

290. Until the end of 1997 in several branches and enterprises with altogether 5 million employees collective agreements have been concluded providing for even better conditions for part-time retirement. The pay increase ranges between 20% and 40% of the part-time income; predominantly at least 85% of full-time income is reached. Contributions to statutory retirement insurance are mostly increased to 90%, in some enterprises even to 100%. Quite often part-time retirement is, however, limited to a certain percentage of the workforce (3%–5%).

§3. Dismissal

I. Extraordinary and Ordinary Dismissal

291. Since the origins of labour law, dismissal as a possibility of unilateral termination of the labour contract has been accepted as a legitimate instrument.[166] According to the liberal philosophy, nobody should be forced to remain in a relationship he or she does not wish to continue. Thus, either party could terminate the contractual relationship by ordinary dismissal. The only condition was to observe a term of notice. If, e.g., in cases of grave misconduct or for other urgent reasons, it was not tolerable for either of the two parties to continue the employment relationship until the notice period had expired, the weapon of extraordinary dismissal, terminating the contract without a term of notice, could be used. It should be pointed out, however, that originally the length of the notice period was up to the individual

165. For a more thorough discussion *cf.* Schmidt, in Blanpain and Weiss, *supra*, pp. 353–367.
166. For a description of the historical background *cf.* A. Seifert & E. Funken-Hötzel, *Wrongful Dismissals in the Federal Republic of Germany*, Comp. Lab. L. & Pol' J. 487 et seq (2004).

parties. In other words, the parties were free, by individual agreement, to reduce the period of notice to a very short time. Since in the nineteenth century, for reasons explained in the introduction, employees did not have any bargaining power, they consequently had to agree to very short periods of notice. This is why in fact it was generally possible to dismiss employees within a short time and, as already explained, without any justification.

II. Development and Basic Idea of Protection Against Dismissal

292. Protection against unfair dismissal does not focus on extraordinary dismissal without notice but on ordinary dismissal with terms of notice. The reason for this is very simple: for an extraordinary dismissal, a specific objective cause had to be given from the very outset, whereas ordinary dismissal originally could be declared without any justifying reason whatsoever. Until today, this is still the case if an employee wants to quit a job. In other words, protection against unfair dismissal exclusively deals with dismissals declared by the employer.

293. The first attempt at providing legal protection against unfair dismissal was embodied in the first Act on BRG of 1920. According to that Act the employer was, for the first time, and also in cases of ordinary dismissal, legally obliged to give reasons. Under certain conditions the works council was allowed to intervene and eventually to appeal to court. The works council, however, could under no circumstances finally prevent the dissolution of the employment contract. The dissolution of the employment contract was always left open to the employer provided if he paid a certain indemnity imposed by the court. This very first and rather modest step of protection against unfair dismissal was partly reduced by the Nazis. In resuming, it is important to note that, until the FRG was founded, protection against unfair dismissal only meant protection against evident and excessive abuses of the employer's power to dismiss. However, even this protection was rather ineffective. The KSchG of 1951 was not only the result of a government and parliamentary initiative but was also the outcome of a basic consensus reached between the top organizations of unions and employers' associations. Thus from the very outset this Act enjoyed a very specific legitimacy and authority. The basic idea of the 1951 KSchG, amended several times since then, is to reverse the traditional structure of ordinary dismissal declared by the employer. Until 1951, the regular case was that such a dismissal was lawful, and only in exceptional cases was regarded as illegal. Since 1951, ordinary dismissals have usually been regarded as illegal, and legality has become the exceptional case. This has consequences mainly for the question of who has to prove what.

294. The law on protection against dismissal can only be understood if the works council's role is taken into account. The same is true for the staff council in the public sector. Since there are only marginal differences between the powers of the two bodies, the following explanations focus exclusively on the powers of the works council (*see* paragraphs 312–316).

III. Common Rules for All Types of Dismissal

295. The first step of improving job security in Germany was the extension of the minimum duration of the term of notice. In the course of history different rules for manual workers and white-collar workers were developed. The minimum term of notice for manual workers was two weeks, for white-collar workers six weeks. These minimum periods were extended according to seniority; again, the rules for white-collar workers were more favourable than those for manual workers. The Federal Constitutional Court, however, considered all these distinctions incompatible with the general principle of equal treatment as laid down in Article 3 paragraph 1 GG.[167] In 1993 a new law was therefore passed, equalizing the situation for manual workers and white-collar workers. Since that time, the minimum term of notice has been four weeks for all employees (Section 622 paragraph 1 BGB). After two years of employment, the notice period is extended to one month, after five years to two months, after eight years to three months, after ten years to four months, after twelve years to five months, after fifteen years to six months and after twenty years to seven months, always to the end of the respective last month (Section 622 paragraph 2 BGB). During a probation period, which may not exceed six months, the term of notice is only two weeks (Section 622 paragraph 3 BGB).

296. It should be stressed that the minimum term of notice may be reduced by collective agreement: only for parties to an individual labour contract are the terms laid down in Section 622 paragraphs 1 and 2 BGB a strict minimum (there are only a few narrow exceptions to paragraph 1 under Section 622 paragraph 5 BGB). The underlying idea is that parties to a collective agreement, at a given time in a given branch and region, know better what is appropriate than the legislator's overall and long-term perspective would allow. Of course, parties to collective agreements are not prevented from raising the minimum term of notice and from extending it in favour of employees. In most branches, this is the normal pattern. Minimum terms of notice as laid down in Section 622 paragraphs 1–3 BGB prevent the parties to an individual employment contract only from reducing the period; they are free to extend them. If they do so, however, the following rule resulting of Section 622 paragraph 6 BGB must be observed: the term of notice the employer has to observe cannot be shorter than the term the employee must conform to when he or she himself or herself gives notice of dismissal. This, however, does not mean that the terms of notice for employer and employee always have to be of corresponding duration: the term of notice the employee respects may be shorter than the term of notice the employer has to comply with.

297. According to Section 623 BGB, in force since May 2000, any dismissal has furthermore to be given in writing. Otherwise, the dismissal is null and void.

167. Federal Constitutional Court, 30 May 1990 – 1 BvL 2/83 et al., *Arbeitsrechtliche Praxis*, No. 28 §622 BGB.

298. Furthermore, it is important to note that any dismissal, whether lawful or not, becomes automatically valid with the consequences that the employment relationship is terminated and that the dismissal can no longer be contested in court, if the employee does not take court action within three weeks after he or she has received the dismissal. This follows from Sections 4–7 KSchG. In this way, the legislator has accommodated the employers' interests in economic planning reliability.

§4. Extraordinary Dismissal

299. According to Section 626 BGB extraordinary dismissal (dismissal without notice) is lawful only provided that 'there are reasons which in view of all circumstances of the case and in evaluating the interests of both parties make it unacceptable for either of the parties to fulfil the contract until the end of the period of notice'. This section covers every labour contract. Reasons justifying extraordinary dismissal may not only be based on misconduct or incompetence but also on severe economic circumstances, which have nothing to do with the employee's behaviour. It is important to stress that all circumstances of the particular case have to be evaluated. That is why any generalization of what is a justified reason for extraordinary dismissal would be totally misleading. The answer to the question of whether or not certain factors justify a dismissal without notice may differ from case to case, depending on the situation. If a dismissal is based on repeated misconduct on the part of the employee, it is, at least in principle, necessary that the employee has prior warning (*Abmahnung*). In other words, the employer must have made perfectly clear that in the case of repeated or continued misconduct the employee will be dismissed (*see* paragraph 307).

300. In order to ensure that the employee is not left in any uncertainty, Section 626 BGB requires that notice of dismissal shall be given within two weeks after the reason for the termination became known. In addition, the dismissing party has to disclose the reason for the dismissal at the request of the dismissed party. However, according to the Federal Labour Court and to the prevailing opinion among labour law scholars,[168] violation of this rule does not render the dismissal void.

§5. Ordinary Dismissal

I. The Applicability of the Act on Protection Against Dismissal

301. The central provisions of the KSchG have always not been applicable to small establishments below a minimum size.[169] However, the scope of exemption

---

168. *Cf.* J.-M. Niemann, in *Erfurter Kommentar zum Arbeitsrecht*, ed. R. Müller-Glöge et al, 2020, Verlag C.H. Beck, §626 BGB para. 243 with further proofs.

169. However even in small establishments there are a minimum of social aspects to be considered; Federal Labour Court, 21 Feb. 2001 – 2 AZR 15/00, *BAGE*, vol. 97, pp. 92–106; *cf. also* the annotation of M. Schmidt, *International Labour Law Reports* 293–303 (2001).

provided for in Section 23 KSchG has been changed several times. Until 1985, establishments with five or fewer employees (apprentices not included) were exempted from the application of the KSchG, no matter whether or not the employees concerned were full-time employees. The scope of this exclusion was extended by the Act on Improvement of Employment Opportunities (BeschFG) of 1985. Since then, only employees having been employed for at least 10 hours a week or 45 hours a month have had to be considered in the calculation of the necessary minimum number of employees. The idea was to give incentives to employ part-time employees. When in view of increasing unemployment in the early 1990s the view that dismissal protection constituted a deterrent for employment became more and more popular, the 1996 Act on the Improvement of Employment Opportunities (*see* paragraph 271) was passed, raising the minimum number of employees from more than five to more than ten. At the same time the rule according to which part-time employees are taken into account was changed: part-time employees with a regular working time of not more than 10 hours should be taken into account as 0.25, part-time employees with a regular working time of not more than 20 hours as 0.5, and finally part-time employees with a regular working time of not more than 30 hours as 0.75 employees. By raising the minimum number of employees required for the applicability of the KSchG to an establishment, the legislator hoped to stimulate 'small' employers to employ more persons; the new modus of considering part-time employees was motivated by the aim of avoiding indirect discrimination.[170] Since it was highly disputed whether the raising of the threshold had had the expected effects it was lowered again to more than five employees immediately after the change of government in 1998. At the same time, the modus for considering part-time employees was changed. From January 1999 on, the KSchG has been applicable to establishments employing more than five employees; part-time employees with a regular working time of not more than 20 hours are taken into account as 0.5, and part-time employees with a regular working time of not more than 30 hours count as 0.75. The second prerequisite is that the employee must have been employed by the same employer for at least six months. Hence, probation clauses, which are generally limited to a duration of less than six months, are only of marginal relevance. Their only effect is that the short (two weeks') minimum term of notice during probation periods is applicable, no matter what the contractual term of notice may be.

302. In 2003, the same government that had amended Section 23 KSchG only a few years before decided to re-amend it by raising the threshold from five to ten employees again but conserving the old threshold for employees covered by the lower threshold at 31 December 2003. Consequently, employees whose employment contracts have been concluded in 2004 or later only enjoy dismissal protection if the establishment they are employed in has more than ten employees (apprentices excluded). Those appointed before 2004 are covered by the KSchG if they are employed in an establishment employing usually more than five employees (apprentices excluded). For the calculation of the latter threshold, those employees employed in 2004 and later are not to be taken into account.

170. Seifert & Funken-Hötzel, *supra*, pp. 487 et seq.

II. The Concept of Social Justification

303. According to Section 1 KSchG, ordinary dismissal is normally socially unjustified and therefore unlawful. Section 1 paragraph 2 KSchG lists three exceptions, which render a dismissal legal. Thus, if the legality of a dismissal is contested it is up to the employer to prove that the prerequisites of such an exceptional case were met at the time when the employee to be dismissed received the declaration of dismissal. There are three kinds of reasons possibly justifying an ordinary dismissal: to do with the employee's person, the employee's behaviour, or economic reasons.[171]

A. Reasons Concerning the Employee's Person

304. The notion of 'reasons concerning the employee's person' refers to a situation in which the employee is unable to fulfil the requirements of his or her job. The main example of this category is illness. However, it should be pointed out that the economic interest of the employer in dismissing a sick employee must be carefully balanced against the interests of the employee who is ill. Thus, it is necessary to examine the details of the economic impact, the impact on the organization and on work performance, the impact on other employees, the possibility of a transfer, the duration of the employment, etc. One of the decisive factors to be taken into consideration is the size of the enterprise.[172] Large enterprises are considered to cope more easily than small enterprises with the problems created by sick and therefore temporarily absent employees. In short, the dismissal is lawful only if, after an evaluation, it turns out to be necessary as a last resort.

305. In cases of chronic disease and long-lasting sickness, the labour courts tend to be very reluctant to recognize a dismissal as lawful; this is especially true for large enterprises. The most serious problem, however, concerns the dismissal of employees who are frequently sick for short periods. In such cases, the courts were more ready to accept the dominance of the employer's economic interests.[173] Since it is not sufficient that the cause for dismissal existed in the past, everything depends on the question of whether or not the illness will continue in future. This, under usual circumstances, is difficult to predict. Thus the question arises of who should bear the burden of proof. The Federal Labour Court has decided that, because he or she is the one who best knows the condition of his or her health, it is up to the

171. Seifert & Funken-Hötzel, *supra.*
172. Federal Labour Court, 10 Mar. 1977 – 2 AZR 79/76, *Arbeitsrechtliche Praxis*, No. 4 §1 KSchG 1969 *Krankheit.*
173. Federal Labour Court, 23 Jun. 1983 – 2 AZR 15/82, *Arbeitsrechtliche Praxis*, No. 10 §1 KSchG 1969 *Krankheit.*

employee to prove that he or she will not be sick in the future.[174] This rule meant that it is not very difficult to dismiss an employee who has frequently been sick for short periods.

306. In recent years, however, dismissal due to illness has become much more difficult. The reason for this is the regulation on company integration management (*Betriebliches Eingliederungsmanagement* – BEM) in Section 164 paragraph 2 SGB IX. This stipulates: 'If employees are unable to work because of illness for more than six weeks without interruption or repeatedly for more than six weeks within a year, the employer shall clarify with the responsible representative body within the meaning of § 176 [SGB IX], and in the case of severely disabled persons also with the representative body for severely disabled persons, with the consent and participation of the person concerned, the possibilities of how the incapacity for work can be overcome as far as possible and with what benefits or assistance renewed incapacity for work can be prevented and the job can be retained.' The employer is thus obliged to offer long-term sick employees or those with frequent short illnesses a BEM. With the help of the BEM, ways can be found to maintain the job by reorganizing the workplace or by continuing employment under different working conditions.[175] The Federal Labour Court has set high hurdles here in order to consider a dismissal in the absence of a BEM to be nevertheless proportionate. The court had ruled: 'Only if the implementation of the BEM could not have produced positive results, its absence is harmless. In order to demonstrate that the dismissal complies with the principle of proportionality and that he had no milder means of overcoming the disease-related disturbance of the employment relationship than the termination notice, the employer must demonstrate the objective uselessness of the BEM. To this end, the employer must present in detail and comprehensively why it would not have been possible to continue working at the previous workplace, nor to adapt or change the workplace to suit the employee's needs, nor could the employee have been employed at a different workplace with a different job, i.e., why a BEM could not have helped to counteract new periods of illness or the continuation of incapacity to work and to maintain the employment relationship (…). If, on the other hand, it is conceivable that a bEM could have produced a positive result, i.e., that the joint search for measures to reduce absenteeism or to overcome incapacity to work would have been successful, the employer must regularly be reproached for having given "premature" notice of termination.'[176]

---

174. Federal Labour Court, 25 Nov. 1982 – 2 AZR 140/81, *Arbeitsrechtliche Praxis*, No. 7 §1 KSchG 1969 *Krankheit*; 9 Jun. 1989 – 2 AZR 19/89, *Arbeitsrechtliche Praxis*, No. 21 §1 KSchG 1969 *Krankheit*.
175. *See* K. Nebe, Individueller Anspruch auf Durchführung eines BEM-Verfahrens, *Article B18/2011*, under www.reha-recht.de.
176. Federal Labour Court, 13 Mai 2015 – 2 AZR 565/14, *Neue Juristische Wochenschrift (NJW) 2016*, p. 109.

B. Reasons Concerning the Employee's Behaviour

307. The notion of 'reasons concerning the employee's behaviour' refers to nothing other than misconduct such as repeated absenteeism without exculpation or repeated tardiness; insult, theft or other criminal offences towards the employer or other employees; drug consumption at the workplace; manipulation of the time-keeping system, etc. Since again all the circumstances of the particular situation must be taken into account, it is impossible to list all the types of misconduct justifying dismissal. The reasons justifying ordinary dismissal due to reasons concerning the employee's behaviour differ from reasons justifying an extraordinary dismissal as regards gravity and intensity of the misconduct. Only grave misconduct may lead to an extraordinary dismissal. However, since a dismissal is always supposed to be the *ultima ratio*, an employee behaving unacceptably can generally be dismissed only if he or she has received and ignored a prior warning (*see* paragraph 299), explaining unmistakably that the behaviour is unacceptable and that he or she will be dismissed if he or she continues to behave this way.

308. The question of whether or not mere suspicion of misconduct may be a reason for extraordinary or ordinary dismissal (*Verdachtskündigung*) is fiercely debated. The Federal Labour Court accepts mere suspicion of misconduct as a reason for dismissal provided that the following three preconditions are fulfilled: if the employee is suspected of having committed grave misconduct, if the suspicion is strong and if the necessary investigations did not prove the suspicion to be unfounded. During the investigations, the employer may suspend the employee from his or her duty to work, but the employer is nevertheless obliged to pay remuneration.

C. Economic Reasons

309. A cause for dismissal for economic reasons may be external influences (economic crisis, etc.) as well as measures taken by the employer (introduction of new technologies, measures of rationalization, etc.). The dismissal is justified if, due to the economic situation, it has become impossible for the employer to retain the employee any longer. If the dismissal is contested in court, it is up to the employer to prove the details of the economic situation and the necessity for dismissal.[177] The decision of whether or not to take particular organizational measures (introduction of new technologies, measures of rationalization, etc.) leading to a dismissal is, however, not subject to judicial control.[178] It is considered to be part of management's prerogative even, as will be shown in Part II (*see* paragraphs 625–633), if the works council is involved.

---

177. H. Oetker, *Erfurter Kommentar zum Areitsrecht,* ed. R. Müller-Glöge et al, 2020, Verlag C.H. Beck, §1 KSchG paras 211 et seq.
178. Federal Labour Court, 30 Apr. 1987 – 2 AZR 184/86, *Arbeitsrechtliche Praxis*, No. 42 §1 KSchG 1969 *Betriebsbedingte Kündigung.*

310. If, in a case of dismissal for economic reasons, it is necessary to select employees to be dismissed, the selection must be made taking into account 'social aspects'. The idea is that those who would suffer most from the effects of a dismissal should be the last to be dismissed. Originally, the notion of 'social aspects' was not defined in Section 1 paragraph 3 KSchG. The courts interpreted it as referring to all possible factors defining the social situation of a person (age, seniority, marital status, number of children, economic status, etc.). In other words the notion 'social aspects' refers to a very complex phenomenon which is not easy to assess. Instead of focusing on certainty, practicability and simplicity, as for example the seniority rule used in many countries, Section 1 paragraph 3 KSchG aimed at social justice in each individual case. The 1996 amendment of the KSchG (*see* paragraph 293) reversed that valuation: in order to promote certainty, practicability and simplicity the notion 'social aspects' was replaced by three exclusive criteria: 'seniority, age and obligations to pay maintenance'. Furthermore, the legislator established in Section 1 paragraph 3 sentence 2 KSchG the employer's option to exempt certain employees from the social selection to be made, provided that the continuation of their employment was necessary, particularly due to their knowledge, competency and performance or in order to safeguard a balanced personal structure of the establishment. It has to be pointed out that the conditions for this exemption, by court interpretation, have become very restrictive.[179] In addition, a new instrument was introduced: the so-called list of names in Section 1 paragraph 5 KSchG. If, in the case of a change of establishment in the terms of Section 111 BetrVG (*see* paragraph 626), works council and employer were able to agree upon a list of names of those employees to be dismissed the KSchG presumed that the dismissal of these employees was justified by economic reasons, the correctness of the social choice made by employer and works council being subject to judicial review of a very limited kind only. All these amendments, however, were also repealed in 1999 (*see* paragraphs 271, 301) and reintroduced again with minor amendments only a few years later by the very same legislator (*see* paragraph 302). Since January 2004, the social aspects to be taken into account have again been enumeratively listed in Section 1 paragraph 3 sentence 1 KSchG. The three criteria of 1996 – seniority, age and obligation to pay maintenance – have been complemented by a fourth: disability. The option in Section 1 paragraph 3 sentence 2 KSchG as well as the list of names in Section 1 paragraph 5 KSchG were reintroduced.

D. Impossibility of Further Employment

311. Even if there is an accepted cause for a dismissal, it is still considered to be socially unjustified and therefore void if the employee can be transferred to a comparable job with comparable working conditions, either immediately, after retraining, or after further training. In the latter case, the expenses for retraining should not exceed a reasonable level, taking into account the financial resources of the employer. Moreover, the dismissal is socially unjustified and void if the employee has agreed to be transferred to a job with poorer working conditions if such a job is

179. H. Oetker, *Erfurter Kommentar zum Areitsrecht, supra*, §1 KSchG paras. 342 et seq.

available. According to the case law of the Federal Labour Court, the possibility of transfer to any establishment of the enterprise is subject to examination, no matter whether or not there is a works council or how it reacts.[180] Even in cases of dismissal for reasons concerning the employee's behaviour, in cases where the source of misconduct can be eliminated by transfer, the possibility of a transfer, according to the Federal Labour Court, should be examined.[181]

§6. The Role of the Works Council in Dismissal Cases

312. Before any dismissal, whether it is ordinary or extraordinary, the employer is, according to Section 102 paragraph 1 BetrVG, obliged to consult the works council. If he fails to fulfil this obligation, the dismissal is null and void. The employer has to inform the works council of the employees to be dismissed, of the type of dismissal (ordinary or extraordinary), of the reason for the dismissal, of the date the dismissal will take effect, of the criteria applied for selection, of the examination of the possibilities of a transfer, etc.[182] In short, the works council is entitled to receive all information necessary to check the legality of the dismissal. It has to be stressed that the works council always has to be consulted before the dismissal is declared; a violation of this rule cannot be corrected later. In addition, it must be pointed out that before terminating the employment of a severely disabled employee, the representative body for severely disabled persons must also be consulted. If the employer fails to do so, the termination is also void according to the legal consequence of Section 178 paragraph 2 sentence 3 SGB IX introduced in 2017.

313. In the case of extraordinary dismissal, the works council has three days to agree or to declare reservations in writing. If the works council does not react within this period, its consent is statutorily assumed. No reservations declared by the works council in due time and in due form prevent the employer from dismissing the employee. Such reservations have no legal effect whatsoever, except that, later in court, the position of the dismissed employee may be better than in a situation where the works council has agreed to the dismissal or has done nothing. In fact, however, things are quite different. Since, as will be shown in Part II (*see* paragraphs 575 et seq.), the employer in many ways depends on the works council's cooperation, he or she tends to avoid conflict with it. This is why quite often, especially in big enterprises, the factual position of the works council is much stronger than it appears under the law.

314. In the case of an ordinary dismissal, the works council has one week to react; it can agree, it can do nothing, it can declare reservation in writing or it can

180. Federal Labour Court, 22 May 1986 – 2 AZR 612/85, *Arbeitsrechtliche Praxis*, No. 4 §1 KSchG 1969 *Konzern*.
181. Federal Labour Court, 22 Jul. 1982 – 2 AZR 30/81, *Arbeitsrechtliche Praxis*, No. 5 §1 KSchG 1969 *Verhaltensbedingte Kündigung*.
182. Seifert & Funken-Hötzel, *supra*, pp. 487 et seq.

object to the dismissal in writing. If the works council does not react its consent is assumed by law. None of the works council's possible reactions prevents the employer from dismissing the employee. The only reaction that may have some effect is a declaration of objection. However, before discussing the effects of a declaration of objection, the conditions will be sketched briefly. They are listed in Section 102 paragraph 3 BetrVG:

1. in selecting the employee for dismissal, the employer has not taken account or has not taken sufficient account of social aspects;
2. the measure contravenes a guideline drawn up pursuant to Section 95 (*see* paragraph 187);
3. the employee to be dismissed can be employed in another job in the same establishment or in another establishment of the undertaking;
4. the employee can continue to be employed after reasonable retraining or further training; or
5. the employee can continue to be employed under changed contractual conditions and has agreed thereto.

315. As regards the examination of the application of the social aspects or the availability of possibilities of transfer, the works council is supposed to be in a better position than the individual employee is. The works council can improve control of the selection procedure by so-called guidelines for selection of employees (Section 1 paragraph 4 KSchG, Section 95 BetrVG). Nevertheless, it should be pointed out that the legislator has restricted the scope of such guidelines in cases of dismissal. It is not possible to reduce the factors to be taken into account to one single factor and thereby pervert the aim and complexity of Section 1 paragraph 3 KSchG. There has to be a minimum of at least four factors: age, seniority, disability and maintenance duties. Thus, guidelines for selection of employees in cases of dismissal are primarily an instrument for listing the different factors and putting them in an order of priority. In fact, however, as in the case of guidelines for selection of employees in cases of hiring, such guidelines exist only in a minority of enterprises. One of the main reasons for the hesitation of works councils in initiating such guidelines may be that they are afraid of being pushed into a role of responsibility for the conditions of dismissal. For if works council and employer have agreed upon the factors to be taken account of, and upon the order of priority among those factors, a selection of employees to be dismissed can only be contested as regards gross incorrectness in court (Section 1 paragraph 4 KSchG).

316. If the works council, in due time and in due form, has declared its objection, there are two legal consequences to be considered: first, when the employer gives notice of dismissal he or she must, at the same time, hand over the written declaration of objection to the dismissed employee. This in fact means that the employee is receiving a strategic idea of how to fight the dismissal in court. This explains why the frequency of lawsuits in cases in which the works council has declared its objection is significantly higher than in other cases. Unfortunately, there are no recent empirical studies providing a safer and more precise base for evaluation. Second, if the dismissed employee brings an action against his or her employer in court he or she has to be actually employed until the end of the lawsuit, provided that he or she wishes to be so. However, it must be stressed that, at the same time, Section 102 BetrVG provides a tool for the employer to relieve himself or herself from this obligation by obtaining a court injunction. Among other causes, the claim for obtaining an injunction is justified if the continuation of the employment would put an 'intolerable economic burden' on the employer. It is evident that, in view of the fact that a lawsuit for dismissal protection can last several years, that burden is proven in all but exceptional cases. This is why only a small percentage of employees entitled to work until the end of the lawsuit in fact succeed in doing so.

§7. Reinstatement Versus Financial Compensation

317. The individual employee has the right to initiate a lawsuit to contest the legality of the dismissal. According to law, the normal remedy is reinstatement. However, even if the dismissal is unlawful and therefore void, the court may according to Section 9 KSchG, upon the employer's application, dissolve the contract. The employer may request the dissolution of the contract if 'further fruitful cooperation cannot be expected'. The facts proving this requirement may be created during the lawsuit. If the court grants the employer's request, the employer must pay indemnities to the employee. Section 10 KSchG only fixes the maximum amounts of such indemnities, generally up to twelve months' wages; for employees older than 50 years of age having been employed for at least fifteen years, fifteen months' wages; and for employees older than 55 years of age having been employed for at least twenty years up to eighteen months' wages. It is up to the court to determine the exact amount, taking into account the circumstances of the particular case. The mere fact that, even if the dismissal is unlawful, the possibility of judicial dissolution of the employment relationship is available steered the protective machinery away from integration and led it to compensation. The dismissed employee was usually aware of the fact that in the end he or she could not prevent the dissolution of the contract but only obtain a compensation. Hence, his or her strategy was to aim at significantly higher compensation than that granted by the court in accordance with the legal framework. This led to early compromises in the courts of first instance since usually the employer was ready to pay a higher compensation if that meant that the lawsuit could be terminated quickly. This explains why empirical research of the late 1970s and early 1980s concluded that, contrary to the model favoured by law, reinstatement was the rare exception and financial compensation rather the normal pattern.

318. Dissolution, however, was only a real threat as long as the dismissed employee was no longer integrated into the company's workforce during the lawsuit. This made it easy to pretend that 'further fruitful cooperation' was no longer possible. In 1985, however, the Federal Labour Court, in addition to the scheme of

Section 102 BetrVG (*see* paragraphs 314–316), developed the following pattern.[183] In spite of the uncertainty as to the question of whether or not the dismissal was lawful and therefore terminated the employment relationship, the dismissed employee has no right to be actually employed except in very exceptional cases where the dismissal is evidently illegal. But if, according to the decision of the labour Court of First Instance, the dismissal is considered to be illegal, the dismissed employee is entitled to continue working for the remaining period of the lawsuit at all appellate levels until the final decision. In other words, once there is a strong indication of the illegality of the dismissal, the employee's interest in continuing working prevails over the employer's interest. The new approach meant a radical change. It is difficult to convince the court of the impossibility of fruitful cooperation as long as the employee continues to be employed. Therefore, the employee is no longer ready to agree to a compromise on compensation in first instance but tries by all means to get a judgment. If this is favourable for him or her he or she has an unrestricted right to be reinstated for the rest of the lawsuit. This, however, implies that the employer no longer can be sure that his or her claim for dissolving the contract will be successful. In short and to make the point: the new Federal Labour Court's approach has succeeded in establishing reinstatement as a practical remedy. This has mainly led to the fact that, before dismissing an employee, each employer checks even more carefully whether the dismissal is lawful. Hence, dismissals not meeting the legal requirements are becoming rarer. In big companies, where a huge staff of legal experts is available, they virtually no longer occur. In small and medium-sized companies, however, due to the lack of expert knowledge, the situation is different. If today large companies want to get rid of an employee without being able to justify a dismissal they try to reach a mutual agreement on a contract of termination by offering much more financial compensation than had been the case before 1985.

319. Since court proceedings in matters of dismissal protection often end in a compromise agreement providing for financial compensation Section 1a KSchG, establishing an 'easy to handle, modern and unbureaucratic alternative solution', was introduced in 2004. Accordingly, the employee being dismissed for economic reasons may be entitled to receive a financial compensation of 0.5 of the monthly salary for every year that he or she has been continuously employed if (1) the employee does not take court action against the dismissal, and if (2) the employer has informed the employee in the dismissal notice that the dismissal is based on economic reasons and that the employee may claim compensation if he or she does not take court action. It is important to note that Section 1a KSchG does not limit in any respect the parties' right to conclude compromise agreements on financial compensation. This means that the introduction of Section 1a KSchG has in fact hardly changed anything.

183. Large Senate (*see* para. 362), 27 Feb. 1985 – GS 1/84, *Arbeitsrechtliche Praxis*, No. 14 §611 BGB *Beschäftigungspflicht.*

320. For reasons of legal certainty the factual situation at the time when the employee to be dismissed receives the declaration of dismissal is decisive for judging the lawfulness of a dismissal. Changes of fact, which occur during the notice period or after the termination of the employment relationship, cannot be taken into account. Several reasons for dismissal, however, are not founded on present facts but on a scenario of future events (i.e., the employee's future state of health, the enterprise's future closing down). If the expected events do not occur it seems to be contrary to natural justice simply to refer the employee to the validity of the dismissal. This is why the Federal Labour Court has granted a claim to re-engagement. Originally, a claim to re-engagement was granted only in cases of reasons concerning the employee's behaviour. In 1997, however, the Federal Labour Court for the first time acknowledged a claim to re-engagement in the case of a dismissal for economic reasons.[184] According to the Federal Labour Court the following principles apply: if a dismissal for economic reasons is based on the employer's forecast that he or she will not be able to employ the employee after the expiration of the notice period, and if that forecast proved to be incorrect during the notice period the employee is entitled to be re-engaged. Such a claim to re-engagement is, however, subject to two conditions: the first being that the employer, relying on the validity of the dismissal, has not yet made arrangements and the second being that it is not unreasonable to oblige him or her to continue the employment relationship.

While the law on protection against dismissal generally also applies to executive staff, there is a very important exemption in this respect laid down in Section 14 KSchG. The contracts of executive staff, who have the power to hire and fire other employees, can be dissolved more easily: the only condition is payment of financial compensation. The employer does not need to give reasons if he or she applies for the judicial termination of the employment relationship for employees of this group in exchange for financial compensation. The same applies to a narrowly limited group of risk carriers of major institutions whose annual fixed remuneration exceeds three times the contribution assessment ceiling in the statutory pension insurance. This regulation was included in Section 25a paragraph 5a of the German Banking Act (Kreditwesengesetz) in 2019 as part of the Brexit Tax Accompanying Act (Brexit-Steuerbegleitgesetz). In this way, it should be easier to terminate the employment contracts of top bankers in the future, comparable to those of executive staff.

§8. Dismissal Protection for Specific Groups

I. Pregnancy and Parenthood

321. According to Section 17 MuSchG it is forbidden to dismiss a woman during the period from the beginning of her pregnancy until the minimum of four months after she has given birth to a child or had a miscarriage beyond the twelfth week of pregnancy. Only in very exceptional cases in which the continuation of the

184. Federal Labour Court, 27 Feb. 1997 – 2 AZR 160/96, *Neue Zeitschrift für Arbeitsrecht*, 1997, pp. 757 et seq.

employment relationship would be absolutely unacceptable for the employer can a pregnant woman or a woman who has recently given birth to a child be dismissed – provided that the *Land* Office for Labour Inspection gives its consent. Since the prerequisites for such an exception are extremely tough, these cases do not play any role in practice. Similar rules apply to parents taking parental time. According to Section 18 BEEG a parent taking parental time cannot be dismissed during the leave which may last up to three years per child (*see* Section 15 BEEG) – unless further employment is absolutely unacceptable for the employer and the *Land* Office for Labour Inspection gives its consent. It must be stressed, however, that contracts concluded for a definite period end when the definite period has expired, even if a dismissal would be void.

II. Disabled Employees

322. According to Section 168 SGB IX, severely disabled employees or persons treated as such can only be dismissed with the consent of the administrative agency in charge of disabled persons. This applies to ordinary as well as to extraordinary dismissals. The SGB IX limits the discretionary powers of the administrative agency. Furthermore, the representative body for severely disabled employees must also be consulted before the employment relationship is terminated. Otherwise, the termination is invalid under the provision of § 178 paragraph 2 sentence 3 SGB IX, which was introduced in 2017 by the Federal Partition Act (*Bundesteilhabegesetz*).

III. Apprentices

323. According to Section 22 of the BBiG, apprentices can be dismissed without any prerequisites and without a minimum term of notice during the probation period. After this period, employers can only extraordinary dismiss apprentices, i.e., under the conditions previously mentioned (*see* paragraphs 299–300).

IV. Members of Employee Representative Bodies

324. According to Section 15 KSchG, members of works councils and other bodies of the works constitution, as well as members of staff councils in the public sector, can, during their term of office and within a period of one year thereafter, only be dismissed extraordinarily. During the term of office, the employer furthermore needs the works council's consent to the dismissal. If the works council refuses its consent, the employer may appeal to the labour court to supersede the works council's consent. The labour court must grant the employer's request if a cause for extraordinary dismissal is given. For members of the body organizing the works council's election and for those who are mere candidates for works council membership, there is also a specific protection granted in Section 15 KSchG. During the period between their nomination until six months after the publication of the election result these persons can only be dismissed by extraordinary dismissal. Until the date of the publication of the outcome of the election, the works council's consent is required under the same conditions as explained above.

V. Protection by Collective Agreements

325. Some collective agreements exclude ordinary dismissals for specific groups of employees (e.g., those over 53 years of age in some sectors of the metal industry, white-collar workers who have been employed for at least fifteen years in the public service, etc.). In these cases, only extraordinary dismissals are allowed. Whether or not these provisions contravene the ban of age discrimination as provided for in Sections 1, 7, 10 AGG (*see* paragraphs 329–331) remains to be seen.

§9. Protection Against Discriminatory Dismissal

326. The AGG also applies to dismissals. This follows from Section 2 No. 2 AGG. Accordingly, discrimination on any of the grounds mentioned in Section 1 No. 2 AGG is illegal in relation to *inter alia* dismissals and measures concerning the termination of an employment relationship. Nevertheless Section 2 paragraph 4 AGG provides that for dismissals only the general and specific provisions on dismissal protection apply, particularly the KSchG, including provisions on dismissal protection for working mothers and parents (*see* paragraphs 301 et seq., 321), for disabled persons (*see* paragraph 322) etc. However, none of these provisions contains any explicit ban on discrimination on any grounds. Any attempts to interpret the KSchG in accordance with Directives 2000/43/EC, 2000/78/EC and 2002/73/EC are doomed to failure not only because its scope of application is limited (to employees having been employed for at least six months in establishments employing more than ten employees) but also because the statutory criteria to be taken into account raise questions as to their compatibility with Directives 2000/43/EC and 2000/78/EC. Therefore, Section 2 paragraph 4 AGG has to be disregarded. Hence, any dismissal contravening the ban on discrimination guaranteed in Section 7 paragraph 1 AGG is null and void. This legal consequence already results from general rules of civil law, i.e., Section 134 BGB, and is simply put straight into Section 7 paragraph 2 AGG. In addition, the employee may claim compensation for any material and non-material damages in accordance with Section 15 paragraphs 1 and 2 AGG (*see* paragraph 181).

327. From among the various exceptions the AGG allows, those granted in terms of Sections 9 and 10 Nos 4–6 AGG are the most interesting for dismissal. Regardless of Section 18 (*see* paragraphs 176 et seq.), unequal treatment on grounds of religion or belief is also permissible if, in respect of employment by religious communities, by any institution assigned to them irrespective of its legal form or by associations having made the collective ministration of religion or belief their task, a certain religion or belief constitutes a justified occupational requirement, taking into account either the self-conception of the respective religious community or association or the kind of activity to be performed. This follows from Section 9 paragraph 1 AGG. The ban of discrimination on grounds of religion and belief furthermore does not, according to Section 9 paragraph 2 AGG, affect the right of any of those religious communities, institutions assigned to them irrespective of their legal form or associations having made the collective ministration of religion or belief their task referred to in (1) to ask for loyal and honest conduct within the meaning of their respective self-conception from their employees.

328. Section 10 No. 4 AGG provides that the fixing of age limits for admission or entitlement to retirement or invalidity benefits under schemes of occupational systems of social security, including the fixing of different ages for employees or groups or categories of employees under those schemes, may not constitute discrimination on grounds of age. The same is true for the use of age criteria in actuarial calculations in the context of such schemes. By passing Section 10 No. 4 AGG, the German legislator has used the option granted by Article 6 paragraph 2 of Directive 2000/78/EC. Section 10 No. 4 AGG explicitly refers only to age thresholds for admission or entitlement to retirement or invalidity benefits. It does not apply to provisions in collective agreements or in employment contracts providing that, if the employee leaves the undertaking, prospective benefits are portable only if a certain age limit has been reached. Such provisions, however, seem to be incompatible with Section 10 sentences 1 and 2 AGG. There is no legitimate aim conceivable justifying such agreements. Particularly the argument, that younger persons still have enough time to build up entitlement to occupational pensions cannot be regarded as legitimate within the meaning of Section 10 AGG.

329. According to Section 10 No. 5 AGG, an agreement providing for the automatic termination of the employment relationship at a time when the employee may apply for old age pension does not constitute age discrimination, notwithstanding Section 41 SGB VI. According to the latter provision, the employee's right to receive an old age pension may neither be regarded as a reason justifying the termination of the employment relationship in terms of the KSchG (*see* paragraphs 301 et seq.)[185] nor does the employee's age as such justify a dismissal under the KSchG. As a consequence, a dismissal due to the employee's age is valid only if the employer can show that the employee is no longer able to fulfil the requirements of his or her job.[186] This is why clauses providing for an automatic termination of the employment relationship at a certain age are very common in Germany. They cannot only be found in individual employment contracts but also in collective agreements and in works agreements (*see* paragraphs 453 et seq., 634 et seq.). Prior to the coming into effect of the AGG, such clauses providing for the automatic expiry of the employment relationship at the age of 65 were deemed to be valid under German law on condition that the employee was in fact economically safeguarded by a

185. Settled case law of the Federal Labour Court since dec. of 28 Sep. 1961, *Arbeitsrechtliche Praxis*, No. 1 §1 KSchG 1951 *Personenbedingte Kündigung*.

186. In a decision of 28 September 1961, *Arbeitsrechtliche Praxis*, No. 1 §1 KSchG 1951 *Personenbedingte Kündigung*, the Federal Labour Court had indicated that, in exceptional cases, 'a proper age structure' may be regarded as a reason justifying a dismissal of older employees due to economic reasons under the KSchG. This decision, issued at a time of full employment, was and still is highly disputed.

statutory old age pension.[187] With the gradual increase of the standard age limit in the statutory pension insurance, the age limits must also be interpreted in such a way that they refer to the possible retirement age, which currently can mean an increase of the relevant age up to 67.[188] According to sentence 3, which was introduced in 2014 in Section 41 SGB VI, if the employment relationship is to be terminated when the standard retirement age is reached, it may be agreed that the date of termination will be postponed, if necessary several times. This continued employment for a limited period was confirmed by the CJEU.[189]

330. Whether or not Section 10 No. 5 AGG stating that such clauses may not constitute age discrimination is compatible with Article 6 of Directive 2000/78/EC is highly debatable. For such clauses have to be regarded as 'dismissal conditions' within the meaning of Article 3 paragraph 1(c) of Directive 2000/78/EC. The scope of Directive 2000/78/EC is limited in several respects. An exception for age thresholds terminating the employment relationship, however, can be found neither in Article 3 paragraph 1 nor in other provisions. Clauses providing for an automatic expiry of the employment relationship at a certain age are hence generally subject to Article 6 of Directive 2000/78/EC – notwithstanding consideration No. 14 of Directive 2000/78/EG explaining that the directive 'shall be without prejudice to national provisions laying down retirement ages'. First, consideration No. 14 – and consideration No. 13 – do not relate to retirement ages laid down in collective agreements and individual contracts but to the age limits as conditions for access to the domestic systems of social security.[190] Second, the material scope of a directive cannot be restricted by considerations alone.[191] The crucial question hence is whether there is a legitimate aim justifying clauses providing for the automatic expiry at a certain age. Such a legitimate aim may in particular be assumed in cases in which the termination of the employment relationship is appropriate and necessary to protect the employee's or third persons' health and safety, as e.g., in the case of pilots and aviation engineers.[192]

187. Federal Labour Court, 20 Nov. 1987, *Arbeitsrechtliche Praxis*, No. 2 §620 BGB *Altersgrenze*. This of course applies even more if the employee is entitled to benefits from an occupational pension scheme, *cf.* 18 Jul. 1978, *Arbeitsrechtliche Praxis*, No. 9 §99 BetrVG 1972; 21 Apr. 1977, *Arbeitsrechtliche Praxis*, No. 1 §60 BAT; 19 Sep. 1985, *Arbeitsrechtliche Praxis*, No. 11 §77 BetrVG 1972.
188. Federal Labour Court, 13 Oct. 2015 – 1 AZR 853/13, *BAGE* 153, 46.
189. CJEU, 28 Feb. 2018 – C-46/17, ECLI:EU:C:2018:131.
190. W. Boecken, 'Die Altersgrenze von 68 Jahren für Vertragsärzte aus EG-rechtlicher Sicht', *Neue Zeitschrift für Sozialrecht*, 2005, pp. 393 et seq., p. 394.
191. For a more detailed argumentation *cf.* M. Schmidt & D. Senne, 'Das gemeinschaftsrechtliche Verbot der Altersdiskriminierung und seine Bedeutung fuer das deutsche Arbeitsrecht', *Recht der Arbeit*, 2002, pp. 80–89, pp. 84 et seq.
192. In such cases, the Federal Labour Court even accepts a retirement age of 60, *cf.* dec. of 25 Feb. 1998, *Arbeitsrechtliche Praxis* No. 11 §1 TVG *Tarifverträge: Luftfahrt*, with further proofs; *cf. also* dec. of 31 Jul. 2002 – 7 AZR 140/01 with annotation by M. Schmidt, *International Labour Law Reports* 407–414 (2002).

331. In the past, the Federal Labour Court found that, provided that the employee was entitled to statutory old age pensions, age limits in collective agreements were usually justified by the employer's interest in a proper age structure and in predictable personnel and junior staff planning[193] on the one hand and by the fact that a transparent age limit was fairer than an otherwise necessary close observation of any signs of decline in performance and more considerate than having to prove in court that the employee was, due to his or her age, no longer able to perform his or her contractual duties on the other. The latter argument, however, is not convincing at all. It simply deprives employees of their statutory right to claim unlawful dismissal.[194] The former argument that transparent age limits are necessary to establish a predictable planning of personnel and junior staff eventually simply provides help for employers not be obliged to employ employees above a certain age. Neither aim is legitimate within the meaning of Article 6 of Directive 2000/78/EC. The only aim that can be regarded as legitimately justifying age limits terminating the employment relationship is the intention to create employment and promotion chances for younger employees. Whether or not a fixed age limit is justified for a certain sector of occupation hence depends on the employment situation of that sector. In sectors where the majority of employees – whether voluntarily or due to health reasons – retire long before they have attained the age limits for entitlement to the ordinary statutory old age pension (*Regelaltersgrenze*), fixed age limits are unnecessary to create employment and promotion chances for younger employees. Only in sectors where vacancies are altogether limited, where employees usually work until they have reached the age limit for ordinary statutory old age pensions and where many of them would like to continue working beyond that age, may statutory age limits for retirement be compatible with Article 6 of Directive 2000/78/EC. Therefore, Section 10 No. 4 AGG should be interpreted very restrictively. Of course it is true that, in a decision of 2007[195] concerning Spanish law, the CJEU has stated not only that 'promoting employment' was a legitimate aim of public interest in terms of Directive 2000/78/EC but also that the Member States and the social partners at national level enjoy broad discretion in their choice, not only to pursue a particular aim in the field of social policy but also in the definition of measures capable of achieving it. Whether or not the CJEU will approve this view in respect of German collective agreements not explicitly referring to employment promotion remains to be seen.

332. In social plans (*Sozialplänen*) in terms of the BetrVG (*see* paragraph 629), benefits may be distributed in accordance with age or length of service provided that the parties to the social plan, i.e., employers and works councils, have established provisions providing for a grading of redundant payments clearly taking into account labour market employability, essentially depending upon age, by a comparatively strong emphasis on age. This follows from Section 10 No. 6 AGG. The same applies if they have excluded from the benefits of the social plan employed

193. Dec. of 20 Nov. 1987, *BAGE*, vol. 57, p. 30.

194. C. O'Cinneide, *Diskriminierung aus Gründen des Alters und Europäische Rechtsvorschriften* (2005), p. 7.

195. 16 Oct. 2007 – C-411/05 (*Palacios de la Villa*), ECLI:EU:C:2007:604.

persons who are economically secure because they are, as the case may be after entitlement to unemployment benefits, entitled to statutory old age pensions. Section 10 No. 6 AGG has been criticized for stating meaningless and self-evident matters at the same time, but leaving the crucial question – when labour market chances differ so much that a grading of benefits may be taken into account – unanswered.[196] Only one point seems to be clear: the widespread practice of considering age as an immediate factor with the consequence that benefits which rise continuously together with age cannot be sustained.[197]

§10. Collective Redundancy

333. In the legal system of Germany, collective redundancy is primarily regarded as a cumulation of individual dismissals. In other words, in cases of collective redundancy the requirements previously mentioned for individual dismissals should also be observed (*see* paragraphs 291 et seq.). The definition of 'collective redundancy' is a very narrow one. Only if a comparatively high proportion of the workforce is to be dismissed within a period of thirty days is the employer obliged to inform the Employment Agency in advance. According to Section 17 paragraph 1 KSchG, the proportion of employees to be dismissed is as follows: in establishments with more than 20 and less than 60 employees at least 5 employees; in establishments with at least 60 and less than 500 employees at least 10% of the employees, or at least 25 employees; in establishments with a minimum of 500 employees at least 30 employees.

334. The Employment Agency plays a certain role in the context of collective redundancy. However, it has only very limited powers. This is the result of experiences in the 1920s. In that period, for a certain time a state authority was entitled to prohibit collective dismissal if the employer did not meet the requirements established by law. In this context, it is especially important to mention that collective dismissal was only considered legally permissible if the employer could show that collective dismissal could not be prevented even by a reduction in working time (and correspondingly a reduction in the remuneration) for all employees of a plant. There was a limit to the extent of a reduction: it was not necessary to go below twenty-four hours per week. The details of this regulation, however, are not important. It is much more important to stress that it was built on the idea that collective dismissals, at least in principle, could be prevented by a temporary reduction of working time. This strategy turned out to be an illusion. It very soon became clear that in view of the economic crisis of the 1920s this mechanism placed too much of a burden on companies. Instead of preventing collective dismissals, it led on the contrary to collective dismissals of an even larger number of employees. It turned out to be a strategy for speeding up the collapse of companies. This explains why

196. G. Annuß, 'Das Allgemeine Gleichbehandlungsgesetz im Arbeitsrecht', *Betriebs-Berater*, 2006, p. 1629, p. 1634.
197. *Cf.* U. Schweibert, 'Alter als Differenzierungskriterium in Sozialplänen', *Festschrift Deutscher Anwaltverein* (2006), p. 1001.

the law was changed so soon. The state authority's powers were dramatically reduced: it was no longer authorized to prohibit collective dismissals but merely to impose a delay of several weeks, and even this in only very extreme and rare cases. This experience had two important effects for further development: first, it made clear that labour law could not simply ignore economic factors, and second, it led to the insight that flexible rules were more appropriate than rigid ones. Even today, the Employment Agency has to be involved before every collective redundancy. The employer has to meet two requirements. One of them is frequently violated, the other is usually met.

335. According to Section 17 paragraph 1 KSchG, the employer is obliged to inform the Employment Agency in writing before making the individual employees redundant. Before notifying the Employment Agency, Section 17 paragraph 2 KSchG obliges the employer to inform the works council of the reason for the planned redundancies, of the number and professions of the employees to be made redundant, of the number and professions of employees employed in the company on a regular basis, of the period within which the redundancies are to be executed and of the intended criteria for selecting the employees to be made redundant. This information also has to be given in writing. In addition, the employer is obliged to give any further information the works council is asking for. Section 17 paragraph 2 KSchG forces the employer to discuss with the works council all possibilities of preventing the redundancies, of reducing their number, and of mitigating their negative impacts. The works council is supposed to comment in writing on the employer's intention. This written comment as well as a copy of the information given to the works council has to be attached to the employer's notice to the Employment Agency, as provided for in Section 17 paragraph 3 KSchG. These annexes are a precondition of the notice's validity. If the employer can prove that in spite of being informed properly the works council has not reacted, the notice may be handed over to the Employment Agency without the works council's comment. Among other data, the employer's notice to the Employment Agency has to contain information on the sex, the age, the professional qualification and the nationality of the employees to be dismissed; a copy of this notice has to be handed over to the works council. The works council is entitled to comment again on this notice and to pass this comment directly on to the Employment Agency. In this case, it is the employer who is entitled to receive a copy of the works council's comment. Even though it is true that employers usually comply with their obligation to inform the works council and Employment Agency in advance, it should at least be mentioned that a strategy to escape this obligation, which is used quite often, is to keep the number of dismissals slightly under the legal minimum constituting a collective redundancy.

336. The Employment Agency's powers to influence the employer's decision to dismiss a larger number of employees are only marginal. According to Section 18 KSchG, it cannot prevent but only delay a collective dismissal for a maximum duration of two months. In addition, the Employment Agency has the competence to facilitate short-time work for the period of delay. According to Section 87 BetrVG (*see* paragraph 621), the employer can generally introduce short-time work only with the works council's consent. If this consent cannot be reached the arbitration committee has to make a decision replacing the consensus between works council and employer. If, however, the Employment Agency permits the reduction of working time in this specific context, the works council's consent is no longer required. The rationale of the requirement to give notice and of the Employment Agency's power to delay the collective dismissal and to facilitate short-time work is again simple. The idea is to use the delay to find alternative solutions in the labour market for those being dismissed. It is evident that this expectation cannot be met if the situation in the labour market is characterized by unemployment, and in particular by long-term unemployment, as has been the case in the old FRG since the early 1970s and as is the case in East Germany to an even more dramatic extent.

337. Until recently it was clear that 'redundancy' (*Entlassung*) in terms of Section 17 KSchG did not refer to the expression by the employer of his or her intention to put an end to the contract, i.e., to the dismissal (*Kündigung, see* paragraph 291), but to the actual cessation of the employment relationship on the expiry of the period in the notices of redundancy.[198] This interpretation was based on the wording of Section 17 KSchG on the one hand – the German term *Entlassung* is not identical with the term *Kündigung* – and on the purpose of Sections 17, 18 KSchG on the other for these provisions aim at purposes of labour market policy. The Employment Agency should have the chance to induce in time measures aiming at avoiding or at least deferring of burdens of the labour market and to provide other jobs for the redundant employees. In its contentious decision in the case *Junk*[199] the CJEU, however, convincingly argued that Articles 2–4 of the Directive 98/59/EC on collective redundancies must be construed as meaning that the event constituting redundancy consists in the declaration by an employer of his or her intention to terminate the contract of employment. The wording of the directive already indicated this result. In its versions in other languages than German, the term used in the place of *Entlassung* either covers at the same time both of the events or refers rather to the expression by the employer of his or her intention to terminate the contract of employment. Moreover, Article 2 paragraphs 1 and 2 as well as Article 3 paragraph 1 showed that the obligations to consult and to notify arise prior to any decision by the employer to terminate contracts of employment. The Federal Labour Court hence could not help but change its case law.[200] Consequently, any dismissal given before the collective redundancy has been notified in terms of Section 17 paragraph 1 KSchG is null and void.

338. The administrative control of collective dismissals is rather unimportant when compared with the role of the works council. It has to be stressed that the works council has specific tools affecting a collective dismissal and its effects, the so-called compromise of interests (*Interessenausgleich*) and the so-called social plan (*Sozialplan*). Both instruments will be explained in Part II in the context of institutionalized employee participation (*see* paragraphs 628–629).

---

198. Federal Labour Court, established case law, *cf.* dec. of 13 Apr. 2000 – 2 AZR 215/99, *Arbeitsrechtliche Praxis*, No. 13 §17 KSchG 1969.
199. Dec. of 27 Jan. 2005 – C-188/03, *European Court Reports*, 2005, I-885.
200. Dec. of 23 Mar. 2006 – 2 AZR 343/05, *Arbeitsrechtliche Praxis*, No. 21 §17 KSchG 1969.

§11. TRANSFER OF THE ESTABLISHMENT

339. Whereas the employee's death always terminates the labour contract, different rules apply when it is the employer who 'dies'. Except for employment relationships of a very personal character, the employer's inheritor takes the employer's place. It should also be stressed that insolvency does not automatically terminate the contract either.[201] The legal consequences of a sale, a hiring out, a leasing, or a renting of the establishment, or a department of the establishment, for the employment relationships within that establishment had been a matter of discussion for a long time. According to the rules of civil law, such events were regarded as lawful reasons for dismissal and therefore actually led to loss of employment. It was at the discretion of the new owner or leaseholder whether to conclude new contracts with the employees dismissed by the (old) owner. Labour courts tried to develop and to offer appropriate solutions, which remained highly contested. In 1972, the legislator finally passed Section 613a BGB stipulating that in such cases the employment relationship was being transferred to the new owner or leaseholder. This regulation, however, turned out to be insufficient for the very reason that only rights and duties laid down in the individual contract were transferred but not the rights and duties arising from collective agreements and works agreements. In addition, this deficit was held to be incompatible with Directive 77/187/EEC as adopted in 1977. That is why, in 1980, the legislator amended Section 613a BGB. Since that time not only the continuation of the employment relationships has been guaranteed, but also the transfer of rights and duties arising from collective sources – albeit in a very complicated manner. Section 613a BGB has to be interpreted in the light of Directive 77/187/EEC. This is why this area of law has fundamentally been shaped by the decisions of the CJEU.

340. The German legislature did not define the term 'transfer'. For quite a while, the definition used by the Federal Labour Court differed from that used by the CJEU in two respects. First of all, the Federal Labour Court regarded the transfer of tangible or immaterial assets as indispensable.[202] Second, it held the view that the objective possibility of continuing or resuming the operation would be sufficient to assume a transfer in terms of Section 613a BGB.[203] Since 1997, following the CJEU's decision in *Ayse Süzen*,[204] the Federal Labour Court has disengaged from these views[205] and has adopted the CJEU's formula.[206] As a consequence, initial contracting out and contracting back in are today regarded as subcategories of a

201. Federal Labour Court, 16 Sep. 1982 – 2 AZR 271/80, *Arbeitsrechtliche Praxis*, No. 4 §22 KO.
202. *Cf.* dec. of 25 Feb. 1981 – 5 AZR 991/78, *Neue Juristische Wochenschrift*, 1981, p. 2212; more recently 27 Apr. 1995 – 8 AZR 197/94, *Neue Zeitschrift für Arbeitsrecht*, 1995, p. 1155.
203. Established case law *cf.* Federal Labour Court, 12 Feb. 1987 – 2 AZR 247/86, *Arbeitsrechtliche Praxis*, No. 67 §613a BGB; 16 Jul. 1998 – 8 AZR 81/9, *Neue Zeitschrift für Arbeitsrecht*, 1998, p. 1233.
204. Dec. of 11 Mar. 1997, case C-13/95, *European Court Reports*, 1997, I-1259.
205. As regards (1): established case law since dec. of 22 May 1997, *Neue Zeitschrift für Arbeitsrecht*, 1997, p. 844; as regards (2) established case law since dec. of 22 May 1997 – 8 AZR 101/96, *Neue Juristische Wochenschrift*, 1997, 3188.
206. Established case law, *cf.* for example dec. of 27 Oct. 2005 – 8 AZR 568/04, *Arbeitsrechtliche Praxis*, No. 292 §613a BGB, with further proofs.

transfer. However, the Federal Labour Court – in that respect in accordance with the CJEU – insists that no transfer is given if only the activity or function is transferred (*Funktionsnachfolge*); a transfer is hence not given if the new contractor takes on neither material nor immaterial assets nor employees.[207]

341. The most complicated problem today is how to differentiate the transfer of a mere function from the transfer of an undertaking in branches where no material assets are required or where services are delivered with equipment of the contractor. If a service provider loses such a client to a competitor together with the contract of services the obligation to use the client's equipment, previously used by the initial service provider, is transferred to the new service provider. Depending on the kind of services and the equipment, rather narrow guidelines may result, determining the new provider's decision how to organize the service, even if he or she had not taken over any kind of organizational concept of his or her predecessor. As a consequence, not only the services but also the organizational concept before and after the change of provider can resemble each other very strongly. In order to differentiate a transfer of an undertaking/establishment in terms of Section 613a BGB from a mere transfer of functions, the Federal Labour Court had developed the following line: a transfer of equipment presupposes their transfer for independent commercial use (*eigenwirtschaftliche Nutzung*), i.e., independent commercial use of the equipment taken over by a contractor is decisive in establishing whether or not there has been a transfer of equipment.[208] Following the CJEU's decision in *Carlito Abler*[209] the *Land* Labour Court Düsseldorf has asked the CJEU whether or not the Federal Labour Court's view was compatible with the directive.[210] In its decision in *GueneyGoerres*[211] the CJEU explicitly answered that question in the negative. Among German scholars, the CJEU's decision is criticized because it is very unclear now how a mere transfer of functions can be distinguished from a transfer of undertaking.[212]

342. According to the Federal Labour Court's established case law the employee whose employment relationship is supposed to be transferred automatically to the new owner or leaseholder had the right to contradict the transfer and opt to remain employed by the old employer.[213] This right, which had been derived from the employee's right of personality as guaranteed in Article 2 paragraph 1 GG, is especially important in cases in which only a part of an establishment is transferred. Due to a decision of the CJEU referring to a rather different case in the Netherlands it

207. Dec. of 22 Jan. 1998 – 8 AZR 243/95, *Arbeitsrechtliche Praxis*, No. 173 §613a BGB; more recently 27 Oct. 2005 – 8 AZR 568/04, *Arbeitsrechtliche Praxis*, No. 292 §613a BGB.
208. Established case law, recently dec. of 17 Apr. 2003 – 8 AZR 253/02, *Arbeitsrechtliche Praxis*, No. 253 §613a BGB, with further proofs.
209. Dec. of 20 Nov. 2003, C-340/01, *Neue Zeitschrift für Arbeitsrecht*, 2003, p. 1385.
210. Dec. of 5 May 2004 – 10 Ca 11334/03, *NZA Rechtsprechungs-Report*, 2004, p. 597.
211. Dec. of 15 Dec. 2005 – C-232/04 and 233/04, *Neue Zeitschrift für Arbeitsrecht*, 2006, p. 29.
212. *Cf.* only M. Schlachter, 'Betriebsübergang bei "eigenwirtschaftlicher Nutzung" von Betriebsmitteln des Auftraggebers', *Neue Zeitschrift für Arbeitsrecht*, 2006, p. 80.
213. Federal Labour Court, 2 Oct. 1974 – 5 AZR 504/73, and 22 Apr. 1993, *Arbeitsrechtliche Praxis*, Nos 1 and 103 §613a BGB; *cf.* U. Preis, *Erfurter Kommentar zum Areitsrecht,* ed. R. Müller-Glöge et al, 2020, Verlag C.H. Beck, §613a BGB paras. 101 et seq.

was, for a while, highly contested whether or not the employee's right to oppose the transfer of his or her employment relationship as developed by German courts was compatible with the Directive 77/187/EEC.[214] In the meantime, however, the CJEU has expressly confirmed this compatibility.[215] According to Section 613a paragraph 5 BGB as introduced in 2002 in order to implement Directive 2001/23/EC, either the transferor or the transferee, either of the two, has to inform the employees concerned by a transfer in advance in text form (*Textform*) of: the date or proposed date of the transfer, the reason for the transfer, the legal, economic and social implications of the transfer for the employees and any measures envisaged in relation to the employees. Section 613a paragraph 5 BGB applies in any case of a transfer in any establishment, irrespective of whether or not the employees would have been entitled to elect a works council, a staff council or executive staff representatives.

343. Any dismissal for reason of transfer of an establishment or of parts of an establishment is null and void. The Federal Labour Court is applying this rule very strictly: if there is any indication that the transfer could have caused the dismissal it is considered to be invalid.[216] This prohibition against dismissal also applies to situations in which the KSchG is not applicable either because the establishment is too small or the employee has not yet been employed for at least six months. Hence, in cases in which dismissals are generally lawful without a justifying reason justification is necessary if transfer of undertakings is at stake. However, Section 613a paragraph 4 BGB explicitly allows dismissals on different grounds, particularly dismissal for economic reasons in terms of the KSchG (*see* paragraphs 309–311).

§12. Dismissal to Change Working Conditions

344. If the employer wants to change the working conditions of the employee (e.g., to transfer him or her to another job or to reduce his or her salary) and the employee does not agree the employer has no choice but to use the weapon of dismissal to reach his or her goal. This dismissal is understood to be a regular dismissal (whether it is extraordinary or ordinary), combined with an offer to continue the employment relationship under amended conditions. If the employee accepts the offer he or she accepts to work for worse working conditions with the consequence that the old employment relationship is terminated; if he or she refuses the offer he or she risks the dismissal taking effect and losing the job. In order to escape this risk the legislator has provided a specific mechanism. According to Section 2 KSchG, an employee who does not wish to accept the amended working conditions is not forced to refuse the offer and thereby risk losing his or her job. He or she can also accept the offer and at the same time declare a reservation. The implication of the reservation is that the justification of the dismissal can still be contested in court. If the dismissal is unjustified, the former working conditions apply; if it is justified,

---

214. Dec. of 5 May 1988 – cases 144 and 145/87 (*Berg* et al.), *European Court Reports*, 1988, p. 2559.
215. 16 December 1992 – case C-132/91 et al. (*Katsikas*), *European Court Reports*, 1992, I-6577.
216. Federal Labour Court, 16 May 2002 – 8 AZR 319/01, *Arbeitsrechtliche Praxis*, No. 237 §613a BGB No. 237.

the new working conditions apply. Nevertheless, the employment relationship continues in any case. The remaining question to be examined is whether the change of working conditions is socially justified, whether it is for reasons concerning the employee's personality, for reasons concerning the employees' behaviour, or for economic reasons. Here the same principles apply as explained previously (*see* paragraphs 303 et seq.). However, the standards are generally lower because it is not the termination of the contract but only the change of working conditions that is the subject of the dispute.[217] Since the danger of losing the job is eliminated by this mechanism, it is evident that the employer may not request judicial dissolution of the employment contract.

345. If the employee accepts the offer to change the working conditions and, at the same time, declares a reservation the new conditions are nevertheless applicable until a final court decision is reached. If the change of working conditions turns out to be socially unjustified, and therefore illegal, the employee must be reinstated in accordance with the original working conditions and is entitled to receive the pay difference he or she lost by working temporarily under the new (worse) conditions.

346. As in all other cases of dismissal, the works council has to be consulted before each dismissal to change working conditions. The works council's possible reactions are the same as explained previously (*see* paragraphs312–316).

347. Quite often kinds of remuneration (benefits, premiums, etc.) are granted by way of uniform contracts concluded with all employees or at least a group of them. If an employer wants to reduce labour costs by reducing these kinds of remuneration, evidently dismissal to change working conditions would be available. However, it would have to be examined for each individual employee whether or not such a modification was justified. If they were involved, the labour courts would have to check whether this justification stood up. In view of the fact that in such cases the employer's cost reduction strategy is not focusing on the individual employee but on all employees as a collective, the instrument of dismissal turns out to be very impractical. In searching for a more appropriate instrument to modify working conditions in such cases, the question arose whether this aim could be achieved by works agreements as concluded between works council and employer (*see* paragraphs 634–636). This, however, is very problematic because the relationship between works agreement and individual contract is governed by the principle of more favourable conditions, meaning that the standards as set by works agreements can – regarded from the employee's perspective – be improved by individual contract. Consequently, it would not be possible to lower standards based on individual contract by works agreements. For several years the Federal Labour Court developed a perspective to overcome this obstacle: the uniform conditions based on uniform contracts were no longer conceived as belonging to the category of individual contract but understood as being 'quasi-collective' with the consequence that they could be changed by works agreements. The courts, however, were, at the same

217. Federal Labour Court, 6 Jun. 1973 – 2 AZR 450/72, *Arbeitsrechtliche Praxis*, No. 1 §626 BGB *Änderungskündigung*.

time, given the power to examine whether the modification remained within tolerable limits. This approach more and more came under attack for it was accused of mixing up individual and collective categories in a non-permissible way.

348. In 1986, the Federal Labour Court has developed a new pattern.[218] First, it corrected the former approach by stating that, in cases of uniform conditions and contracts, the principle of more favourable conditions still applies. Second, it changed the meaning of this principle for just these cases of uniform employment contracts: a works agreement is not to be compared to the position of the individual, referring to the difference between works agreement and individual contract, but to the position of the collective, i.e., the total sum of money spent for the respective remuneration by works agreement and by the uniform individual contracts is to be compared (so-called collective principle of more favourable conditions). According to this principle the works agreement may reduce standards for the individual employee only if the total sum of money to be spent is not reduced. This, of course, means that it is only possible to restructure distribution between the employees by works agreement, but not to reduce labour costs as a whole. This, in effect, means that the position of the individual contract was strengthened. The collective principle of more favourable conditions, by the way, only applies to monetary questions. As far as non-monetary issues are concerned, the individual principle of more favourable conditions is strictly applied again. It has, however, to be stressed that the solution as developed by the Federal Labour Court is highly controversial. It may well be that a re-evaluation will take place.

218. Large Senate (*see* para. 362), 16 Sep. 1986 – GS 1/82, *Arbeitsrechtliche Praxis*, No. 17 §77 BetrVG 1972.

Chapter 8. Covenant of Non-competition, Employee Inventions

§1. Covenant of Non-competition

349. It is generally understood to be one of the worker's ancillary contractual duties not to compete during the duration of the employment contract with his or her employer.[219] The employer may be interested in limiting the worker's freedom of competition even after the termination of the contract. Such a non-competition clause, in principle, is considered valid. But since such clauses lead to the fact that the worker, even after the termination of the contract, is prevented from making optimum use of his or her skills it was found to be necessary to protect the worker's interest. Therefore, Sections 74–75f HGB provide specific provisions regulating detailed standards to be observed in such cases. Originally, these provisions were applicable only to white-collar workers with commercial functions. White-collar workers with technical functions enjoyed a much more fragmentary protection provided by Section 133f GewO. Nevertheless, the Federal Labour Court decided that the principles laid down in Section 133f GewO were applicable to all employees, no matter whether their function was commercial or technical, and no matter whether they were manual workers or white-collar workers.[220] In 2003, this case law was codified in Section 110 GewO. Accordingly, employer and employee may agree to limit the employee's occupational activities after the termination of the employment contract. Sections 74–75f HGB apply *mutatis mutandis*.

350. The basic structure of the regulation provided by Sections 74–75f HGB is as follows. The covenant of non-competition must be in writing, the limitation of the freedom to compete cannot exceed a period of two years after the contract has been terminated, and for the time of non-competition the employer has to pay the employee a yearly sum of money corresponding to at least half of one year's salary the employee received before the contract was terminated. Besides, this clause is valid only if the employer has a justified business interest in the employee's non-competition and if the covenant, in view of the region, the time and the subject of non-competition, does not cause unreasonable disadvantages for the employee, taking into account the circumstances of each individual case.

§2. Employee Inventions

351. The legal basis for the law on employee inventions is the Act on Employee Inventions (*Arbeitnehmererfindungsgesetz*– ArbNErfG) of 1957. This Act, however, applies only to inventions in the technical field, which may lead to a patent or a registered design. For other inventions, there is no statutory regulation. According

219. Long established case law, *cf.* Federal Labour Court, 26 Sep. 2007 – 10 AZR 511/06, *Arbeitsrechtliche Praxis*, No. 4 §61 HGB with further proofs.
220. Dec. of 16 Aug. 1990 – 2 AZR 113/90, *Arbeitsrechtliche Praxis*, No. 10 §611 BGB *Treuepflicht*.

to the 1957 ArbNErfG, there are three types of inventions to be distinguished: service inventions, free inventions and proposals for improvements (Sections 2–4 ArbNErfG). Service inventions are inventions made in the course of the individual labour contract. They may arise out of work performed by the employee or at least based on experience the employee has acquired in his or her job. In the case of such inventions, the employee has mainly three duties (Sections 5–17 ArbNErfG): the employee must keep the invention secret, is not allowed to exploit the invention and has to inform his or her employer. The employer can make limited or unlimited use of the invention, and if he or she does, the employee is entitled to claim financial compensation. Details are regulated in the 1957 Act. The employer may decide to release the invention, which means that the employee is entitled to make any use of it he or she wishes. Free inventions are those made during the period of the employment relationship but not in connection with the work or experience and knowledge connected with the particular job. It also does not matter whether or not the invention was made during working hours. The only requirement is that it was invented while there was an employment relationship. In this case the employee is, according to Sections 18 and 19 ArbNErfG, obliged to inform his or her employer of the invention immediately, unless the invention has nothing to do with the products or services of the enterprise concerned. If the employer wants to claim that the employee's invention is not a free invention but indeed a service invention he or she has to do so in writing within three months. Proposals of improvements are not inventions in a technical sense, which may lead to a patent or a registered design. However, according to Section 20 ArbNErfG these proposals put the employer in a similar privileged position as an invention in the technical sense would put him or her: it is up to the employer to implement and make use of the proposal if he or she is ready to pay the financial compensation regulated in the ArbNErfG.

352. As far as proposals for improvements are concerned, the works council has a right to co-determination of all regulations concerning the handling of such proposals as granted in Section 87 paragraph 1 No. 12 BetrVG (*see* paragraphs 618–621). As regards proposals for improvements covered by the 1957 ArbNErfG the question of payment of financial compensation is not subject to co-determination. As far as other proposals are concerned (in the clerical sector), payment of financial compensation cannot be enforced by the works council. However, once the employer decides to pay such compensation the details are subject to co-determination in terms of the aforementioned provision.

Chapter 9. Settlement of Individual Labour Disputes

§1. The System of Labour Courts

I. Basic Structure

353. In Germany, labour courts are the principal mechanism of conflict resolution, in individual as well as in collective labour disputes.[221] The roots of the system date back to the nineteenth century, but the real starting point of labour courts, as a special branch of the court system, is the ArbGG of 1926. Until then, ordinary courts for civil law matters had jurisdiction in labour disputes. The legal basis for the structure, jurisdiction and procedure of today's labour judiciary is primarily the ArbGG of 1953, revised in 1979.

354. The German labour court system is three-tiered: labour courts of first instance (*Arbeitsgerichte* – ArbG), *Land* labour courts (*Landesarbeitsgerichte* – LAG) in the second instance and at the apex the BAG.

355. While there are 638 ordinary courts of first instance, there are only 110 labour courts of first instance in Germany today.[222] Hence, in many cases the travelling distance to the competent labour court is longer than to the competent ordinary Court of First Instance. It has, however, to be stressed that there are no indications that this fact affects the readiness to initiate law suits.

356. In the old FRG 14 *Land* labour courts were existing: one for each of the eleven *Länder* of the original FRG and in addition another one in Bayern (Munich and Nuremberg) and two others in Nordrhein-Westfalen (Cologne, Düsseldorf and Hamm). After the unification *Land* labour courts have been established in each of the five new *Länder* in the territory of the former GDR. On 1 January 2007, the *Land* labour courts of Berlin and Brandenburg were merged to form the largest *Land* labour court of all, the LAG Berlin-Brandenburg. Prior to this, the two *Länder* had already merged their *Länder* courts of social security, of finances and of administration. Consequently, the overall number of *Land* labour courts is now eighteen.

357. Only a very small percentage of the costs for the courts on all three levels is covered by the courts' own collection of fees. Labour courts of first instance as well as *Land* labour courts are financed by the *Länder*. The *Länder* are also responsible for the establishment of the courts and the delineation of the judicial districts

221. For the basic features of this system *see* M. Weiss, *Labour Dispute Settlement by Labour Courts in Germany*, Indus. L. J. 1 et seq. (1994); M. Weiss, *The Crucial Role of Courts in German Labour Law*, in B.J. Mulder et alii (eds.).Sui Generis. Festskrift til Stein Evju, Oslo 2016, 730 et seq.

222. BMJV, *Gerichte des Bundes und der Länder am 15. Mai 2017*, https://www.bmjv.de/SharedDocs/Downloads/DE/PDF/Anzahl_der_Gerichte_des_Bundes_und_der_Laender.pdf?__blob=publicationFile&v=2.

(Sections 14, 33 ArbGG). The major trade unions and employers' associations in the respective *Land*, however, should be consulted before such a decision is taken.

358. The Federal Labour Court is administered by the Federal Minister of Labour and Social Affairs (*Bundeministerium für Arbeit und Soziales*) in consultation with the Federal Minister of Justice (*Bundesjustizministerium*) (Section 40 paragraph 2 ArbGG). From its establishment in 1957 until 1999 the Federal Labour Court was situated in Kassel (Hesse); in November 1999, it moved to Erfurt (Thuringia) in the territory of the former GDR.

359. As follows from Sections 16, 17, 20 and 21 ArbGG, labour courts of first instance are composed of one or more panels, each with a career judge (*Berufsrichter*) as chairperson and two honorary judges (*ehrenamtliche Richter*), one from the employer and one from the employee side. In a court with more than one panel, the jurisdiction of the individual panels is determined by an organizational chart set up by the courts themselves.

360. *Land* labour courts, as courts of second instance, have exclusive jurisdiction for appeals against decisions of the labour courts of first instance (Section 64 ArbGG). As a rule, their jurisdiction extends throughout one *Land* (but for the already indicated exceptions of Bavaria and North Rhine-Westphalia). Likewise, those of the labour courts of first instance, the panels of the *Land* labour courts are composed of one career judge and two honorary judges from the ranks of employers and employees (Sections 35–39 ArbGG).

361. Judgments handed down by a *Land* labour court may, under specific conditions, be appealed to the Federal Labour Court, which, in the meantime comprises ten divisions, called 'senates'. Each senate consists of three career judges and two honorary judges from employer and employee sides (Sections 41–44 ArbGG). Since the Federal Labour Court exclusively focuses on questions of law and, consequently, is not deciding on the facts of a case, the professional element has more weight than in courts of lower instances where the decision on facts is also at stake.

362. At the Federal Labour Court there is also a so-called Large Senate (*Großer Senat*) provided for by Section 45 ArbGG. The Large Senate is composed of the court President, one career judge from each of those senates, which are not chaired by the court President, and six honorary judges serving in the Federal Labour Court, three from the employers' side and three from the employees' side. If one senate of the Federal Labour Court wishes to deviate from a decision made by another senate or by the Large Senate itself, the senate wishing to deviate is obliged to refer the matter to the Large Senate. Furthermore, matters of fundamental importance may be referred to the Large Senate if this seems necessary for the development of the legal system or in order to guarantee uniformity of decisions. The explicit competence to decide in matters required as regards the development of the legal system means that, in fact, the Large Senate is, within narrow limits, entrusted with tasks similar to those of the legislator.

363. The sequence of appeals within the labour court system normally leads to the fact that the Federal Labour Court has the final say in labour law matters. However, even the Federal Labour Court's decisions can be challenged for being not compatible with the Federal Constitution. The Federal Labour Court, like any other court, is of course not entitled to deviate from the provisions of the Constitution. If one of the parties thinks that the Federal Labour Court's decision violates the Constitution, it may file a complaint of unconstitutionality (*Verfassungsbeschwerde*) at the Federal Constitutional Court. This instrument is used with increasing frequency, especially in areas in which the Federal Labour Court's decisions fundamentally influence industrial relations (*cf.* paragraphs 410, 413, 453, 455).

364. If a subject matter is governed not only by German law but also by law of the EU, and if the latter plays a determining role in deciding the case at stake, labour courts of first instance and *Land* labour courts may, and the Federal Labour Court must in accordance with Article 267 TFEU, refer any doubts as to the interpretation of Union law to the CJEU in Luxembourg for a preliminary ruling. The decision of the CJEU is, due to the principle of supremacy of Union law, binding on German labour courts of all instances as well as on the Federal Constitutional Court. If the Federal Labour Court, contrary to Article 267 TFEU, does not make a referral to the CJEU despite the relevance of a question of Union law, this may constitute a breach of the constitutional guarantee of the statutory judge (Article 101 paragraph 1 sentence 2 GG).[223]

II. The Judges

A. *Career Judges*

365. The career judges of the labour courts of first instance and of the *Land* labour courts are appointed by the authority determined by the individual *Land*, usually the Minister of Labour and Social Affairs. They are selected by the Minister of Labour and Social Affairs, jointly with the respective *Land* Minister of Justice, aided by an advisory committee consisting of three benches, equally representing the state's major trade unions, the employers' associations and the judiciary of the labour court system in the respective *Land*. In some *Länder* the committee may have additional members, all of whom are selected by the Minister of Labour and Social Affairs of the respective *Land*. Employers' associations and trade unions provide lists of candidates, among whom the minister chooses the members of the advisory committee. The committee members representing the judiciary of the labour court system are appointed by the Minister of Labour and Social Affairs in consultation with the Minister of Justice.

366. The career judges at the Federal Labour Court are appointed by the Federal President on joint proposals of the Federal Minister of Labour and Social Affairs

223. Federal Constitutional Court, 10 Dec. 2014 – 2 BvR 1549/07, *Neue Zeitschrift für Arbeitsrecht (NZA)* 2015, 375.

and the election committee for federal judges, a body composed of the *Land* Ministers of Labour and Social Affairs and an equal number of members elected by the Federal Parliament, as guaranteed in Article 95 GG. There is no advisory committee consisting of trade union and employers' association representatives on federal level – this only exists at *Land* level.

367. As a rule, the career judges of the courts of all three levels, after three years of service, are appointed for life, i.e., until they reach retirement age and thereby are entitled to the old age pension. They can be recalled only under very restricted circumstances. Any transfer – even if this means a promotion – is invalid without the respective judge's consent. Career judges of the Federal Labour Court must, according to Section 42 paragraph 2 ArbGG, have a minimum age of 35. In the courts of lower instance, there is no such minimum age requirement. Of course, all career judges have studied law and passed the two state examinations. In addition, at least in principle, they have already specialized in labour law when they join the court. This means that they usually are at least 26 years old.

B. Honorary Judges

368. Honorary judges (*ehrenamtliche Richter*) of the labour courts of first instance and of the *Land* labour courts are, in terms of Sections 20 and 37 ArbGG, appointed for a term of five years by the Minister of Labour and Social Affairs of the respective *Land* from lists submitted by the trade unions, certain other labour organizations and employers' associations of the respective judicial district. These organizations may nominate whomever they think to be capable of serving as an honorary judge. In actual practice, the honorary judges nominated by the trade unions are usually trade union officials; on the employer's side, they may be employers' association officials, members of the management board of companies, individual employers, or other trusted persons.

369. In selecting the honorary judges, the Minister of Labour and Social Affairs of the respective *Land* must also take account of minority organizations. This duty is usually carried out with regard to the number of members the proposing organization has. The organizations on either side can limit the margin of choice by proposing together only as many candidates as positions for honorary judges are to be filled.

370. The honorary judges on the benches of the labour courts of first instance must be at least 25 years old (Section 21 ArbGG). In the *Land* labour courts, the minimum age is 30 (Section 37 paragraph 1 ArbGG), in the Federal Labour Court it is 35 years (Section 42 paragraph 2 ArbGG). Honorary judges must be German citizens. In order to become an honorary judge in a *Land* labour court a person should have served in the same capacity at a labour Court of First Instance for at least five years. Honorary judges on the Federal Labour Court are supposed to have special insight in labour law and labour matters. This requirement is considered to be met if they have served for at least five years in the same capacity in a labour Court of First Instance or in a *Land* labour court.

371. Just like career judges, honorary judges at the labour courts are independent. They can neither be recalled or transferred and nor are they bound by instructions. At least according to the law, the organizations nominating them have no possibility of exerting influence on the court performance of 'their' honorary judges. In actual practice, this may be different. This, however, is an area of mere speculation. There are no empirical data whatsoever. In the decision-making process, the votes of the honorary judges carry as much weight as those of the career judges, which at least theoretically opens up the possibility of outvoting career judges in the labour courts of first instance and in the *Land* labour courts. In actual practice, however, this hardly ever seems to happen.

III. Parties and Their Representatives

372. In Germany, unlike many other countries, not only trade unions but also and first of all individual employees can be parties on the labour side to cases heard in labour courts. Trade unions have no means of preventing an employee from going to court. This pattern corresponds with the deeply rooted concepts of individual autonomy, individual dignity and equal treatment of all individuals. The employees' access to court, however, is to be evaluated ambiguously. Even though most lawsuits are initiated by employees, and not by employers, it has to be stressed that in more than 80% of those lawsuits initiated by employees, the complaint is filed after or in the course of termination of the employment relationship. During an existing employment relationship, employees are usually afraid to bring a conflict to court. Whether or not they are right, they fear revenge. There is no doubt that the fear of revenge would decrease if collective actors had the exclusive responsibility of initiating a lawsuit.

373. In disputes involving questions of employee participation under the BetrVG, the following may be a party to legal proceedings: the works council, employers' associations, or individual employers. The relationship between individual employers and employers' associations corresponds to that between employees and trade unions.

374. In labour courts of first instance, parties to a dispute may represent themselves, but also may be represented by counsel. Under the 1926 ArbGG, attorneys (*Rechtsanwälte*) were excluded from representing parties in labour courts of first instance; only trade union representatives were allowed to act as counsel. The question of who should be allowed to represent litigants was subject to a very fierce debate throughout the Weimar era. Nowadays, this debate is only of historical interest. According to Section 11 ArbGG 1957 attorneys as well as legal aid representatives of trade unions, or representatives of employers' associations for litigants from the employers' side respectively, are allowed to represent litigants in labour courts of first instance. While legal aid representatives of employers' associations are usually fully fledged lawyers, this does not apply to legal aid representatives of trade unions. Trade unions offer them specific training programmes to provide the knowledge necessary to be able to act on behalf of litigants. Representation by attorneys is increasing, whereas use of legal aid representatives of trade unions is declining. In the period from 1953 to 1978 representation by attorneys in labour courts of first instance almost doubled (from 28% to 47%), whereas use of legal aid representatives dramatically decreased (from 33% to 20%). Figures that are more recent are not available.

375. While representation by counsel is optional in labour courts of first instance, it is required at higher levels. In *Land* labour courts litigants still can choose between attorneys and legal aid representatives of trade unions or employers' associations (Section 11 paragraph 2 ArbGG 1957), as is the case in the labour courts of first instance.

376. In cases heard by the Federal Labour Court, representation by an attorney is obligatory (Section 11 paragraph 2 ArbGG). The limitation on attorneys at this level is an implication of the rule that the Federal Labour Court only deals with questions of law and not with points of fact.

377. In ordinary courts of civil law, attorneys were admitted only for a specific judicial district until 1999. In the labour court system, this has always been different. Any attorney admitted to practise in Germany can represent his or her clients before any labour court of any instance in the country. The Federal Labour Court especially is very unhappy with this rule, since the majority of lawyers representing cases in the Federal Labour Court appear only once or twice a year; only very few appear more often. This means that the Federal Labour Court has quite often to deal with attorneys inexperienced in questions of labour law.

IV. Procedure

378. Labour court proceedings are based on the same general principles as proceedings in ordinary courts of civil law (Sections 46 paragraph 2, Section 4, paragraph 6, Section 2, paragraph 5 ArbGG). The ArbGG 1957, however, contains several modifications designed to guarantee simple, expeditious and inexpensive proceedings (Section 9 paragraph 1 ArbGG).

379. According to Section 54 ArbGG, every case brought before a labour court begins with what is called a conciliation hearing (*Gütetermin*), heard by the chairperson sitting alone. The purpose of this procedure is to bring about a compromise between the parties. To this end, the chairperson is required to discuss the whole dispute with the parties as regards the facts of the matter and the legal position and in light of an assessment of the evidence presented. In the course of the conciliation hearing, the judge quite often indicates to the disputants his or her legal opinion, thereby influencing substantially the willingness of the parties to reach a compromise. If both parties agree the conciliation hearing may even be continued in an additional hearing, which must take place at an early date. The conciliation hearing may result in one of the three following options: either the action is withdrawn, or a compromise is agreed upon, or a date is set for an adversarial hearing before the entire panel. Even if the attempt at conciliation fails, the court is obliged, during the entire proceedings that may follow, to try to reach a settlement. Approximately 30% of the cases are settled in the conciliation session. The number of compromises reached throughout the whole proceedings is even higher, and significantly higher than in ordinary courts. For labour court judges it is quite often a question of prestige to achieve a high number of compromises.

380. Labour courts, like ordinary courts of civil law, are only involved upon the motion of a party; they are bound to base their decisions on facts brought forward and established by the parties to the dispute. This procedure, however, will often put the employee not represented by (qualified) counsel at a disadvantage, as he or she usually has little or no knowledge of the law and for this reason may fail to put in a specific claim, or may neglect to bring forward facts because he or she does not understand their legal significance. In such a situation, the court may compensate for these deficiencies in its conduct of the proceedings. According to the ZPO, applicable also in labour law proceedings, the presiding judge is obliged to see that all details relevant to the case are brought forward and that proper applications are filed. Applied to labour court procedure this means that the judge is obliged to take the initiative himself or herself, to ask questions and make proposals of his or her own. Hence, the court's task is not limited to hearing and to deciding the case but also comprises, to a certain extent, intervention in favour of the weaker party.

381. The principle of expeditiousness plays an important role in labour court proceedings. If a compromise cannot be reached in the conciliation hearing, it is the chairperson's responsibility to prepare the proceedings in such a manner that the case can be terminated in one session, if possible (Section 56 ArbGG). To this end, the chairperson can summon witnesses and experts, request all official documents and ask for opinions without being bound by the parties' applications. The chairperson may also request the conflicting persons to appear personally, as is actually done in most cases. The period for filing an answer to a complaint and the period indicated in the summons are shorter than in ordinary civil court procedure. The duration of proceedings (in judgment proceedings) before the labour courts of the first instance is about 3.2 months[224] and before the *Länder* labour courts about 7.8 months.[225]

382. If proceedings cannot be terminated in the first session, a date for continuation must be announced at once. If proceedings can be terminated, a judgment is pronounced, as a rule immediately following the hearing (Section 57 ArbGG). The principle of expeditiousness is certainly to a great extent responsible for the fact that more than a third of the disputes pending in the labour courts of first instance are settled within three months.

224. Statistisches Bundesamt, *Rechtspflege – Arbeitsgerichte – 2018*, p. 56.
225. *Ibid.*, p. 108.

383. German labour court proceedings recognize two forms of appeal: the first on points of law and points of fact, and the second on points of law only. According to Section 66 ArbGG, decisions of labour courts of first instance may be appealed to *Land* labour courts within one month. Appeal to the *Land* labour court is permissible, in terms of Section 64 ArbGG, if the appeal has either been explicitly admitted by the labour Court of First Instance, if the gravamen is worth more than EUR 600, if the existence or termination of an employment relationship is at stake or if, under certain further conditions, the decision to be appealed is a judgment in absence. According to Section 64 paragraph 3 ArbGG, an appeal has to be admitted if either the dispute is of fundamental importance, or deals with matters relating to collective bargaining in a wider sense, or if the decision of the labour Court of First Instance is based on a deviation *inter alia* from a decision of the higher *Land* labour courts. The *Land* labour court reviews the case in complete detail, both on points of law and points of fact.

384. From decisions of *Land* labour courts appeal (on questions of law only) may be lodged to the Federal Labour Court, provided that the *Land* labour court has explicitly allowed this, within one month (Sections 72 and 74 ArbGG). Leave to appeal must be granted if the dispute is of fundamental importance or if the decision of the *Land* labour court deviates *inter alia* from a preceding ruling of the Federal Labour Court. If leave to appeal is denied there is a specific procedure to nevertheless reach a reviewing decision of the Federal Labour Court. In cases under review by the Federal Labour Court, no new facts may be put forward; the facts established by *Land* labour courts are not subject of discussion there, as the Federal Labour Court is strictly confined to questions of law.

V. Costs

385. Labour court proceedings are less expensive than other court proceedings. Court fees are set in proportion to the amount at issue. In cases dealing with protection against dismissal, for example, the 1957 ArbGG limits the reference value to three times the amount of the respective employee's monthly salary (Section 42 paragraph 4 Act on Court Fees (*Gerichtskostengesetz* – GKG)). Court fees amount to only a small percentage of this sum; they are to be paid by the losing party.

386. Distribution of attorney fees follows a different pattern. In the first instance, each party, also the winning party, must bear the costs of its own counsel (Section 12a paragraph 1 ArbGG). The purpose of this regulation is to minimize the employee's financial risk; he or she would otherwise, should he or she lose the case, be required to pay the fees of his or her employer's attorney. For trade union members, however, this rule has no importance since trade unions provide legal counsel at no cost. This, by the way, is for many employees the main reason for joining a trade union. Hence, trade unions serve in a way as a sort of legal expenses insurance.

387. In the second and third instances, the losing party must bear the attorney fees of both parties. In the *Land* labour court, a union member may again be represented by a legal counsel offered by his or her trade union free of charge. At this level, however, union membership does not automatically imply free legal counsel. The trade unions decide in each individual case whether they are willing to offer legal aid for the second instance, depending on their evaluation of the employee's chances to win the dispute. The reason for this practice is simple: trade unions do not want to waste money.

388. If one of the parties is not in a position to pay the costs of the proceedings without jeopardizing his or her family's income, there is a possibility of applying, under certain circumstances, for state legal aid (*Prozesskostenhilfe*) and consulting assistance (*Beratungshilfe*) for pre-litigation advice by a lawyer.

§2. The Role of Labour Courts in Settling Individual Disputes

389. Labour courts have jurisdiction in disputes of rights. The distinction between individual and collective labour disputes, though made in German law, is of no relevance for the jurisdiction of the labour courts: it covers both types of disputes. There are – as will be shown later on – some procedural peculiarities if specific types of collective labour disputes are at stake.

390. In matters of individual labour law, the jurisdiction of the labour courts comprises all types of cases listed in the ArbGG 1957. In most of these cases, the labour courts have exclusive jurisdiction, meaning that, even if the participants wish, the case may not be heard by another court. There is only a small margin of manoeuvre within which it is left to the conflicting parties to decide whether to have the case heard by a labour court or by an ordinary court of civil law matters.

391. According to Section 2 ArbGG 1957, labour courts have exclusive jurisdiction in matters involving civil legal disputes between employer and employee arising from an employment relationship, in questions relating to the existence or non-existence of an employment contract, as regards obligations remaining after the dissolution of an employment contract, and, in addition, in civil legal disputes involving torts, in so far as these are connected with the employment relationship. This means that labour courts have exclusive jurisdiction over virtually all legal conflicts between employer and employee arising from the employment relationship. In this context, the notion 'employee' includes manual workers, white-collar workers, apprentices and even employee-like persons (Section 5 ArbGG).

392. In labour law conflicts, the courts are involved mainly on employees' initiative. Statistical evidence shows that individual employees, trade unions or works councils, initiate the overwhelming majority of all complaints.

393. The following figures show the development between 1981 and 2005 (a specific type of cases referring to collective labour law is not included; this will be included in Part II, *see* paragraphs 694 et seq.).

394. Survey on the activities of the labour courts of first instance:[226]

Year	*1981*	*1997*	*2006*	*2018*
Disputes still pending at the beginning of the year	104,138	262,599	146,765	96,677
New complaints	347,520	659,185	467,807	320,094
– initiated by employees, trade unions or works councils	333,974	637,486	460,747	304,729
– initiated by employers or employers' associations	13,358	21,373	6,884	14,627
– initiated by state agencies	188	326	176	25
Total number of disputes	451,658		614,572	416,771
Disputes settled within the year	350,053	672,804	476,906	319,381
– by judgment on the merits	32,690	53,103	36,892	23,109
– by other judgments	40,348	87,231	47,623	24,020
– by compromise reached in court	125,734	266,276	249,065	202,341
– otherwise (e.g., withdrawal of suit)	151,281	266,194	143,326	69,911

226. For these and the following figures for 1981 and 1997 *cf.* Bundesministerium für Arbeit und Sozialordnung (ed.), *Tätigkeit der Arbeitsgerichte 2006* (Berlin) and for 2018 *cf.* Bundesministerium für Arbeit und Soziales (ed.), *Tätigkeit der Arbeitsgerichte 2018* (Berlin).

Year	*1981*	*1997*	*2006*	*2018*
Issues				
Remuneration	165,690	249,485	170,588	124,424
Holidays/holiday bonus	11,380	19,331	18,867	
Dismissals	145,972	320,362	231,588	173,096
Reference/correction of reference	5,924	15,939	30,817	
Damages	5,794	4,951	4,541	
Classification	1,866	9,484	1,735	2,993
Others	46,911	167,708	138,704	112,125
More than one issue	42,679	107,952	109,465	17,292
Duration from filing the complaint until settlement				
(a) *In dismissal cases*				
– up to 1 month	50,307	62,765	65,308	51,103
– 1–3 months	57,592	123,601	97,258	81,034
– 3–6 months	23,817	65,117	46,090	32,269
– 6–12 months	10,589	53,487	27,261	16,164
– more than 12 months	1,571	23,395	6,811	2,764
(b) *In all other cases*				
– up to 1 month	59,000	57,545	55,546	33,793
– 1–3 months	69,930	123,057	87,739	49,251
– 3–6 months	23,379	70,551	42,070	26,462
– 6–12 months	19,498	80,422	37,528	20,070
– more than 12 months	30,370	23,395	11,295	6,471

Year	*1981*	*1997*	*2006*	*2018*
Disputes not yet settled at the end of the year	101,605	248,980	137,666	97,329

These figures show a significant increase of workload. Although only about 25% of the working population lives in the new *Länder* (*see* paragraph 24), the number of disputes has almost doubled since unification. As a consequence, the period within which the cases are settled has extended. As far as issues are concerned there has been a shift. The number of disputes concerning remuneration, dismissals and classification has risen disproportionately.

395. Survey on the activities of the *Land* labour courts

Year	*1981*	*1997*	*2006*	*2018*
Appeals still pending at the beginning of the year	5,720	15,865	12,337	9,117
New appeals	14,133	28,477	20,793	13,548
Total number of appeals	19,853	44,342	33,130	22,665
Disputes settled within the year	13,974	27,062	22,042	13,472
– by judgment on the merits	5,302	8,536	7,284	4,546
– by other judgments	168	286	192	246
– by compromise reached in court	4,363	8,812	8,463	4,607
– otherwise (e.g., withdrawal of suit)	4,041	9,428	6,103	4,073
Duration from filing the appeal until settlement				

Year	*1981*	*1997*	*2006*	*2018*
(a) In dismissal cases				
– up to 3 months	2,727	3,865	2,775	999
– 3–6 months	2,481	4,448	4,133	1,741
– 6–12 months	822	3,423	3,385	1,923
– more than 12 months	398	1,252	904	636
(b) In all other cases				
– up to 3 months	3,183	4,410	2,626	1,346
– 3–6 months	2,304	4,086	3,597	2,548
– 6–12 months	1,176	3,543	3,165	2,828
– more than 12 months	833	2,035	1,457	1,451
Appeals not yet settled at the end of the year	*5,879*	*17,280*	*11,088*	*9,185*

At appeal level the slowing down of appeals in the period between 1990 and 1997 is the most significant feature shown by these figures.

396. Survey on the activities of the Federal Labour Court

Year	*1981*	*1997*	*2006*	*2018*
Appeals still pending at the beginning of the year	1,629	858	762	846
New appeals	576	774	1,117	591
Total number of appeals	2,205	1,632	1,879	1,437

Year	*1981*	*1997*	*2006*	*2018*
Appeals settled within the year	804	775	817	679
– by judgment on the merits	396	587	511	338
– by other judgments	48	–	2	2
– by compromise reached in court	220	60	80	133
– by withdrawal of appeal	120	110	176	149
– otherwise	20	18	48	18
In cases of appeals settled by judgment on the merits duration from filing the appeal to settlement				
– up to 6 months	3	34	15	32
– 6–12 months	14	175	334	113
– 1–2 years	379	378	162	150
– more than 2 years	–	–	–	43
Appeals not yet settled at the end of the year	1,401	857	86	758

The most striking element shown by these figures is the fact that the workload of the Federal Labour Court, contrary to that of the labour courts of first instance, has decreased since 1990 and is still below the number of appeals pending in 1981.

§3. Complaint Procedure

397. The 1972 BetrVG was the first statutory Act providing for a complaint procedure under German law. Sections 84–86 BetrVG 1972 stipulate that an employee, who feels that he or she has been discriminated against, has been treated unfairly, or has otherwise been put at a disadvantage by the employer or by any other employee of the plant, has the following options. He or she may complain to the competent authorities in the plant, either personally or with the help of a works council member. He or she may also complain to the works council, which, provided that the complaint appears justified, must use its influence on the employer to bring about a remedy. If the complaint refers to a conflict of rights, the employee may also lodge it at the labour court. The employee may choose any of the foregoing options or a combination of them. Thus, he or she may first lodge a complaint directly to the establishment's authority; if unsuccessful, the employee may lodge the complaint to the works council, and if he or she is still not satisfied and the conflict is one of rights, the employee may finally involve the labour court. However, he or she may as well skip the first two steps and go directly to court, or omit only the first step and address his or her complaint to the works council.

398. If employer and works council disagree as regards the justification for the complaint, the works council may appeal to the arbitration committee. From this stage on, the procedure to be followed depends on whether the complaint involves a conflict of interests or a conflict of rights. In a conflict of interests, the decision of the arbitration committee supersedes any agreement between employer and works council. However, either of these two bodies may appeal to the labour court arguing that the arbitration committee has exceeded its jurisdiction. If the complaint involves a conflict of rights, the decision of the arbitration committee can only serve as a recommendation to employer and works council on how the case should be settled. Parties to a collective agreement, as well as the parties to a works agreement, have the competence to regulate details of their complaint procedure voluntarily. Thus, the parties may replace the arbitration committee by a complaint committee whose structure is not defined by law.

399. In everyday life at an establishment level, the initiation of the complaint procedure as established in Sections 84–86 BetrVG is, however, rather the exception than the rule. This is why in 1989 the IG Media concluded a collective agreement for the printing industry specifying the complaint procedure for the area of occupational health and safety and started a campaign mobilizing employees to avail themselves of their right to complain. Two years later, 70% of the works councils, which had been interviewed about the effects of the specification of the complaint procedure answered that nothing had changed. Evidently, employees prefer to settle complaints, which do not end up in a lawsuit, on the shop floor with personnel management and without any subsequent formal procedure whatsoever.

Part II. Collective Labour Law

Chapter 1. Freedom of Association

§1. Notion and Historical Developments

400. The expression 'freedom of association', as used here, refers to the right of employees and employers to organize themselves in order to safeguard their occupational interests. Freedom of association has to be understood in its broadest sense. It is not restricted to the right to set up associations, but also comprises a whole range of rights without which the right to organize would lose much of its meaning. Such additional rights not only refer to the right of the associations to decide on their organizational structure and administration, but also to the right to decide freely on their activities.

401. In the history of freedom of association in Germany, three main periods should be distinguished. (1) Until 1869, freedom of association was not legally recognized but subject to penal sanctions. (2) Between 1869 and 1918, freedom of association was semi-legalized, meaning that it was recognized in principle but at the same time prevented from being used effectively. (3) Since 1918, with the exception of the Nazi period, freedom of association has been fully recognized as the leading principle of collective labour law.

402. In the Prussian Trade Act (*Preussische Gewerbeordnung*) of 1845, each strike or each persuasion to strike was liable to be punished by imprisonment of one year. The GewO 1869 abolished all provisions, which prohibited and punished the freedom of association. However, even though freedom of association was recognized in principle, there were still severe restrictions imposed on associations. According to the law, members could not only leave an association whenever they liked, it was moreover impossible for an association to establish any sort of legal framework which could have led to legal obligations for its members. Thus, the internal structure of associations was not backed by law. Court proceedings were not available if members did not follow the associations' policy rules. The second, more important restriction, was the following: even though it was no longer punishable to strike, to 'try to persuade others to strike by use of threat' was still punishable by imprisonment. Interpretation of this formula by the courts led to the fact that the term 'threat' was understood in a very broad sense, including practically every verbal attack on those to be persuaded (e.g., those who refused to participate in a strike were called 'strike breakers' or 'blacklegs'). Thus it became possible to punish those who were the active leaders trying to mobilize others. There was a third restriction, perhaps the most important one: according to the rules governing the structure of associations in general, there were special prerequisites for associations acting in the area of social policy. They still needed the permission of the state authorities. Permission had to be granted if certain conditions were fulfilled, but the danger of not getting permission or losing permission still remained. In order to be acknowledged as a legal entity, associations acting in the area of social policy had to fulfil another condition – they had to present a list of all members. Unions refused to comply with this condition for the obvious reason that they did not want to enable the state authorities to control their membership. This is why unions failed to become legal persons. Although all these restrictions were abolished, the unions retained this attitude. Even today, most unions are still not organized as legal entities.

403. The Weimar Republic finally brought full recognition of freedom of association. Article 159 of the WRV guaranteed ‘every individual and every occupation’ the freedom of association ‘to safeguard and improve working and economic conditions’. This is where Article 9 paragraph 3 of the present Constitution has its roots. Article 9 paragraph 3 GG also guarantees ‘to everyone and to all occupations’ the right ‘to form associations, to safeguard and improve working and economic conditions’. Article 9 paragraph 3 GG also states that ‘agreements which restrict or seek to impair this right shall be null and void’. This provision has become by far the most important legal source for collective labour law in Germany. Wherever there are gaps, doubts, or ambiguities, the problem is solved by recourse to this provision. Important parts of the present law on collective agreements, and virtually the whole law on industrial conflict, are nothing more than a result of court interpretation of Article 9 paragraph 3 GG.

404. In spite of the fact that in the past it was the employees’ freedom of association which was threatened and which had to be acquired, it is not only this aspect of freedom of association that Article 9 paragraph 3 GG refers to. Just like Article 159 WRV, Article 9 paragraph 3 GG is understood as covering employees’ freedom of association as well as employers’ freedom of association. In view of the different status of employers and employees in society, this certainly does not mean that the implications are the same for both sides. In view of the fact that constitutional recognition of freedom of association is mainly a result of the employees’ fight for this freedom, Article 9 paragraph 3 GG would be distorted if it were applied equally to both sides. Thus, for every implication of this constitutional guarantee, the past and factual differences between employers and employees must be kept in mind.

§2. Individual Freedom of Association

405. Neither the state nor anybody else may prevent employees or employers from setting up an association to safeguard and improve working or economic conditions, a so-called collective industrial organization (*Koalition*), or from being a member of a collective industrial organization. The practical impact of this guarantee of the so-called individual freedom of association has consequences, particularly for the individual employment relationship. The employee – and the employer – is protected against any kind of discrimination resulting from the use of his or her freedom of association. This follows from Article 9 paragraph 3 sentence 2 GG. Accordingly, agreements that restrict or seek to hinder this right are null and void; measures directed to this end are illegal. Thus, it is evident that employment contracts obliging an employee not to become, or not to remain a union member, so-called yellow dog contracts, are void. The member of a collective industrial organization is not only protected against discrimination but is also entitled to all activities guaranteed to the association as such by the constitutional guarantee of freedom of association. And here again, these activities are protected against discrimination. Whereas these principles are not contested on a theoretical level, the implications in particular cases – What does discrimination mean? Who has to prove it? etc. – are highly disputed.

406. In Germany the freedom to form an association,[227] to join an association, to remain in an association and to be active in an association, is called 'positive freedom of association'. Whereas it is perfectly clear that Article 9 paragraph 3 GG focuses on this aspect of freedom of association, it is highly contested whether and how far the freedom not to join an association or to leave an association, the so-called negative freedom of association is protected by this very article. In spite of the fact that the negative freedom of association has never been endangered, the Federal Labour Court interprets Article 9 paragraph 3 GG as guaranteeing also this aspect of freedom of association.[228] The 'negative' freedom is simply regarded as the mirror image of the 'positive' freedom of association. The actual debate is not so much about the legitimacy of the protection of the 'negative' freedom of association as such – in this respect, the discussion mainly focuses on the question of whether this freedom is guaranteed by Article 9 paragraph 3 GG or rather by Article 2 paragraph 1 GG, guaranteeing the freedom of one's personality – but on the boundaries between 'positive' and the 'negative' freedom of association.[229] While it is uncontested that closed shops or union shop arrangements violate the 'negative' freedom of association, the question arises of how far a union is allowed to provide privileges for its members in order to increase the attractiveness of the association and thereby stimulate membership. To quote one example: by using the instrument of collective agreement unions tried to establish clauses safeguarding additional payments for union members only by prohibiting the employer from voluntarily granting non-union members the same benefits. In 1967 this conflict between the 'positive' freedom, backing a union in increasing its attractiveness, and the 'negative' freedom, backing non-union members in their wish not to be tempted to join a union, was solved in favour of the 'negative' freedom by the Federal Labour

227. For a detailed discussion on the freedom of association *see* A. Seifert, 'Koalitionsfreiheit', in M. Weiss and A. Gagel, *Handbuch des Arbeits- und Sozialrechts* (2003), Baden-Baden, §28.
228. Large Senate (*see* para. 362), 29 Nov. 1967 – GS 1/67, *Arbeitsrechtliche Praxis*, No. 13 Art. 9 GG.
229. *Cf.* W. Linsenmaier, *Erfurter Kommentar zum Areitsrecht,* ed. R. Müller-Glöge et al, 2020, Verlag C.H. Beck, Art. 9 GG paras. 32 et seq. with further proofs.

Court.[230] In other words, the clauses preserving privileges to union members were held to be void. This decision provoked a critical discussion. Many observers thought that the court had overestimated the negative freedom of association.[231] The Federal Labour Court, however, did not repeal its view, but has confirmed it in several recent decisions.[232] Nevertheless, the discussion of whether or not trade unions are entitled to reserve certain benefits for their members is still ongoing.[233]

§3. Collective Freedom of Association

407. The German Constitution not only guarantees the individual's freedom of association but also protects collective industrial organizations that have been set up to guard and promote the employment and economic conditions of their members, i.e., the so-called collective freedom of association. It is generally agreed that a constitutional guarantee of the individual's freedom of association would be useless if the organization itself was not constitutionally protected. This is why Article 9 paragraph 3 GG is understood as protecting the associations' existence, their organization, and their activities.

408. Of course, only those associations, which seek to safeguard and improve working conditions, so-called collective industrial organizations, fall within the scope of Article 9 paragraph 3 GG. From what has been said so far, it is evident that free membership must be the organizational basis of such associations. In addition to this self-evident implication of Article 9 paragraph 3 GG, the Federal Labour Court has developed a whole range of prerequisites to be fulfilled by associations that want to enjoy the protection of Article 9 paragraph 3 GG and to carry out certain activities reserved to associations within the meaning of this provision. For example, only associations fulfilling certain criteria are allowed to participate in collective bargaining and to conclude collective agreements. These prerequisites will be explained in detail later (*see* paragraphs 453 et seq.).

409. The collective freedom of association raises further difficult questions. When is the existence of the organization endangered? Does this have to be evaluated from a short-term, a medium-range, or a long-term perspective? And what are the activities protected by this constitutional guarantee? One of the main activities of collective industrial organizations is, of course, collective bargaining. Hence, it

230. Dec. of 29 Nov. 1967 – GS 1/67, *Arbeitsrechtliche Praxis*, No. 13 Art. 9 GG.

231. *Cf.* B. Weller, 'Zur Frage der Differenzierungsklausel', *Arbeit und Recht*, 1970, 161–166; U. Zachert, 'Renaissance der tariflichen Differenzierungsklausel?', *Der Betrieb*, 1995, 322–325.

232. Dec. of 21 Jan. 1981 – 4 AZR 547/86, *BAGE* 54, p. 113; 21 Jan. 1987 – 4 AZR 486/86, *Der Betrieb*, 1987, p. 492; 23 Mar. 2011 – 4 AZR 366/09, *BAGE* 137, 23.

233. *Cf.* R. Waltermann, Differenzierungsklauseln im Tarifvertrag in der auf Mitgliedschaft aufbauenden Tarifautonomie, *HSI-Schriftenreihe Band 15*, Frankfurt/Main 2015; W. Däubler, 'Tarifliche Leistungen nur für Gewerkschaftsmitglieder?', *Betriebs-Berater*, 2002, pp. 1643–1648; F. Gamillscheg, 'Ihr naht euch wieder, schwankende Gestalten – "Tarifbonus" für Gewerkschaftsmitglieder', *Neue Zeitschrift für Arbeitsrecht*, 2005, pp. 146–150; M. Franzen, 'Vorteilsregelungen für Gewerkschaftsmitglieder', *Recht der Arbeit*, 2006, 1.

is accepted that Article 9 paragraph 3 GG also guarantees so-called autonomy in collective bargaining (*Tarifautonomie*).[234] It is, however, controversial to what extent this autonomy is exactly protected from interference.[235] The answers to these questions are still subject to much controversy, as will be shown when describing specific aspects of the law on collective agreements, the law on industrial conflict and the law on institutionalized employee participation (*see* paragraphs 453 et seq., 512 et seq., 650 et seq.).

I. The Doctrine of Core Area

410. Until recently, the Federal Constitutional Court held the view that Article 9 paragraph 3 GG only safeguarded activities which were 'imperative for the preservation and protection of the association's continued existence'.[236] Among those activities is the right to recruit members and to communicate with members. However, even if an activity was agreed to be covered by Article 9 paragraph 3 GG, the question arose of how far this activity was protected in view of the fact that it might conflict with the rights of others. To quote an example: whether or not the right of trade unions to recruit members and to communicate with members includes the right to enter an establishment in order to launch promotion or information activities is highly controversial. In the past, the line developed by the Federal Constitutional Court and the Federal Labour Court, balancing the right to freedom of association of the trade union and the employers' rights of property, was as follows.

411. Employees who are members of a trade union were entitled to advertise among their colleagues for trade union membership and to inform about the activities of their union.[237] Trade union propaganda may in particular include advertising by means of posters, and distributing a trade union journal or other information papers. These activities, however, are lawful only during breaks. Furthermore, they have to be carried out without making demands upon the employer's property, i.e., in-plant mailboxes. Furthermore, care has to be taken that 'the peace within the establishment' is not disturbed by such activities and that 'nobody [is] insulted'. But if trade union members are employed in an establishment, the employer is not obliged to allow an external trade union member to enter the establishment in order to distribute propaganda, since if a trade union is already represented in an establishment, the right to enter the establishment is not imperative for the trade union in order to make use of its constitutionally guaranteed freedom of activity.[238] The

234. *Cf.* only Federal Labour Court, 18 Feb. 2003 – 1 AZR 142/02, *Arbeitsrechtliche Praxis*, No. 163 Art. 9 GG *Arbeitskampf* with further proofs.
235. *Cf.* Federal Constitutional Court, 3 Apr. 2001 – 1 BvL 32/97, *Arbeitsrechtliche Praxis*, No. 2 §10 BUrlG Kur; annotated by M. Schmidt, *International Labour Law Reports* 413–423 (2001).
236. For example dec. of 2 Jul. 1979 – 1 BvR 335/78, *Arbeitsrechtliche Praxis*, No. 61a Art. 9 GG *Arbeitskampf* with further proofs.
237. Federal Constitutional Court, 14 Nov. 1995 – 1 BvR 601/92, *Arbeitsrechtliche Praxis*, No. 80 Art. 9 GG.
238. Federal Constitutional Court, 17 Feb. 1982 – 2 BvR 384/78, *Arbeitsrechtliche Praxis*, No. 9 Art. 140 GG.

question of whether a trade union not represented in an establishment is entitled to enter it in order to inform employees about trade union activities and distribute propaganda has not yet been fully resolved. Such a right is frequently denied with reference to the possibilities of advertising and giving information about trade union activities outside the establishment.[239] In 2010, however, the Federal Labour Court decided that a union from outside the company must be granted access once every six months for the purpose of recruiting members.[240]

412. It is clear that the criteria developed by the courts are very vague. Thus everything depends on the interpretation of Article 9 paragraph 3 in specific cases. Two examples of cases decided by the Federal Labour Court may illustrate the problem. In the first case, union members wore on their working hard hats, which belonged to the employer, a union badge.[241] The badges could easily be removed without the hats being damaged. A balance had to be struck between the right of the union to put out propaganda and the employer's guarantee of private property as to the hats. Priority was given to the employer's rights for the reason that the way the union exerted its right to distribute propaganda was not compatible with the principle of proportionality. Since there were other effective forms of putting out propaganda, it was not necessary to make use of the employer's property. In the second case, the union had advertised by means of posters.[242] These posters not only drew attention to the union's activities concerning working conditions, but also to other services not related to working life but traditionally offered by unions, i.e., insurances for all kinds of risks, legal aid for lawsuits outside the labour law area, etc. The Federal Labour Court decided that this kind of advertising was covered by the constitutional guarantee based on Article 9 paragraph 3 GG. This more recent decision shows a tendency to broaden the scope of the guarantee of propaganda activities. In quoting these examples, it should be stressed that the purpose here is not to describe in detail the boundaries of the union's right to issue propaganda, but to show the uncertainty of these boundaries with their many dimensions. It is also intended to show that these boundaries are not static but subject to gradual change depending on change in the courts' attitudes. Finally, it has to be pointed out that the right to distribute propaganda is only taken as an example; the same holds true for all other activities backed by the constitutional guarantee.

II. Renunciation of the Doctrine of Core Area

413. In November 1995, the Federal Constitutional Court redefined the scope of Article 9 paragraph 3 GG by explicitly renouncing its core area formula.[243] The court stated that – contrary to its former rulings – the scope of Article 9 paragraph 3 GG was not limited to activities, which were imperative for the preservation and

239. *Cf.* B. Boemke, *Münchener Handbuch zum Arbeitsrecht,* R. Richardi & O. Wlotzke ed., Verlag C.H. Beck, §289 para. 13.
240. Federal Labour Court, 22 Jun. 2010 – 1 AZR 179/09, *BAGE* 135, 1.
241. Dec. of 23 Feb. 1979 – 1 AZR 172/78, *Arbeitsrechtliche Praxis*, No. 30 Art. 9 GG.
242. Federal Labour Court, 30 Aug. 1983 – 1 AZR 121/81, *Arbeitsrechtliche Praxis*, No. 38 Art. 9 GG.
243. Dec. of 14 Nov. 1995 – 1 BvR 601/92, *Arbeitsrechtliche Praxis*, No. 80 Art. 9 GG.

protection of the continued existence of the association but protected all activities which were specific for collective industrial organizations, i.e., trade unions and employers' associations. Not all activities covered by Article 9 paragraph 3 GG, however, are automatically lawful: Article 9 paragraph 3 GG still has to be balanced with other conflicting constitutional guarantees such as, for example, the right to private property as guaranteed in Article 14 GG (*see* paragraph 448). For example, the Federal Labour Court[244] has decided that it follows from the freedom of association as granted in Article 9 paragraph 3 GG that is up to the collective industrial organization to decide where, by whom and how to canvass new members. A trade union may even decide to send duly authorized agents into the establishment. However, this right of course conflicts with the employer's domestic authority as granted in Article 13 GG, with his or her rights of property guaranteed in Article 14 GG, and with his or her right to free occupational and economic activity in Article 12 GG which may be affected if the flow of work and the peace within the establishment is disturbed. However, it has to be borne in mind that the employer's relation to a trade union responsible for his or her establishment cannot be the same as the relation to an uninvolved third party. On the contrary, employer and trade union have a number of direct and indirect legal relations. Therefore, trade unions may have a right of access to the establishment. However, whether the trade unions' right of access following from the freedom of association prevails over the employers' above-mentioned fundamental rights cannot be stated in general. Everything depends on the circumstances of the case at stake, i.e., on the one hand the dimension and intensity of the right of access of trade union representatives not employed in the establishment, its frequency, its duration and the time of the visits and the number of external trade union representatives; and the employer's interest in an undisturbed operation and peace in the establishment, his or her interests in secrecy and in security and the expenses resulting for the employer. In an earlier decision,[245] the Federal Labour Court has found that a police trade union may not display a list of signatures in order to canvass support for the trade union's demand for more jobs of police career civil servants. In that case, the police trade union's freedom of association had to give way to the principle of legality of administration granted in Article 20 paragraph 2 GG. These decisions demonstrate that finding the proper balance between the conflicting fundamental rights or principles in a certain case at stake is very difficult and highly unpredictable. One may very well raise the question whether the Federal Labour Court should not have exerted judicial self-restraint and called for the legislator to regulate these matters instead.

---

244. Dec. of 28 Feb. 2006 – 1 AZR 460/04, *BAGE*, vol. 117, pp. 137–151; annotated by A. Seifert, *International Labour Law Reports* 85–98 (2007).
245. Of 25 Jan. 2005 – 1 AZR 657/03, *BAGE*, vol. 113, pp. 130–137.

Chapter 2. Trade Unions and Employers' Associations

§1. Definition of Collective Industrial Organizations

414. Since there is no statutory definition of the term 'trade union' and 'employers' association', these central terms of collective labour law have to be defined by case law. In addition to the self-evident implications of the guarantee of collective freedom of association (*see* paragraphs 407 et seq.), the Federal Labour Court has established further criteria to be met by collective industrial organizations in terms of Article 9 paragraph 3 GG.[246] When developing that list, the court has had to balance two conflicting interests: on the one hand, only strong trade unions, being able to put pressure on the employers' side, guarantee appropriate results for collective bargaining. On the other hand, if the requirements for acknowledgement were too demanding, it would become very difficult for new trade unions to be recognized. Established trade unions are of course interested in keeping newcomers out. For more often than not, the formation of new trade unions is at the expense of established trade unions' membership. And all in all, the density of German trade unions has been steadily declining (*see* paragraph 426). (1) The association must be established for unlimited duration. An ad hoc association is not sufficient for the simple reason that there should be a guarantee that the association will continue to exist, at least for the duration for which the collective agreement has been concluded. Otherwise, there would be no party liable for the execution of the agreement. (2) A corporate structure is required: the association must be organized in a way guaranteeing its continuity even if members leave and new persons join. (3) Associations in terms of Article 9 paragraph 3 GG have to follow the principles of democratic decision-making. Since associations are acting on behalf of their members there should be a guarantee that members are able to influence the activities of their association. This is why associations have to follow the principles of democratic decision-making in their collective policy decisions. (4) The association may only consist of members belonging to either the employees' side or employers' side. This requirement of clear-cut division leads to the question of how far, for example, associations of executive staff may be understood to be employees' unions in view of the fact that many of their members carry out managerial functions. According to the contention of the Federal Labour Court, this requirement is fulfilled as long as top executive staff do not dominate the association. (5) The fifth criterion is again based on the same idea as the third and the fourth ones: an employees' association may also not be restricted to one establishment but must be an interplant association. The roots of this attempt to prevent so-called company unions again date back to the Weimar era when company unions turned out to be identical with 'yellow unions'. The solidarity basis relying on the coherence of external links and exceeding the scope of one establishment is supposed to be the best guarantee for independence. (6) An association in terms of Article 9 paragraph 3 GG must be independent from its social antagonist. This criterion is mainly a reaction to experiences of the Weimar

246. Dec. of 21 Nov. 1975 – 1 ABR 12/75, *Arbeitsrechtliche Praxis*, No. 6 §118 BetrVG 1972; of 15 Mar. 1977 – 1 ABR 16/75, *Arbeitsrechtliche Praxis*, No. 24 Art. 9 GG; of 14 Feb. 1978 – 1 AZR 76/76, *Arbeitsrechtliche Praxis*, No. 58 Art. 9 GG *Arbeitskampf*.

era when so-called yellow unions turned out to be mere employers' instruments undermining the labour movement. (7) Associations in terms of Article 9 paragraph 3 GG must be independent from third parties, such as e.g., the state, political parties or the churches. Neither government nor a political party may be in a position to influence the strategies of such an association. This requirement does not stop an association from aiming at political goals similar to those of a political party. The political orientation of an association is its own autonomous decision. Hence, the requirement of independence from the state and from political parties intends nothing other than to guarantee this autonomy.

§2. Organization and Structure of Trade Unions

I. General Pattern

415. As previously mentioned, a characteristic feature of today's union structure in Germany is the fact that different political and ideological wings are amalgamated in one association. This means that within the union movement there is no political or ideological fragmentation (so-called principle of amalgamated unions). There are, however, exceptions to this general pattern: the Christian unions, which for many years played only a marginal role but have become more important since the mid-1990s (*see* paragraph 429).

416. The second important characteristic of unions in Germany is the fact that they are mainly organized on an industry or a branch basis (for an exception *see* paragraphs 417–418 and 431). This means that a union is open to all employees in the industry concerned, no matter which trade or occupation they are engaged in. This again implies that there is only one union for all employees of the branch or industry. Industry or branch in this context should be understood in a very broad sense. Thus, for example the Metal Workers' Union (*IG Metall*) covers the automobile industry as well as the electrical industry, the shipbuilding industry, the machine building industry and the computer industry to mention just a few.

417. Again there are unions which do not fit in this industry- or branch-based pattern, e.g., the Union of Education and Science (*Gewerkschaft Erziehung und Wissenschaft* – GEW), which is not open to all employees of an establishment but only to those who have specific professions and occupations in the system of education and science.

418. The other exception to that rule, the White-Collar Workers' Union (*Deutsche Angestellten-Gewerkschaft* – DAG), vanished in 2001, when the DAG merged with four other unions, with the German Union of Post Employees (*Deutsche Postgewerkschaft* – DPG), the Union of Trade, Banking, and Insurance (*Gewerkschaft Handel, Banken und Versicherungen* – HBV), the Union of Workers in Media (*Industriegewerkschaft Medien – Druck und Papier, Publizistik und Kunst – IG Medien*) and the Union of Public Services, Transport, and Traffic (*Gewerkschaft*

Öffentliche Dienste, Transport und Verkehr – ÖTV) to form the United Union for Services (*Vereinigte Dienstleistungsgewerkschaft* – ver.di).[247]

419. Although career public servants are treated differently from employees and are not covered by labour law (*see* paragraph 29), they do enjoy freedom of association. That is why they are not only allowed to form a union but also to found associations of their own with the umbrella organization being the German Federation of Career Public Servants (*Deutscher Beamtenbund* – dbb). It should, however, be added that the dbb and its member unions do not exclusively represent career civil servants but also employees.

420. In addition to these unions, there are a number of associations, which organize higher-level white-collar workers. The umbrella organization, comprising six member organizations, is the Association of Executive Staff (*Deutscher Führungskräfteverband* – ULA).

II. The DGB and Its Member Unions

421. The most important trade unions are those organized in the DGB. Members of this federation are not individual employees but unions. At the beginning of the 1990s, the DGB embraced sixteen individual trade unions. Since that time, however, several mergers have taken place. In 1995 the Union of Horticulture, Agriculture and Forestry, a rather small union having difficulties in existing on its own, merged with the Union of Building and Construction Industries to form the Union of Construction, Agriculture and Environment (*Industriegewerkschaft Bauen-AgrarUmwelt* – IG BAU); at the same time and for the same reason the Union of Mining and Energy (*Industriegewerkschaft Bergbau und Energie*) merged with the Union of Chemical, Paper and Ceramic Industries (*Industriegewerkschaft Chemie-Papier-Keramik*) and the small Union of Leather Industries (*Industriegewerkschaft Leder*) to form the Union of Mining, Chemical and Energy Industries (*Industriegewerkschaft Bergbau, Chemie, Energie* – IG BCE). In 1998, the Union of Textile Industries (*Gewerkschaft Textil-Bekleidung* – GTB) merged with the Metal Workers' Union (*Industriegewerkschaft Metall* – IGM) in 1998, and in 2000 the Union for Timber and Plastics Industry (*Gewerkschaft Holz und Kunststoff* – GHK) followed suit. Since the merger between four DGB member unions and the DAG to ver.di has taken place in 2001, the DGB has consisted of only eight trade unions (*see* paragraph 426).

422. According to the standing rules of the DGB, member unions must coordinate their fields of organization. These can be altered only in agreement with the union or unions concerned and with the DGB itself. To quote an example, when in 1978 the Police Union (*Gewerkschaft der Polizei* – GdP) became a member of the

247. For an interim assessment more than five years after the merger *cf.* B. Keller, 'Ver.di – quo vadis?', *WSI-Mitteilungen*, 2007, p. 467.

DGB, the ÖTV was asked to recommend to its members working for police departments to transfer to the GdP. At the same time, the GdP advised its members not employed in police service to move to the ÖTV. Thus, overlapping and competition is eliminated between unions organized in the DGB. There is, however, one exception to this principle. The GEW is, as already mentioned, open to employees employed in establishments covered by ver.di. Thus, a certain amount of competition is inevitable. Membership rolls of the DGB trade unions include manual workers, white-collar workers and career public servants (as far as these unions cover the public sector). Disputes between affiliated unions can be settled by arbitration according to the Constitution of the DGB. According to their standing rules and programmes, the DGB and its member unions are politically neutral, that is they are not organized along party lines and do not adhere to any ideology. However, it should be mentioned that in reality the DGB unions are politically closer to the SPD than to any other party.

423. The DGB, financed by dues paid by the individual unions, has a mainly policy-making function, although member unions are not bound by its policies. The DGB does not conclude collective agreements; this competence lies with its member unions. The DGB can mediate in inter-union disputes if asked to do so. Its main role is that of a spokesman for the labour movement on the one hand, and of a coordinator of the policies of its member unions on the other hand.

424. The organizational structure of the DGB and its member unions is uniform as regards all important aspects. Member unions are national associations and are divided into federal, district and local levels. Some unions also have a *Land* level organization, sandwiched between the district and federal levels. Others also have local plant branches. Governing bodies of the individual unions are, at every level, the assemblies of delegates or members, the executive board, and at federal level, the executive board. The highest governing body of each individual union is the federal convention, which meets every three or four years. The federal convention should ideally reflect the membership structure of the respective union, but in practice, this is often not the case. Women, for example, are still underrepresented at the convention in proportion to their numbers among the members. It is the function of the convention to elect the federal executive board, to vote on changes in the standing rules, and to formulate the basic principles of union policy. It may very well be doubted to what degree the convention actually performs this last function. The assumption that union policy is more likely to be determined by the executive board than by the delegates is not entirely without foundation; the board has a multitude of opportunities to influence the formation of opinion within the convention. Between convention sessions, the federal executive board is the ultimate authority. It consists of almost all unions of delegates elected at district conferences and members of the federal executive board. At federal level the administration is carried out by the executive board, at lower levels by subordinate *Land* or district boards, and local administrative boards.

425. The DGB itself consists of a federal association, *Land* associations, district associations and numerous local branches. At every organizational level of the

DGB, there is an executive board and an assembly of delegates (at the local level an assembly of members). The assembly of delegates is made up of members from the individual unions. The federal convention of the DGB is, like the conventions of the individual unions, the highest governing body. It is an assembly of delegates elected by members of all the unions, meeting every three years. Individual unions are represented according to their membership strength. This means that large unions, such as the *IG Metall* and ver.di, have the strongest positions. These two unions in fact dominate the DGB's policy. Besides the federal convention, the executive council is the highest decision-making body of the DGB. It consists of members nominated by the individual unions, the federal executive board and the district chairpersons of the DGB. The authority of the executive council is so far-reaching that it may be regarded, more or less, as the main decision-making body of the DGB. As in the individual unions the executive board carries out the daily business of the DGB. The federal executive board of the DGB comprises the managing board (eight members and a chairperson) and the chairperson of each of the DGB member unions.

426. In Germany, the rate of unionization remained for a long time rather stable, somewhere between 30% and 40%. In 1970, 30.5% of the workforce were organized in DGB member unions, in 1990 this applied to 31% of the workforce (the few per cent organized in unions not belonging to the DGB not included). After unification, the rate climbed up to 38%, due to a higher degree of unionization in the territory of the former GDR. In the meantime, there has been a significant loss of members throughout the union movement. At the end of 2018 only 5,974,951 employees,[248] i.e., 17% of all employees subject to compulsory social insurance respectively 13% of all employed persons in Germany[249] were organized in DGB member unions. Of all trade union members organized in DGB member trade unions, 38% belong to IG Metall and 33% to ver.di. Another 10.6% are organized in IG BCE, 4.7% in GEW, 4.1% in IG BAU, 3.3% in the food workers union NGG (*Gewerkschaft Nahrung-Genuss-Gaststätten*), 3.2% in GdP and 3.1 in the railway and transport union EVG (*Eisenbahn- und Verkehrsgewerkschaft*).[250] Over the years, the two biggest unions – IG Metall and ver.di – have even extended their position of organizing formerly about half of all to 70% of the members of the DGB unions today, thereby strengthening their dominant position.

427. In the old FRG, the ratio between male and female trade union members almost remained the same. Until the mid-1980s, the number of female trade union members amounted to about 20% of all trade union members, and then slightly increased. Until the end of 1992, this figure climbed up to 32.1%. Within the territory of the old FRG, the women's share was 25% whereas in the territory of the former GDR it amounted to 48%. This shows that the average increase of female members was mainly due to the structure in East Germany, which always has known

248. Member statistics of the *DGB*, https://www.dgb.de/uber-uns/dgb-heute/mitgliederzahlen/2010.
249. In 2018, there were 32,870,228 employees subject to compulsory social insurance and in total 44,838,000 employed persons in Germany, *cf.* Bundesagentur für Arbeit (ed.), *Der Arbeitsmarkt in Deutschland 2018, supra*, tab. IV.1a.
250. *DGB*, https://www.dgb.de/uber-uns/dgb-heute/mitgliederzahlen/2010.

a high rate of female employment and of unionization of females. Until 2018, the percentage of female trade union members in Germany as a whole had only slightly decreased to 33.7%.[251]

III. Other Confederations and Their Members

A. *The Federation of Career Public Servants*

428. The German Federation of Career Public Servants (*Deutscher Beamtenbund*– dbb) is the umbrella organization of the various *Land* and federal career public servants' associations. Since working conditions and salaries for career public servants are regulated by statutory law the dbb does not take part in collective bargaining and, at least according to the prevailing opinion among judges and labour law scholars, is not allowed to take part in industrial action.[252] Thus, the main function of the dbb is to lobby for better working conditions. In this context it should be pointed out that career public servants (*Beamte*) (*see* paragraph 29) were unknown in the former GDR. After the unification, this type of employment relationship has been reintroduced in East Germany, with the consequence that the constituency of the dbb has been enlarged.

B. *The Federation of Christian Unions*

429. The Federation of Christian Unions (*Christlicher Gewerkschaftsbund Deutschlands* – CGB), founded in 1959 is the umbrella organization of Christian unions organized on an industry-wide basis. In 1997, allegedly 302,874 employees were organized in CGB member unions. Up-to-date membership figures are not available. Until recently, the Christian unions were only marginally relevant. In the second half of the 1990s, however, the employers of the East German metal industry 'discovered' the Christian Metal Workers' Union (*Christliche Gewerkschaft Metall* – CGM) as a bargaining partner a lot more conciliatory than *IG Metall.* For example, the collective agreement 'Phoenix', ended in 1998, provided for working conditions considerably worse, from the employees' point of view, than those in comparable collective agreements concluded with the *IG Metall*. The *IG Metall* was trying to fight such undercutting by filing actions for judgments declaring that the Christian Metal Workers' Union, due to its very low number of members, is not a collective industrial organization as guaranteed in Article 9 paragraph 3 GG. In March 2006, however, the Federal Labour Court decided otherwise.[253] In a recent ruling from 2018, the Federal Labour Court had to deal with the question of whether a trade union affiliated to the CGB, the salaried employees' union DHV, might not

251. *Ibid.*
252. Federal Constitutional Court, 6 Jun. 1958 – 1 BvR 1/52, *BVerfGE*, vol. 8, pp. 1–18; 30 Mar. 1977 – 2 BvR 1045/75, *BVerfGE*, vol. 44, pp. 249–283; *cf.* also H. Otto, *Münchener Handbuch zum Arbeitsrecht,* R. Richardi & O. Wlotzke ed., Verlag C.H. Beck, §285 fn. 191 et seq.
253. Dec. of 28 Mar. 2006 – 1 ABR 58/04, *BAGE*, vol. 117, pp. 308–336.

be eligible for collective bargaining, as there are doubts as to whether it meets the requirements for the necessary enforcement and performance capacity. However, the court did not finally decide this question, but referred the case back to the lower instance, since the facts of the case (e.g., the actual number of members of the DHV) must first be further clarified.[254]

C. *The Association of Executive Staff*

430. The ULA is an umbrella organization consisting of 17 member organizations organizing about 70,000 executive staff employees. The largest association, the Association of Academic and Leading Personnel in the Chemical Industries (*Führungskräfte-Verband Chemie* – VVA), has a membership of about 30,000. Member associations of ULA are conceived to be something in between employees' trade unions and employers' associations. That is why it is very doubtful how far they are entitled to take part in collective bargaining and in industrial action, as will be explained later (*see* paragraph 505). They are not only an organization of executive staff in a strict sense, but for higher-ranking employees in general.

IV. Other Unions

431. Besides the unions organized in the DGB or any other trade union confederation, there are a few smaller unions, not belonging to any trade union confederation, that are nevertheless highly effective in representing their constituency's interests because their members are highly qualified and work in important positions so that strike action is very effective. For example, the Marburg Federation (*Marburger Bund*), founded in 1947, represents 114,000 physicians (employees as well as career public servants). The Association Cockpit (*Vereinigung Cockpit*), founded in 1969, represents 9,600 pilots of commercial aircrafts and commercial helicopters as well as flight engineers. The Independent Organization of Flight Attendants (*Unabhängige Flugbegleiter Organisation* – UFO) (*see* paragraph 455) founded in 1992, represents above 10,000 members.

§3. Organization and Structure of Employers' Associations

I. Employers' Associations in the Private Sector

432. For employers, at least in principle, two associations are available, in which they may be organized. They usually belong to both: to a national association of a branch of industry at federal level (e.g., for the metal industries) and to a multi-industry *Land* association grouping all trade associations together at *Land* level. Like employees' associations, employers' associations are, as a rule, organized on

254. Federal Labour Court, 26 Jun. 2018 – 1 ABR 37/16, *BAGE*, vol. 163, p. 108.

three levels: local or district, *Land* and federal level. Unlike trade unions, employers' associations are usually organized as legal entities. As on the trade union side, there is an amalgamated system without ideological fragmentation.

433. The federal trade associations as well as the multi-industrial *Land* associations belong to an umbrella organization, the Confederation of German Employers' Associations (*Bundesvereinigung der Deutschen Arbeitgeberverbände* – BDA). According to its standing rules, it is the BDA's task to represent the socio-political interests of employers beyond the scope of one *Land* or one economic sector. Its members are not bound by its policies. Neither the BDA nor the multi-industrial associations participate in collective bargaining. Collective bargaining falls within the exclusive competence of the individual employers' trade organizations (*Arbeitgeberverband*). The BDA, however, does issue recommendations as to bargaining strategies.

434. As far as the degree of organization among German employers is concerned, no exact figures are available. Thus, only trends can be reported. The main trend to be reported is that, while it had been relatively high for a long time, the degree of organization among German employers has been rapidly declining to ca. 62% in 2006[255] (percentage of employees employed by organized employers). The reasons for this development are multifaceted. Among them are the economic problems arising after the unification, in particular in the territory of the former GDR, the growth of a new generation of entrepreneurs (in the new *Länder*, in new branches as software, telecommunication, etc.) reluctant to participate in traditional structures, the increasing competitive pressure due to European Monetary Union and globalization, etc. Some employers' associations have tried to react to that development by offering two different kinds of membership: the regular membership implying that members are bound by collective agreements concluded by the employers' association (*see* paragraph 453), and a non-regular membership (*OT-Mitgliedschaft*) meaning that non-regular members are entitled to all the services offered by the association but are not bound by collective agreements. Whether or not such non-regular memberships are lawful was highly contested.[256] In 2006, the Federal Labour Court finally answered this question in the affirmative.[257] It found no general legal objections if the standing rules of an employers' association provide for a kind of membership without being bound by the collective agreements concluded by the association. According to the court's view, freedom of association as granted in Article 9 paragraph 3 GG also protects the collective industrial organization's right to self-determination of their own organization, the procedure of decision-making and the administration of business. Consequently, the method of internal organization is also covered by the collective industrial organization's right

255. European Commission (ed.), *Industrial Relations in Europe 2006*, p. 37.
256. W. Däubler, 'Tarifausstieg – Erscheinungsformen und Rechtsfolgen', *Neue Zeitschrift für Arbeitsrecht*, 1996, pp. 225 et seq.
257. Dec. of 18 Jul. 2006 – 1 ABR 36/05, *Arbeitsrechtliche Praxis*, No. 19 §2 TVG *Tarifzuständigkeit*; annotated by A. Seifert, *International Labour Law Reports* 401–416 (2007).

to activities granted by Article 9 paragraph 3 GG. In 2010, the Federal Constitutional Court confirmed that this case law of the Federal Labour Court on the statutory structure of such a non-regular membership in an employers' association (with a clear distinction between members bound by collective bargaining agreements and those not bound) is in conformity with the Constitution.[258] Today, about 47.8% to 61.1% of employers' associations offer this kind of non-regular membership and about half of their members make use of it.[259] The second trend to be reported is that, even though employers' associations in Germany cover all types of enterprises – whether big, medium-sized or small – within the same organization, the organization rate of small enterprises is significantly lower than that of big enterprises.

II. Employers' Associations in the Public Sector

435. In the public sector there are two employers' associations, one for the *Länder*, the Association of German *Länder* (*Tarifgemeinschaft Deutscher Länder*– TDL), and one for the municipalities, the Municipal Employers' Association (*Verband kommunaler Arbeitgeber* – VKA). The latter is a confederation of member organizations organized within the region of a *Land*.

436. Collective bargaining is sometimes carried out jointly by the two organizations, and sometimes by the two organizations in cooperation with the federal government. For a long time, both organizations were, for example, together with the federal government, parties to the Federal Collective Agreement for White-Collar Workers in the Public Service (*Bundes-Angestelltentarifvertrag* – BAT). However, this long-lasting cooperation has been loosened recently. The more it turned out that collective bargaining had to do with the distribution of costs between the Federation and the individual *Länder* on the one hand, and municipalities on the other hand, the more difficult it became to maintain the joint bargaining structure. Since 1 October 2005, the BAT has been replaced by the Collective Agreement for the Public Sector (*Tarifvertrag für den öffentlichen Dienst* – TVöD), concluded by the Federal Minister of Internal Affairs and by the VKA on the one hand, and since 1 November 2006 by the Collective Agreement of the *Länder* (*Tarifvertrag für die Länder* – TV-L), concluded by TDL, on the other hand. While the TVöD applies to employees of the Federation and of the municipalities, the TV-L is applicable to the employees of most *Länder* (all except Berlin and Hesse). On the employees' side, both collective agreements have been signed by ver.di, GEW and GdP.

§4. Legal and Factual Position of Trade Unions

437. As previously indicated, trade unions in Germany lack the status of a legal entity. This deficit, however, should not be overestimated. Since trade unions are in

258. Federal Constitutional Court, 1 Dec. 2010 – 1 BvR 2593/09, NZA 2011, 60.
259. M. Behrens & M. Helfen, Sachzwang oder Programm? Tarifpolitische Orientierungen und OT-Mitgliedschaft bei deutschen Arbeitgeberverbänden, *WSI-Mitteilungen 6/2015*, pp. 452, 454.

fact more or less treated as if they were legal entities. Step by step they gained privileges granted by statute or by court decisions. Just one single example may illustrate this development: according to Section 50 ZPO as amended until 2009, associations that are not legal entities can be plaintiffs in a lawsuit only under rather intricate conditions. Not only the association as such but all its members must act as plaintiffs. For an association of the size of today's trade unions the application of this requirement meant that it was practically impossible to initiate a lawsuit. As a result of a change in the law in 2009, associations without legal capacity are now also actively entitled to take legal action. Especially for the reason of the former law, Section 10 ArbGG grants trade unions the same position as legal entities. This, however, applies only to matters dealt with in labour courts. In ordinary civil law matters, the remaining gap has been bridged by decisions of the Federal Court of Justice (*Bundesgerichtshof* – BGH), even before 2009.[260] The court took note of the important factual situation of trade unions. Due to this factual situation, and in spite of the statutory situation, the court decided that trade unions could initiate a lawsuit under the same conditions as if they were legal persons. In other words, their legal status no longer indicates the real legal powers that unions enjoy.

438. From a financial point of view, trade unions are still powerful organizations. In former times, DGB unions even ran quite a few big companies, for example a huge building company, a huge bank (*Bank für Gemeinwirtschaft* – BfG) and a publishing company for most of the trade union publications (*Bund-Verlag*). Today, however, they have reduced these activities significantly. The reduction of involvement in businesses is mainly due to mismanagement and to situations where top managers ended up in conflicts of loyalty. The reduction of business activities, however, does not necessarily imply a decrease of financial power. DGB trade unions have accumulated quite significant financial resources, last but not least real estate.

439. The role of trade unions as organizations representing employees' interests is generally accepted and uncontested in Germany. Trade unions are not only factually integrated in society but they have quite a few institutionalized rights of participation. These rights are not limited to matters of the labour market but go far beyond this scope. Unions are, however to a rather limited extent, integrated in boards dealing with educational and cultural matters, on the boards of mass media, in institutions dealing with economic and social security matters, in the labour court system (*see* paragraphs 368–371) and social security court system, to give only some idea of the multitude of their activities.

440. In addition to their function in improving and safeguarding working and economic conditions, unions offer a wide variety of services to their members (e.g., travel agencies, all kinds of insurance).

---

260. Of 6 October 1964 – VI ZR 176/63, *Arbeitsrechtliche Praxis*, No. 6 §54 BGB; 11 July 1968 – VII ZR 63/66, BGHZ, vol. 50, pp. 325–335; for more recent legislation *see* Federal Labour Court, 15 May 2019 – 7 ABR 35/17, *Neue Zeitschrift für Arbeitsrecht* 2019, 1595.

Chapter 3. Collective Bargaining

§1. Level and Scope of Collective Bargaining

I. Level of Collective Bargaining

441. According to the main legal foundation for collective bargaining, the TVG 1949, amended in 1969, parties to a collective agreement may be on the employees' side trade unions only.[261] On the employers' side, either individual employers or an employers' association may be party to a collective agreement. The umbrella organizations of each side may also conclude collective agreements if the competence to do so is part of the duties regulated in their standing rules, or if they are authorized to do so by their member associations. Thus, theoretically, and in accordance with the law, the DGB as well as the BDA could be authorized by their member organizations to conclude collective agreements. Since individual unions or individual employers' associations have little interest in such a complete centralization of collective bargaining powers, passages to this effect are included neither in the DGB standing rules nor in those of the BDA. The responsibility and the competence for collective bargaining hence lies with the respective trade unions.

442. As far as the distribution of power to decide on claims for collective bargaining within trade unions is concerned, it is the federal executive board, which has the final say in most unions. In most DGB unions, the federal executive board is authorized to make binding decisions not only on the claims but also on the conclusion and termination of an agreement if it is applicable nationwide. These powers, to a rather high degree, extend to regional agreements as well. This implies that the terms and conditions of collective agreements in East Germany are, to a great extent, decided in West Germany, where the headquarters are.

443. A collective agreement between a trade union and a single employer is also called 'company agreement' (*Firmentarifvertrag*). If the agreement is signed by an employers' association one speaks of an 'area collective agreement' (*Flächentarifvertrag*). Area collective agreements may cover a certain region of an industry or the entire territory of the FRG for a certain industry or branch. In most industries, the territory of Germany is divided into different regions for the purpose of collective bargaining. It is up to the associations to decide on the boundary of such regions. In some cases, these regions are identical with the territory of a *Land*, but if this is the case it is for accidental reasons only. Tradition and practical considerations explain why these regions differ from industry to industry.

---

261. For more details to the role of Trade Unions in collective bargaining *see* M. Weiss, *German Trade Unions: Their Role in Collective Bargaining*, in *Trade Unions and Non-employee Representation in Europe – the Current State of Play and Prospects for the Future* 33 et seq (J. Carby-Hall & M. Rycak ed. 2016).

444. If collective bargaining takes place at industry or branch level, two effects are almost inevitable. First, the conditions laid down cannot take account of particular circumstances in individual companies. Thus, of necessity, the standards must be vague and ambiguous. Second, since the agreements cover a huge number of enterprises and employees, public attention and public pressure is rather significant. Parties to collective agreements hence have no choice but to act in an economic and responsible manner. This means that, at least in general, the minimum standards laid down in collective agreements cannot exceed the possibilities of small companies within the respective industry. This is why collective agreements are quite often only of limited relevance for the more prosperous sectors within an area covered.

445. Collective agreements concluded at company level between a trade union and a single employer are still the exception. In 2018, company collective agreements covered only 8% of employees in the old FRG and 11% of employees in the former GDR.[262] Only 2% of establishments were bound by company collective agreements.[263] For example, company-level collective agreements can be found in the formerly state-owned undertakings that have been privatized: for Deutsche Bahn AG, Deutsche Post AG and Deutsche Telekom AG highly complicated company and group collective agreements apply. In the telecommunications sector, air traffic sector and the mineral oil industry company collective agreements are very common, as well as in private services.

446. In the mid-1990s, however, in East Germany as well as in West Germany the problem arose that more and more companies had difficulty in coping with the minimum conditions as laid down in area collective agreements. This was the starting point of different developments altogether undermining the diffusion grade of area collective agreements of the traditional type (*see* paragraph 638).[264] On the one hand, coverage by area collective agreements has been steadily declining since,[265] because employers either did not join or left their associations or became OT members (*see* paragraph 434). In the old FRG, collective agreement coverage has declined from 69% of employees covered in 1996 to 61% in 2004 and to 56% in 2018; at the same time in the former GDR this percentage has decreased from 56% to 45% in 2018. The figures are even more impressive if one looks at the percentage of establishments covered: in 2018, area collective agreements directly covered

262. Destatis, *Tarifbindung von Arbeitnehmern*, https://www.destatis.de/DE/Themen/Arbeit/Arbeitsmarkt/Qualitaet-Arbeit/Dimension-5/tarifbindung-arbeitnehmer.html.
263. WSI-Tarifarchiv (based on data of IAB Betriebspanel), *Tarifbindung 2018*, https://www.boeckler.de/pdf/ta_tarifbindung_betriebe_2018.pdf.
264. For more information *see* R. Bispinck & T. Schulten, 'Decentralisation of German Collective Bargaining? Current Trends and Assessments from a Works and Staff Council Perspective', *WSI-Mitteilungen*, Special Issue 2003, pp. 24–33.
265. For the following figures *cf.* WSI (ed.), *Tarifhandbuch 2006, supra*, p. 42; WSI-Tarifarchiv (based on data of IAB Betriebspanel), *Tarifbindung 1998–2018*, https://www.wsi.de/de/tarifbindung-15329.htm.

27% of establishments in the old FRG and 17% of those in the former GDR.[266] These low figures for collective bargaining coverage are put into perspective, however, by the fact that about 30% of establishments not directly covered state that they were geared to the area collective agreement. This, of course, is no guarantee that the area collective agreement is applied correctly and completely. It indicates, however, that the area collective agreement is still a framework of reference. The reasons for the discrepancy between coverage of employees and coverage of establishments is that in bigger establishments union density is usually higher than in small and medium-sized enterprises. On the other hand, collective agreements were made more flexible. The actors at plant and enterprise level were empowered to deviate within certain limits from these minimum standards. The effect is a decentralization of bargaining power and bargaining activities, at least to a certain extent. Works councils as bodies of institutionalized employee participation are thereby integrated in the structure of collective bargaining, as will be shown below (*see* paragraph 638).

II. Scope and Subject of Collective Bargaining

447. Collective agreements cover virtually all areas of the private and the public sector. Until the beginning of the economic crisis in the mid-1970s, collective bargaining concentrated mainly on remuneration and other economic benefits, including financial and other compensation in cases of rationalization. Since the 1980s, however, other issues have become more and more important, e.g., reduction and flexibility of working time, job security, vocational training, etc.[267] Due to the challenges resulting from the transformation of the economy through increasing digitalization, job security and qualification of employees is a particularly important aspect in current and future wage negotiations.

448. Collective bargaining is understood to be the main implication of the guarantee of collective freedom of association as provided in Article 9 paragraph 3 GG. Thus, the question arises: what are the subjects envisaged by the formula according to which collective bargaining is supposed to 'safeguard and improve working and economic conditions'? In other words, how far is it possible to regulate matters, which have traditionally been subject to managerial prerogative by collective agreement? The notion 'working and economic conditions', taken as an isolated formula, could be used in a broad sense including decisions on investment, prices, etc. However, it should be realized that Article 9 paragraph 3 GG is just one of several, and conflicting, fundamental rights guaranteed in the Constitution. The Constitution equally guarantees the right to private property and means of production in Article

266. WSI (ed.), *Tarifhandbuch 2006, supra*, tab. 6.3; WSI-Tarifarchiv (based on data of IAB Betriebspanel), *Tarifbindung 1998–2018*, https://www.wsi.de/de/tarifbindung-15329.htm.

267. For more detailed information *see* the *Tarifhandbuch*, annually published by the WSI in Bund-Verlag, Cologne; *see further* the regular overviews published by R. Bispinck & WSI-Tarifarchiv in *WSI-Mitteilungen*, Bund-Verlag, Cologne; *see also* WSI Collective Agreement Archive, 'Bargaining Policy in the German System of Industrial Relations', *WSI-Mitteilungen*, Special Issue 2003, pp. 34– 41.

14 GG. Thus, according to the prevailing opinion among labour law scholars, the phrase 'working and economic conditions' is used as a kind of residual category. Collective agreements may only provide data for the decisions of management; the decision as such is subject to the employers' freedom as guaranteed in Articles 12 and 14 GG. Collective agreements may fix the costs for managerial decisions by setting standards for remuneration, holiday, working hours, etc. and may regulate the effects of such decisions, e.g., consequences in cases of rationalization. However, the decision whether or not to engage in a business at all, whether or not to invest, etc., remains subject to managerial prerogative.[268] However, so as not to give a wrong impression, it should be pointed out that this boundary is not very clear but is subject of an intense debate. In future it may well be that the formula 'working and economic conditions' may be used in a broader sense including also areas so far understood to be the exclusive field of managerial freedom. In a decision of 2007[269] the Federal Labour Court has found, for example, that strike action de facto aiming at preventing the employer from closing a plant and shifting production by putting enormous strike claims was lawful. The court explicitly declined to control the strike claim extent for fundamental reasons.

449. Since 1974, due to an amendment to the TVG, collective agreements may not only cover employees but also 'employee-like' persons (*see* paragraph 85). This, however, does not apply to commercial agents, even though they are 'employee-like' persons (*see* paragraph 87). According to the HAG it is also permitted to regulate working conditions of homeworkers (*see* paragraphs 89–91) by collective agreement. Nevertheless, it should be stressed that the legal possibilities to conclude collective agreements for homeworkers and other 'employee-like' persons are used only to a very limited extent.

III. Collision of Collective Agreements

450. It can happen that different trade unions conclude collective agreements with one employer, which regulate the same working conditions for a company, e.g., the pay structure. In such cases, these are referred to as conflicting collective agreements (*Tarifkollision*). The question is what effects the collective agreements have in this case and how they relate to each other. Since 1957, the principle of uniform collective agreements (*Tarifeinheit*) has applied in Germany based on the Federal Labour Court's case law, according to which in principle only one collective agreement should apply in a company. However, the court abandoned this principle in 2010, because the TVG had not regulated the relationship of conflicting collective

268. *Cf.* further proofs at W. Linsenmaier, *Erfurter Kommentar zum Arbeitsrecht*, ed. R. Müller-Glöge et al, 2020, Verlag C.H. Beck, Art. 9 GG para. 75.
269. Dec. of 24 Apr. 2007 – 1 AZR 252/06, AP No. 2 §1 TVG *Sozialplan*.

agreements and it had doubts about the constitutional conformity of the principle.[270] Subsequently, an employer could be bound by several collective agreements and had to observe all of them (so-called collective majority or collective plurality).[271] In the meantime, the competition situation among some unions had increased and the legislator feared that the collision of collective agreements would jeopardize the functioning of collective bargaining autonomy.[272] The legislator therefore decided to return to the principle of uniform collective agreements and adopted the Uniform Collective Bargaining Act (*Tarifeinheitsgesetz*) in 2015. However, he made some changes to the old legal situation.[273]

451. According to the new Section 4a paragraph 2 sentence 2 TVG, the following now applies: 'Insofar as the areas of application of collective agreements of different unions, which are not identical in content overlap (conflicting collective agreements), only the legal provisions of the collective agreement of the union, which has the most members in an employment relationship at the time of conclusion of the last conflicting collective agreement in the company (majority collective agreement) are applicable in the company.' However, a trade union whose collective agreement does not apply because it does not have a majority in the company has the possibility under Section 4a paragraph 3 TVG to reproduce the legal provisions of the applicable collective agreement of the other trade union. This means that it is entitled to conclude a collective agreement with the same provisions where there has been an overlap with its own collective agreement. The regulation has raised various questions, such as how to prove that there is a 'majority' in the company without the employer knowing how many members the union has in the company.

452. After a constitutional complaint was lodged against the law by comparatively smaller trade unions, the Federal Constitutional Court ruled in 2017 that the Uniform Collective Bargaining Act is essentially compatible with the Constitution.[274] However, it also laid down requirements for the protection of minority trade unions whose collective agreements are superseded.[275]

§2. PARTIES TO A COLLECTIVE AGREEMENT

453. As already mentioned, collective agreements may, according to Section 2 TVG, be concluded on the employees' side by trade unions and on the employers'

270. Federal Labour Court, 7 Jul. 2010 – 4 AZR 549/08, *Neue Zeitschrift für Arbeitsrecht 2010*, pp. 1068 et seq.
271. M. Franzen, *Erfurter Kommentar zum Areitsrecht*, ed. R. Müller-Glöge et al, 2020, Verlag C.H. Beck, § 4a TVG, para. 1.
272. *Bundestagsdrucksache* 18/4062, p. 8.
273. *Cf.* M. Franzen, *Erfurter Kommentar zum Areitsrecht*, ed. R. Müller-Glöge et al, 2020, Verlag C.H. Beck, § 4a TVG, para. 1.
274. Federal Constitutional Court, 11 Jul. 2017 – 1 BvR 1571/15, *BVerfGE 146*, 71.
275. For more details *see* K. Bepler, Ein Zwischenurteil? – Bemerkungen zum Tarifeinheitsurteil des Bundesverfassungsgerichts, *Arbeit und Recht 2017*, pp. 380 et seq.

side either by a single employer or by employers' associations. There is no statutory definition of the notions 'trade union' and 'employers' association'. Thus, the question arises of whether any group of employees or employers may be entitled to be a party to a collective agreement, or whether certain requirements must be met in order to be allowed to conclude a collective agreement. If any association were allowed to participate in collective bargaining, the danger that the system of collective bargaining could lose its function would be a permanent threat. This is exactly the view of the Constitutional Court which puts it the following way:

> it cannot be the purpose of Article 9 paragraph 3 GG that every association of employees or employers should be admitted to participate in collective bargaining. The starting point for any further consideration should be that it is the purpose of the system of collective bargaining to produce a reasonable structure of working conditions This purpose requires that the ability to participate in collective bargaining must be based on certain prerequisites.[276]

In other words, since the system of collective bargaining is understood to be a system which must produce a certain result the conditions which guarantee this result must be regulated by law. As a consequence, certain prerequisites must be fulfilled by any association, whether trade union or employers' association, in order to be accepted as a party to collective agreements.

454. In addition to the criteria of a collective industrial organization (*see* paragraphs 408, 414) a trade union in terms of Section 2 TVG has to fulfil three further requirements. First of all, the requirement of willingness to engage in industrial action, however, only applies in principle. Meanwhile more and more exceptions are granted. If, for example, an association of employed medical doctors for ethical reasons declares that it refuses to resort to industrial action this is supposed to be justified. For the Federal Labour Court has indicated in the meantime that it may depend on the occupation, or on the hierarchical position of the employees organized in an association, whether or not the willingness to engage in industrial action is a precondition for an association within the meaning of Article 9 paragraph 3 GG.[277] Other means may be just as effective to exert pressure, e.g., the use of the media to attract public attention, etc. In short, the willingness to engage in industrial action as a condition for being a party to a collective agreement depends on the circumstances.

455. Much more important than the willingness to engage in industrial action – and heavily disputed – is the requirement of sufficient power to exert pressure on the employers' side (*Durchsetzungskraft*). Since the TVG considers a single employer to be powerful enough to be a party to collective bargaining, this is necessarily valid also for an employers' association. The necessity of sufficient power

276. Dec. of 18 Nov. 1954 – 1 BvR 629/52, *Arbeitsrechtliche Praxis*, No. 1 Art. 9 GG.
277. Federal Labour Court, 25 Nov. 1986 – 1 ABR 22/85, *Neue Zeitschrift für Arbeitsrecht*, 1987, pp. 492 et seq.

is based on the assumption that proper functioning of the autonomous system of collective bargaining would be undermined if powerless associations were allowed to participate in collective bargaining. However, it creates a barrier for new associations claiming to be trade unions and stabilizes already established large trade unions. Therefore, and also due to an intervention of the Federal Constitutional Court,[278] the Federal Labour Court has gradually lowered the standards of this criterion since the 1980s.[279] Today an employees' association must possess the necessary power to guarantee that the social counterparty cannot simply ignore a bargaining offer.[280] For an appropriate compromise of interests with socially pacifying effects may only be reached if the employees' association is able to exert as much pressure as necessary to cause the employers' side to engage in collective bargaining. The employees' association has to be taken seriously by its social antagonist in order to safeguard that working conditions are not unilaterally determined by the employers' side but are in fact negotiated between both parties to the collective agreement. Whether or not an employees' association has such power has to be determined taking into account all the circumstances of the respective case. One criterion possibly decisive to judge the power to exert pressure is the number of members. The unclear membership figures were also a reason why, for example, the eligibility of the union DHV to negotiate collective agreements was doubted.[281] However, as the Federal Labour Court emphasized in the case of the UFO,[282] the association's power is to be judged in relation to its regional and occupational scope determined by the association itself. Within this scope, the association must be able to stand up to the employers' side. If an association has only a small number of members, the ability to exert sufficient pressure on the social antagonist may also result from the fact that its members are specialists who work in key positions and, in case of industrial action, cannot or can only with difficulty be replaced at short notice. In addition, the sufficient power of an employees' association may also be concluded from the fact that it has already actively participated in collective bargaining. Even though collective agreements concluded by other (established) trade unions are simply copied, this can be an indication for the association's power, unless these collective agreements are be regarded as sham or courtesy collective agreements.

456. The final criterion distinguishing a trade union from a mere association in terms of Article 9 paragraph 3 GG concerns its organizational structure. According to the more recent, but nevertheless established case law of the Federal Labour Court a trade union must be able to perform its tasks.[283] The conclusion of collective agreements needs to be prepared. For that purpose, a trade union has to watch and to forecast economic developments and other framework conditions in order to

278. Dec. of 20 Oct. 1981 – 1 BvR 404/78, *Arbeitsrechtliche Praxis*, No. 31 §2 TVG.
279. Dec. of 16 Nov. 1982 – 1 ABR 22/78, *Arbeitsrechtliche Praxis*, No. 32 §2 TVG.
280. *Cf.* Dec. of 14 Dec. 2004 – 1 ABR 51/03, *Arbeitsrechtliche Praxis*, No. 1 §2 TVG *Tariffähigkeit*; *cf.* M. Schmidt, *ILLR* 51–64 (2005).
281. *Cf.* Federal Labour Court, 26 Jun. 2018 – 1 ABR 37/16, *BAGE*, vol. 163, p. 108.
282. *Cf.* Dec. of 14 Dec. 2004 – 1 ABR 51/03, *supra.*
283. *Ibid.*, with further proofs.

develop demands to be negotiated. In addition, the factual implementation of a collective agreement has to be controlled and secured. The results of collective bargaining, usually constituting a compromise, have to be communicated and accomplished within the association. In order to be recognized as a trade union competent to conclude collective agreements, an employees' association must hence guarantee proper performance of these tasks. However, as the Federal Labour Court stated, no abstract requirements can be set up in this respect. It all depends whether or not the association is capable of fulfilling its tasks within the frame of its self-determined scope of competences. If the association's self-determined scope covers the whole territory of Germany and employees of a variety of occupations and professions, usually considerable equipment also all over Germany will be required. If, however, a trade union limits its scope to one occupational group, concentrated to a few focal points as is the case with UFO, a comparatively small, centralized organization may suffice to negotiate collective agreements effectively, to control and safeguard their implementation and to attend to members. Usually, an effective organization will require a full-time team of employees. However, as the court put it, the employment of full-time employees is not an indispensable requirement of a trade union.

§3. Content and Effect of a Collective Agreement

457. As far as the content of a collective agreement is concerned, two parts must be distinguished: the obligatory part and the normative part (Section 1 TVG). The obligatory part contains the rights and obligations between the parties to the collective agreement, the normative part regulates the working conditions, the modalities of conclusion and termination of an employment contract and questions pertaining to the establishment and its legal structure. In addition, the question arises of how to deal with conflicting collective agreements, i.e., if there are several collective agreements of possibly competing trade unions for a company.

I. Obligatory Part

458. The rights and duties of parties to a collective agreement may be established by explicit clauses in the collective agreement. Since the TVG does not define the legitimate scope of these rights and duties, the question arises whether such rights and duties necessarily refer to questions, which can be dealt with in the normative part. Since obligations established in the obligatory part are binding on nobody other than the parties to the collective agreement, there is no reason for such a limitation. Some labour law scholars nevertheless regard the indicated limits as compulsory. However, it should be stressed, that at least so far, this controversy has been of almost no practical importance. Two duties are binding on the parties to a collective agreement, even if they are not explicitly mentioned in the collective agreement: the peace obligation (*Friedenspflicht*) and the duty to exert influence (*Einwirkungspflicht*). These duties are deemed to be inherent in the very existence of the collective agreement. Even if parties to a collective agreement explicitly contracted out of those duties, they would nevertheless apply. Any abrogation would be null and void.

459. The peace obligation places the parties to the collective agreement under an obligation to maintain industrial peace for the duration of the agreement in question. Specifically, neither of the parties may seek to push through demands to alter the existing content of the agreement by taking any form of industrial action. Since this obligation is limited to the content of the agreement in question, it is called a 'relative peace obligation'. It does not, however, preclude industrial action aimed at achieving a collective agreement on terms and conditions not already laid down in the content of the agreement in question. Consequently, if parties to a collective agreement wish to prohibit any industrial action for the duration of the collective agreement (so-called absolute peace obligation) a specially agreed arrangement is necessary. In practice this possibility is, however, not used at all.

460. The duty of parties to a collective agreement to exert their influence implies that they must use the means available to them under the law of associations to ensure that their respective members duly abide by the provisions of the agreement. However, the duty to exert influence does not oblige them to take steps against every individual breach of the agreement, for instance if an employer is temporarily failing to pay the collectively agreed rates of pay because of financial difficulties. Its intention is rather to ensure that the provisions of the agreement are generally upheld among members and to prevent any deliberate moves to undermine these provisions, e.g., by means of industrial action contravening the peace obligation.

II. Normative Part

461. The normative part of a collective agreement contains provisions, which apply to all employment relationships with normative effect. As a matter of principle laid down in Section 4 paragraph 1 TVG, normative provisions have direct and mandatory effect on all employment relationships bound by the collective agreement, i.e., these relationships are automatically invested with the content of the agreement, irrespective of any other arrangement agreed upon between employer and employee. Two types of normative provisions are to be distinguished: those relating to the individual employment relationship in its strict sense (individual normative provisions) on the one hand, and those relating to the establishment, to the law on works constitution and on joint institutions set up by the parties to the collective agreement (collective normative provisions) on the other hand.

A. Individual Normative Provisions

462. Individual normative provisions may regulate the content, the conclusion and the termination of the individual contract of employment. Normative provisions on conclusion and termination of a contract of employment regulate the conditions and formalities for entering into and ending an employment relationship. Normative provisions regulating the content of the employment contract may include all provisions covering the entire range of matters that can be the subject of a contract of employment from pay to working hours, aspects of job protection, working conditions, skills, etc. They can also cover matters merely allied to the employment relationship such as employee liability or time limits for asserting entitlements. Any individually agreed arrangements conflicting with individual normative provisions of a collective agreement are null and void, and are replaced by the collectively agreed regulation. Divergences from the collective agreement are lawful only provided that they are expressly permitted by the agreement or if they contain more favourable conditions for the employee, the so-called principle of favourability (*Günstigkeitsprinzip*).

463. According to Section 3 paragraph 1 TVG, individual normative provisions are legally binding only if both parties to the individual contract of employment, employee and employer, are members of the respective party to the collective agreement, i.e., if the employee is organized in the contracting union and is employed by an employer who is a member of the contracting employers' association. To repeat once again: the employee's membership in the union, which has concluded the respective collective agreement is not sufficient for entitlement to the minimum standards guaranteed in a collective agreement. In addition, the employer has to be a member of the employers' association, which has concluded the respective collective agreement on the employers' side. It is self-evident that normative provisions only apply to the region and to the industry the agreement has been concluded for.

464. In most enterprises, however, union members as well as non-union members are employed. That means that there are two different legal regimes applicable to the two groups of employees. At least according to law, the employer could insist on granting non-union members working conditions below the minimum standards provided for by collective agreements. Such a practice would not violate the principle of equal treatment. Nevertheless, it would constitute a strong incentive for trade union membership. As a consequence, in order not to provide such an incentive, an employer who is bound by a collective agreement usually grants the working conditions laid down in that agreement to all his or her employees, whether they are union members or not.

465. Working conditions, especially remuneration, are in fact often granted at a level, which is higher than the minimum standards laid down in collective agreements. Hence, it may well be that the actual level of remuneration is not affected by a wage increase due to collective bargaining. This is why trade unions tried to establish clauses in collective agreements according to which factual remuneration is taken as the basis for the calculation of wage increases in order to guarantee that the increase is paid in addition to what has been paid already. According to the Federal Labour Court, however, such clauses are illegal mainly because they limit the space for individual agreements in favour of the employee.[284] In the court's view, they deviate from the collective agreements' function to set minimum conditions and nothing else.

B. Collective Normative Provisions

466. Among the collective normative provisions, two types of norms are to be distinguished: normative provisions referring to employee representation and participation in the establishment on the one hand, and provisions focusing on employees as members of the workforce of the establishment on the other hand. Clauses extending the statutory rights of works councils may illustrate what is meant by the first category. Rules regulating access to certain facilities in the establishment, e.g., the use of the telephone for personal purposes, the modalities of gate inspections, the use of parking areas, etc. are examples of the second category. In short, these regulations exceed the scope of the individual employment relationship.

467. Collective normative provisions apply directly and mandatorily to all establishments of an employer, which belong to the contracting employers' association, no matter whether or not the employees are members of the contracting trade union. Consequently, distinctions between union and non-union members are not to be drawn. The differentiation between the applicability of individual normative provisions and collective normative provisions is based on practical considerations: patterns set by collective normative provisions only operate in practice if they are applied homogeneously. The distinction between individual normative provisions and collective normative provisions is not always easy. However, in view of the different scopes of application it has to be made in every single case. Hence, in practice this differentiation is a source of never-ending controversy.

C. Normative Provisions on Common Institutions

468. To provide specific services (additional vocational training, etc.) or specific benefits (additional holiday payments, payments in addition to social insurance benefits, etc.) unions and employers' associations may establish institutions by collective agreement. These institutions are administered by the associations of both sides. They are financed by the members of the employers' associations. These institutions exist mainly in areas with a large number of small or medium-sized enterprises (the most prominent example is the *Sozialkassen der Bauwirtschaft* – SOKA-Bau – in the building industry). The rights and duties of these institutions and the members of the employers' associations as well as the rights and duties of these

---

284. Dec. of 13 Jun. 1958 – 1 AZR 591/57, *Arbeitsrechtliche Praxis*, No. 2 TVG §4 *Effektivklausel*; of 16 Sep. 1987 – 4 AZR 265/87, *Arbeitsrechtliche Praxis*, No. 15 TVG §4 *Effektivklausel*.

institutions and members of the unions can be laid down in normative provisions in collective agreements. As a consequence, these institutions may sue the members of the employers' association if they refuse to pay their contributions, and the union members may sue the institution if it does not provide the services or benefits the employees are entitled to according to the collective agreement.

§4. Formal Requirements, Duration

469. According to Section 1 paragraph 2 TVG, a collective agreement must be in writing. In addition, the employer has to place the text of the collective agreement at the employees' disposal (Section 8 TVG). Finally, every collective agreement must be entered in the register of the Federal Ministry of Labour (Section 6 TVG). Registration has, however, no significance in terms of the legal validity of a collective agreement.

470. Collective agreements are usually concluded for a definite period and end automatically when this period expires. Whether concluded for a definite or for an indefinite period, they can always be terminated earlier by mutual agreement. Ordinary dismissal with terms of notice is possible, provided that this is explicitly stipulated in the agreement. In exceptional situations, when it becomes intolerable for a party to a collective agreement to be bound by the collective agreement, an extraordinary dismissal may be justified. That follows from the principle that it must always be possible to terminate any permanent legal relationship for good cause earlier than originally agreed. For a very long time, extraordinary dismissal of collective agreements simply did not happen in Germany. This changed in 1993, when several employers' associations of the East German metal branch as well as employers' associations of the East German iron and steel industry declared an extraordinary termination of collective agreements which had been concluded in 1991 and which provided for a step by step increase of wages in East Germany up to 100% of the West German level until April 1994. After massive strikes, the parties to the collective agreement finally agreed *inter alia* to postpone the adaptation of East German wages to West German standards until mid-1996. Under what conditions an extraordinary termination of a collective agreement can be justified the Federal Labour Court had to decide for the very first time in 1996.[285] Accordingly, high demands should be made for a good reason justifying an extraordinary termination of a collective agreement. Moreover, the court declared, it followed from the principle of *ultima ratio* that, before a party to a collective agreement could declare a collective agreement to be extraordinarily terminated, it should have attempted to bargain with the other party to the collective agreement for an adjustment of the collective agreement to its economic possibilities. Virtually all other questions, however, still remain unanswered.

285. Federal Labour Court, 18 Dec. 1996 – 4 AZR 129/96, *Arbeitsrechtliche Praxis*, No. 1 §1 TVG *Kündigung*.

471. Neither employers nor employees can escape the binding effect of a collective agreement by leaving the employers' association or the trade union. If they were members of the contracting associations at the time of conclusion of the collective agreement, it applies to them until its termination (Section 3 paragraph 3 TVG). After the termination of a collective agreement, the normative part remains in effect until a new collective agreement is concluded (Section 4 paragraph 5 TVG). But for the period between the termination of the old collective agreement and the conclusion of a new collective agreement normative provisions cease from being rigid minimum standards which cannot be abrogated by an individual agreement. Now it is legally possible to agree individually on conditions below the standards set by normative provisions.

§5. Extension of Collective Agreements by Order Imposing Extension

472. The fact that the scope of application of collective agreements is limited to employees who are members of the trade union, which is a party to the collective agreement, can lead to disadvantages for employees covered by a collective agreement, particularly in a period of economic crisis. In times of high unemployment and a corresponding surplus of labour, employers may prefer to hire non-union members, whom they can pay below collectively negotiated wages. This is exactly what happened in the economic crisis during the Weimar era. Due to that experience, the legislator of the 1949 TVG provided for the possibility to extend the scope of application of an existing collective agreement to non-organized employers and employees within the region and industry covered by the respective collective agreement. This instrument, granted in Section 5 TVG, is called 'order imposing extension' (*Allgemeinverbindlicherklärung*). It is particularly used in branches where there are a large number of small non-organized employers, i.e., in the building industry or in retail distribution.[286]

473. By means of an order imposing extension, duties are imposed on non-organized employers and non-organized employees. Hence, the question arose of how far this mechanism was compatible with the so-called negative freedom of association. The Federal Constitutional Court decided, however, that the order imposing extension does not contravene this freedom.[287] Thus, the mechanism as such is no longer controversial. Furthermore, an imposed collective agreement shall be complied with by the employer even if he is bound by another collective agreement.

474. The order imposing extension is issued by the Federal or *Land* Minister of Labour and Social Affairs, depending on the territorial scope of the collective agreement, upon a joint application of the parties to the collective agreement and in agreement with a committee comprised of three representatives each from the umbrella associations of employees and employers. Decisions of this committee are

286. WSI (ed.), *Tarifhandbuch 2006, supra*, tab. 6.2.
287. Federal Constitutional Court, 24 May 1977 – 2 BvL 11/74, *BVerfGE*, vol. 44, pp. 322–353.

made by simple majority, thus allowing either side, voting en bloc, to prevent the extension of the agreement. A further condition for an order imposing extension is that the order is deemed to be in the public interest, notably because terms and conditions of employment in the area concerned would otherwise fall below the generally prevailing level. Until the amendment of Section 5 TVG in August 2014, it was also a further condition that employers bound by collective bargaining agreements employ no less than 50% of the employees covered by the collective bargaining agreement. After the amendment of the provision, the extent of the collective bargaining coverage only plays a subordinate role, namely as a possible criterion for deciding whether a public interest exists. According to Section 5 paragraph 1 sentence 2 TVG, this is usually the case if either the collective agreement has become of predominant importance in its scope for the shaping of working conditions or if the safeguarding of the effectiveness of the collective agreement's standard-setting against the consequences of undesirable economic developments requires an order imposing extension. Collective agreements establishing common institutions of unions and employers' associations (*see* paragraph 468) may also be ordered imposing extension in order to ensure its operation under the provisions of Section 5 paragraph 1a TVG.

475. It should be stressed that an order imposing extension does not have any influence on the content of the agreement. The minister is not entitled to change anything, as this would be a violation of the autonomy of parties to a collective agreement to decide exclusively on the content of a collective agreement.

§6. Extension of Collective Agreements by Governmental Decree

476. In the building and construction industry, an additional mode of extension of collective agreements is provided for in the Act on Posting of Workers (*Arbeitnehmerentsendegesetz* – AEntG) of 1996. Since January 1999, the extension of a collective agreement can also be achieved by governmental decree. Contrary to the above described proceeding resulting in an order imposing extension (*see* paragraphs 472–475), the extension of a collective agreement by governmental decree does not require the consent of the committee of representatives of the umbrella organizations of both sides of industry. This new procedure has been established due to the difficulties in achieving the committee's consent to the extension of collective agreements in the building and construction industries providing for minimum wages also applicable to posted workers. In August 1999, the Federal Minister of Labour for the first time exercised this new competence and issued a decree extending a collective agreement on minimum wages of a 9.63 in the former FRG and of an 8.31 in the former GDR in the building and construction industry that has been updated several times since. Since 2005, further collective agreements for subconstruction work, e.g., for painters and varnishers, for roofers and for demolition workers have been extended by governmental decree. In addition, since the AEntG has been detected as a tool for fixing collectively agreed minimum wages for any branches (*see* paragraph 255), collective agreements for building cleaners and letter services have been extended.

477. Like an order imposing extension, a governmental decree imposing extension requires that the legal provisions of this collective agreement be applied to all employers and employees covered by and not bound by it and that this appears necessary in the public interest (Section 7 AEntG). Even in the building and constructing industries, however, a collective agreement may not be extended against the will of both parties to the collective agreement: a governmental decree imposing extension may be issued only on condition of a joint application of the parties to the collective agreement. Moreover, before issuing a decree imposing extension the employers and employees falling under the geographical scope of the collective agreement and the parties to the collective agreement must be consulted.

478. Since its amendment by the Collective Bargaining Autonomy Strengthening Act (*Tarifautonomiestärkungsgesetz*) 2014, the AEntG is no longer restricted to the sectors expressly mentioned in the AEntG, but is open to all sectors. The procedure for the adoption of the statutory instrument is governed by Section 7a AEntG. The legal provisions of a nationally applicable collective agreement can be extended in a generally binding manner if this appears necessary in the public interest and, in particular, if predatory competition via wage costs can be counteracted. In addition, a joint application by the parties to the collective agreement to be extended is also required. With the extension of the AEntG to all industries, a second industry-related system of minimum protection of working conditions was introduced in addition to the general statutory minimum wage.[288]

479. A special regulation exists for the care sector, as a large number of church owned and church-related companies are active there. The procedure in accordance with Section 7a AEntG has been adapted to take account of the church's right of self-determination. The special provisions of Sections 10–13 AEntG apply there. A Commission decides on recommendations for establishing minimum working conditions. The Commission consists of eight members, who are appointed by the Federal Ministry of Labour and Social Affairs, taking into account proposals made by the parties to collective agreements in the care sector and by the employee and employer sides. The proposed working conditions can then be applied by statutory decree to all employers and employees who fall within the scope of the recommendation. If a collective agreement in the care sector pursuant to Section 7a AEntG is to be extended by statutory decree, this will take precedence. Section 7a paragraph 1a AEntG stipulates that religious communities, in whose areas commissions have been formed to determine working conditions in the care sector on the basis of Church law, are to be involved in the procedure for determining minimum working conditions.[289]

288. T. Lakies, in Deinert, Heuschmid, Zwanziger (ed.), *Handbuch Arbeitsrecht*, § 49 paras 8 et seq.
289. *Cf.* Justification of the legislator for the Long-Term Care Wage Improvement Act (*Pflegelöhnev-erbesserungsgesetz*), *Bundestagsdrucksache 19/13395*, p. 2.

Chapter 4. Dispute Resolution

§1. From Dispute Resolution by State Authorities to Voluntary Joint Dispute Resolution

480. After the First World War, when the Republic of Weimar was founded, collective bargaining became subject to detailed legal regulation. In this context, the Act on Dispute Resolution of 1923 is of specific relevance. According to this Act, dispute resolution boards composed of representatives of trade unions and employers' associations, chaired by a president nominated by the state, had to be established. Their primary task was to mediate on the request of one of the parties. It was up to the parties to accept their proposals or not. There were, however, two important exceptions. First, the board was authorized to intervene, without having been requested to do so by one of the parties, provided that this intervention was suitable in view 'of the public interest'. And second, the proposal of the board could be imposed on the parties if this was 'necessary for economic and social reasons'. It was exclusively up to state agencies to decide whether those conditions were fulfilled.

481. This system of dispute resolution by state authority (*staatliche Schlichtung*) was conceived to be an exception to the normal rule. However, in the course of the Weimar era, it became more and more important, primarily in the mining industry, the iron industry, the metal industry and the textile industry. In 1929, more than half of all collective agreements were the results of dispute resolution by state authority. The effect was discouraging for trade unions as well as for employers' associations. Trade unions later on considered this mechanism as an instrument for weakening their strength: since it was clear that the state would finally determine the standards of working conditions, they relied too much on the state instead of keeping up their autonomous power. Employers' associations did not agree at all with the intervention of the state. In their view, the costs imposed by state dispute resolution reached an amount, which could not be tolerated from an economic point of view. In short, looking back, both actors opposed the system of dispute resolution by state authorities as being inadequate. That is why it was clear that the re-establishment of such a system had no chance after the Second World War. The present situation can only be understood as a reaction to the experiences of the Weimar era.

482. After the Second World War, an Allied Control Council Act (*Kontrollratsgesetz* – KRG) on Dispute Resolution Machinery in Labour Conflicts was passed in 1946. This Act is still valid today. It gives absolute priority to voluntary dispute resolution agreements by trade unions and employers' associations. According to this Act, it is exclusively up to the parties to decide whether such a procedure should be established and if so, how it should be organized. Only as a subsidiary element for cases in which a voluntary procedure either does not exist or turns out to be unsuccessful does the Act offer an additional aid to the parties to reach an agreement. The *Länder* have to establish dispute resolution boards. Those boards are standing committees, established by the *Land* Ministers of Labour and Social

Affairs. They consist of an equal number of representatives of both sides, chaired by a neutral president, who is nominated by the *Land* Minister of Labour and Social Affairs, in agreement with the trade unions and employers' associations from a list compiled by the Labour Department in cooperation with those organizations. However, it has to be stressed that such a board can only intervene upon the request of both parties. The decisions of the board are binding on the parties only if they have agreed in advance that this should be so. Otherwise it remains up to them whether or not they accept the proposal of the board.

483. The frame provided by the KRG was specified by various *Land* Acts. The details of all those specifications, however, can be ignored for a very simple reason: dispute resolution by state authorities as a last resort in case of failure of autonomous voluntary procedures as established by the KRG does not play any role in practice. It exists on paper, but not in reality. The exclusive pattern in practice is joint dispute resolution established by agreement between the parties (*vereinbarte Schlichtung*). However, even the practical impact of joint dispute resolution procedures should not be overestimated. The huge number of collective agreements, at least so far, is a result of free collective bargaining without involvement of dispute resolution.

484. In an agreement between the DGB and BDA of 1954, the following basic terms were fixed:

> Thereby the DGB and the BDA as well as their member associations are obliged to take serious efforts to primarily conclude collective agreements by way of free negotiations. If those negotiations do not lead to a result it is the common conviction of DGB and BDA that state boards should not be involved in dispute resolution in collective bargaining, but only joint dispute resolution boards based on voluntary agreements. This, however, requires that the necessary preconditions for such a voluntary system are established by the contracting parties.

The same agreement contains a model of such an agreement on joint dispute resolution which is recommended to the member associations. At the same time, member associations were urged to conclude corresponding agreements as quickly as possible. They, of course, were free to modify the model agreement offered by DGB and BDA. It is interesting to note that the model agreement already offered two alternative types of joint dispute resolution boards: one only composed of the contracting parties, the other chaired by a neutral president.

485. Meanwhile agreements on the establishment of joint dispute resolution cover all areas of the private sector. It has to be stressed, however, that there is no homogeneous pattern; it differs from industry to industry and from sector to sector. In order to give an idea of the wide range of variety, three agreements on the establishment of joint dispute resolution are selected to illustrate this phenomenon: the agreement for the food industry, the agreement for the metal industry and the agreement for the chemical industry.

§2. The System of Voluntary Joint Dispute Resolution

I. Composition of Joint Dispute Resolution Boards

486. One basic difference refers to the structure of the joint dispute resolution boards. In the food industry, two instances are provided for: a board of first instance, and a board of appeal. The board of first instance consists exclusively of trade union representatives and representatives of employers' association, four from either side. Each group of representatives elects a chairperson. Those two chairpersons act as presidents, both having equal rights. The board of appeal, consisting also of four representatives of each side, is chaired by a neutral president. This president is selected from a list compiled by agreement of the two sides. The list contains three names. If the two parties cannot agree on whom to select within three days after the appeal has been initiated, the choice is made by lot.

487. The metal industry has a board for joint dispute resolution in general and a board for special dispute resolution during strike and/or lockout. The board for joint dispute resolution in general is composed of two representatives of each side, and two presidents of whom only one is entitled to vote. The two presidents are to be nominated by agreement of both sides. If no agreement is reached either side has the right to nominate one of the two presidents. The question of who has the right to vote, and who is prevented from voting, has again to be resolved by agreement. If agreement cannot be reached immediately, the issue has to be decided by lot. The composition of the special dispute resolution board is basically the same. There are, however, not only two but three representatives of both sides.

488. In the chemical industry, the board is composed of three representatives of each side. It is exclusively up to the board members to elect a president among themselves. The presidency, however, has to rotate between union representatives and employers' association representatives.

489. In spite of all these differences one common feature has to be underlined: there is always a distinction between regional boards for regional agreements and national boards for industry-wide agreements.

II. Initiation of the Joint Dispute Resolution Procedure

490. According to the agreement for the food industry, it is sufficient that one of the two parties takes the initiative to involve the joint dispute resolution board; the other side is obliged to participate. The initial step, however, has to meet some formal requirements (a written, detailed description of the issues at stake, etc.). If joint dispute resolution fails to be successful at the first attempt, either party may appeal to the board of appeal in the same way.

491. According to the agreement for the metal industry, joint dispute resolution is only available either before negotiations take place, or after negotiations have failed. Failure either has to be agreed upon by both sides or has to be declared in writing by one side to the other. After negotiations have failed both parties can jointly initiate the dispute resolution within two days. If this does not happen either party can unilaterally initiate joint dispute resolution within another day. Such a unilateral attempt of initiation, however, leads to joint dispute resolution only if the counterparty, within another period of two days, agrees to participate. In other words, neither side has the power to impose joint dispute resolution on the other. This in particular applies to the special joint dispute resolution during a strike or lockout, which can only be involved on mutual request of both sides.

492. Just like the agreement for the metal industry, the agreement for the chemical industry allows joint dispute resolution only on condition that negotiations have already taken place and that failure of negotiations has been declared by at least one party. There is, however, an exception which can only be understood in view of the fact that German law does not recognize a duty to bargain. That is why the agreement for the chemical industry allows access to joint dispute resolution if negotiations on a new collective agreement or on a new subject matter are refused by the counterparty. If within a period of thirty days no consensus on a date for the beginning of negotiations is reached, joint dispute resolution can be initiated. In the chemical industry, unlike the metal industry, either side has the right to impose joint dispute resolution on the other side unilaterally. The other side is obliged to participate.

III. Joint Dispute Resolution and Peace Obligation

493. In Germany, as has already been explained (*see* paragraph 458), industrial action on matters regulated in a collective agreement is prevented until the collective agreement expires or is terminated. In some agreements on joint dispute resolution, this relative peace obligation is extended beyond the termination of the collective agreement. The agreement for the food industry prevents industrial action for the duration of the joint dispute resolution procedure. While in the agreement for the metal industry a comparable provision is missing, strikes and lockouts are prohibited for a period of four weeks after termination of the former agreement. The furthest reaching prolongation of the peace obligation is laid down in the agreement for the chemical industry: strike ballots, strikes, or lockouts may only be initiated after unsuccessful termination of the joint dispute resolution procedure. In other words, in the chemical industry joint dispute resolution has to precede industrial conflict.

IV. Procedure and Effects of Joint Dispute Resolution

494. There is one feature common to all industries: none of the boards meets in public. Whereas in the food industry it is up to the board whether experts or persons who can give information are invited, this is different in the two other industries. In the chemical industry, each side can bring its own experts and/or persons who can give information. In the metal industry, the situation is a little more complicated. Both sides are free to make offers in this respect. However, if the board decides to hear an expert or another person of one side, the other side has the right to bring in an equivalent person.

495. According to all three agreements, the board has to hear the parties and to evaluate the documents, etc. presented by the parties. It is, however, mainly up to the board itself to develop specific procedural rules; the agreements contain no procedural rules. According to all three agreements, the boards primarily have to make an effort to stimulate an agreement between the parties instead of presenting a proposal themselves.

496. In the food industry, a recording clerk has to write minutes. These minutes, however, are to be kept secret. The recording clerk as well as the members of the board are obliged to keep the content of the proceedings secret. Even if the clauses in the other two agreements are not as detailed, the regulations are the same. In the food industry, the board decides with simple majority. No board member may abstain from voting. Normally it is up to the parties whether they accept the proposal of the board. However, there is one important exception: if, at least six of the eight board members have voted for the board decision it is binding on the parties. If the board of first instance does not reach a decision, or if its decision is not accepted by the parties, the board of appeal can be involved. For the decisions of the board of appeal almost the same as for the board of first instance applies: it is generally up to the parties whether or not they accept it, but if seven of the nine board members have voted for the decision it is binding on the parties. Parties may, however, also agree in advance that they will be bound by each of the board decisions. This agreement cannot be repealed later.

497. In the metal industry, there is a provision according to which the board has to propose a decision within a certain period. The proposal has to be in writing. Decisions are also made by simple majority. However, the decision is in no case binding. It is always up to the parties to accept the proposal or to refuse it. It is, however, possible to agree in advance that the decision of the board will be binding. This effect can be restricted to board decisions by qualified majority or to unanimous board decisions. There is no difference between the procedure in general joint dispute resolution and in joint dispute resolution during strikes and lockouts. In the chemical industry, board decisions based on the simple majority of votes are binding. Finally, it should be mentioned that the expenses of the joint dispute resolution machinery in all three industries are shared by the parties.

§3. The Function of Joint Dispute Resolution

498. Joint dispute resolution aims to serve two purposes: to promote an agreement and to prevent strikes and lockouts or, at least, to terminate strikes and lockouts. It has to be kept in mind that negotiations in different branches do not take place at the same time every year. Usually a big trade union is put in the role of a trendsetter, and the others more or less follow. Thereby a fairly homogeneous overall pattern is established. It is usually either IG Metall or ver.di, which plays the role of a trendsetter. In those trendsetting situations joint dispute resolution is customarily not used to prevent a strike. If a collective agreement cannot be reached easily, industrial action has to be taken in order to show each side's constituency that every attempt is being made to improve the results of bargaining. Nevertheless, once strikes (and lockouts) have started, joint dispute resolution is usually used to terminate the conflict. And here joint dispute resolution has proved to be a rather successful instrument, defining the pattern of the final outcome. This is due to quite a few factors. In both sectors, in the public services as well as in the metal industry, external mediators play a decisive role. They are usually people of high authority, capable of promoting compromises and especially of selling those compromises to the general public. As already indicated these bargaining rounds – especially the trendsetting bargaining round – enjoy high public attention. Public opinion is shaped by all kinds of statements: figures and evaluations published by different economic research institutes, figures and evaluations published by the advisory Economic Research Council which delivers an annual report on the economic perspectives to government, the view of government on the economic perspective and, of course, the views of the two counterparties of the bargaining table are published in the media. This mixture of information discussed daily in all media helps to create an understanding that an agreement should be fixed within a certain range. The mediator's main task is to convince parties to a collective agreement that his or her proposal meets this expectation. Hence, the support of the general public and the support of the constituency of each side is more or less guaranteed. In order to ensure this goal the media are involved once the joint dispute resolution board is making a proposal. The media's positive reaction, at least in principle, guarantees the approval of the proposal by the parties and their constituency. This analysis, of course, would be incomplete without mentioning that the general public and the media consider strikes (and lockouts) to be something which has to be stopped quickly. This attitude, of course, helps to support the attempts at joint dispute resolution.

499. Once the trendsetting bargaining round is terminated, bargaining in other branches starts. In this context, joint dispute resolution is quite often used to prevent a strike. In such a situation, there is not much need to go on strike for reasons of legitimacy. Hence, joint dispute resolution can serve a preventive function. It normally turns out to be sufficient to enable the party representatives at the bargaining table to sell the results to their respective constituencies.

500. As far as political mediation is concerned, it never works if politicians try to interfere directly in the conflict. This rather alienates parties to a collective agreement and is considered to be an attack on their constitutionally guaranteed autonomy in collective bargaining. However, to shape public opinion by spreading statements in the media is a very efficient strategy of political joint dispute resolution, which is used regularly.

501. On the whole the system of voluntary joint dispute resolution has turned out to be an instrument which helps a great deal to promote suitable compromises without infringing the autonomy in collective bargaining of the parties involved.[290] If from time to time individual politicians or legal scholars are pleading for a revival of dispute resolution by state authorities – especially for the public sector – this should not be taken too seriously. At least so far, such attempts have remained irrelevant and will probably remain irrelevant in the future.

502. Since, however, no third-party intervention is able to force the parties to reach an agreement, the only remaining instrument to put pressure on the parties is industrial action. This is why the legal regulation of industrial action is very important for the structure and functioning of the German system of collective bargaining.

§4. The Complementarity Between Collective Bargaining and Industrial Action

503. Even if in Germany virtually no statutory provisions refer to industrial action, this matter is nevertheless regulated in detail. Law on industrial action, however, is almost exclusively judge-made law. Since the legislator remained inactive, the labour courts, when dealing with cases of industrial conflict, had no choice but to develop legal rules on industrial action. The basis for these rules was and still is Article 9 paragraph 3 GG. As has already been mentioned, this article deals with freedom of association. Originally, the term 'industrial action' was not even included in this article. In connection with the so-called Emergency Acts (*Notstandsgesetze*) of 1968, Article 9 paragraph 3 GG has been amended to include a provision according to which certain emergency measures may not be directed against industrial action, declared by associations of either side, to safeguard and to improve working and economic conditions. It is perfectly clear that this amendment does not define the legal boundaries of industrial action. The only implication, which can be derived from this amendment, is the following: if industrial action is constitutionally protected against measures of emergency industrial action must be legal, at least to a certain extent.

504. In 1968, when Article 9 paragraph 3 GG was amended, the law on industrial action, as developed by the courts, was already well established. The basic and still leading decision of the Federal Labour Court originates from 1955.[291] In that decision, the basic structure of the law on strikes and the law on lockouts was outlined. Meanwhile, the court has refined and modified this original position in many decisions.

---

290. For more details *see* M. Weiss, *Dispute Resolution in German Employment and Labour Law*, Comp. Lab. L. & Pol'y J. 101 et seq (2013).
291. Large Senate (*see* para. 362), 28 Jan. 1955 – GS 1/54, *Arbeitsrechtliche Praxis*, No. 1 Art. 9 GG *Arbeitskampf*.

505. According to the established case law of the Federal Labour Court, industrial action has to be understood as being exclusively complementary to collective bargaining. To put it differently: industrial action is only allowed in so far as its purpose is the achievement of a collective agreement, and the achievement of aims that can be regulated in a collective agreement. Any industrial action for other purposes, whatever they may be, is understood to be illegal from the very outset. A very important implication of this interrelationship between collective bargaining and industrial conflict is the following: measures of industrial action may legally only be carried out by parties competent to conclude a collective agreement (*see* paragraphs 453 et seq.). For the employees' side, this means that a strike can only be called by a trade union. The right to strike, as derived from Article 9 paragraph 3 GG, is understood to be an extension of the collective freedom of association (*see* paragraphs 407 et seq.). The consequence of this understanding is that all strikes declared by a group of employees, which are not backed by the union, so-called wildcat strikes, are illegal, no matter what their goals may be and no matter how justified these goals are. Thus, it may be said that in Germany the right to strike is in fact a trade union right and not a right of the individual. Even if the unions are exclusively allowed to call out a strike, non-union members in establishments covered by a strike are entitled to participate in that strike. In fact, it is usual practice that non-union members participate in strikes.

§5. Factual Development of Industrial Conflict

506. Compared to most other industrialized countries, Germany has had very little industrial action until today. Statistics for the period between 1970 and 2018 are as follows.[292]

	Strikes[293]		*Lock-Outs*[294]		*Strikes and Lock-Outs*
Year	*Employees Participating (1,000)*	*Working Days Lost (1,000)*	*Employees Affected (1,000)*	*Working Days Lost (1,000)*	*Working Days Lost (1,000)*
1970	184	93	–		93
1971	334	2,599	202	1,884	4,483
1972	23	66	–		66
1973	179	545	–		545
1974	250	1,051	–		1,051

292. For the period 1970 to 2004: WSI (ed.), *Tarifhandbuch 2006, supra*, tab. 9.1.; and for the period 2005 to 2018: Bundesagentur für Arbeit (ed.), *Streikstatistik (Jahreszahlen), Deutschland 2018*, tab. 1.
293. Including simultaneous lockouts.
294. Disregarding simultaneous strikes.

	Strikes[293]		*Lock-Outs*[294]		*Strikes and Lock-Outs*
Year	*Employees Participating (1,000)*	*Working Days Lost (1,000)*	*Employees Affected (1,000)*	*Working Days Lost (1,000)*	*Working Days Lost (1,000)*
1975	36	69	–		69
1976	117	412	52	122	534
1977	34	24	–	–	24
1978	299	2,548	188	1,733	4,281
1979	63	405	15	78	483
1980	45	128	–	–	128
1981	253	58	–	–	58
1982	40	15	–	–	15
1983	94	41	–	–	41
1984	399	2,921	34	869	3,790
1985	78	35	–	–	35
1986	116	28	–	–	28
1987	155	33	–	–	33
1988	34	42	–	–	42
1989	44	100	–		100
1990	257	364	–	–	364
1991	208	154	–	–	154
1992	598	1,545	–	–	1,545
1993	133	593	0	0	593
1994	401	229	–	–	229
1995	183	247	–	–	247
1996	166	98	0	0	98
1997	13	52	0	0	52
1998	4	16	0	0	16
1999	199	79	0	0	79
2000	7	11	–	–	11
2001	61	27	0	0	27
2002	428	310	–	–	310
2003	57	163	–	–	163
2004	101	51	–	–	51
2005	17	19	–	–	19
2006	169	429	–	–	429

	Strikes[293]		*Lock-Outs*[294]		*Strikes and Lock-Outs*
Year	*Employees Participating (1,000)*	*Working Days Lost (1,000)*	*Employees Affected (1,000)*	*Working Days Lost (1,000)*	*Working Days Lost (1,000)*
2007	106	286	–	–	286
2008	154	132	–	–	132
2009	28	64	n.a.	3	67
2010	12	25	n.a.	1	26
2011	11	70	–	–	70
2012	22	86	–	–	86
2013	67	150	–	–	150
2014	58	155	–	–	155
2015	230	1,092	–	–	1,092
2016	215	209	n.a.	0	209
2017	61	129	n.a.	0	129
2018	682	571	–	–	571

507. These figures, however, are not very illuminating. They do not distinguish between the classical indefinite strike to exert pressure on the counterparty until a compromise is reached, and other strike tactics, especially the strategy of so-called new mobility (*neue Mobilität*) as developed in the late 1970s. This strategy replaces the big strike for an indefinite time by short strikes that, day by day, are shifted from one establishment to another within the region covered by the collective agreement to be reached. While the strike traditionally takes place after negotiations, these strikes are called during negotiations in order to exert pressure on the employers and to accelerate proceedings.[295] Their aim is to warn the employers that in the event of failure of negotiations the conflict will increase. That is why these strikes are called 'warning strikes'.

508. Strike activities principally occur in specific sectors. Two trade unions more or less dominate the scene: the *IG Metall* and ver.di. For example in 2007 and 2014, however, a very small but exclusive trade union – the Union of Locomotive Drivers (*Gewerkschaft der Lokführer* – GdL) – which is not a member of the DGB but of the dbb, attracted a lot of public attention by striking for several days. The same happened in recent years with strikes by trade unions of pilots and medical doctors employed in hospitals.

295. O. Ricken, *Münchener Handbuch zum Arbeitsrecht,* R. Richardi & O. Wlotzke ed., Verlag C.H. Beck, § 265 para. 5 and § 266 para. 6 et seq.

509. In the period between 1960 and 1984, there have been seven major lockouts: in 1963 and in 1971 in the metal industry in Baden-Württemberg, in 1976 in the printing industry nationwide, and in the metal industry in Baden-Württemberg, in 1978–1979 in the steel industry in North Rhine-Westphalia, and in 1984 in the metal industry in Hesse and Baden-Württemberg. It is important to stress that, since 1984, lockout factually no longer matters. This is mainly due to the new strike pattern. All former lockouts were carried out by the employers' associations in response to indefinite strikes called by unions. The strategic purpose of lockouts was to increase the number of employees affected by industrial action. Thereby the number of employees entitled to strike benefits from the strike-conducting union was increased. Thus, lockout has mainly to be understood as an instrument for putting financial pressure on the unions. For legal as well as for factual reasons it is very difficult to use the lockout to reach the same goal responding to warning strikes in the context of 'new mobility'. Lockout is, as already explained, only used in the private sector. It is a phenomenon almost exclusively confined to the metal and printing industries.

510. New technologies have led to a close interdependence of operations of different enterprises within an industry, and even between enterprises of different industries. Thus, for example, the automobile industry depends on all kinds of supplies produced by other enterprises. New technologies admit management without stockpiling of supplies so that costs can be reduced. The supplies, which are needed, are called for and delivered daily. This interdependence clearly shows that any industrial action in an enterprise of an ancillary supplier must quickly affect the enterprises depending on the supplies. This is why it is not surprising at all that unions more and more tend to call for strikes in enterprises of ancillary suppliers in order to gain the maximum effect with comparatively few employees on strike. This also explains the fact that an increasing number of employees although neither being on strike nor being locked out are nevertheless indirectly affected by industrial action. This is reflected by the figures referring to industrial action in the metal industry in 1984: 57,000 employees were on strike, 155,000 were locked out, and 195,000 were unable to work because their plants were indirectly affected. As will be shown later, the legal treatment of these employees indirectly affected by industrial action has become one of the main problems of the law on industrial conflict.

511. Even if wildcat strikes, in whatever form, are illegal they do happen from time to time, and especially in the territory of the former GDR they play an important role. Whether this will be a temporary or a permanent phenomenon is difficult to predict.

§6. Basic Features of Strike Law

I. The Normal Strike Pattern

512. In addition to the requirements implied by the complementarity of strike and collective bargaining as outlined previously (*see* paragraphs 503–504), the Federal Labour Court has established prerequisites for a legal strike. Originally, according to the decision of the Federal Labour Court of 1955, the most important criterion for the evaluation of the legality of a strike was the principle of 'social adequacy' (*Sozialadäquanz*).[296] This principle refers to what is generally accepted in society as being legal. However, since it is just this question which is controversial, the principle could not solve the problem and only served as a basis of legitimacy for the development of the real criteria. Since it became obvious rather early on that the principle of social adequacy was not helpful at all in resolving the problem, the Federal Labour Court in 1971 applied another principle as the governing principle of strike law, the principle of proportionality (*Verhältnismäßigkeitsprinzip*).[297] According to this principle, the use of industrial action must be suitable and necessary to reach the intended purpose, and may not be inappropriate to reach the intended purpose. In other words, the principle of proportionality tends to prevent the abuse of strikes. Nevertheless, the problem remains to draw the borderline between proper use and abuse. Due to the vagueness of this principle governing the strike law, the discretionary powers of the courts in specifying the law on industrial action are almost unlimited.

513. From the principle of proportionality the Federal Labour Court has mainly derived the following specific prerequisites:

- a strike must respect the peace obligation;
- a strike must be fair;
- a strike must be the last resort;
- a strike must be preceded by a secret ballot of union members.

514. According to the Federal Labour Court, not only would a strike violate the peace obligation (*see* paragraphs 458 et seq.), but any activity initiating a strike. In other words before the peace obligation has expired, no preparation for industrial action may legally be carried out.[298]

515. The requirement of a 'fair strike' implies that the strike is not intended to destroy the enterprises that are subject to the strike. However, the Federal Labour Court has indicated that the requirements of a fair strike may also be infringed if

296. Large Senate (*see* para. 362), 28 Jan. 1955 – GS 1/54, *Arbeitsrechtliche Praxis*, No. 1 Art. 9 GG *Arbeitskampf*.
297. Large Senate (*see* para. 362), 21 Apr. 1971 – GS 1/68, *Arbeitsrechtliche Praxis*, No. 43 Art. 9 GG *Arbeitskampf*.
298. Fundamentally Federal Labour Court, 31 Oct. 1958 – 1 AZR 632/57, *Arbeitsrechtliche Praxis*, No. 2 §1 TVG *Friedenspflicht*.

the strike reaches a certain level of intensity.[299] Even a particularly long strike could theoretically be regarded as unfair. In actual practice, however, this requirement does not matter, and it is very unlikely that this will change in future. The strike pattern, as carried out in Germany, generally seems to meet the requirement of a fair strike.

516. The most important of the above-mentioned limitations of the freedom of unions to strike, at least until recently, was the requirement that a strike may only be carried out as a last resort. This so-called principle of *ultima ratio* (*Ultima ratio-Prinzip*) implies that all means of negotiation must be exhausted and joint dispute resolution must be attempted before a strike can be called.[300] Of course, it is up to the trade union to declare that negotiations have failed if it seems that further negotiations would be useless. Seriousness and execution of negotiations is definitely not subject to judicial control. However, as will be shown in the following passage on warning strikes, the Federal Labour Court has changed the meaning of this principle and thereby almost abolished it.

II. The Warning Strike

517. Spontaneous short strikes in one or more enterprises, lasting not more than a few hours, were traditionally called and backed by unions during bargaining rounds. The extent of these activities was, however, marginal. There was no developed strategy for utilizing warning strikes as a means of pressure. They remained more or less isolated incidents within the bargaining rounds. Nevertheless, according to the rules established by the Federal Labour Court, it was perfectly clear that warning strikes could not be legal as they violated two requirements of a lawful strike: they were not preceded by a strike ballot, and they were not used as a last resort but during negotiations.

518. This traditional view changed when, in 1976, the Federal Labour Court had to decide on the lawfulness of a short strike of a few hours in one establishment, which remained the single action of this kind during all following bargaining rounds within the respective industry and region.[301] The court evidently wanted to legalize warning strikes for the very simple reason that in the past it had quite often turned out that those small 'warning strikes' led to a quicker compromise, thereby eliminating the necessity for a big strike. Thus, with regard to the principle of *ultima ratio*, the court stated:

> the principle is only meant for a strike of a longer duration or a strike of an indefinite period If the only intention of a strike is to promote negotiations by

299. Dec. of 21 Apr. 1971 – GS 1/68, *supra*.
300. Federal Labour Court of 21 Apr. 1971 – GS 1/68 in *Arbeitsrechtliche Praxis*, C. H. Beck, GG Art. 9 GG *Arbeitskampf* No. 43.
301. Federal Labour Court, 17 Dec. 1976 – 1 AZR 605/75, *Neue Juristische Wochenschrift*, 1977, p. 1079.

> demonstrating the counterpart the employees' readiness to go on strike, then this mild pressure, by way of a short warning strike, may be exerted before means of negotiation are exhausted.

In other words, the criterion of *ultima ratio*, and the requirements of a preceding strike ballot, only apply to a normal strike, but not to warning strikes. Since 1976 consequently it has become controversial where to draw the demarcation line between a 'normal strike' and 'warning strike', the latter being characterized by mild pressure and short duration.

519. In this situation – as has already been mentioned – the *IG Metall* and the former Union for the Printing Industry (*IG Druck*) developed the strategy of so-called new mobility. This strategy consisted in 'warning strikes' rotating within the area to be covered by a collective agreement and conducted during negotiations (*see* paragraph 516). The question was whether or not these local short strikes, based on a highly developed union strategy, fell under the category 'normal strike' or under the category 'warning strike'. In the first case they would have been unlawful since the above-mentioned prerequisites for a lawful strike (secret strike ballot, principle of *ultima ratio*) were not met, whereas they would have been lawful in the second case. For the unions, the strategy of 'new mobility' has a great advantage when compared to a 'normal strike'. Due to the obligation to pay strike benefits granted in the unions' standing rules, a normal strike has become very expensive for German trade unions. However, a strike along the lines of 'new mobility' is very cheap, as the union does not pay any benefits at all. Thus, for the unions it was crucial whether 'new mobility' was lawful. In 1984, the Federal Labour Court confirmed the legality of the strikes conducted in the framework of 'new mobility' by categorizing them as being warning strikes.[302] This decision provoked strong opposition from the employers' side. Employers and employers' associations questioned the constitutionality of this decision. They argued that the system of free collective bargaining, as guaranteed by the Constitution, would be endangered by the fact that, due to the lawfulness of the strategy of 'new mobility', the employees' side had become too powerful, thereby destroying the balanced negotiation procedure.

520. As already indicated, in the meantime the Federal Labour Court has changed its position fundamentally. It is no longer willing to differentiate between a 'normal strike' and a 'warning strike' as regards the applicability of the principle of *ultima ratio*.[303] Consequently, both types of strike come under this principle. At the same time, however, the court has significantly reduced the conditions to be fulfilled in order to meet the requirements of *ultima ratio*. This means in practical terms that it is now much easier to go on strike even at an early stage of negotiations. According to the Federal Labour Court, the principle of *ultima ratio*:

---

302. Federal Labour Court, 12 Sep. 1984 – 1 AZR 342/83, *Arbeitsrechtliche Praxis*, No. 81 Art. 9 GG *Arbeitskampf*; M. Weiss, 'Die neue Arbeitskampfrechtsprechung des BAG', *Kritische Vierteljahresschrift für Gesetzgebung und Rechtswissenschaft*, 1986, pp. 366 et seq.
303. Dec. of 21 Jun. 1988 – 1 AZR 651/86, *Arbeitsrechtliche Praxis*, No. 108 Art. 9 GG *Arbeitskampf*.

> does not require a formal declaration that collective bargaining has broken down as a prerequisite for initiating industrial action of any kind. That initiation rather reflects the free declaration of the party concerned, a declaration which is not open to review and, hence, solely determining, that it considers the possibilities of reaching an understanding without recourse to pressure to be exhausted. This means that there is no later determining point of time as from which industrial action other than warning strikes becomes lawful. There is a uniform point as from which a warning strike, like any other form of industrial action, is not excluded, even though collective bargaining continues … .

The implication of this new approach is simply that the principle of *ultima ratio* has more or less become meaningless.

521. As an implication of this new approach strike ballots can no longer be considered to be a precondition of a lawful strike. This, however, remains more or less irrelevant in practical terms. As far as a normal strike is at stake for which the union would have to pay strike benefits, the union is evidently interested in limiting the strike frequency. A strike ballot is a very efficient instrument to serve this goal. Therefore, the standing rules of trade unions require that a strike ballot which is held before a strike (other than a warning strike) can be called out. Hence, even if the law does not require a strike ballot, in practical terms it remains a precondition of a strike.

522. In 2015, the trade union IG Metall used the so-called twenty-four-hour strike[304] as a new means of industrial action for the first time. This represents a path between warning strike and enforcement strike. This is neither a short warning strike of only a few hours, nor is it a full-scale enforcement strike, but something in between, in order to be able to escalate the collective bargaining further. The twenty-four-hour strike can be seen as an extension of the warning strike. In contrast to the classic warning strike, however, the striking workers are to receive strike pay. During the strike phase, negotiations will continue, but the pressure will be increased significantly. If a company is paralysed for twenty-four hours, the production losses are much greater than if it were only a warning strike. Of course, this can also increase the damage significantly, especially in closely networked production processes.

III. The Solidarity Strike

523. For a long time it has been unclear to what extent a solidarity strike (*Unterstützungsstreik*) may be legal. In 1985, the Federal Labour Court clarified at least first basics.[305] Accordingly, the strike to be supported has to be lawful as regards

304. *Cf.* S. Greiner, *Das arbeitskampfrechtliche Verhältnismäßigkeitsprinzip*, Frankfurt a.M. 2018, pp. 21 et seq.
305. Dec. of 5 Mar. 1985 – 1 AZR 468/83, *Arbeitsrechtliche Praxis*, No. 85 Art. 9 GG *Arbeitskampf*; dec. of 12 Jan. 1988 – 1 AZR 219/86, *Arbeitsrechtliche Praxis*, No. 90 Art. 9 GG *Arbeitskampf*; *cf.*

the criteria outlined above. Moreover, the motive of the solidarity strike must be the benefit of those to be supported, and not the benefit of those striking due to solidarity. Only if the solidarity strikers do not intend to change their own working conditions do they not violate the peace obligation incumbent upon them. But even if these two conditions are fulfilled, a solidarity strike is lawful only in very exceptional cases, for example if an employer, whose establishment is the target of a solidarity strike, has previously given up neutrality by taking over production from employers involved in the industrial action. A similar exceptional case would occur if enterprises involved in industrial action, and enterprises that were targets of solidarity strikes, could from an economic point of view be regarded as an entity. These examples of exceptions, presented by the Federal Labour Court, showed that the court regarded solidarity strikes as almost always unlawful. The scope of the exceptional cases was much too narrow to allow solidarity strikes to become a relevant feature of industrial conflict in Germany.

524. The evaluation given just now has been approved by the fact that it took more than twenty years for the Federal Labour Court to have a chance to reconsider its ruling of 1985.[306] In fact, the court took a possibly far-reaching decision, which seems to indicate a general change of understanding of the right to strike. It started off by stating that, since the protection of Article 9 paragraph 3 GG was not limited to a certain core area of collective freedom (*see* paragraphs 407 et seq.), the right to support the lawful strike demands of others was generally granted, even if the trade union conducting the main strike to be supported was not identical with the trade union conducting the solidarity strike. In such a case, the peace obligation is usually not infringed because the peace obligation is binding only in respect of the matters already regulated in a collective agreement between the two parties (*see* paragraphs 458 et seq.). The central principle limiting the right to support a strike of others by a solidarity strike, however, is the principle of proportionality (*see* paragraph 512). (1) Accordingly, a solidarity strike must not be obviously unsuitable to support the main strike. In such a case, the solidarity strike does not serve the enforcement of collective bargaining demands. It is, however, up to the trade union calling out its members for a solidarity strike to decide whether a solidarity strike is suitable to support the main strike. The fact, however, that the employer confronted with a solidarity strike can neither fulfil the strike demands of the main strike nor persuade the employers' association to fulfil the strike demands, does not mean that the solidarity strike was generally unsuitable for increasing the pressure on the social counterparty and influencing the main strike. The solidarity shown by strikers may strengthen the readiness to strike of trade union members conducting the main strike, particularly if they belong to the same trade union. In addition, there are many informal links and ways to influence the main strike. (2) A solidarity strike must not be unnecessary to support the main strike. Again, however, it is up to the union to decide what is necessary. (3) Eventually, a solidarity strike should be proportional. Here again, the fundamental rights of the trade union resulting from

M. Weiss, 'Die neue Arbeitskampfrechtsprechung des BAG', *Kritische Vierteljahresschrift für Gesetzgebung und Rechtswissenschaft*, 1986, pp. 366 et seq.

306. Dec. of 19 Jun. 2007 – 1 AZR 396/06, *Arbeitsrechtliche Praxis*, No. 173 Art. 9 GG *Arbeitskampf*.

Article 9 paragraph 3 GG have to be balanced with the employers' rights granted in Articles 12 and 14 GG in every single case (*see* paragraph 413). Hence, a solidarity strike would be disproportionate if the main strike supported by the solidarity strike was illegal, e.g., because the main strike infringed the peace obligation. Besides, the following circumstances have to be taken into account. (a) Is the employer subject to the solidarity strike connected with the employer subject to the main strike, e.g., because both belong to the same group? (b) Has the employer subject to the solidarity strike already interfered with the main strike and hence infringed its neutrality? (c) How long and how intense is the solidarity strike? Does is have supportive character or does it actually replace the main strike? In the case at stake, the Federal Labour Court found that the solidarity strike was not unlawful because both employers – one publishing house, one printing company – belonged to the same group.

IV. The Political Strike

525. In Germany, the term 'political strike' is used for any strike intended to put pressure on the state administration or on the legislator, no matter whether or not working and economic conditions are concerned.[307] This, however, does not refer to strikes in which the state, in its function as an employer of employees in the public service, is a party to a collective agreement.

526. From what has been explained so far it follows that a political strike must always be illegal simply because it does not aim at achieving a collective agreement. However, the prevailing scholarly opinion even regards a political strike as unconstitutional.[308] As far as the protagonists in a political strike try to put Parliament under pressure, the constitutional guarantee of the freedom of the members of Parliament is supposed to be violated. But even if a strike is not directed against Parliament the strikers are considered to violate the Constitution since the citizens' power to elect the members of Parliament is regarded as also being a limitation of citizens' engagement in state legislation and administration. This very questionable opinion has been elaborated with reference to a strike which the unions had called out in order to influence Parliament in passing the BetrVG 1952. This strike was no general strike, but only a two-day strike in the newspaper industries. In the meantime, this view has been confirmed by *Land* labour courts. The Federal Labour Court has never discussed the matter further but simply referred to its original decision.

307. O. Ricken, *Münchener Handbuch zum Arbeitsrecht,* R. Richardi & O. Wlotzke ed., Verlag C.H. Beck, § 266 para. 10.
308. *Cf.* O. Ricken, *Münchener Handbuch zum Arbeitsrecht,* R. Richardi & O. Wlotzke ed., Verlag C.H. Beck, § 272 para. 39.

527. While the traditional opinion is still supported by many scholars, an increasing group of scholars is questioning this approach.[309] Meanwhile it has turned out that working and economic conditions are to a great extent regulated by state intervention. Collective bargaining is only one mechanism among others, which is becoming less important than state regulation. This is why the question arises whether Article 9 paragraph 3 GG does not, at least to a certain extent, also guarantee so-called political strikes. Of course, the guarantee would be limited to cases concerning working and economic conditions, and perhaps a distinction would have to be made between strikes for an indefinite period and strikes for a definite period.

V. Apprentices as Strikers

528. As already indicated above (*see* paragraph 147), according to Section 10 paragraph 2 BBiG, the rules and principles governing the labour contract apply to apprentices unless the BBiG itself expressly states otherwise, and unless the application of labour law would be incompatible with the nature and the aim of apprenticeship. The main controversy as regards this provision concerns the question of whether apprentices are entitled to strike. One opinion favours equal treatment with other employees for the simple reason that, in view of strike and collective bargaining, their situation is the same.[310] Another view denies this right arguing that the purpose of vocational training would exclude strike participation. In 1984 and 1985 the Federal Labour Court decided that apprentices enjoy the right to strike, at least for short strikes according to the pattern of 'new mobility'.[311] As far as strikes of longer duration are concerned, the question has still not been explicitly decided. However, strikes of a longer duration are rather the exception than the norm today. In addition, according to later decisions of the Federal Labour Court, the legal requirements for a warning strike and a 'normal' strike are the same today (*see* paragraph 513).

VI. Career Public Servants as Strikers

529. The fact that career public servants are denied the right to strike is one of the most controversial issues of German law on industrial action. The relationship between career public servants and the public employer is considered to be no employment relationship. Consequently, labour law does not apply at all (*see* paragraph 29). Specific rules of public law govern the relationship between career public servants and their employers. As a consequence, career public servants on the

309. *Cf.* W. Däubler, 'Das Grundrecht auf Streik – eine Skizze', *Zeitschrift für Arbeitsrecht*, 1973, pp. 200, 222, with further proofs.
310. O. Ricken, *Münchener Handbuch zum Arbeitsrecht, supra*, § 272 para. 20; M. Weiss & D. Marx, 'Das Streikrecht Auszubildender', *Arbeit und Recht*, 1982, pp. 329 et seq.
311. Dec. of 12 Sep. 1984 – 1 AZR 342/83, *Arbeitsrechtliche Praxis*, No. 81 Art. 9 GG *Arbeitskampf*; M. Weiss, *Kritische Vierteljahresschrift für Gesetzgebung und Rechtswissenschaft*, 1986, pp. 366 et seq.

one hand enjoy, especially as far as job security, social benefits and old age pensions after retirement are concerned, significant privileges compared to employees. On the other hand, the duty of loyalty towards the state that career public servants have to comply with is much more extensive than that resulting from an employment relationship. This implies that the employer's right to issue instructions is more far-reaching than in an employment relationship. Wages and other working conditions are fixed by the legislator. There is no collective bargaining whatsoever.

530. This distinction between career public servants and regular employees in the public sector can only be explained historically. It dates back to the German Reich before the First World War. Already during the Weimar era, it was very controversial whether this structure should be maintained. After the Second World War there was and still is an ongoing debate about whether or not the structure of employment relationships in the public sector, and mainly in the public service, should not be subject to fundamental reform aiming at a structure abandoning this specific type of career public servant relationship. Up until now, it has been mainly due to the strong lobby of career public servants' associations that this debate remained without any results.

531. A 'career public servant' cannot be defined in functional terms. Career public servants are found in the public administration as well as – still on a small scale – in the postal services or in the railway services. Although postal and railway services were privatized in 1994, and although legal entities of civil law generally cannot employ career public servants, the legislator factually allowed privatized post and railway enterprises to employ career public servants. Career public servants may be schoolteachers, university professors, members of the police or of the fire brigades, administrators of the public health service or of the public energy service, etc. Even within specific institutions of the public sector it is almost impossible to identify a career public servant by the function performed. Quite often it is merely accidental whether a specific function is performed by a career public servant or by a normal employee. The postman distributing letters, the secretary in an administrative office in a ministry, the driver of a railway engine may all be career public servants or normal employees, etc. Examples to show how arbitrary the distinction has become could be given on a never-ending scale. This is the background to be kept in mind when discussing the exclusion of career public servants from the right to strike. The similarity between the real employment situation of career public servants and that of other employees makes it more and more difficult to perceive the justification for the structural difference.

532. During the last few years in quite a few areas, career public servants have indicated that they are no longer willing to take this exclusion for granted. Mainly schoolteachers, in spite of being career public servants, have participated in strike-like activities claiming better working conditions.

533. There is no statute denying career public servants the right to strike. The ban on strike of career public servants is rather derived from general rules laid down in the Constitution and from general principles governing the law of career public servants. This position is fully backed by the decisions of the competent Federal Administrative Court (*Bundesverwaltungsgericht*) and, to a large extent, by scholars.[312] The main reasons to deny career public servants the right to strike are the following. Since the working conditions of career public servants are fixed by legislation, any strike for better working conditions would necessarily have to be directed against Parliament; according to German law, such a strike, however, would be an illegal political strike (*see* paragraphs 525–527). Furthermore, a career public servant's right to strike is considered to be incompatible with the duty to loyalty as stated in Article 33 paragraph 4 GG. In Article 33 paragraph 5 GG, the traditional principles governing the status of career public servants are guaranteed; the exclusion of the right to strike is considered to be part of those principles. Finally, the denial of the right to strike is regarded as a proper compensation for the privileges career public servants enjoy. These are only the most prominent examples of a long list of reasons justifying career public servants' exclusion from the right to strike.

534. It well may be doubted whether the exclusion of career public servants from the right to strike irrespective of their specific functions is compatible with Article 6 No. 4 of the European Social Charter, or with ILO Conventions Nos 87 and 98, all ratified by Germany. Evidently, those international regulations have a functionally oriented and much more confined perspective of what groups of employees may be excluded. In order to avoid further trouble with international law, Germany has renounced ratifying ILO Conventions Nos 151 and 154.

535. In 2014, the Federal Administrative Court had to decide whether civil servant teachers were allowed to strike. The court referred to the case law of the European Court of Human Rights (ECtHR). The ECtHR had ruled in landmark judgments on Article 11 European Convention on Human Rights (ECHR) that it could be compatible with the freedom of association to prohibit strikes by members of the civil service exercising sovereign authority on behalf of the state. In this context, the ECtHR understands the term members of the public administration within the meaning of Article 11 paragraph 2 sentence 2 ECHR not in terms of status but in terms of function (task).[313] The Federal Administrative Court came to the conclusion that teachers at German public schools are not members of the state administration within the meaning of Article 11 paragraph 2 sentence 2 ECHR because they do not exercise genuine sovereign functions. It stated that it was the task of the legislator to resolve this conflict between the status-related ban on strikes under Article 33 paragraph 5 of the GG and the function-related guarantees under Article 11 of the ECHR and to bring about a balance by means of practical concordance.[314] A constitutional complaint was lodged against this decision. In June 2018, however,

312. Federal Administrative Court, 3 Dec. 1980 – 1 D 86/79, *Neue Juristische Wochenschrift*, 1981, p. 1283.
313. EctHR, 12 Nov. 2008 – No. 34503/97 (Demir and Baykara); EctHR, 21 Apr. 2009 – No. 68959/01 (Enerji Yapi-Yol Sen).
314. Federal Administrative Court, 27 Feb. 2014 – 2 C 1/13, *BVerwGE 149*, 117.

the Federal Constitutional Court ruled: 'The ban on strikes by civil servants in Germany is in line with the principle that the Basic Law should be compatible with international law and in particular with the guarantees of the European Convention on Human Rights'.[315] A complaint was subsequently lodged before the ECtHR to clarify whether the ban on strikes in German law is compatible with Article 11 ECHR. The complaint is still pending.[316]

VII. New Forms of Industrial Action Beyond the Strike

536. Trade unions are not limited to the classic form of strike – in its variations – in order to build up pressure on the employer in collective bargaining. The principle of freedom to choose the means of industrial action makes it possible to use other means of industrial action to enforce collective bargaining demands.[317]

537. In 2009, the Federal Labour Court had to decide whether a strike-accompanying action such as a flash mob is also permissible.[318] The background was a flash mob action in a retail company organized by the trade union ver.di. In this action, many people were shopping for low-value items in a coordinated manner at the same time, in order to block the checkout area for a longer period of time, and others were filling their shopping trolleys at the same time, in order to leave them at the checkout or elsewhere in the branch offices. The trade union flash mob action also involved people who were not members of the trade union or who were employees of the company. The Federal Labour Court ruled that such a flash mob action, which is used in a publicly accessible company to cause a short-term and surprising disruption of operational processes in order to exert pressure on the employer to enforce collective bargaining targets, is not generally inadmissible. However, the employer must have effective means of defence at its disposal. In addition, proportionality must be maintained. The Federal Constitutional Court had later endorsed this assessment.[319]

§7. Basic Features of the Law on Lock-Out

I. The Notion of Equal Bargaining Power: From a Formalistic to a Substantive Concept

538. Since the early years of the FRG, the law on lockout has undergone substantial changes. The approach originally developed by the Federal Labour Court in

315. Federal Constitutional Court, 12 Jun. 2018 – 2 BvR 1738/12, 2 BvR 1395/13, 2 BvR 1068/14, 2 BvR 646/15, *BVerfGE 148*, 296.
316. Application No. 59433/18.
317. *Cf.* S. Greiner, *Das arbeitskampfrechtliche Verhältnismäßigkeitsprinzip*, Frankfurt/Main 2018, pp. 50 et seq.
318. Federal Labour Court, 22 Sep. 2009 – 1 AZR 972/08, *BAGE 132*, 140.
319. Federal Constitutional Court, 26 Mar. 2014 – 1 BvR 3185/09, *Neue Juristische Wochenschrift 2014*, pp. 1874 et seq.

its fundamental decision of 1955 was very formalistic: both sides, trade unions and employers' (associations) had to be treated equally; consequently both sides had to have equally powerful means of industrial action.[320] According to this conception of so-called parity of weapons (*Waffengleichheit*), lockout was regarded as being lawful under the same conditions as strikes. The legal basis for both was Article 9 paragraph 3 GG.

539. However, although the Federal Labour Court in its decision of 1955 pretended to treat both sides equally, it drew a very important distinction: lockout, if used as a weapon of defence against a strike, was supposed to have stronger legal effects in order to be efficient. Thus, while a strike only suspends the employment contract, a lockout was supposed to terminate the contract. This part of the decision of the Federal Labour Court was heavily criticized. In 1971, the Federal Labour Court finally revised its decision by stating that a lockout usually has a mere suspending effect.[321] Only in very exceptional cases may a lockout terminate the contract, for example during lengthy and particularly heated industrial conflicts and as a weapon against an illegal strike. However, it should be stressed that since 1971 the terminating effect of lockouts has actually no longer been relevant.

540. In the 1970s, it was not the effect but the legality of lockouts that was subject to controversy. This was mainly due to the fact that at that time the number of employees affected by industrial action was increased enormously by lockouts (*see* paragraph 506). The unions, which had to pay strike benefits to their members being locked out, claimed that lockouts should be considered illegal because they tended to destroy the union's bargaining power. In 1980, the Federal Labour Court finally took a position in this controversy.[322] The court gave up its approach of formalistic equal treatment of strike and lockout as developed in 1955. Instead, it favoured a substantive approach, focusing on the so-called balance of bargaining power (*Arbeitskampfparität*).

541. According to this concept, the strike is understood to be an indispensable lever in collective bargaining. Collective bargaining would be nothing but 'collective begging' if trade unions did not have the right to strike.[323] However, what is true for a strike is not in the same way true for a lockout. A lockout is generally not required to keep the balance of bargaining power. Hence, a lockout is generally not legal. However, there is an exception: if only a small proportion of employees in the region covered by the collective agreement are on strike, competition among employers may be affected and, as a result, solidarity among employers may be endangered. Consequently, in such a case lockouts are to be permitted.

---

320. Large Senate (*see* para. 362), 28 Jan. 1955 – GS 1/54, *Arbeitsrechtliche Praxis*, Art. 9 GG *Arbeitskampf* No. 1.
321. Large Senate (*see* para. 362), 21 Apr. 1971 – GS 1/68, *supra*.
322. Dec. of 10 Jun. 1980 – 1 AZR 168/79 and 1 AZR 822/79, *Arbeitsrechtliche Praxis*, Nos 64 and 65 Art. 9 GG *Arbeitskampf*.
323. *Cf.* Federal Labour Court, 10 Jun. 1980 – 1 AZR 822/79, *BAGE 33*, 140.

542. Following this logic, two important questions had to be solved. What is meant by 'such a small proportion of employees within the region', and what volume of lockout is legally permitted? Evidently, the answer is not given in Article 9 paragraph 3 GG. Thus, the court had no choice but to develop a model of its own. Accordingly, the top limit for lockouts is 50% of the employees in the area covered by a collective agreement. If 50% or more than 50% of the employees within the area are already on strike no further lockout is permitted because then so many enterprises are affected that the solidarity among employers is not endangered. If up to 25% of the employees within a bargaining area are on strike employers may react by locking out another 25%. If more than 25%, but less than 50% of the employees within a bargaining area, are on strike employers may lockout up to 50%. The limits chosen are rather arbitrary and can only be explained by taking into consideration the case in which they have been developed. In 1978 in the metal industry out of 500,000 employees, only 90,000 went on strike. As a reaction, the employers' association locked out another 120,000. Thus, finally 210,000 employees were engaged in strikes or affected by lockouts. Although such a huge number of employees had been locked out, the Federal Labour Court, after having developed the rules explained above, was able to consider the lockout as being lawful. After all, the number of those being locked out remained under 25%. The Federal Constitutional Court has finally confirmed the decision of the Federal Labour Court.[324]

543. The main effect of this decision is the fact that unions are now able to calculate in advance the possible maximum number of employees being locked out. Even though there is no doubt that the position of the Federal Labour Court developed in 1980 has limited the legal scope of lockout, it should be borne in mind that, according to the normal strike pattern as conducted in Germany, lockout has always remained possible. Unions would never voluntarily ask 50% or more of the employees of a region to go on strike. On the contrary, they would rather tend to keep the number of strikers as small as possible in order to limit their financial burden.

544. According to the Federal Labour Court, it is forbidden to treat non-union members different from union members in situations of lockout. In some cases, employers only locked out union members, keeping the non-union members and paying them remuneration. In other cases, both union and non-union members were locked out, but employers voluntarily paid compensation for lost wages to non-union members. All these strategies, however, are considered to be a violation of the collective freedom of association (*see* paragraphs 407 et seq.) since they aim at reducing the attractiveness of union membership.[325]

545. It should be stressed that lockout is only discussed, and in practice only plays a role, as an instrument of defence against a strike. The so-called offensive

324. Dec. of 26 Jun. 1991 – 1 BvR 601/92, *Arbeitsrechtliche Praxis*, No. 117 Art. 9 GG *Arbeitskampf*.
325. Dec. of 10 Jun. 1980 – 1 AZR 331/79, *Arbeitsrechtliche Praxis*, No. 66 Art. 9 GG *Arbeitskampf*; M. Weiss, 'Die neue Arbeitskampfrechtsprechung des BAG', *Kritische Vierteljahresschrift für Gesetzgebung und Rechtswissenschaft*, 1986, pp. 366 et seq.

lockout is merely of theoretical interest. There can, however, be no doubt that such a lockout would be incompatible with the reasoning of the Federal Labour Court in its decision of 1980.

II. Assignment of Non-strikers as an Instrument of Defence

546. Employers may try to transfer the work to be done by strikers to employees who are not on strike, either to employees within the same establishment or enterprise, or to employees of other enterprises. According to the Federal Labour Court employees are not obliged to perform such work thus acting as strike breakers (blacklegs).[326] Solidarity among employees prevents such a duty. In other words, employers may have recourse to the indicated strategy only on condition that non-striking employees voluntarily agree to do the work previously performed by strikers.

547. In the past, temporary workers were increasingly used as strike breakers. Under the previous legal situation, temporary workers were not obliged to work for a hirer if the latter was directly affected by an industrial dispute. However, in some cases, temporary workers were put under massive pressure to act as strike breakers. It has become apparent that the right to refuse performance is not sufficient due to the special situation of temporary workers. The ban on the use of temporary workers in industrial disputes under collective bargaining agreements could not be effectively enforced in practice either.[327] For this reason, an explicit prohibition was included in §11 AÜG with effect from April 2017 to use temporary workers if the respective company is directly affected by an industrial dispute. However, this is not to be understood as a general prohibition of employment and does not apply if the hirer ensures that temporary workers do not take over activities that were previously performed by employees who are on strike. In addition, however, the temporary worker is still generally not obliged to work for a hirer if the hirer is directly affected by an industrial dispute.

548. In the public sector, the strategy of using non-striking personnel to undermine the effect of a strike has been a very controversial issue for two reasons. First, according to the rules developed by the Federal Labour Court, a lockout would be legally impossible since in the public sector competitiveness does not matter. Second, there is a group of persons who are not allowed to strike and who therefore are available to perform the work normally done by the strikers, i.e., career public servants (*see* paragraphs 29, 78, 428). According to recent decisions of the Federal Administrative Court and the Federal Labour Court, the assignment of career public servants as strike breakers (blacklegs), effectively demonstrated in defence against

326. Dec. of 22 Mar. 1994 – 1 AZR 622/93, *Arbeitsrechtliche Praxis*, No. 130 Art. 9 GG *Arbeitskampf*.
327. *Cf* Bundestag document (*Bundestagesdrucksache*) 18/9232, p. 27.

a strike in the Post Office, was held to be legal.[328] According to these decisions, the public employer was supposed to have the power to assign career public servants even for work below their respective usual standard of work. Career public servants were not entitled to refuse to perform such work. In particular, the Federal Labour Court underlined that the possibility of assigning career public servants as strike breakers should be seen as a substitute means of defence for non-available lock-outs. The requirement of a balance of bargaining power, as developed in the decisions on lockouts, was therefore deemed to be met. In 1993 the Federal Constitutional Court rejected this position.[329] Whereas before all courts involved in the matter had considered the assignment of career public servants as strike breakers to be lawful, it has been banned since then. The main argument of the Federal Constitutional Court is very simple: the powers of the state towards career public servants cannot be determined by courts but only by Parliament. This means that the assignment of public servants as strike breakers is unlawful as long as it is not explicitly allowed and regulated by an Act of Parliament. It can be predicted that such an Act will never be passed. This means that the assignment of career public servants as strike breakers will also be outlawed in future.

§8. Legal Effects of Strikes and Lock-Outs

I. The Individual Contract of Employment

549. During strikes and lockouts the employment contract continues. A legal strike and a lawful lockout only suspend the employment contract of those who are legally participating in the strike.[330] This suspension refers to the main duties of the parties. Ancillary duties remain as far as they focus on the continuity of the employment relationship.

550. Since strikers and those who are locked out lose their right to remuneration for the duration of the strike or lockout respectively, it is important to mention that those who are organized in the union concerned are entitled to strike benefits from the union. Non-union members do not receive anything. As a general rule, the strike benefit paid by unions amounts to about two-thirds of net wages.

551. Employees participating in an illegal strike are contravening the employment contract. This may have two consequences: they may have to pay damages

328. Federal Administrative Court, 10 May 1984 – 2 C 18.82, *Arbeitsrechtliche Praxis*, No. 87 Art. 9 GG *Arbeitskampf*; Federal Labour Court, 10 Sep. 1985 – 1 AZR 262/84, *Arbeitsrechtliche Praxis*, No. 86 Art. 9 GG *Arbeitskampf*.
329. Federal Constitutional Court, 3 Mar. 1993 – 1 BvR 1213/85, *Arbeitsrechtliche Praxis*, No. 126 Art. 9 GG *Arbeitskampf*.
330. Dec. of 10 Jun. 1980 – 1 AZR 168/79 and 1 AZR 822/79, *Arbeitsrechtliche Praxis*, Nos 64 and 65 Art. 9 GG *Arbeitskampf*.

and/or they may be dismissed.[331] As far as dismissal is concerned, an ordinary dismissal for reasons concerning the behaviour of the employee and even, under certain circumstances, an extraordinary dismissal may be lawful. If an illegal strike has been called by a trade union, however, employees may rely upon the lawfulness of the strike. Consequently, in such cases the danger of dismissal is almost excluded. Only in very rare cases may evaluation of the circumstances in a particular case lead to the result that a dismissal is considered to be justified. This, however, is different in cases of wildcat strikes, in which no union is involved. However, even participation in wildcat strikes is not always a reason for dismissal. It, on the one hand, depends on the question of how far the employer himself or herself has provoked the wildcat strike. On the other hand, the degree of participation plays a role, at least in general. Only those who have initiated the wildcat strike, but not those who have only participated without holding any specific position, may be dismissed.[332] It should be stressed that, in spite of the law, in most cases in which employees have been participating in illegal strikes they do not have to face sanctions. However, the mere possibility of those sanctions remains an effective threat.

II. Tort Liability

552. If a strike is illegal, a trade union can be made liable for damages caused by strike. Given the financial circumstances of the unions, this is not merely a theoretical threat. In 1970, the assets of the sixteen DGB unions were estimated at DM 1,434 billion, and that of the DAG at DM 100 million. Figures that are more recent are not available. A few unions have agreed upon liability limits with employers' associations. The joint dispute resolution agreement between the Federal Metal Employers' Association (*Gesamtmetall*) and the Metal Workers' Union (*IG Metall*), to quote one example, set a limit of DM 1 million. Up to the present, employers have only called upon the courts to state the unions' liability for damages, but have not raised actions for performance. One reason for this restraint might be the reluctance to publish economic data in order to prove the damage caused; another could be fear of negative effects, which the execution of such a judgment would have on the relations between employers' associations and trade unions.

553. A trade union is liable to pay damages where local organizers of the strike cause damage by excessive activities not covered by the right to strike. The union has a far-reaching obligation to ensure that no excessive activities take place.

331. Federal Labour Court, 21 Oct. 1969 – 1 AZR 93/68, *Arbeitsrechtliche Praxis*, No. 41 Art. 9 GG *Arbeitskampf*; 14 Feb. 1978 – 1 AZR 103/76, *Arbeitsrechtliche Praxis*, No. 59 Art. 9 GG *Arbeitskampf*.

332. Federal Labour Court, 14 Feb. 1978 – 1 AZR 103/76, *supra*.

§9. The Duty to Uphold Essential Supplies and Services

554. The principle of proportionality is the only available criterion of the legality of strikes and lockouts in essential services. According to this principle, the interests of third persons as well as the interests of the population in general may not be affected in a disproportionate way. Or, as the Federal Labour Court put it in a leading decision of 1971:

> In our society, where everything is connected and interlinked, strikes and lockouts not only affect those participating in industrial action but also those not participating as well as third persons and the public in general. Therefore, industrial action has to meet the requirement of proportionality. This means that economic conditions have to be taken into consideration, and that public interest may not be violated in an evident manner.[333]

555. This vague and unspecific formula is, of course, unable to provide exact criteria for specific cases. It is rather a source of speculation of what could be the implication for specific areas and situations. There is a widespread consensus, however, that this formula does not imply that strikes in any specific area where essential services are provided would be completely prohibited. According to the by-far prevailing view among labour law scholars, the consequence of the principle of proportionality is the establishment of emergency services, otherwise the strike is considered to be illegal.[334] There is also a widespread consensus that the life, health and safety of people have to remain unaffected: they always have priority over the right to strike. All these limitations of the right to strike apply equally to the public and to the private sector, no matter whether a plant is a public entity or privately owned.

556. While it is relatively easy to reach a consensus on the abstract level, this is different as regards implications that are more concrete. Of course, a strike of physicians or nurses in a hospital has to be performed in a way not affecting the health and life of their patients. Of course, a strike in a pharmaceutical plant must not lead to the effect that no medicaments are available to those who need them. Of course, water, gas and electricity cannot be cut off in a way endangering health and life of people. Of course, a strike of garbage collectors has to be performed in a way not affecting health and life of the population. There is even a consensus that services have to be provided beyond health, life and safety: transport, postal services, information by media, just to mention some examples. This consensus, however, does not solve the problem. The question remains to what extent these services are to be provided in specific situations. Among labour law scholars, quite a few attempts have been made to specify this extent for specific essential services. The result of these attempts, however, is nothing other than a list of different suggestions of what could possibly be the specific impact of the general formula. Some favour arrangements coming pretty close to a strike prohibition, others prefer a more limited

333. Dec. of 21 Apr. 1971 – GS 1/68, *supra*.

334. *Cf.* W. Linsenmaier, *Erfurter Kommentar zum Arbeitsrecht,* ed. R. Müller-Glöge et al, 2020, Verlag C.H. Beck, Art. 9 GG paras 134, 168.

restriction on strike activities. Whether or not in a real conflict the courts would follow those suggestions, remains an open question.

557. So far the Federal Labour Court has only clarified that emergency services may not be defined and organized by the employer alone, but in cooperation with trade unions. What would have to be done in a case of non-agreement is still fairly unclear. There is a debate whether the labour courts could replace such an agreement by an injunction then: in the absence of real case material, however, nobody can give a clear answer. The list of open questions is long. Who chooses the employees for emergency services – trade unions, the employer, employers' associations or they all together in a sort of concerted action? Who is entitled to supervise and give directives to the emergency employees – the employer, or trade unions, or all together? Who is liable if an emergency employee causes damages – the employee or the union behind him? The list of open questions of this kind can be prolonged almost endlessly. In view of this legal uncertainty, it sounds like a miracle, but actual conflicts on those issues almost never seem to arise or at least almost never reach court level. As indicated at the beginning of this monograph, this is due to the actors involved. Trade unions do everything to act in a responsible way in helping to provide emergency services. For them, it is a question of maintaining legitimacy and authority within society. This self-restraint seems to be much more effective than any law possibly could be.

558. In the context of strikes in essential services, one area has gained specific attention: the media. In view of the fact that freedom of information, freedom of expression and freedom of the press are important constitutional guarantees, the question arose whether or not strikes in newspaper companies, in radio and television institutions could be legal at all. After a rather heated controversy, a broad consensus has been reached that no special rules apply to this area.[335] As everywhere else, the principle of proportionality requires that emergency services are provided whose extent again is as unclear as the extent of emergency services in any other area. Due to the fact that the *IG Druck* has merged with two other unions to form the *IG Medien*, now integrated into ver.di, this consensus has meanwhile been contested by some scholars.[336] In order to reopen the discussion they emphasize the danger of a strike paralysing all media. Now the question whether or not there should not be at least a prohibition of a strike affecting printed and electronic media at the same time is put more seriously than before. However, no result can be reported yet. It may, however, be predicted that no significant change will happen.

---

335. *Cf.* M. Weiss, 'Sonderarbeitskampfrecht der Presse?', *Arbeit und Recht*, 1984, pp. 97 et seq.
336. H. Brox & B. Rüthers, *Arbeitskampfrecht* (2nd edn 1982), para. 96.

§10. The Position of Employees in Enterprises Indirectly Affected by Industrial Action

I. The Employer's Duty to Pay Remuneration

559. As previously explained (*see* paragraph 268) the so-called theory of spheres meant that employees in enterprises indirectly affected by industrial action lost their right to remuneration if they could no longer be employed due to industrial action. Since a strike was considered to be a cause originating from the employees' sphere, and since all employees were considered to be a coherent entity, unified by solidarity, employees indirectly affected by a strike had to bear the risk of losing remuneration. Even if the scope of industrial action was extended by a lockout the result remained the same: the strike was the first cause, without a strike there would have been no lockout, therefore the theory of spheres was also applied to this case.

560. In 1980, the Federal Labour Court renounced the theory of spheres.[337] Accordingly, any proper solution to the problem had to be in accordance with the legal rules on industrial conflict. Whereas so far the focus had been on the cause of the disturbance of work performance, the focus was now shifted to the effects of payment of remuneration. The question to answer now is whether payment of remuneration or non-payment of remuneration will influence the balance of bargaining power between the parties to an industrial conflict so that this balance is endangered. Evidently, this problem cannot be solved on an empirical basis. The labour courts thus have almost unlimited discretionary power to establish rules. According to the Federal Labour Court, employees belonging to the industry the industrial conflict refers to lose their right to remuneration, no matter whether or not they belong to the regional area covered by the intended collective agreement. If they do not belong to the industry the industrial conflict refers to, they, at least in principle, retain their right to remuneration. However, there is again an exception: if there is a close economic interrelationship between the enterprises in industrial conflict and those being indirectly affected they lose their right to remuneration. The result is almost the same as it was according to the former theory of spheres. Evidently the danger that employers indirectly affected, which would have to pay remuneration, could exert pressure on employers involved in industrial conflict in order to terminate the conflict, was given more weight than the danger that employees indirectly affected and remaining without remuneration could equally exert pressure on the union to terminate the conflict.

II. The Role of the Works Council

561. As previously mentioned short-time work can only be introduced with the consent of the works council (*see* paragraph 228). Short time in this sense includes temporary reduction of the normal working hours, whether it is daily or weekly

337. Dec. of 22 Dec. 1980 – 1 ABR 2/79 and 1 ABR 76/79, *Arbeitsrechtliche Praxis*, Nos 70 and 71 Art. 9 GG *Arbeitskampf*.

working hours that are shortened, and whether it is completely stopped for a certain time. Thus, there is no doubt that cases in which, due to industrial conflict, work cannot be carried out elsewhere are covered by this notion. Therefore, the question arises whether the agreement of the works council is also required in such a case. This question has become very controversial due to the fact that it is quite often doubtful whether it is really necessary to stop work, and if so, how far and to what extent (in time and in scope) it is necessary. Evidently, it makes a difference whether the employer has the power to decide alone, or whether his or her decision is subject to control of the works council, and possibly subject to changes imposed by the arbitration committee. In 1980, the Federal Labour Court solved the problem in a very Solomonic mode: 'Whether or not work shall be stopped is exclusively up to the employer to decide, but the modalities of the work stoppage must be agreed by the works council.'[338] Thus the works council is, at least to a certain extent, empowered to control the employer's decision, since in fact the two questions of whether to stop work, and how to do it, are closely related.[339]

III. The Neutrality of the State and the Duty of the Employment Agency to Pay Unemployment Benefits

562. According to SGB III, unemployment benefit is not only paid in case of unemployment in its strict sense, but also to employees affected by short-time work. Thus, the question arises of how far employees affected by industrial conflict and thereby losing their right to remuneration are entitled to these benefits. Today Section 160 SGB III answers this question.

563. Before explaining the content of Section 160 SGB III, it should be stressed that, according to the standing rules of German trade unions, employees who have lost their right to remuneration because work can no longer be performed in indirectly affected establishments do not receive trade union strike benefits. Thus, if they are not entitled to unemployment benefit, the only way to finance their living is social assistance. But first of all, social assistance benefits are very low, and second and more important, social assistance benefits are only paid to persons who can prove that they have no financial resources whatsoever. The latter condition would be fulfilled only by a very small proportion of the respective employees. Finally, it should be mentioned that, even if the conditions can be fulfilled, there is still quite often a very strong psychological barrier to applying for social assistance. In short, if no unemployment benefit is paid it is inevitable that a trade union, which has called out for strike, is under pressure from the indirectly affected employees, either to stop industrial conflict or to pay them strike benefit (if they are union members). This clearly shows that the ability of unions to call a strike depends very much on how this question is regulated.

338. Dec. of 22 Dec. 1980 – 1 ABR 2/79 and 1 ABR 76/79, *supra*.
339. *Cf.* co-determination in companies indirectly affected by industrial action D. Klocke, *Das BetrVG und der Arbeitskampf im Betrieb*, Frankfurt/Main 2019, p. 86.

564. Section 160 SGB III is based on the idea that the state should be neutral in relation to parties to an industrial conflict. Three implications are derived from this idea which always were and still are uncontested: (1) those on strike or being locked out never receive unemployment benefit; (2) those indirectly affected being employed in the industry involved in the conflict, and belonging to the region covered by the intended collective agreement never receive unemployment benefit; (3) those indirectly affected but not belonging to the industry involved in the conflict always receive unemployment benefit. Thus, there is only one group whose treatment has become controversial: those indirectly affected and being employed in the industry involved in the conflict, but not belonging to the region covered by the intended collective agreement.

565. A former version of Section 116 of the Act on Employment Promotion (*Arbeitsförderungsgesetz* – AFG), later on amended first as Section 146 SGB III and later as Section 160 SGB III, was specified by the so-called Decree on Neutrality (*Neutralitätsanordnung*) of 1973. Accordingly, the persons belonging to this latter group were in principle entitled to unemployment benefit. However, there was a very important exception. The right to unemployment benefits was excluded if the bargaining claims of the union in the region the employee belonged to, were 'equal in kind and in extent' to the claims of the union in the region where the industrial conflict was taking place. The idea underlying this formula was that unemployment benefit should not be paid if the cause of industrial conflict was based on a collective agreement, which was to become the model for all collective agreements in the whole industry. In 1984, when the Metal Workers' Union in all regions claimed a reduction of the weekly working time from forty to thirty-five hours, the meaning of this formula became controversial. The problem was that reduction of working time was not the only claim being subject to negotiation within the bargaining round. In fact, there were also other claims relating to remuneration, fringe benefits, holidays, etc. As far as these additional claims were concerned, there were slight differences from region to region. Thus, the question had to be answered whether the above-mentioned formula applied already if only the main and predominant claim was identical, or if its application required that all claims were identical. In preliminary lawsuits leading to injunctions by social security courts, the second interpretation was favoured leading to the effect that employees indirectly affected by industrial action and belonging to the industry in which the industrial conflict was taking place but not belonging to the region covered by the intended collective agreement were entitled to unemployment benefits.

566. In view of these experiences, Section 116 AFG was amended in 1986. Since that time, entitlement to unemployment benefits is excluded if, in the area the indirectly affected employee belongs to, a union has laid a claim 'equal in kind and in extent to a dominant claim of the region where the industrial conflict takes place, without being identical', and if 'most probably the essential parts of the results reached in an industrial conflict will be transferred to the other region'. The decision if, in a particular case, these requirements are met is incumbent on the so-called committee of neutrality (*Neutralitätsausschuss*), composed of employees' and employers' representatives, and chaired by the President of the Federal Employment Agency. This decision is subject to judicial control. While so far only claims officially laid by a trade union have been taken into consideration, it is now sufficient that 'the behaviour of the party to the collective agreement may lead to the conclusion that this claim is understood to be laid'. Due to the centralized structure of German trade unions and due to the tendency to preserve solidarity within a union by homogeneous working conditions, at least the main claims laid by unions in a bargaining round are more or less equal. Hence, it is perfectly clear that the new formula will lead in almost all cases to the result that unemployment benefits will not be paid. Not very surprisingly, this intervention of the legislator has provoked the strongest trade union opposition for many years. In 1995 the Federal Constitutional Court examined the constitutionality of the amended version of Section 116 AFG (today: Section 160 SGB III) and has answered it in the affirmative.[340] However, the court said that the regulation was 'still' constitutional at the time. It is highly questionable whether this statement is still true over twenty years later. The actual conditions in the metal and electrical industry have since then changed further to the detriment of the trade unions, due to the many interdependencies between the industrial companies. Today's Section 160 paragraph 3 SGB III could therefore be partly unconstitutional under parity aspects in the meantime.[341]

§11. Injunctions

567. It is highly controversial how far injunctions may be used in industrial conflict to prevent unlawful industrial action. The normal effect of an injunction is the preliminary regulation of a certain question subject to final regulation by a regular court procedure at a later date. In cases of injunctions to prevent unlawful industrial action the factual result, however, would be final. If a strike was prevented during an industrial conflict it would not help at all if, later on, the strike was declared lawful. The opportunity to exert pressure on the counterparty can often not be delayed because the conflict will already be settled. In spite of these doubts concerning the function of injunctions in industrial conflict, the labour courts are using the instrument on motion of the parties involved. However, they have increased the prerequisites to be fulfilled. Injunctions on industrial conflict may only be granted against industrial action, which is obviously unlawful. Nevertheless, it should be stressed that these injunctions do happen from time to time and are by no means only of theoretical interest.[342]

340. Dec. of 4 Jul. 1995 – 1 BvF 2/86, *Arbeitsrechtliche Praxis*, No. 4 §116 AFG.
341. E. Kocher et al., *Noch verfassungsgemäß? Fernwirkungen bei Arbeitskämpfen in der Automobilindustrie und die Verfassungsmäßigkeit des § 160 Abs. 3 SGB III*, Frankfurt/Main 2017.
342. *Cf.* O. Ricken, *Münchener Handbuch zum Arbeitsrecht,* R. Richardi & O. Wlotzke ed., Verlag C.H. Beck, § 276 paras 29 et seq.

§12. CONCLUDING REMARKS

568. Even though statistics show that industrial conflict does not happen frequently in Germany, the law on industrial conflict is nevertheless of predominant importance for the understanding of German labour law. Due to their traditional legalistic approach, unions as well as employers' associations act along the lines laid down by legal rules. Thus, the law on industrial conflict defines the power relationship between the two sides of industry. Consequently, the structure of free collective bargaining is mainly determined by the rules on industrial conflict. Recently, the controversies on this very definition of power relations have increased and have become stronger and stronger, and the acceptability of the decisions of the Federal Labour Court for parties affected has evidently decreased. Thus, it is not surprising at all that at present practically all important problems of the law on industrial conflict are subject to judicial control by the Federal Constitutional Court. It is an open question, however, whether or not the court will be able to fulfil the expectations, which are placed on its ability to act as a kind of 'super-legislator'.

569. To foreign observers it may be strange that the aspect of financial compensation for those who are affected by industrial action plays such a dominant role. This has to do with a specific mentality built up by the very early introduction of an extended social security system. Consequently, the idea that there has to be financial compensation for any risk may be more relevant than in many other countries. Due to this mentality, unions are widely understood to mainly serve as an insurance against loss of remuneration in case of strike and lockout. And if the unions fail to meet this expectation it has to be the social security system which pays, in this case unemployment insurance.

Chapter 5. Institutionalized Forms of Employee Participation: The Works Constitution

§1. Notion and Historical Development

570. The term 'works constitution' (*Betriebsverfassung*) refers to the institutionalized system of employee representation by works councils in the private sector and by staff councils in the public sector. The following explanations will focus on the private sector. The public sector is only mentioned in so far as the structure is significantly different. The system of works constitution is probably the most important characteristic of labour law in Germany. It has implications for virtually all aspects of individual and collective labour law.

571. To understand the system as it is at present, it should be borne in mind that the works constitution is not by any means the invention of the labour movement. During the nineteenth century, as a reaction to the growth of the labour movement, employers voluntarily established some rudimentary form of employee participation. There were essentially two reasons for doing this: to keep trade unions out of the establishment and to provide the employer's policies at plant level with more legitimation. In 1891, conservative groups first introduced in Parliament, against strong opposition from the Social Democratic Party and from the trade unions, an Act governing employee participation. Later, due to political changes and to changes in the strategic concept of the main part of the labour movement, the unions began to support the idea of employee participation at plant level. They were thinking in terms of limiting the decision-making powers of employers on all matters, especially in the economic sector, by establishing democratic structures within the plant. And, of course, their conception was employee participation controlled by unions. However, in 1920, when the first Act on BRG was enacted, a compromise had to be found which would appeal to the conservative parties, which still held the majority in Parliament. Therefore, the 1920 BRG resembled more closely the models established by employers in the nineteenth century than it resembled the ideas developed by unions. The dualistic system of representation by unions and representation by works councils being independent from the unions was confirmed. Thus, it can be said that the BRG 1920 was enacted in spite of the unions and not because of them.

572. After 1920, the unions tried to overcome the institutional separation between them and the works councils. They also tried to broaden the scope of matters to be controlled by works councils, particularly to include economic questions. When, after the downfall of the Nazi regime, the works council system was re-established in 1952, the unions were not satisfied at all because these two basic expectations were not met. That is why they protested against the adoption of the new BetrVG by calling out a strike in the newspaper industry in 1952 (*see* paragraph 526). However, Parliament did not change its opinion, and the unions fought the BetrVG 1952 from the very outset. When finally in 1972 the BetrVG was fundamentally amended, the unions' demands were to a certain extent granted, with the result that the dualistic system is no longer as strict as it was before, and that the matters covered falling under the competences of works councils were significantly extended.

573. New technologies on the one hand and the demand for more flexible working patterns on the other hand have led to the fact that many establishments are organized in a way differing from the organizational structure the BetrVG 1972 has been based on. Increase of telework, of outsourcing, of flexible patterns of cooperation between different establishments – these are only a few examples for that development. It has given rise to a discussion of whether or not the BetrVG 1972 should be amended in order to adopt notions such as e.g., 'establishment' to the changed circumstances. In 2001, the BetrVG 1972 was eventually amended. The amendment was supposed to improve the conditions for the application of the BetrVG in small and medium-sized establishments, to adapt the traditional organizational structures to an ever-changing reality, to improve the resources available to the works council and to increase the works council's powers in certain areas.[343]

574. Whereas the BRG 1920 covered both sectors, the private sector as well as the public sector, this is not the case today. While the private sector is governed by the BetrVG 1952, amended in 1972, the public sector is covered by the BPersVG of 1955, as amended in 1974. For the personnel of the different *Länder* respective *Land* Staff Representation Acts apply, differing more or less from the BPersVG.

§2. The Works Constitution in the Private Sector

I. The Basic Organizational Structure

575. Unlike in many other countries, works councils in Germany are exclusively made up of employee representatives. Works councils act as counterparties of management. Their members are elected by secret ballot of all employees of the establishment (industrial unit, plant, office) over 18 years of age. Employees over 18 years of age who have been employed for at least six months, may be elected (Section 8 BetrVG). According to Section 21 BetrVG, the term of office for works council members is four years. Re-election is possible and not limited in any way.[344]

576. According to Section 1 BetrVG, every establishment with at least five employees over 18 years of age, three of them having been employed for at least six months, is required by law to establish a works council. Nevertheless, many small and medium-sized establishments do not have a works council. Only larger

343. For more details *see* M. Weiss, *Modernizing the German Works Council System: A Recent Amendment*, The Int'l J. Comp. Lab. L. & Indus. Relations 151–264 (2002); M. Behrens, 'The New German Works Constitution Act in Practice', *WSI-Mitteilungen*, Special Issue 2003, 56–65.

344. For more details *see* M. Weiss, *Cooperative Industrial Relations: The German Example and its Impact*, in *The Role of the State and Industrial Relations* 127 et seq (A. Perulli & T. Treu eds, 2019).

enterprises fully comply with the law. It is up to the employees of the respective establishment whether they establish a works council. There is no sanction if they fail to do so, but obviously, employees who do not establish a works council voluntarily abandon all the rights invested in the works council by law.[345]

577. In principle, and according to the law, works councils are institutions still separate from trade unions. They represent all employees of an establishment whether or not they are union members. Nevertheless, in spite of the institutional separation between unions and works councils, there are close links. Meanwhile the unions have succeeded in influencing the composition of works councils. The vast majority of works council members are also trade union members. Their share among the works council members has remained to be relatively stable. The 1989 amendment of the BetrVG has made it even easier for trade unions to present lists of candidates: not only where – as it was regulated before – a works council so far did not yet exist but in any establishment where the trade union is represented by at least one member, the trade union can present a list of candidates (Section 14 paragraph 3 BetrVG). The fear that this would lead to an increased representation of small trade unions and to a decrease of DGB representation, at least so far, has not been confirmed. The figures of the elections of 1981 and 1994, the first election after the unification, are as follows. Unfortunately, more recent detailed figures are not available.

	1981	*1994*
Number of establishments	35,343	40,039
Total number of works council members	190,193	220,245
	= 100%	= 100%
DGB members	147,184	165,570
	= 77.4%	= 75.8%
White-collar union members	5,703	3,855
	= 3.0%	= 1.8%
Members of other unions	1,068	2,737
	= 0.6%	= 1.2%
Non-union members	36,238	46,249
	= 19.0%	= 21.2%

The figures show that the distribution of mandates remained more or less stable, even after the unification. The most important competitors of the DGB unions are

345. For more information *cf.* J. Addison, et al., *German Works Councils Old and New: Incidence, Coverage and Determinants*, IZA Discussion Paper No. 495, 2002.

non-unionized candidates. More recent surveys show that – based on the organizational areas of the trade unions ver.di, IG Metall and IG BCE – an average of 27.6% of works council members were not union members in 2014.[346]

578. According Section 9 BetrVG, the size of a works council depends on the number of employees in the establishment. In establishments with up to twenty employees, it has only one member, in establishments with more than twenty and up to fifty employees, there should be three members, etc. In establishments with more than 7,000 and up to 9,000 employees, the number of works council members reach 31 employees. Above this level, for each additional 3,000 employees the number of works council members increases by two.

579. Since the amendment of 2001 manual workers and white-collar workers are no longer treated as separate groups. Formerly, the proportion of representatives of each group in the works council depended on the proportion of each group of the total workforce of the plant. According to the BetrVG 1972, the normal practice is for each group to elect its candidates by separate secret ballot. However, the majority of each group may decide that a joint election should be held, and this has become the usual practice.

580. If works councils are established in different establishments of a multi-plant enterprise, they must form a company works council (*Gesamtbetriebsrat*) (Section 47 BetrVG). Each works council with up to three members appoints one of its members; every works council consisting of more than three members appoints two of its members to the company works council. Men and women should be represented adequately. It is important to note that the works councils of individual establishments are not subordinate to the company works council. According to Section 50 BetrVG, the company works council is only authorized to deal with matters, either which cannot be regulated at the level of the individual establishment or which are delegated to it by an individual works council. If there are several company works councils in one group of enterprises, it is up to the company works councils to establish a group works council at the level of the parent company (*Konzernbetriebsrat*) (Section 54 BetrVG). Each company works council would have to appoint two of its members. However, even if the BetrVG 1972 opens this channel to establish a group works council, group works councils only play a marginal role in actual practice.

581. According to the 1996 Act on European Works Councils (*Europäisches Betriebsrätegesetz* – EBRG), implementing Directive 94/45/EC, in Union-scale undertakings with at least 1,000 employees in the Member States and at least 150 employees in each of at least two Member States furthermore a European works council with rights to information and consultation may be established,[347] while in

346. I. Artus et al., *Betriebsräte ohne Gewerkschaften? Zur Praxis und Problematik gewerkschaftsferner betrieblicher Mitbestimmung*, Düsseldorf 2019, p. 15.

347. For further information *see* M. Weiss, 'European Works Councils', Germany, *IEL*, suppl. 219 (April 1999).

European companies, according to the 2004 Act on Employee Involvement in a European company (*SE-Beteiligungsgesetz* – SEBG), implementing Directive 2001/86/EC, European company works councils have to be established. In European Cooperative Societies, according to the 2006 Act on Employee Involvement in a European Cooperative Society (*SCE-Beteiligungsgesetz* – SCEBG), implementing Directive 2003/72/EC, SCE works councils are to be set up.

582. If a works council consists of at least nine members, according to Section 27 BetrVG an executive committee (*Betriebsausschuss*) to deal with current routine affairs should be established. Much more important is the fact, however, that in establishments with more than 100 employees the works council may even delegate specific functions and rights to the executive committee or other committees in terms of Section 28 BetrVG. These committees play an important role in practice.

583. According to Section 106 BetrVG, in enterprises with usually more than 100 employees, a so-called economic committee dealing with economic affairs (*Wirtschaftsausschuss*) must be appointed by the works council (or by the company works council in a multi-establishment enterprise). The economic committee consists of at least three and at most seven members (Section 107 paragraph 1 BetrVG). One of the members of the economic committee has to be a member of the works council in order to establish a communication link. All other members shall be employees of the enterprise, but do not need to be works council members. The reason why non-works council members may be appointed to the economic committee is very simple: the legislator wanted to permit persons who are experts on economic matters to be appointed. This is why, according to Section 107 paragraph 1 sentence 2 BetrVG, it is even possible to appoint executive staff to the committee on economic affairs. In actual practice, however, this possibility is never used.

584. According to Section 42 BetrVG 1972, all employees of an establishment should meet four times each year. These so-called works meetings (*Betriebsversammlungen*) take place during working hours; remuneration is guaranteed (Section 44 BetrVG). According to Section 43 BetrVG, works meetings are initiated and chaired by the works council. The works council reports on its activities. The employer must be invited to the works meetings (Section 43 paragraph 2 BetrVG). The employer, or his or her representative, is entitled to address the works meeting. At least once a year the employer, or his or her representative, must report to the works meeting on matters of personnel policy and social affairs in the establishment, as well as on the economic situation of the establishment, including the future outlook. It is evident that the works meeting is important as a communication link between the works council and its constituency. Nevertheless, in this area the statutory provisions do not correspond with reality. Empirical studies show that only in a small proportion of establishments are four works meetings per year held. In most establishments, the number is lower, and in quite a few establishments no works meetings take place at all.

585. Employees under 18 years of age are neither entitled to elect nor permitted to become works council members (Sections 7 and 8 BetrVG). Furthermore, the interests of juvenile employees may need particular attention. This is why, according to Section 60 BetrVG 1972, in each establishment employing at least five juveniles (employees under 18 years of age and apprentices under 25 years of age) a juvenile delegation (*Jugend- und Auszubildendenvertretung*) should be elected. The organizational structure, as well as the election procedure is very much identical to that of the works council. However, it must be stressed that the juvenile delegation is not entitled to act directly as a counterparty to management. The efficiency of the juvenile delegation depends on its cooperation with the works council, which also represents the interests of juvenile employees, and with the employer. In order to make this cooperation effective, the juvenile delegation is entitled to send one of its members to attend any meeting of the works council.

586. Neither works council meetings, nor committee meetings, nor works meetings take place in public session (Section 30 sentence 4 BetrVG).

II. Executive Staff in the Works Constitution

587. According to the BetrVG, executive staff are not covered by works council representation. Members of this group are neither permitted to participate in the election of works council members, nor can they be elected. As previously indicated, the definition of this group was very controversial when the Act was amended in 1972 (*see* paragraph 94). According to the original version of Section 5 BetrVG 1972, persons were regarded as being executive staff:

> who by their status and under their contract of employment:
>
> 1. are entitled on their own responsibility to engage and dismiss employees on behalf of the establishment or one of its departments; or
> 2. are endowed with general authority or full power of representation (*Prokura*), the latter also being important in relation to the employer; or
> 3. essentially carry out other duties on their own responsibility which are normally assigned to them because of their particular experience and knowledge in view of the importance of the said duties for the existence of the establishment.

It was this third alternative in particular, which led to problems. The formula was so vague that everything depended on its interpretation. It was once again the task of the labour courts to draw the borderline. According to the Federal Labour Court, only those persons are excluded from the structure of works council representation who have managerial functions, who enjoy significant discretionary powers in decision-making and who, in view of the very nature of their function, are acting as counterparties of the employees represented by the works council.[348] The scope of this group has been narrowed down tremendously by the Federal Labour Court.

348. Federal Labour Court, 23 Jan. 1986 – 6 ABR 51/81, *Arbeitsrechtliche Praxis*, No. 32 §5 BetrVG 1972; 25 Oct. 1989 – 1 ABR 76/79, *Arbeitsrechtliche Praxis*, No. 42 §5 BetrVG 1972.

Employees belonging to middle management or to research staff, just to mention two groups, are not members of the executive staff within the meaning of the BetrVG.

588. Since the definition as developed by the courts has turned out to be rather vague, the legislator tried to specify the notion by an amendment to the BetrVG in 1989 further. Since that time, Section 5 paragraph 3 BetrVG has excluded employees who normally carry out other duties that are of importance for the existence and development of the undertaking or establishment and the performance of which requires special experience and knowledge if, in doing so, they either take decisions substantially without instruction or have a major influence on such decisions; this may also be the case if there are certain preconditions such as provisions of law, fixed programmes or directives or if they are required to work as a team with other executive staff. The change in substance is, however, marginal. Whether the more specified definition helps to provide a clear enough demarcation line to be helpful in actual practice may well be doubted.

589. In many enterprises, the group of executive staff excluded from works council representation established its own representative body based on an agreement between this group and the employer. There was no homogeneous pattern as to organizational structure and rights of these representative bodies. They existed in about 330 enterprises. In all cases, they only dealt with matters concerning the group of executive staff.

590. Hence in 1989, the Act on a Representative Body for Executive Staff (*Sprecherausschussgesetz* – SprAuG) has been passed, providing a legal basis for executive staff representation. According to the SprAuG, a representative body for executive staff may be elected in establishments regularly employing at least ten members of executive staff. It is up to the executive staff whether such a body is to be formed. The ballot may be subject to a revote, and the decision may be revised. The election is conditional on a corresponding classification procedure carried out by the electoral boards for the election of works councils and representative bodies for executive staff: only executive staff as such are eligible to vote and eligible for election. If an establishment has fewer than ten employees classed as executive staff, they are added to the number of executive staff employed in the geographically nearest establishment of the same company in which the quorum is met. By majority vote of all executive staff in a company usually employing at least ten members of executive staff altogether, a single company-level representative body for executive staff can be formed which is responsible for the establishments of the entire company. A general representative body for executive staff must be formed if there are several such bodies at an individual establishment level within one company. A group representative body for executive staff can be formed with the agreement of the general representative bodies of the group member companies, together employing at least 75% of the executive staff employed by the group of companies as a whole.

591. The term of office of these representative bodies is also four years. Their size depends on the number of executive staff employed in the establishment or company concerned. Members of such bodies do not enjoy entitlements comparable to those of works council members – neither release from work, nor retention of grading, nor special protection against dismissal. Representative bodies of executive staff are confined to information and consultation rights. They have neither rights of veto nor co-determination rights. Whether or not the formally weak position, however, corresponds with a weak position in actual reality remains an open question. So far, empirical evidence is lacking.

III. The Role of Unions Within the Works Constitution

592. As previously mentioned, unions have overcome the institutional pattern of dual representation due to the fact that a great number of works council members are also union members. In addition, the BetrVG grants unions, which are represented in establishment specific rights. First of all, all unions are granted initiating functions. Thus in establishments without a works council they may initiate a works meeting during which the employees may decide whether or not they want to establish a works council (Section 17 paragraph 3 BetrVG). Or, if for a certain period no works meeting has taken place, unions may enforce it in terms of 43 paragraph 4 BetrVG. However, it should be stressed that these initiating functions in practice evidently play a very marginal role. Otherwise, the widespread non-existence of works councils or the non-conduct of works meetings would not be possible. More important than the initiating functions of trade unions are their controlling functions. The unions have extended rights to control the works council election procedure and may even file a motion to reach the nullification of a works council election by court decision if legal rules were not properly applied (Section 19 paragraph 2 BetrVG). If a member of the works council or the works council as such has violated its duties of office, the union may achieve a court decision excluding a works council member from office or dissolving the works council (Section 23 paragraph 1 BetrVG). Even if the employer violates the duties imposed on him or her by the BetrVG, it is again the unions, which are according to Section 23 paragraph 3 BetrVG, entitled to initiate the imposition of sanctions by the labour courts. Although works meetings do not take place in public sessions, external union representatives have a right to be present (Section 46 BetrVG). At the request of at least one-fourth of the works council members or at the request of the majority of one group (manual workers or white-collar workers), an external official of a union represented in the works council is entitled to participate in the works council meeting (Section 31 BetrVG). The same rule applies to committee meetings, including meetings of the economic committee.

593. In order to guarantee the effective use of the specific rights of unions, Section 2 paragraph 2 BetrVG provides that, after having notified the employer or his or her representative, agents of unions, which are represented within an establishment, shall be granted access to the establishment.

594. According to Section 37 paragraph 6 BetrVG, works council members are entitled to participate in training courses at the employer's expenses. These courses are supposed to provide the knowledge works council members need to fulfil their task (for details, *see* paragraph 602). These courses are almost exclusively offered by trade unions. This evidently is an important instrument for trade unions to make sure that works council members act in their spirit.

595. To obtain a correct picture of the influence of trade unions on works council policy, however, one has to go far beyond the formal structure of the works council system. Informally in some branches and especially in larger corporations, the unions dispose of so-called trusted representatives (*Vertrauensleute*) inside the establishment, who in some cases are appointed by the union and in other cases are elected by the union members employed in the establishment. These trusted representatives are considered to be the communicating link between trade union members and trade union administration. In addition, they support, influence and sometimes to a certain extent even control works council activities. Their influence varies from establishment to establishment and from branch to branch. The same is true for their organizational structure.

IV. The Legal Status of Works Council Members

596. During their term of office works council members cannot be recalled by their constituency; this can only be achieved by a labour court decision, which may be initiated either by a union represented in the establishment, or by one-fourth of the employees, or by the employer (Section 23 paragraph 1 BetrVG). An individual works council member may be removed from office or the works council as a whole may be dissolved only if the member or the council itself respectively has violated the BetrVG in a grievous manner or neglected the duties pertaining to office. Such claims are very rarely taken to court, however, and enjoy little success if dealt with there. In other words, once the works council members are elected they can in general be sure of remaining in office until the end of term.

597. As already mentioned above, works council members (as well as members of juvenile delegations) enjoy far-reaching protection against dismissals. This protection turned out to be ineffective in the case of apprentices who were members of the juvenile delegation. Since the contract of apprentices is always concluded for a definite period, and since a contract for a definite period terminates automatically when the period has expired, no dismissal is necessary to terminate the employment relationship with an apprentice. This is why protection against dismissal turned out to be useless. In 1974, the BetrVG was therefore amended. Apprentices who are members of the juvenile delegation and whose contract expires during office are entitled to be employed afterwards. According to Section 78a BetrVG, the employer can only refuse further employment if facts are given which would justify a dismissal of a works council member.

598. According to Section 78 BetrVG, works council members may neither enjoy privileges nor suffer disadvantages because of holding office. This general rule is specified mainly by the following three provisions: first, works council members are not entitled to receive additional payments or benefits as a compensation for holding office. Second, it is guaranteed that their remuneration will always attain the same level it would have attained if they had not become works council members. Employees who are, at the beginning of the term of office, in a situation comparable to that of a works council member, are taken as a point of reference. It should be stressed that this guarantee of keeping the level of remuneration is applicable no matter what kind of work the works council member actually performs. It further implies that a works council member is entitled to wage increases comparable to what employees get. On the contrary, works councils must not be favoured because of their professional activities. In questions of an appropriate further development of the remuneration, this is sometimes a difficult assessment. Third, and most important, there is a guarantee of retaining occupational skills and occupational standard. This guarantee refers to the risk that the employer could be tempted to keep the level of remuneration but to employ the works council member nevertheless in a mode, which does not correspond with his or her occupational skills. Moreover, the works council member could otherwise be excluded from further vocational training, which other employees may enjoy. The guarantee intends to prevent these effects. All these guarantees are extended until one year after the term of office has expired. This may imply, in particular cases in which the works council member, due to his or her office, did not have a chance to participate in vocational training before that the employer must provide all possibilities of vocational training within this period of one year.

599. Works council members are entitled to be released from their duty to work without loss of pay 'to the extent necessary for properly carrying out their functions, taking into account the size and nature of the establishment' (Section 37 paragraph 2 BetrVG). In other words, the time of being released from work is not fixed; it depends on the circumstances of the particular case. According to the rules developed by the labour courts, it is up to the works council members to decide what time is necessary to carry out their functions.[349] Only in situations of evident and excessive abuse could the employer refuse to release a works council member from his or her duty to work.

600. If the establishment exceeds a certain minimum number of employees a certain minimum of works council members must be entirely released from their duty to work for their whole term of office (Section 38 paragraph 1 BetrVG). This obligation does not apply to establishments with fewer than 200 employees. While in plants with at least 200 and up to 500 employees, at least one works council member must be entirely released, this figure increases to 12 members in plants with between 9,000 and 10,000 employees. In plants with more than 10,000 employees, one further member of the works council must be released for each additional 2,000

349. Federal Labour Court, 15 Mar. 1995 – 7 AZR 643/94, *Arbeitsrechtliche Praxis*, No. 105 §37 BetrVG 1972.

employees. The law provides only for a minimum standard. The minimum standards provided by law may be extended or modified by collective agreements or works agreements.

601. The possibility of entire release from the duty to work is one of the most important features of the German works constitution. Its effects are very ambiguous. On the one hand, this leads to a professionalization of works council members, which evidently increases the efficiency of the works council. On the other hand, it is difficult for these professional works council members to be reintegrated into the rank and file when their term of office expires. This is why these members tend to do everything to be re-elected and to treat their term of office in the works council as a lifetime career. Thus, the danger cannot be denied that a bureaucratic power structure could thereby be established which tends to remain in power.

602. As already mentioned, works council members are entitled to attend training courses insofar as the knowledge imparted is necessary for the activities of the works council. In order to be able to attend these courses they are entitled to be released from their duty to work without loss of pay.[350] The employer has to bear the expenses for attending these courses. This provision has led to many controversies. Hundreds of cases dealt with in labour courts have meanwhile brought some clarification. Referring to the question of who is allowed to offer such courses, it is generally agreed that of unions may offer works council training courses. As already pointed out, in actual practice the large majority of such training programmes are offered by unions. Thereby the unions have a very important weapon for influencing works council policy.

603. Referring to the question of what may be the subject of such training courses, it is agreed that not only works constitution law may be taught but the curriculum may be extended to information on economic, ergonomic and labour law problems connected with works council activities.[351] Meanwhile, the real issue is the question of how many members of the works council may attend such courses, how often they are entitled to attend and how long these courses may last. The Federal Labour Court tends to decide these problems along the lines of the principle of proportionality, meaning that there should be a reasonable relationship between the size and the financial resources of the establishment on the one hand, and the number of works council members attending these courses, the frequency and the length of these courses on the other hand.[352] This leads to the fact that training opportunities in large prosperous enterprises are better than in marginal enterprises where the economic conditions may not be as good. Since in the latter case the works council would have to be especially efficient in order to protect the employees

350. Federal Labour Court, 28 Jun. 1995 – 7 ABR 55/94, *Arbeitsrechtliche Praxis*, No. 48 §40 BetrVG 1972.
351. *Cf.* U. Koch, *Erfurter Kommentar zum Arbeitsrecht,* ed. R. Müller-Glöge et al, 2020, Verlag C.H. Beck, § 37 BetrVG para. 14.
352. Federal Labour Court, 31 Oct. 1972 – 1 ABR 7/72, *Arbeitsrechtliche Praxis*, No. 2 §40 BetrVG 1972; 8 Feb. 1977 – 1 ABR 124/74, *Arbeitsrechtliche Praxis*, No. 26 §37 BetrVG 1972.

against the negative effects of economic crisis, it may be doubted whether the view of the Federal Labour Court is really a proper solution to this problem.

604. In addition to the training just mentioned, each member of the works council is, only once during each term of office, entitled to three weeks' paid release in order to attend a seminar to broaden his general educational level. Newcomers in their first term are even entitled to four weeks of paid release for educational purposes (Section 37 paragraph 7 BetrVG).

605. It is the employer who bears all the expenses arising from the activities of the works council, as is explicitly laid down in Section 40 BetrVG. In addition, the employer must provide the necessary accommodation, facilities (including books and periodicals on labour law), and office staff required for meetings, consultations and day-to-day operation of the works council. The extent of this duty to pay works council expenses is very controversial. Again, proportionality used in the sense previously explained has become the decisive criterion in handling this problem.

606. The employer must provide the works council with all the information (including the files) the works council needs in order to carry out its tasks properly (Section 80 paragraph 2 BetrVG). Under certain, rather restricted conditions the works council is entitled to call on the advice of experts (Section 80 paragraphs 3 and 4 BetrVG). This restriction is due to the fact that the expenses are borne by the employer. This is why in actual practice mainly union officials fulfil the function of providing expert advice to works councils free of charge. This support of works council activities is becoming increasingly important.

V. Legal Restrictions on Works Council Activities

607. Works councils are required by Section 74 paragraph 1 BetrVG to cooperate with the employer in good faith. Consequently, industrial action as a means of conflict resolution is explicitly prohibited in Section 74 paragraph 2 BetrVG. This, of course, does not mean that works council members are not allowed to participate in legal strikes called out by a trade union in order to achieve a certain result in collective bargaining. However, according to the prevailing view among labour law scholars, the works council as a representative body must remain neutral even during a lawful strike.[353] Subject to controversy is the question whether, and in how far, the participation and co-determination rights of the works council are suspended during a strike. At present uncertainty prevails. In general, the participation rights in industrial disputes generally remain in force and can only be restricted in individual cases.[354]

353. *Cf.* T. Kania, *Erfurter Kommentar zum Arbeitsrecht,* ed. R. Müller-Glöge et al, 2020, Verlag C.H. Beck, §74 BetrVG para. 11.
354. *Cf.* D. Klocke, *Das BetrVG und der Arbeitskampf im Betrieb*, Frankfurt/Main 2019.

608. The works council must furthermore refrain from any activity within the establishment promoting a political party (Section 74 paragraph 2 sentence 3 BetrVG). The labour courts have extended this concept: all political activities, whether or not they promote political parties, are forbidden.[355] This duty to act apolitically does not apply to matters of collective bargaining policy, social and economic policy. But even on these latter matters the works council is only permitted to take a stand if the establishment is directly affected. If this latter prerequisite is met, the opinion of a works council may even be identical to the opinion expressed by a political party. In summary, it should be stressed that, on the whole, the law treats establishments as an apolitical arena.

609. All works council activities endangering the 'peace within the establishment' in terms of Section 74 paragraph 2 BetrVG or the proper performance of work are forbidden. This again is a very vague and unspecific formula. Theoretically, it could be used to narrow the scope of works council activities tremendously. But in fact, the approach of the labour courts is different, the formula is understood to be a borderline for extreme cases. Thus, its practical importance is only marginal.

610. According to Section 79 BetrVG works councils are prevented from divulging information classified by the employer as secret. This applies only to information acquired by virtue of holding the office of a works council and explicitly declared to be secret by the employer. The ban on divulging information does not apply to the exchange of information between members of the works council. The works council is free to provide such information to the company works council, to the group works council, to the employee representative on the supervisory board and to the arbitration committee. Quite often, such secrets may be the basis for the decision of a works council on specific matters. Nevertheless, it is not possible for the works council to communicate on this very basis with its constituency. This also applies to works meetings. This communication obstacle may have and often in fact has the effect that activities of a works council are not transparent to its constituency. It thereby is a source of alienation between the works council and its constituency.

VI. The Arbitration Committee

611. Since strikes and lockouts as a means of conflict resolution are expressly prohibited a special dispute settlement body, called the arbitration committee (*Einigungsstelle*), is provided for in Section 76 BetrVG.[356] There are two possibilities: the formation of a permanent arbitration committee and of an ad hoc arbitration committee for each case as required. In practice, the permanent committee is never

355. Federal Labour Court, 28 Apr. 1976 – 1 BvR 71/73, *Arbeitsrechtliche Praxis*, No. 2 §74 BetrVG 1972; 13 Sep. 1977 – 1 ABR 67/75, *Arbeitsrechtliche Praxis*, No. 1 §42 BetrVG 1972.

356. *Cf. also* E. Kocher, *The Regulation of Conflicts in the German Industrial Relations System: Legal and Extra-Legal Institutions and Procedures*, Transfer 654–669 (2002).

used because it is believed that actions of a permanent body could be predicted if one knew in advance the persons on the committee.

612. The arbitration committee consists of a certain number of members appointed by the employer, an equal number appointed by the works council and a neutral president who chairs the committee. The BetrVG does not prescribe the number of members to be appointed by each side. This is to be determined by agreement between works council and employer. Works councils tend to favour a larger number of members than employers. If an agreement cannot be reached, either side may request that the labour court decides the matter. The law establishes a special procedure guaranteeing the establishment of an arbitration committee in Section 76 paragraph 5 BetrVG. The procedure is a very rapid one, which enables a decision to be reached within a few days. If one side, in spite of a court decision, refuses to appoint members, the arbitration committee may function without them.

613. It is up to the employer and to the works council to decide whom to appoint as members of their side. Usually, a majority of the members belong to the enterprise, either as executives on the employer's side or as employees on the works council side. However, quite often, also trade union officials or officials of employers' associations are appointed. Other external members are selected only if expert knowledge is required which goes beyond the qualifications of union officials or officials of employers' associations. The law does not specify who should serve as the 'neutral' president of the committee. It can be any person on whom the employer and works council can agree. Since the neutral president as chairperson has a key role in the committee employer and works council hardly ever reach consent on the person to be selected. Therefore, Section 76 paragraph 2 BetrVG provides that if the parties cannot agree the labour court shall appoint the President of the arbitration committee. This explains why career judges of the labour court constitute about 95% of all arbitration committee presidents. Since the 'neutral' president is paid quite well, serving as President of an arbitration committee is a source of extra income for judges. However, in view of the intention of the legislator to provide for a quick and flexible conflict resolution procedure as an alternative to the court procedure it is highly questionable if it is appropriate for active labour court judges to serve as presidents on arbitration committees.

614. The costs of the arbitration committee, like all other costs of the works constitution, are to be borne by the employer. This is explicitly provided for in Section 76a BetrVG. Initially there was no provision on the specification of these costs. Hence, the Federal Labour Court developed basic rules according to which the internal members of the arbitration committee (those who belong to the enterprise) did not receive any honorarium. However, the external members appointed by the works council had to be paid if the works council could not find qualified persons to serve without pay. This led to the fact that usually the external members had to be paid, including union officials. This helps to explain why, as previously mentioned, the employer tries to keep the number of arbitration committee members as low as possible – the employer has to pay them as well as he or she has to pay the 'neutral' chairperson.

615. The already mentioned 1989 Amendment of the BetrVG confirmed this rule in principle. There was, however, an important innovation. The legislator tried to limit the amount of costs by introducing criteria for the honorarium to be paid: the time needed to act properly in the committee, the difficulty of the conflict at stake and compensation for loss of other income due to the activity in the arbitration committee. The Federal Minister of Labour and Social Affairs is entitled to specify these vague criteria further by decree. So far, any attempt to pass such a decree has failed. The reason is very simple: it would lead to a reduction of honorarium and thereby of costs. Neither the judges involved nor trade unions nor works councils are interested in such a reduction. Whereas for judges the focus is on additional income, trade unions and works councils are interested in keeping the costs of the arbitration committee as high as possible to retain it as a deterrent instrument. The alliance of these interests so far succeeded in delaying the minister's decree. It may well be doubted whether this is a helpful strategy to maintain the legitimacy of the works constitution.

616. Since the arbitration committee was conceived by the legislator as a rapidly operating and flexible body, virtually no procedural rules are prescribed for it. The committee itself develops its procedure. However, since in the majority of cases professional labour judges serve as committee presidents, the procedure tends to resemble that used in labour courts, an inflexible and lengthy one. Section 76 paragraph 3 BetrVG only requires that after oral proceedings the committee shall adopt its decisions by a majority vote. In order to avoid a committee decision appearing to have been imposed on the parties, the chairperson does not participate in the voting during the first ballot. If there is a tie and a second ballot becomes necessary, the chairperson does vote to ensure that there will be a majority decision.

617. In reaching its decision, the arbitration committee must have due regard to the interests of the establishment and to the interests of the employees concerned. Employer and/or works council may appeal to the labour court within two weeks of the date of notification of the awards. On appeal, the court is allowed to consider only if the committee has exceeded its discretionary powers. The court cannot annul the decision of the committee. In practice, appeal to court in cases of conflict of interests is very rare, meaning that the final decision is reached by the arbitration committee. The law requires that decisions of the arbitration committee are recorded in writing, signed by the chairperson and forwarded to employer and works council. It is important to note that during the deliberations of the committee outsiders are not admitted. The exclusion of the public is considered necessary to permit compromises to be reached in resolving conflicts.

VII. Competences of the Works Council

A. *Specific Rights of Participation*

618. Under the BetrVG the works council is granted a whole range of specific rights of participation, ranging from a mere right to information and a right to be consulted over a right to control and of veto to the most important right of all: the right to co-determination. In matters in which these rights apply, the decision-making process is no longer the prerogative of management. The works council can insist on participation to the extent granted by law. Co-determination in this context means that management cannot take any decisions without the consent of the works council. In the absence of a consensus, any move by management would be judged to be illegal. However, co-determination means even more: it gives both sides an equal voice in the decision-making process. Therefore, at least in principle, either side can take the initiative and call for a new settlement.

619. As an illustration of how the decision-making process in cases of co-determination works, the example of a conflict over short-time working may be useful. Whether management or the works council wants to introduce short-time working, in any case an agreement must be reached. This agreement should clarify the following questions: whether short-time working is to be introduced at all, when it is to start, how long it will last, which groups of employees will be affected, etc. In short, every single aspect is subject to co-determination. If management and works council do not succeed in reaching an agreement, the conflict is referred to the arbitration committee. Once the committee has decided, its decision is binding on both parties, management and works council. If either management or the works council is not satisfied with the decision of the arbitration committee, it can appeal to the Labour Court. However, as has already been indicated, in such cases the controlling power of the courts is very limited.

620. The participation rights of the works council are subdivided into three areas, covering social matters, personnel matters and economic matters. Personnel matters include personnel planning and vocational training as well as hiring, transfer, or dismissal of employees. Economic matters are defined as everything concerning the economic policy of management, whether it is investment, production, marketing and so on. The most difficult area to understand is that of social matters. These can have an enormous economic impact, thus it is not easy to separate this area entirely from that of economic affairs. The general understanding is that social matters are those relating only to the social consequences of economic decisions.

621. It is the area of social matters in which the works council has the most extensive right to co-determination. The cases in which the works council enjoys this strong position are exhaustively enumerated in Section 87 BetrVG thereby being the most important provision of the BetrVG. Provided that the matter is neither settled by statutory law nor by collective agreement, the works council has a right of co-determination in the following enumerated cases:[357]

(1) matters relating to the organization of the establishment and the conduct of employees in the establishment;

357. For details *see* T. Klebe in Däubler, Klebe, Wedde (ed.), *BetrVG Betriebsverfassungsgesetz*, 17. Edition, Frankfurt/Main 2020, § 87.

(2) the beginning and end of daily working hours, including breaks, and the distribution of working hours among the various days of the week;
(3) temporary reductions or increases in normal working hours in the establishment;
(4) the time, place and nature of the payment of remuneration;
(5) the preparation of general principles governing leave and of the leave schedule and the specification of the time at which individual employees take their leave if the employer and the employees concerned fail to agree;
(6) the introduction and use of technical devices designed to monitor the conduct or performance of employees;
(7) provisions for the prevention of industrial accidents and occupational diseases and for health protection pursuant to the statutory law or safety provisions;
(8) the form, organization and administration of social facilities whose scope is confined to the establishment, undertaking or group;
(9) the allocation and withdrawal of accommodation let to employees in consideration of the existence of an employment relationship and the general stipulation of conditions governing the use of such accommodation;
(10) questions relating to wage structures in the establishment, and in particular the drawing up of principles governing remuneration, and the introduction and application of new methods of remuneration and changes thereto;
(11) the specification of piece and bonus rates and comparable performance-related remuneration, including rates per unit time;
(12) principles governing the suggestion system in the establishment;
(13) principles governing the performance of group work; group work within the meaning of this provision exists if, as a part of the establishments' routines, a group of employees performs a task assigned to it essentially on its own authority.

In social matters other than those mentioned in Section 87 BetrVG, the works council has no statutory right to co-determination. Works council and employer are, however, nevertheless completely free to conclude works agreements. But, contrary to works agreements as regards matters enumerated in Section 87 BetrVG, such agreements cannot be compelled by the works council. According to Section 88 BetrVG it is entirely up to the employer whether or not to conclude such voluntary works agreements in social matters beyond Section 87 BetrVG.

622. The above list of social matters, enumerated in Section 87 BetrVG, shows that introduction and use of new technologies is only covered by the right to co-determination if technical devices are 'designed to monitor the employees' behaviour or their performance'. It should be stressed that the Federal Labour Court in many decisions has gradually extended the scope of application of this provision.[358] In cases in which Section 87 No. 6 BetrVG is not applicable the works

358. Federal Labour Court, 14 Sep. 1984 – 1 ABR 23/82, *Arbeitsrechtliche Praxis*, No. 9 §87 BetrVG 1972 *Überwachung*; 22 Mar. 1986 – 1 ABR 12/84, *Arbeitsrechtliche Praxis*, No. 14 §87 BetrVG 1972 *Überwachung*; S. Simitis, 'Mitbestimmung als Regulativ einer technisierten Kontrolle von Arbeitnehmern', *Neue Juristische Wochenschrift*, 1985, pp. 401 et seq.

council nevertheless enjoys some sort of co-determination right provided by Section 91 BetrVG. However, this right to co-determination applies only under very restricted conditions and can never prevent the introduction or change of technological equipment. Section 91 BetrVG requires that, as a result of such a measure, a special burden is imposed on the employees, and, furthermore, that the introduction or the change of technological equipment is in obvious contradiction to the non-contested findings of ergonomics relating to job organization based on human requirements. It is important to know that such non-contested findings of ergonomics are very rare, and where they exist, new technological equipment is usually adapted anyway. Thus, cases of obvious contradiction to these findings are rare. Even if all conditions are fulfilled, it is not the technological change that is subject to co-determination as such but only the appropriate measures to obviate, relieve, or compensate for the additional stress thus imposed. All possibilities to reduce the harmful effects of new technological equipment must be taken into consideration. It should be mentioned that this rather theoretical and impractical right to co-determination refers not only to the introduction of new technologies, but also to all changes of work, work performance and work environment. As it has turned out, the implementation of new technologies is easier if it is introduced under full participation and with the approval of the works council. Therefore, especially in large enterprises, there are some cases in which management and works council have extended the co-determination powers of the works council by voluntary works agreement. However, in spite of these experiences, the employers' side as a whole rejects such an extension of the rights to co-determination.

623. In personnel matters a right to co-determination exists only in very few aspects, for example as regards the content of guidelines for selection (*see* paragraph 315 referring to hiring and referring to dismissal), the content of written questionnaires (*see* paragraph 186) and the establishment of general criteria for the evaluation of test results (*see* paragraph 186). As far as in-house vocational training is concerned, the works council has a rather strong position as to selection of training personnel and selection of employees who are allowed to participate in such programmes. In short, whereas the works council position is rather feeble in view of setting up of such programmes, it is strong with regard to their implementation. For the rights of works councils referring to hiring of employees (*see* paragraphs 186 et seq.), for their rights in dismissal cases (*see* paragraphs 312 et seq.) and for their rights in cases of transfer *see* the respective passages (*see* paragraph 200). As far as personnel planning is concerned, the works council has only a right to information and consultation as granted in Section 92 BetrVG.

624. In economic matters, it is the economic committee (*see* paragraph 583) that enjoys specific rights under the BetrVG. However, the competence of the economic committee does not go beyond a mere right to information and consultation. The employer may even refuse to give information if disclosure to the committee members could endanger business secrets.

625. Much more important than the right of the economic committee to information and consultation in economic matters in general are the participation rights of the works council in specific economic decisions, which may cause substantial disadvantages to the workforce of the establishment or for relevant parts of it, so-called substantial alteration to the establishment (*Betriebsänderung*). According to Section 111 BetrVG, the works council enjoys these participation rights in establishments with more than twenty employees. The participation rights of the works council refer to the following decisions: reduction of operations, partial or total closure, transfer of the establishment or transfer of essential parts of it, merger with other establishments, basic organizational changes, basic changes of the purpose or the equipment of the establishment, the introduction of entirely new work methods and production processes.

626. It should be stressed that a mere reduction of the workforce without reduction of the equipment is also understood to be a reduction of operations. Thus, the case of collective redundancy (*see* paragraphs 333 et seq.) is, in principle, included. Nevertheless, 'reduction of operations' in this sense and 'collective dismissal' are not identical. Whereas in the case of collective dismissal the dismissals must be effective within thirty days, there is no such limitation as regards a reduction of operations within the meaning of Section 111 BetrVG. The reduction is understood to be a coherent entity as it is based on the same management decision. A reduction of the workforce may not be a collective dismissal, but it may nevertheless be regarded as a reduction of operations in the sense of Section 111 BetrVG. However, it may also be the other way around: the minimum number of dismissals that add up to a collective redundancy in the sense previously explained (*see* paragraphs 333 et seq.) is lower than the minimum number of dismissals required for a reduction in the sense of Section 111 BetrVG. According to the Federal Labour Court, the minimum level in establishments above 500 employees should be at least 5% (and not only 30 employees as in the case of collective dismissal). The 1985 BeschFG has further limited the scope of a reduction in the sense of Section 111 BetrVG. According to Section 112a BetrVG, in establishments with more than 20 but fewer than 60 employees, the reduction shall be 20% or at least six employees (compared to a minimum of five employees for a collective dismissal), in establishments with at least 60 and fewer than 250 employees, again 20% or at least 37 employees must be affected (compared to 10% or at least 25 employees for a collective dismissal), in establishments with at least 250 and fewer than 500 employees the reduction should be 15% or at least 60 employees (compared to 10% or at least 25 employees for a collective dismissal). Finally, in establishments of 500 employees and more, 10% or at least 60 employees must be affected (compared to the minimum of 30 employees for a collective dismissal).

627. In cases of a substantial alteration to the establishment management must provide the works council with full information in advance. 'Information in advance' means that it has to be given at an early planning stage. 'Full information' means that management has not only to disclose its plans but to supply information on all possible alternatives and modifications which were, or are, taken into account in the particular situation. The idea is to give the works council a proper opportunity to participate by supplying it with the same information that management already has.

628. In addition to supplying information, management is required to reach a so-called reconciliation of interests (*Interessenausgleich*) with the works council (Section 112 BetrVG). This means that management is obliged to try to reach an agreement with the works council on whether, and how, the specific measures envisaged by management have to be carried out. If an agreement is not reached, either side can call in the Executive Board of the Federal Employment Agency for mediation. If his or her mediation is not successful or if neither management nor the works council wants the Federal Employment Agency to mediate, either side may take the issue to the arbitration committee. However, the arbitration committee, if a reconciliation of interests is at stake, has no power to impose a binding decision on the parties, it can only present a proposal. It is up to management and the works council to accept or to reject the proposal. The law provides a procedure to reach a reconciliation of interests, but if the procedure fails to be successful it is up to management to decide. The works council has no legal power to force management in a certain direction.

629. No matter whether or not management has fulfilled its duties to inform the works council and has tried to reach a reconciliation of interests, the works council is always entitled to enforce a so-called social plan (*Sozialplan*) in terms of Section 112 BetrVG. A social plan means nothing less than a special works agreement to compensate or reduce disadvantages for employees in the event of a substantial alteration to the establishment or in cases of insolvency. It is important to state that a social plan is not confined to financial compensation. It may also include programmes on retraining, transfer of employees to other establishments of the enterprise, etc.

630. If an agreement on a social plan cannot be reached, either side is entitled to appeal to the arbitration committee, which then acts as a decision-maker: its decision is binding on both sides (Section 112 paragraph 4 BetrVG). Except in cases of insolvency, which cannot be explained here, there is no minimum or maximum limit for a social plan. According to the formula valid until 1985, the arbitration committee had to make its decision on a social plan 'taking into consideration the social needs of the employees affected as well as the financial strength of the enterprise'. As this very broad formula covered almost any possible decision, judicial control turned out to be totally ineffective. That is why in the BeschFG 1985 the aforementioned formula has been amended. Since 1985, the arbitration committee has had to base its decision on the following principles laid down in Section 112 paragraph 5 BetrVG: a compensation for economic disadvantages, in particular for lower wages, loss of fringe benefits, loss of an expectant right to an occupational pension, moving expenses to a new location, or higher travelling expenses must take into account the particular circumstances of each individual case. The opportunities for affected employees on the labour market must be taken into account. Employees who may be retrained in an adequate job within the same establishment, or in another establishment of the enterprise, or in another enterprise belonging to the same group of enterprises but who nevertheless do not accept the offer of such a job will not receive compensation. A job is not inadequate merely because it is in another town. Finally, the total amount of compensation must not endanger the future existence of the enterprise or the remaining jobs.

631. The restriction of the scope of the term 'reduction of operations', in the sense of Section 111 BetrVG, has led to the effect that the number of cases of collective dismissals in which a social plan can be enforced has decreased. In addition, the 1985 BeschFG has established a privilege for newly established enterprises: no social plan can be enforced in the first four years after the foundation of an enterprise (Section 112a paragraph 2 BetrVG).

632. In view of high unemployment, trade unions and employers' associations have developed models of social plans that give qualification and re-integration into employment priority over financial compensation. When in 1998 in the chemical industry, for example, an enterprise was liquidated, a new enterprise was founded employing those employees who neither retired nor found other jobs. The sole object of the new company was employee training as regards occupational as well as application skills. In order to reach the goal that after two years all employees should have found a job in another – a 'normal' – enterprise, an outplacement service, usually only available for executive staff, was involved. Similar models exist in the banking sector, in the transport (railway) sector, etc.

633. In 1998, the conclusion of such social plans giving re-integration into employment priority over financial compensation found very strong support from the legislator. According to Section 110 SGB III, measures provided for in a social plan aiming at the re-integration of employees who would otherwise not or at least not permanently be integrated into the labour market can be sponsored by the Employment Agency on condition that it can be expected that these persons would otherwise be entitled to other payments of the Employment Agency.

B. Works Agreements

634. Employer and works council may conclude so-called works agreements (*Betriebsvereinbarungen*) not only in matters in which the works council has a right to co-determination but also in all matters relating to labour/management relations in the establishment. Of course, if there is no right to co-determination the works council has no formal power to induce management to sign such an agreement. In cases where the arbitration committee replaces the agreement between works council and employer, the decision of the arbitration committee is understood to be a works agreement (Section 77 paragraph 2 BetrVG).

635. Works agreements must be in writing and signed by both sides (Section 77 paragraph 2 BetrVG). The employer must give employees the opportunity of being conversant with the text of the agreement by displaying it in a suitable place in the establishment. A works agreement may, as a collective agreement, establish rights and duties between the concluding parties (employer and works council). It furthermore may contain individual normative provisions (*see* paragraphs 461 et seq.) and collective normative provisions (*see* paragraphs 466 et seq.). Such normative clauses have an automatic and mandatory effect on the parties to the individual employment relationship. Works agreements may be concluded for a definite or for an indefinite period. Unless otherwise agreed upon, works agreements may be terminated at three months' notice (Section 77 paragraph 5 BetrVG). However, the parties are free to agree on other terms. So far, the same rules apply as previously discussed for collective agreements.

636. For the period between the expiration of a works agreement and the conclusion of a new one, a distinction has to be drawn between agreements on matters in which the works council has a co-determination right and other matters. As to the latter category, the provisions cease to be applicable at the time of expiration. As regards the first category, the same rules apply as to normative clauses of collective agreements (*see* paragraphs 461 et seq.).[359]

VIII. The Relationship Between Collective Bargaining and the Competence of the Works Council

637. According to Section 77 paragraph 3 BetrVG, works agreements dealing with remuneration or other working conditions are only permitted on condition that the same matter is not already regulated in a collective agreement. In that respect, a matter is 'already regulated' if the specific matter is usually regulated in collective agreements in the respective region and branch. In other words, it is not even necessary that a valid collective agreement applies to exclude the permissibility of a works agreement. If a collective agreement exists, it is sufficient that it covers the region and the branch, no matter whether or not it applies to the specific establishment and to the employment relationships within this establishment. This implies that, even in establishments where neither the employer is a member of the employers' association nor the employees are union members, remuneration or other working conditions cannot be regulated by works agreements. This very rigid rule only applies to works agreements on matters in which the works council has no right to co-determination. In these cases, as already mentioned, the works council has no power to induce the management to sign such an agreement. The reason is to prevent the works council from competing with trade unions. Such competition is considered to endanger the strength of the collective bargaining system. Should the system of collective agreements break down, then there would be no adequate substitute at plant level when works agreements cannot be enforced by the works council. Therefore, in order to safeguard the strength of the collective bargaining system, the prerogative of parties to a collective agreement to regulate working conditions must be respected.

---

359. T. Kania, *Erfurter Kommentar zum Arbeitsrecht,* ed. R. Müller-Glöge et al, 2020, Verlag C.H. Beck, §77 BetrVG paras. 100 et seq.

638. According to Section 77 paragraph 3 sentence 2 BetrVG, it is up to parties to a collective agreement to decide whether, in spite of the general rule just explained, works agreements supplementing and specifying the collective agreement are allowed. This may be done by including a so-called opening clause (*Öffnungsklausel*) into the collective agreement.[360] In the past, opening clauses were only rarely included. The main reason for this abstention was that unions feared destroying the homogeneous standards within industry. In the meantime, the situation has dramatically changed. When in the mid-1980s the attempt was made to combine working time reduction with flexibility of working time, it became fairly clear that a collective agreement on regional or branch level could only provide a framework to be specified by works council and individual employer. Thus, the works council became more and more integrated into the structure of collective bargaining.[361]

639. A still very topical example is the collective agreement for the metal industry concluded in 1994. This agreement aims at rescuing jobs by further reducing working time and, at the same time, reducing wages. This, of course, cannot be regulated globally for a whole branch or region, but has to take account of the specific circumstances in individual companies and plants. The collective agreements fixes a weekly working time of thirty-six hours and a certain minimum wage. But it contains a so-called opening clause allowing works council and employer not only to specify the collective agreement, but, within certain limits, to deviate from it. For works council and individual employer two options are available: one referring to all employees and another referring to groups of employees or to parts of the company. As far as the first option is concerned, works council and employer may conclude a works agreement further reducing the weekly working time for all employees from thirty-six hours down to a minimum of thirty hours (or something in-between). In this case, the wages are reduced correspondingly. As a trade-off, dismissal for economic reasons is excluded for the duration of the works agreement. The second option allows the conclusion of a works agreement for groups of employees and/or parts of the company. Again, a reduction of the weekly working time down to a minimum of thirty hours is possible. In this case, the affected employees do not suffer a fully corresponding wage loss. The pattern for partial wage reduction, however, is prescribed in the collective agreement.

640. This example (and many others that could be mentioned) shows that the originally centralized bargaining structure is now looking for a fair balance between

---

360. *Cf.* comprehensively A. Seifert, *Umfang und Grenzen der Zulässigkeit von tarifabweichenden Betriebsvereinbarungen* (2000), pp. 123 et seq.
361. As regards spreading, utilization and importance of opening clauses *cf.* S. Kohaut & C. Schnabel, 'Tarifliche Öffnungsklauseln: Verbreitung, Inanspruchnahme und Bedeutung', *Sozialer Fortschritt*, 2007, pp. 33–40; *cf. also* A. Seifert, *Employment Protection and Employment Promotion as Goals of Collective Bargaining in the Federal Republic of Germany*, The Int'l J. Comp. Lab. L. & Indus. Rel., 343–363 (1999); B. Waas, *Decentralizing Industrial Relations and the Role of Labor Unions and Employee Representatives in Germany*, The Japan Institute for Labour Policy and Training Report (2006), pp. 13–31.

centralized and decentralized bargaining. This, of course, has implications for the power relationship between trade unions and works councils, the latter becoming more and more powerful.

641. Another example of an opening clause, which should be mentioned, is the so-called hardship clause (*Härtefallklausel*). Such a hardship clause was, for example, included in the collective agreement concluded after the industrial conflict about the extraordinary termination of collective agreements in East Germany in 1993 (*see* paragraph 470). The hardship clause stipulates that the parties to the collective agreement, upon application of an employer or of a works council, may agree upon a provision permitting employer and works council to settle a works agreement of limited duration falling below the collective agreement. It is, however, up to the parties to the collective agreement to decide whether a hardship case is given. In the collective agreement, the following cases are acknowledged as hardship cases: prevention of an impending danger of insolvency, safeguarding of jobs, in particular in order to avoid impending dismissals, improvement of chances to stabilization based on a submitted stabilization plan.

642. However, there is still a large number of collective agreements in which the parties to the collective agreement could not agree upon inserting an opening clause into the collective agreement. In such cases works agreements deviating to the employees' disadvantage from the standards laid down in the collective agreement as regards remuneration, working hours, etc. are null and void. This follows from Section 77 paragraph 3 BetrVG. If employer and works council nevertheless conclude such a void works agreement a trade union represented in the establishment may claim to compel the employer to refrain from applying the void works agreement. This is why employers and works councils try to find ways to circumvent the ban of works agreements regulating matters 'already regulated' in a collective agreement. One such strategy of circumvention is that employer and works council bargain upon the necessary cuts. Negotiations result, however, not in a works agreement – such a works agreement would be void – but in amendments to every single individual employment contract (so-called standard type arrangements). Such amendments, of course, require the employees' approval. But in a situation where the works council, for fear of a collective dismissal or a full closing down of the establishment, agrees to a deterioration in working conditions, hardly any employee will dare to reject an offer amending his or her employment contract for the worse.

643. The more often such cases occur, however, the more endangered the system of collective agreement becomes. This is why there has been a very heated discussion among labour law scholars whether or not trade unions should be entitled to take legal action against standard type arrangements regulating matters 'already regulated' in a collective agreement. In 1999, the Federal Labour Court finally, in a very controversial decision, granted such a claim.[362] According to the court, the right of parties to a collective agreement to conclude collective agreements regulating working and economic conditions as guaranteed in Article 9 paragraph 3 GG was otherwise violated. The collective freedom of association was infringed not only by preventing an association from concluding a collective agreement, but also by agreements and measures aimed at frustrating or bypassing a collective agreement. This, however, would not mean that any agreement contravening a collective agreement had to be regarded as violating the collective freedom of association. Single provisions contravening a collective agreement, either in an employment contract or in a works agreement, did not jeopardize the respective collective agreement. Only if a provision in a collective agreement as a collective system was supplanted and should hence be deprived of its core function could a violation of the constitutionally guaranteed freedom of association, however, be asserted. Thus, an infringement of Article 9 paragraph 3 GG required a provision which was intended to have uniform effects and which should replace a provision of a collective agreement. If the works council supported uniform offers to worsen individual employment contracts this requirement was met. Contrary to the principles applicable to the relationship between collective agreements and works agreements as explained *supra* (*see* paragraph 637), these principles, developed by the Federal Labour Court, are, however, applicable only on condition that the collective agreement is binding upon the respective employment relationship.

644. This decision of the Federal Labour Court provoked, as already mentioned, a lot of controversy, especially from the employers' side. Whether or not the trade unions will indeed make use of this new 'weapon', they will have to consider thoroughly. For a trade union, insisting on compliance with the provisions of a collective agreement always risks being blamed for an eventual closing down of the enterprise and the loss of all jobs – a reputation no trade union is very eager to gain. So far, only a few cases have had to be decided.[363]

645. In matters in which the works council has a real right to co-determination, i.e., in matters enumerated in Section 87 paragraph 1 BetrVG, the conflict between collective agreements and the powers of the works council has to be solved in a different way, otherwise any regulation in a collective agreement would lead to the expansion of managerial decision-making powers and diverge from the intention of the BetrVG. Therefore, conflicts are solved as follows: it is still the prerogative of parties to a collective agreement to regulate matters themselves. However, once they have dealt with a matter, this does not mean that the works council completely loses its right to co-determination. First, the position of the works council is affected only

362. Federal Labour Court, 20 Apr. 1999 – 1 ABR 72/98, *Arbeitsrechtliche Praxis*, No. 89 Art. 9 GG; M. Weiss, 'Zum Verhältnis von Individuum und Kollektiv im Arbeitsrecht', in D. Simon & M. Weiss (eds), *Zur Autonomie des Individuums. Liber Amicorum Spiros Simitis* (2000), Baden-Baden, pp. 467 et seq.

363. For example ArbG Marburg, dec. of 3 Jan. 2006 – 1 Ca 671/05, *Arbeit und Recht*, 2006, p. 133; Sächs. LAG, dec. of 13 Nov. 2001 – 7 Sa 118/01, *Arbeit und Recht*, 2004, p. 155; LAG Sachsen-Anhalt, dec. of 8 May 2001 – 9 (5) Sa 723/00, *Arbeit und Recht*, 2002, p. 308; Federal Labour Court, dec. of 13 Mar. 2001 – 1 AZB 19/00, *BAGE*, vol. 97, p. 167.

if the establishment is covered by a collective agreement. Second, co-determination is only excluded if the provision provided for in the collective agreement is so detailed and specific that no room is left for alternative decisions. If there is any leeway for alternative managerial decisions, the right of the works council to co-determination must be respected.

§3. The Works Constitution in the Public Sector

646. As has already been mentioned, only the most evident differences between the works constitution in the private and the works constitution in the public sector will be indicated here. One of the most important differences refers to the organizational structure. As previously shown, the BetrVG 1972 provides works councils at establishment level, company works councils at enterprise level and group works councils at the level of the parent company of a group of enterprises. There is no hierarchy between the three; the main competence remains with the works council (*see* paragraph 580). However, the organizational structure of staff representation in the public sector takes into account that state administration is structured in hierarchical patterns. Consequently, staff representation is organized along these hierarchical patterns: at the lowest level of the public sector establishment, there is a body called staff council (*Personalrat*), at the medium level of the regional public sector establishment there is the regional staff council, and, at top level, the main staff council. Hence, there is a staff council provided for at every level. The minimum size for a public sector establishment to establish a staff council corresponds to the minimum size of establishments in the private sector. The members of the regional staff council, and those of the main staff council, are not appointed by the staff council at lower levels but elected by those employees who are covered by the regional staff council. The same applies to the main staff council. The staff councils at upper levels enjoy the greatest power. Therefore, they need the highest legitimation that can only be provided by a secret ballot of all the employees they represent.

647. If, as laid down in the BPersVG 1974, an agreement between staff council and the head of the public sector establishment is necessary but cannot be reached, the conflict has to be transferred to the next higher level. The final decision is made by agreement between the main staff council and the head of the top public sector establishment. If an agreement cannot be reached, it is the arbitration committee, which is to resolve the conflict. The arbitration committee in the public sector is structured in a way similar to that in the private sector. If, according to the organizational rules of administration, the head of a lower level unit is not authorized to make a decision on a certain matter it is from the very outset up to the staff council at the upper level to handle the matter. The hierarchical system of staff representation in the public sector is not only very complicated but tends to produce decisions at the top level rather than at lower levels.

648. The hierarchical organization of the staff council as just explained also applies to the structure of the juvenile delegation for employees under 18 years of age. The number of members of the staff council corresponds to the number of employees in the public sector establishment. While so far the same principles apply as in the private sector, there is one basic difference: the size of the staff council is limited to thirty-one members.

649. Whereas in the private sector only employees are represented, representation in the public sector is extended to a third group: career public servants (*see* paragraph 29). Each group elects its candidates by secret ballot but the majority of each group may decide on a joint election. Even if the staff council, as a body, represents both groups it should be stressed that in view of personnel matters relating to career public servants the staff council has only a very restricted right to participate. According to a decision of the Federal Constitutional Court of 1959, which was confirmed in 1995, personnel matters of career public servants are subject to the government's prerogative and may hence be subject to employee participation only in a very limited way.[364]

364. Dec. of 27 Apr. 1959 – 2 BvF 2/58, *Neue Juristische Wochenschrift*, 1959, p. 1171; 24 May 1995 – 2 BvF 1/92, *Neue Zeitschrift für Verwaltungsrecht*, 1996, 574.

Chapter 6. Employee Representation on the Supervisory Board

§1. Historical Development

650. As previously mentioned (*see* paragraph 40), participation and democratization of all areas of society became the key words of the labour movement around the turn of the nineteenth to the twentieth century. Workers' representation by works councils was only considered as a first step towards this goal. Democratization of the economy as a whole was the model developed by the labour movement in the Weimar era. According to this model, employee participation at all levels of decision-making (enterprise, region and state) would have to be established. This model, however, remained a programme during the Weimar era.

651. Employee representation on the supervisory board is understood to be one further step towards this goal to change the power structure in the economic field. The first successes in realizing this programme were reached in the mining and the iron and steel industries. After the Second World War, the enterprises in these areas of industry faced the danger of being totally dismembered by the Allied Forces. In order to fight this danger these industries sought the support of the unions. Since the unions had not been affiliated to the Nazi regime, they had an important voice in this context. In order to obtain the support of trade unions the responsible persons of these industries offered equal representation of employees on the supervisory boards of the respective companies in exchange. Thus, a model was established which, after heated controversy, was confirmed by the legislator in 1951 when the Act on Co-determination by Employees on the Supervisory Boards and Management Boards of Undertakings of the Mining and the Iron and Steel Manufacturing Industries (*Montan-Mitbestimmungsgesetz* – Montan-MitbestG) was passed. This historical development explains why, until today, the situation in the mining and the iron and steel industries differs from that in all other German industries.

652. In 1952, the political circumstances had already changed: the danger of dismemberment had been banned. This is why the 1952 BetrVG, which has been replaced by the Act on One-Third Participation (*Drittelbeteiligungsgesetz* – DrittelbG) in 2004, introduced a model of employee representation on the supervisory board, which remained far below the level of representation reached in the mining and the iron and steel industries. In the following years, the unions made great efforts to extend the 1951 model of the mining and the iron and steel industries to all areas of industry. Finally, in 1976 a compromise was reached. The Act on Co-Determination by Employees (*Mitbestimmungsgesetz* – MitbestG) introduced a third model that has to be understood as an attempt to close the gap between the two previous models. This explains why there are still three different models today.

§2. The Role of the Supervisory Board

653. In order to understand the impact of employee representation on the supervisory board, it is necessary to understand the general role of this board within the power structure of an enterprise.[365] Under company law, the supervisory board is a company organ which is required in the case of registered cooperative societies (*eingetragene Genossenschaften*) and public limited companies (*Aktiengesellschaften* – AG); in the case of private limited companies (*Gesellschaften mit beschränkter Haftung*) it is obligatory only if certain preconditions apply, in all other cases it is optional. It should be stressed that, from the very outset, the acts providing employee representation on the supervisory board did not create new bodies. They simply fitted employee representation into the traditional corporate framework, modifying only the composition of the governing bodies. Supervisory boards and management boards, which existed prior to the introduction of employee participation, have retained their traditional functions. The only difference is that these boards are no longer composed exclusively of individuals guided by the interest of the owners.

654. According to the traditional German two boards system of company laws, it is exclusively the management board (*Vorstand*) which represents and manages the enterprise. The supervisory board (*Aufsichtsrat*) has only two basic functions: to elect the members of the management board and to supervise the activities of the management board. The members of the management board are elected by majority vote of the supervisory board for a certain period. In order to fulfil its controlling tasks the supervisory board has an extended right to information. The management board is obliged to supply the supervisory board with comprehensive information on all basic issues referring to the management of the enterprise at least once per year. Besides, the supervisory board or any member of the supervisory board can request at any time additional information on affairs of importance for the enterprise. The management board is statutorily obliged to meet such a request.

655. The shareholder meeting (*Hauptversammlung/ Gesellschafterversammlung*) or even the supervisory board itself may, by majority vote, extend the power of the supervisory board. They are authorized to establish rules according to which several important managerial decisions require the consent of the supervisory board in order to become effective. But even if the supervisory board refuses its consent, the management board may reach a decision in spite of the refusal of the supervisory board: it may appeal to the shareholder meeting which always has the power to overrule the consent of the supervisory board. This possibility cannot be excluded.

656. It should be mentioned that the legal and factual powers of the supervisory board depend on the legal type of company. The supervisory board of a public limited company is, however, still the strongest, when compared to other models of company law, for example to the supervisory board of a private limited company.

365. For more information *cf.* H.-D. Assmann, B. Lange & R. Sethe, 'Chapter 5: The Law of Business Associations', in *Introduction to German Law* 143–177 (J. Zekoll & M. Reimann eds. 2nd edn, 2005); *see also* P. Leyens, *German Company Law: Recent Developments and Future Challenges*, German L. J. 1407–1417 (2005).

657. According to law, members of the supervisory board meet once every quarter of a year, at least twice a year. Since the management board is full-time occupied to manage the enterprise, and since it has access to a staff of experts preparing its decisions, it is perfectly clear that the management board is by far the more powerful body of the two.

§3. The Basic Structure of Employee Representation on the Supervisory Board

I. The Model of the Mining, Iron and Steel Industry

658. The model of the mining, iron and steel industry is based on equal representation of shareholders and employees on the supervisory board, the chairpersonship being reserved for a 'neutral' person, elected by majority vote of both, employee representatives and shareholder representatives. The Montan-MitbestG is, according to Section 1 paragraphs 1 and 2 Montan-MitbestG, applicable to enterprises constituted as public limited companies, private limited companies or incorporated cost-book mining companies employing more than 1,000 employees.

659. The supervisory board, as a rule, consists of eleven members. According to Section 4 Montan-MitbestG, in very big enterprises the number may, under certain conditions described in Section 9 Montan-MitbestG, be extended to fifteen or even twenty-one members. Taking the usual case of a supervisory board with eleven members, shareholders and employees each appoint five members.

660. According to Section 6 paragraph 1 Montan-MitbestG, at least two of the employee representatives must belong to the workforce of the enterprise. The remaining three employee representatives do not need to be employed by the enterprise but may be external representatives. Whereas two of the three external members may in terms of Section 6 paragraph 3 Montan-MitbestG be, and always are, members of the respective unions, the third member (the so-called additional member) must be neither a trade union member nor an employee of the respective enterprise nor have economic interests in the enterprise (Section 4 paragraph 2 Montan-MitbestG). The employee representatives belonging to the workforce of the enterprise are, after consultation of the unions represented in the enterprise, nominated by secret ballot among the works councils of the enterprise (Section 6 paragraph 5 Montan-MitbestG). The candidates for the remaining three seats are proposed by the unions represented in the enterprise. Among those proposed, the representatives are again, by secret ballot, nominated by the works councils of the enterprise. Finally, all nominated representatives have to be formally elected and confirmed by the shareholder assembly. The nominations, however, are binding on the assembly. This follows from Sections 5 and 6 paragraph 6 Montan-MitbestG. The election is only a formality in order to correspond with the original structure of the electoral power of the shareholder assembly.

661. According to Section 8 Montan-MitbestG, the neutral chairperson of the supervisory board is nominated by majority vote of the other members of the supervisory board (shareholder representatives and employee representatives). This nomination is again binding on the shareholder meeting, which should formally elect and confirm the chairperson. If a majority decision on the supervisory board cannot be obtained a rather complicated procedure for nominating a candidate is provided for. If this procedure fails to be successful it is up to the shareholders to decide. A neutral chairperson is necessary to ensure that the supervisory board can overcome a deadlock between shareholder representatives and employee representatives.

662. The Montan-MitbestG 1951 not only provides for employee representation on the supervisory board. It allows for the first time, and so far the last time, employee representation on the management board. As a full member of the management board (enjoying equal rights) an 'employee director in charge of personnel and social affairs of the enterprise' (*Arbeitsdirektor*) must be elected in terms of Section 13 Montan-MitbestG. Contrary to the employee director in charge of personnel and social affairs of the enterprise provided for in Section 33 MitbestG 1976 (*see* paragraph 670), the employee director in terms of Section 13 Montan-MitbestG cannot be elected against the majority of votes of the employee representatives on the supervisory board. However, once elected, the employee director has the same legal status as all other members of the management board.[366]

663. In the period after 1951, it turned out that employee representation in enterprises of the mining and of the iron and steel industries was not very helpful if the representatives did not have access to the supervisory board of the parent enterprise of the group. Therefore, the 1956 Act Amending the Montan-MitbestG (*Mitbestimmungsergänzungsgesetz* – MitbestErgG) extended the model established by the Montan-MitbestG 1951 to the holding company of a group of companies, provided that the group objective was characterized by companies of the group whose main activities took place in the mining and iron and steel industries. Meanwhile it appears that fewer and fewer holding companies fulfil this requirement. The number of controlling companies of groups, which are still active in the mining and iron and steel industries but whose main activities take place in other industries and which therefore would not be covered by the 1951 and 1956 Act, has been increasing. This is why in 1981, after very heated debates, the Act Amending the Montan-MitbestG and the MitbestErgG (*Gesetz zur Änderung des MontanMitbestimmungsgesetzes und des Mitbestimmungs-Ergänzungsgesetzes*) was passed. Accordingly, the 1951 and 1956 Acts, for a period of six years after the date when the activities in the mining, iron and steel industries ceased to be predominant, are still applicable to the controlling company. At the end of 1987, when two of the at that time five controlling companies of groups to which the 1951 Act and the 1981 Act respectively had been applicable would otherwise have failed to

366. For more information on the *Arbeitsdirektor see* K. Blessing & K.-P. Otto, 'The Labour Director – A Manager Trusted by the Workforce', *Mitbestimmung*, 8/2002, p. 66.

qualify for future application of the mining, iron and steel model of employee representation on the supervisory board, the 1981 Act was extended until the end of 1988 and then replaced by the Act Securing Co-Determination in the Mining, Iron and Steel Manufacturing Industries (*Gesetz zur Sicherung der Montanmitbestimmung*). The latter Act *inter alia* dramatically reduced the requirements for controlling companies to be covered by the Acts of 1951 and 1956: instead of a share of mining, iron and steel activities within the group of at least 50%, it is now sufficient that the mining, iron and steel activities sum up to a share of 20% or that at least 2,000 employees are employed in those industries.

664. This enormous increase of the scope of application has led to a hostile reaction of the holding companies affected. One of them initiated a lawsuit claiming that the 1988 Act was incompatible with the Constitution. In 1999, when the claim had been pending for already eight years, the Federal Constitutional Court decided that the 1988 Act was incompatible with the general principle of equal treatment as guaranteed in Article 3 paragraph 1 GG inasmuch as the employment of 2,000 employees suffices for the application of the 1988 Act.[367] According to the Federal Constitutional Court, the principle of equal treatment required that enterprises to which the 1988 Act was applicable should show adequate reference to the mining, iron and steel industry. Such an adequate reference was given as regards the requirement that 20% of the group turnover must be achieved in the mining, iron and steel sector. This, however, did not apply to the alternative condition of 2,000 employees being employed in this sector. The connection of a company to the mining, iron and steel industry could not be ascertained by absolute numbers of employees employed in that industry but only by comparing that number to the total number of employees in the whole group. In the case pending before the Federal Constitutional Court 2,000 employees correlated to 2.5% of all employees – a share too small to prove an adequate reference to the mining, iron and steel industry. Therefore, the 1988 Act was amended by the Second Act Simplifying the Election of Employee Representatives Within the Supervisory Board (*Zweites Gesetz zur Vereinfachung der Wahl der Arbeitnehmervertreter im Aufsichtsrat*) in 2004. The requirement of '2,000 employees' has been replaced by the criterion 'one-fifth of all employees of all group companies'.

665. By the end of the 1980s, the number of enterprises subject to the specific form of employee representation in the mining, the iron and steel industries had fallen to 31. Due to unification, this figure rose to forty-six in 1991, stood at ca. 45–50 in 2006 and in 2011 the number of co-determined companies was again thirty-one. Presently, there is no holding falling under the MitbestErgG. The number of employees in this sector fell during the 1980s from 434,000 in 1985 to 352,000 in 1990. After unification, it briefly rose to 492,000, only to decline to 307,000 by 1994. In 1996, the number of employees in companies subject to this form of co-determination amounted to around 400,000. This means that at least 100,000 employees active outside the mining, iron and steel industry were represented by supervisory boards set up in accordance with the 1951 Act.

367. Dec. of 3 Mar. 1999 – 1 BvL 2/91, *Arbeitsrechtliche Praxis*, No. 2 §3 MitbestErgG.

II. The Model of the One-Third Participation Act

666. The application of this model established by the BetrVG 1952, which has been replaced by the DrittelbG 2004, is again limited to enterprises structured as specific legal forms of a company: as public limited companies, as private limited companies, as incorporated cost-book companies under mining law, as co-operatives, or as mutual insurance companies. With the exception of public limited companies, it depends on the legal and factual status whether or not these enterprises have to establish a supervisory board at all. The DrittelbG only applies where there is a supervisory board. As follows from Section 1 DrittelbG, the enterprises covered by this model must employ more than 500 employees. According to the latest available figures from an evaluation of 2009, there were almost 1,500 companies in which a third of the shares were held, most of which were limited liability companies and stock corporations.[368]

667. According to Section 4 DrittelbG, one-third of the supervisory board members must be employee representatives. The size of the supervisory board depends on the rules of company law. If there is only one or if there are only two employee representative to be elected, they must be persons employed by the enterprise. If more employee representatives are to be elected they should at least include two employees of the enterprise. As regards the remaining employee representatives there are no special provisions. Consequently, it is possible, but not necessary, to elect external candidates. Employee representatives are elected by all employees of the enterprise over 18 years of age (Section 5 paragraph 2 DrittelbG). Works councils as well as one-tenth of the employees of the enterprise, or at least 100 employees, are entitled to put forward lists of candidates (Section 6 DrittelbG).

III. The Model of the 1976 Co-determination Act

668. Like any other Act concerning employee representation on the supervisory board the MitbestG of 1976 is applicable to enterprises of a certain size and constituted as specific legal persons. It covers public limited companies, partnerships limited by shares, private limited companies, incorporated cost-book mining companies and co-operatives, which employ at least 2,000 employees. As far as holding companies of groups of companies are concerned, the MitbestG 1976 is applicable to companies employing fewer than 2,000 employees provided that the holding company and the German group companies together have at least 2,000 employees. The MitbestG 1976, moreover, applies to companies with fewer than 2,000 employees whose structure corresponds to one of the above-mentioned legal forms of companies that are, within a partnership limited by shares, a partner of unlimited responsibility and which employ at least 2,000 employees including the employees of this partnership. As with the other acts on co-determination mentioned above, temporary workers in the company of the hirer are to be counted in determining the

368. I.M.U. (ed.), *Unternehmensmitbestimmung*, 3.9 Wie viele mitbestimmte Unternehmen gibt es in Deutschland?, https://www.imu-boeckler.de/de/unternehmensmitbestimmung-17362.htm.

threshold value if their period of employment exceeds six months (*see* Section 14 paragraph 2 sentence 6 AÜG). The minimum duration of employment is to be understood in relation to the workplace. The decisive factor is whether the company uses temporary workers to fill jobs for more than six months during a year, regardless of whether the temporary workers change jobs and whether they are used in the same or different jobs.[369]

669. In 1996, 728 companies were covered by the 1976 Act. Back in 1983, the figure was 481, since when there has been a steady increase. In 1990, the 1976 Act covered 522 companies. In 1991 one year after the unification, it initially jumped up to 575, and subsequently rose to 719 in 1995. According to the Institute for Co-determination and Corporate Governance (Institut für Mitbestimmung und Unternehmensführung, I.M.U.) of the Hans-Böckler-Stiftung, however, in 2013, 651 companies and in 2018, only 638 companies were covered by the Act.[370] If an enterprise covered by the 1976 MitbestG is a holding company, the employees of the subsidiaries participate in the election of the employee representatives to the supervisory board of the holding company. Therefore, the number of subsidiaries, which are thus indirectly covered by the 1976 MitbestG, is much higher than the number of directly affected enterprises. It should be stressed that foreign subsidiaries are not included. In the mid-1980s the number of employees in enterprises co-determined under the 1976 Act was estimated at around 4.5 million. By 1996, this number had risen to 5.0 million.

670. Similar to the model of the Montan-MitbestG (*see* paragraph 662), an 'employee director in charge of personnel and social affairs of the enterprise' must be appointed according to Section 33 MitbestG 1976. Unlike the employee director under the Montan-MitbestG, the employee representatives on the supervisory board, however, do not possess a right of veto.

671. In enterprises covered by the 1976 MitbestG, the supervisory board consists of an equal number of shareholder representatives and employee representatives (Section 7 MitbestG). The size of the board is determined as follows: in enterprises with up to 10,000 employees 12 representatives, 6 from each side; in enterprises with more than 10,000 and up to 20,000 employees 16 representatives, 8 from each side; and in enterprises with more than 20,000 employees 20 representatives, 10 from each side. The company statutes may enlarge this size. A board consisting of twelve members may be enlarged to sixteen members, and a board consisting of sixteen members may be enlarged to twenty members, which is the maximum.

672. On supervisory boards comprising twelve or sixteen members, two seats and on supervisory boards comprising twenty members, three seats must be reserved for trade union representatives (Section 7 paragraph 2 MitbestG). The

369. Federal Court of Justice, 25 Jun. 2019 – II ZB 21/18, *BGHZ 222*, 266.
370. I.M.U. (ed.), *Unternehmensmitbestimmung*, 3.9 Wie viele mitbestimmte Unternehmen gibt es in Deutschland?, https://www.imu-boeckler.de/de/unternehmensmitbestimmung-17362.htm.

remaining seats on the employees' side (four, six, or seven, depending on the size of the board) are reserved for employees of the enterprise.

673. In holding companies of a group of companies, employees of the holding company as well as employees of the subsidiaries may be elected to the supervisory board. For the purpose of election to the supervisory board, the employees of all subsidiaries of a group are considered to be employees of the holding company.

674. The procedure for the election of employee representatives is provided for in Sections 10–24 MitbestG. It is extremely complicated. Two types of election must be distinguished: direct election by majority vote of all employees of the enterprise, and election by delegates. In enterprises with up to 8,000 employees, direct election is the rule, whereas in enterprises of a larger size election by delegates is the normal procedure. This follows from Section 9 paragraphs 2 and 3 MitbestG. Under certain conditions, employees of enterprises with up to 8,000 employees may decide by majority vote to have an election by delegates, and employees in enterprises larger than this, again by majority vote, may decide to have direct elections.

675. The trade union representatives are always elected by ballot among delegates or among all employees (Sections 16, 18 MitbestG). Candidates may be nominated by all trade unions represented in the enterprise or in the group. However, it is entirely up to the election whether these candidates will succeed or not. Contrary to the provisions for the mining, iron and steel industry, the employees are, in direct elections as well as in elections by delegates, entitled to reject any proposed union candidate. Thus, it is up to the employees of the enterprise to finally decide by whom the union is represented in the supervisory board.

676. According to Section 27 MitbestG, the chairperson and the vice-chairperson of the supervisory board are to be elected by a two-thirds majority among supervisory board members. If in a ballot a two-thirds majority is not attained, the shareholder representatives elect the chairperson. In this case, the employees are entitled to elect the vice-chairperson from among their own group. Due to this rule, the presidency in practice is reserved to the shareholder representatives. Since, contrary to the model in the mining, iron and steel industry, there is no neutral chairperson to overcome a deadlock in the event of a tie, a solution had to be found. According to the solution provided by Section 29 paragraph 2 MitbestG 1976, the final decision in any case rests with the shareholders. If a second ballot has to be held on account of a tie, and if this second ballot again results in a tie the chairperson of the supervisory board has the casting vote. This casting vote is a personal privilege of the chairperson, which cannot be exercised by the vice-chairperson. If the chairperson cannot attend the meeting, he or she may authorize another member of the supervisory board to vote on his or her behalf. This authorization may include the transfer of the casting vote.

677. Employee representatives on the supervisory board are usually trade union members. This applies not only to the external representatives but also to those employed in the respective enterprise or group. The number of non-unionized members is marginal: it ranges around 3%. This, of course, is different as far as representatives of executive staff are concerned: they usually do not belong to a trade union. Statistics on their affiliation to member associations of the ULA are, however, not available.

678. In spite of the fact that the MitbestG 1976 had been passed in Parliament with overwhelming majority, the Federal Constitutional Court, on the initiative of nine enterprises and twenty-nine employers' associations, was asked to examine its constitutionality. This was surprising because the constitutionality of the Montan-MitbestG had never been contested before. Those who appealed to the Federal Constitutional Court claimed that the extension of employees' equal representation on the supervisory board of all industries in the private sector implied a new situation. The alleged violation of the Constitution was mainly based on two aspects: the MitbestG was considered to be incompatible with the constitutional guarantee of private property of means of production as guaranteed in Article 14 GG for according to the plaintiffs' view, owners of enterprises would no longer be free to use their invested capital in the way they wished. Furthermore, they argued that the MitbestG violated their freedom of association as granted in Article 9 paragraph 3 GG. According to the plaintiffs' view, the MitbestG destroyed the strict separation of employers and employees, which is understood to be a condition of the system of free collective bargaining as provided for by Article 9 paragraph 3 GG. In a very notable decision of 1 March 1979, the Federal Constitutional Court dismissed the constitutional complaint and confirmed the constitutionality of the 1976 MitbestG.[371] According to the Constitutional Court, the MitbestG was neither a danger to collective bargaining nor did it prevent the proper functioning of enterprises. Since the final decisions within the supervisory board still rested within the shareholder representatives, the guarantee of private property was not violated. While the constitutionality of the MitbestG 1976 is no longer subject of controversy, the question whether and how far it would be possible to extend employee representation on the supervisory board beyond the level of the MitbestG is still open. In this respect, the decision of the Federal Constitutional Court is rather sibylline.

679. However, whether or not employee representation should be extended beyond the MitbestG 1976 is not the most topical question today. On the contrary, stimulated by the discussion on the European company, by the case law of the CJEU on freedom of establishment[372] and by the fact that German board-level co-determination is rather unique within the EU,[373] there are strong political forces striving for a general restriction of board-level employee representation to a third of board members. For example, the FDP has suggested cutting back board-level

371. Dec. of 1 Mar. 1979 – 1 BvR 532/77 et al., *Arbeitsrechtliche Praxis*, No. 1 §1 MitbestG; *cf.* M. Weiss, 'Zur aktuellen Bedeutung des Mitbestimmungsurteils BVerfGE 50, 290', *Kritische Vierteljahresschrift für Gesetzgebung und Rechtswissenschaft*, 2000, pp. 405 et seq.

372. *See* Ch. Kersting & C. Schindler, *The ECJ's Inspire Art Decision of 30 September 2003 and Its Effects on Practice*, German L. J. 1277–1291 (2003) with further proofs.

373. For an evaluation of German co-determination in the 1990s in international and comparative perspective *see* K. Thelen & L. Turner, *German Codetermination in Comparative Perspective* (1997).

co-determination for corporations of any size to a third of supervisory board seats. The so-called Berlin network on corporate governance strongly favours a separate consultation council.[374] Furthermore early in 2004, the Commission on Co-Determination, established jointly by the Confederation of German Employers' Associations (BDA) and the Federation of German Industries (BDI), has presented a rather elaborate proposal to modernize the system of board-level co-determination.[375] The Commission proposes an agreement solution resembling the one known from European secondary labour law: priority for negotiations between management and employee representatives combined with a statutory fall-back solution. According to the Commission, board-level co-determination should be a matter to be negotiated between management and employee representatives. To structure these negotiations, three statutory model options were suggested. (1) The first option is modelled upon the present model of co-determination under the 1976 MitbestG (*see* paragraphs 668 et seq.). The Act applies to stock corporations – in particular to public and private joint stock companies and limited liability companies – employing more than 2,000 employees, i.e., in 2015 ca. 635 companies. In corporations falling under this act, half of the number of supervisory board seats has to be filled with employee representatives. In order to prevent a parity of votes, the chairperson, who is usually elected from among the shareholder representatives on the supervisory board, has the casting vote. (2) The second option is based on the model of co-determination under the 2004 DrittelbG (*see* paragraphs 666–667). (3) As for the third option, the Commission on Co-determination does not suggest to maintain the third, very strong model of board-level co-determination currently applicable in the coal and steel industries (*see* paragraphs 658–665). Instead, a new one, particularly recommended for corporations with one board only is suggested: the model of a consultation and information body separate from the supervisory board and consisting exclusively of employee representatives.

680. In view of this debate, the former Chancellor Schröder established a Commission on Co-determination, chaired by K. Biedenkopf. Its results were presented in December 2006 to Chancellor Merkel.[376] The Commission found no reason to recommend a fundamental amendment of the German law on co-determination. Instead, the experts recommended a further evolution of the system, based on the experiences of the past decades in order to adapt the system to the changed institutional and economic framework. Particularly, the Commission recommended allowing contractual agreements, deviating from the statutory law, on the status of co-determination in group structures and on the size of the supervisory board. The election procedure should be simplified. And employees employed outside Germany should have the possibility to be elected as a member of the supervisory board. Furthermore, the academic members of the Commission saw no necessity for

374. Berliner Netzwerk Corporate Governance, *Corporate Governance und Modernisierung der Mitbestimmung* (2003), Berlin.
375. Kommission Mitbestimmung von BDA und BDI, *Mitbestimmung modernisieren* (2004), Berlin.
376. Kommission zur Modernisierung der deutschen Unternehmensmitbestimmung, *Bericht* (2006), available at http://www.bundesregierung.de/Content/DE/Artikel/2006/12/Anlagen/2006-12-20-mitbestimmungskommission,property=publicationFile.pdf.

amendments as regards the right of a second vote of the supervisory board chairperson or the appointment of the *Arbeitsdirektor* under the MitbestG 1976 (*see* paragraph 668).

681. Whether the 1974 Co-Determination Act is compatible with Union law has been repeatedly questioned by literary circles in the past. In proceedings before the Berlin Court of Appeal (*Kammergericht Berlin*) in 2015, this question was raised and referred to the CJEU for a preliminary ruling. The objection was that only employees at domestic company locations can participate in the Supervisory Board elections. It was argued that the German system of co-determination thus discriminates against employees abroad in the German parent company. In addition, it could discourage employees from moving to a subsidiary in another EU country, which would constitute an obstacle to the free movement of workers. If the lawsuit had been successful, there would have been a great danger that the co-determination system as a whole would be overturned. In July 2017, the CJEU confirmed the conformity of the Act with EU law.[377] The court stated that the rules on the free movement of workers are not applicable to employees who have never exercised their right to free movement within the Union. This freedom does not guarantee that moving to another EU Member State is neutral from a social point of view. Furthermore, there is a lack of EU harmonization and coordination measures in the area of co-determination. The German provisions on co-determination may therefore be limited to employees who are employed by domestic companies.[378]

§4. Legal Status of Employee Representatives

682. The legal status of employee representatives on the supervisory board and the legal status of shareholder representatives on the supervisory board is identical. Employee representatives have the same rights and duties as supervisory board members representing the owners. There is no subject whatsoever reserved to representatives of one side. Employee representatives share any information accessible to members of the supervisory board and are free to express their views on any matter discussed by the board.

683. According to traditional company law, members of the supervisory board are free to discuss company matters among themselves but are prohibited from disclosing this information to other persons, either inside or outside the enterprise. This duty of secrecy also applies to employee representatives. Thus, employee representatives are unable to communicate with their constituency, discuss issues with them, listen to their views and to transmit these views to the supervisory board. This leads to isolation of the representatives and to alienation from the constituency. The effect is a loss of legitimation of employee representatives on the supervisory board. The

377. CJEU, 18 Jul. 2017 – C-566/15 (Erzberger), ECLI:EU:C:2017:562; *cf.* case note of A. Seifert, in 8 Eur. Lab. L. J. 333-343 (2017).

378. *Cf.* J. Heuschmid, Unternehmensmitbestimmung verstößt nicht gegen Unionsrecht, *Arbeit und Recht 2018*, pp. 245–247.

duty of secrecy even prevents employee representatives on the supervisory board from supplying information to the works council, whereas, as previously shown, in the opposite direction free communication is permitted.

684. The 'interest of the enterprise' is the decisive legal point of orientation for both groups, shareholder representatives and employee representatives. This has led to a new understanding of this traditional criterion. Formerly 'interest of the enterprise' was exclusively understood as meaning the interest of the capital owners.[379] Now it is generally agreed that the notion also covers employee interests.[380] The term has thus become extremely vague, which has led to the fact that, in actual practice, it may be doubted how valid it still is to confine activities of supervisory board members.

685. Equal status of employee representatives and shareholder representatives implies that employee representatives are entitled to equal remuneration. Since remuneration for being a supervisory board member could be a source of corruption, employee representatives on the supervisory board who are trade union members are, according to the standing rules of the unions, obliged to transfer a high percentage of this payment to a union foundation. This duty to transfer the remuneration, of course, does not apply to representatives who are not union members.

686. Shareholder representatives evidently do not need protection against dismissal or a right to participate in vocational programmes in order to become qualified for their jobs. This is different for employee representatives. If they are employed in the enterprise, protection against dismissal may be just as necessary as for members of the works council. Moreover, if they really want to influence the policy of the supervisory board they need to be highly qualified, especially in view of the fact that the representatives on the shareholders' side are usually qualified experts in economic and financial affairs. This is why it would be appropriate to give them a right to participate in vocational programmes without loss of pay, similar to works council members. Nevertheless, due to the principle of equal legal status of employee representatives and shareholder representatives, such instruments taking account of the specific situation of employee representatives do not exist.

687. Even if the situation of employee representatives is not taken into consideration by the MitbestG, the Montan-MitbestG or the DrittelbG, it is generally agreed that employee representatives shall be released from their duty to work to participate in supervisory board meetings without loss of pay.

688. The supervisory board is free to establish subcommittees on all kinds of matters. It has turned out that decisions, once prepared by subcommittees, tend to influence the decisions of the board. This is why the composition of subcommittees is understood to be an important question. According to traditional company law

379. S. Laske, 'Unternehmensinteresse und Mitbestimmung', *Zeitschrift für Unternehmens- und Gesellschaftsrecht*, 1979, pp. 173 et seq.
380. T. Raiser, *Mitbestimmungsrecht* (4th edn, 2002), §25 paras 112 et seq.

there are no restrictions referring to the composition of such subcommittees. Thus, the question arises whether and how this has changed. The acts on employee representation on the supervisory board do not regulate this matter. However, it is evident that subcommittees could become a tool to deviate the purpose of employee representation on the supervisory board. This is why the question arises whether or not subcommittees should be composed in the same way as the board.[381] This is still an open question. The conflict between the traditional rules of company law and the underlying idea of the acts on employee representation should be resolved not only as to the composition of subcommittees, but also in view of quite a few other matters not regulated in these acts.

§5. Characteristic Features of the Reality of Employee Representation on the Supervisory Board

689. As previously mentioned, the shareholder meeting or the supervisory board itself may provide rules whereby in specific cases decisions of the management board require the consent of the supervisory board. The number of such cases has diminished continuously since employee representation has been introduced. According to empirical studies, one-third of all enterprises covered by the MitbestG 1976 do not provide for such a consent requirement. When such cases are listed, they mainly refer to financial and economic activities and not directly to the employment situation in the enterprise. Consequently, access to information is in fact the only remaining field of activity for employee representatives.

690. The practical application of all three models is characterized by the fact that employee representatives on the supervisory board belong to the workforce of the enterprise and in most cases are also works council members. Overall, this has strengthened both instruments of participation. It has especially led to the establishment of informal channels. Since management, for obvious reasons, tends to remain on good terms with the works council, it also tends to prevent conflicts with works council members who are also members of the supervisory board. Therefore, before informing the supervisory board management tends to discuss critical questions with at least the internal employee representatives in informal meetings. The importance of these informal communications is the highest under the model of the Montan-MitbestG where the employee director functions as an important link. It is mainly these informal structures that tend to make employee representation on the supervisory board effective. The effect is a preventive one. Because of this informal communication, the manner in which management presents questions to the supervisory board may have changed quite a bit. This may explain why most decisions within the supervisory board are, in spite of employee representation, made unanimously. The privilege of internal representatives to participate in informal communication often causes tensions between internal and external representatives, which, overall, may lead to a weakening of employee representation on the supervisory board as such.

381. T. Raiser, *supra*, §25 paras 51 et seq.

691. Even though the law states that all members of the supervisory board are equally authorized to deal with all questions arising, employee representatives in fact concentrate mainly on the social aspects of company policies. This leads to the fact that their strategies usually remain reactive.

§6. Transposition of European Directives on Employee Representation

692. In addition to the three German models of employee representation on the supervisory board described above, there are new forms of employee representation evolving, induced by EC law: employee representation in the European Society (*Societas Europaea* – SE) and in the SCE (*see* paragraph 581) as well as in cases of cross-border mergers, the latter regulated by the 2006 Act on Employee Co-determination in Case of an Cross-Border Merger (*Gesetz über die Mitbestimmung der Arbeitnehmer bei einer grenzüberschreitenden Verschmelzung* – MgVG), implementing Directive 2005/56/EC. However, these different acts do not provide a certain model but provide for and allow a wide variety of different forms of employee representation.

693. When an SE is established, the level of participation already existing in the company remains largely protected. However, if the company continues to grow, there are disadvantages in terms of employee involvement compared with other forms of participation. The SE is criticised for being chosen by companies with the motivation to 'freeze' the current level of employee involvement.[382] This can be done in two ways, for example: If the workforce in a national company approaches the threshold of 500 employees, above which co-determination is to be introduced, it can be transformed into an SE. It is then no longer obliged to grant participation rights to its employees if the workforce increases to over 500 employees after the conversion. A further limit is set at 2,000 employees, above which the supervisory board is no longer to be filled with employee representatives not just one-third but half of its members. Furthermore, the size of the supervisory or administrative body can be frozen or fixed by the conversion into an SE, so that its size no longer increases when the workforce increases.[383]

---

382. M. Stolt & E. Wolters, *Arbeitnehmerbeteiligung in der Europäischen Aktiengesellschaft (SE), Ein Handbuch für die Praxis*, Düsseldorf 2012, p. 22.
383. M. Stolt & E. Wolters, *Arbeitnehmerbeteiligung in der Europäischen Aktiengesellschaft (SE), supra*, p. 22.

Chapter 7. The Role of Courts in Collective Labour Law

§1. The Role of Labour Courts

694. Labour courts, like all other courts, have jurisdiction only over disputes of rights and not over disputes of interest. Although this principle is uncontested, it should be stressed that the borderline between the two categories has become less and less clear. Labour courts are exclusively competent in all disputes of rights between parties to a collective agreement or between them and third parties, whether it concerns a dispute arising from collective agreements or whether it concerns a dispute about the existence of collective agreements. The same is true for disputes referring to industrial conflict.

695. The labour courts are not only competent in all matters concerning the works constitution in the private sector as well as in matters referring to the election procedure for employee representatives on the supervisory board, but also in matters concerning the capacity to conclude collective agreements and collective bargaining jurisdiction of employees' and employers' organizations.[384] For decisions in the aforementioned matters there is a special procedure provided for, the so-called *Beschluss* procedure, regulated in Sections 80–98 ArbGG. The basic differences between the *Beschluss* procedure and the ordinary *Urteil* procedure are the following: there are no adversary parties, only interested parties. Furthermore, it is up to the court itself to ascertain the underlying facts from the petitions of interested parties and to take evidence. A conciliation hearing is held only if the chairperson considers this useful.

696. Even if in view of the total workload of labour court cases dealing with matters of collective labour law only represent a small proportion, labour court activities in this field are much more important than those in the area of individual labour law. As shown in the preceding chapters, the structure of collective bargaining, the power relationship between the parties to industrial conflict and the structure of the works constitution are, to a significant extent, shaped by the labour courts.

697. A survey on the activities of labour courts of first instance in so-called *Beschluss* procedures:[385]

384. For more details *see* M. Weiss, *The Crucial Role of Courts in German Labour Law*, in B.J. Mulder et alii (eds.).Sui Generis. Festskrift til Stein Evju, Oslo 2016, 730 et seq.; M. Weiss, *Judge Made Labour Law in Germany*, in *Labour Law into the Future: Essays in honour of Darcy du Toit* 122 et seq (K. Malherbe & J. Sloth-Nielson eds. 2012).
385. The data for 2018 are based on Bundesministerium für Arbeit und Soziales (ed.), *Tätigkeit der Arbeitsgerichte 2018* (Berlin).

	1981	*1990*	*1997*	*2006*	*2018*
Cases still pending at the beginning of the new *year*	2,063	3,781	4,473	4,890	3,943
New applications	5,200	8,654	8,800	12,971	10,292
– initiated by employees, trade unions, works councils	3,365	5,590	5,448	9,783	7,973
– initiated by employers or employers' associations	1,833	3,061	3,342	3,187	2,264
– initiated by agencies of labour administration	2	3	10	1	1
Total number of cases	7,263	12,435	13,273	17,861	14,235
Cases settled within *the year*	5,576	9,242	9,566	13,793	10,238
– by judgment on the merits	1,723	2,674	2,722	3,117	2,624
– by compromise reached in court	1,913	2,650	2,065	3,537	3,837
– otherwise	1,940	3,918	4,779	7,139	3,777

	1981	*1990*	*1997*	*2006*	*2018*
Duration *from application until settlement*					
up to 1 month	1,434	2,288	1,827	3,912	2,805
1–3 months	2,522	3,258	2,937	3,384	2,443
3–6 months	923	1,609	2,298	2,967	2,441
6–12 months	514	1,255	1,414	2,850	1,989
more than 12 months	183	832	1,090	680	560
Cases not yet settled at the end of the year	1,687	3,193	3,707	4,068	3,989

698. Survey on the activities of *Land* labour courts in so-called *Beschluss* procedures:[386]

	1981	*1990*	*1997*	*2006*	*2018*
Appeals *still pending at the beginning of the new year*	362	525	801	614	742
New appeals	874	1,303	1,389	1,682	1,303
Total number of appeals	1,236	1,828	2,190	2,296	2,045
Appeals *settled within the year*	781	1,305	1,457	1,511	1,376
– by judgment on the merits	410	563	558	550	508

386. The data for 2018 are based on Bundesministerium für Arbeit und Soziales (ed.), *Tätigkeit der Arbeitsgerichte 2018* (Berlin).

	1981	*1990*	*1997*	*2006*	*2018*
– by compromise reached in court	116	272	409	458	467
– otherwise	255	470	490	503	401
Duration from appeal *until settlement*					
up to 3 months	351	618	553	610	491
3–6 months	258	367	394	483	354
6–12 months	129	232	367	329	377
more than 12 months	43	88	143	89	154
Cases not yet settled at the end of the year	455	523	733	785	671

699. Survey on the activities of the Federal Labour Court in so-called *Beschluss* procedures:

	1981	*1990*	*1997*	*2006*	*2018*
Appeals still pending *at the beginning of the new year*	165	92	61	66	94
New appeals	77	85	68	86	46
Total number of appeals	242	177	129	152	140
Appeals settled within the year	79	104	75	66	77

	1981	*1990*	*1997*	*2006*	*2018*
Duration *from appeal until settlement by judgment on the merits*					
up to 6 months	–	3	23	4	–
6–12 months	4	32	10	25	2
more than 12 months	52	29	9	11	47
Cases not yet settled at the end of the year	163	73	54	86	63

700. For the role of labour courts in providing speedy decisions by way of injunction in order to prevent unproportionate damages *see* paragraphs 557, 567.

§2. The Role of Other Courts

701. In matters of employee representation, labour courts are, as previously mentioned, only competent insofar as problems referring to the election procedure are subject of dispute. All other problems relating to the field of employee representation on the supervisory board are dealt with by ordinary civil courts. This is a consequence of the fact that ordinary civil courts have jurisdiction in cases of company law. As previously explained, employee representation is embedded into the traditional structure of company law and is thus understood to be an aspect of company law.

702. Ordinary civil courts, among other questions, are competent to decide disputes of rights referring to the internal structure of unions and employers' associations. Thus, for example, a dispute about the question whether or not a member can be excluded would be settled by ordinary civil courts.

703. Disputes of rights relating to staff councils in the public sector come under the jurisdiction of administrative courts. This leads to the fact that similar questions concerning the works constitution in the private sector and the staff constitution in the public sector may nevertheless be answered differently.

704. As far as the question is concerned of how far the Employment Agency may pay unemployment benefits to employees indirectly affected by industrial conflict (*see* paragraphs 510, 559–560), it is up to the competent social security courts to settle respective cases. As previously shown, these questions are closely related to the power relationship in industrial conflicts.

705. Finally, the dominant role of the Federal Constitutional Court in all areas of collective labour law should be kept in mind. It is this court, which shapes the basic structure of collective labour law by examining the compatibility of decisions of other courts as well as examining the compatibility of legislative acts with the Constitution. Insofar, the Federal Constitutional Court may be regarded more and more as a kind of superpower.

Selected Bibliography

Legislation

Kittner, M. (ed.), *Arbeits- und Sozialordnung*, 45rd edn, Bund-Verlag, Frankfurt am Main 2020.

Richardi, R. (ed.), *Arbeitsgesetze*, 96st edn, Verlag C.H. Beck dtv, Munich 2020.

Cases

Bundesarbeitsgericht (ed.), *Sammlung der Entscheidungen des Bundesarbeitsgerichts*, Verlag Recht und Wirtschaft, Heidelberg.

Hueck, A., Nipperdey, H.C. & Dietz, R. (eds), *AP – Arbeitsrechtliche Praxis, Nachschlagewerk des Bundesarbeitsgerichts*, looseleaf, Verlag C.H. Beck, Munich.

Stahlhacke, E. & Ramdohr, L. (eds.), *EzA – Entscheidungssammlung zum Arbeitsrecht*, looseleaf, Luchterhand, Neuwied-Darmstadt.

Journals

Arbeit und Recht (ArbuR), Bund-Verlag, Frankfurt am Main.

Archiv für civilistische Praxis (AcP), Verlag Mohr Siebeck, Tübingen.

Betriebs-Berater (BB), Verlag Betriebs-Berater, Frankfurt am Main.

Der Betrieb (DB), Fachverlag der Verlagsgruppe Handelsblatt GmbH, Düsseldorf.

Europäische Zeitschrift für Arbeitsrecht (EuZA), Verlag C.H. Beck, Munich.

German Law Journal, www.germanlawjournal.com.

Neue Zeitschrift für Arbeitsrecht (NZA), Verlag C.H. Beck, Munich.

Recht der Arbeit (RdA), Verlag C.H. Beck, Munich.

Zeitschrift für Arbeitsrecht (ZfA), Carl Heymanns Verlag, Cologne.

Textbooks

Brox, H., Rüthers, B. & Henssler, M., *Arbeitsrecht*, 19th edn, Kohlhammer, Stuttgart 2016.

Däubler, W., *Arbeitsrecht*, 12th edn, Bund-Verlag, Frankfurt am Main 2017.

Dütz, W. & Thüsing, G., *Arbeitsrecht*, 24th edn, Verlag C.H. Beck, Munich 2019.

Hromadka, W. & Maschmann, F., *Arbeitsrecht*, 7th edn, 2018, *Individualarbeitsrecht*, 7rd edn, 2018; vol. 2, *Kollektivarbeitsrecht und Arbeitsrechtsstreitigkeiten*, 7th edn, Springer-Verlag, Berlin, 2017.

Junker, A., *Grundkurs Arbeitsrecht*, 18th edn, Verlag C.H. Beck, Munich, 2019.

Kokemoor, A., *Sozialrecht*, 9th edn, Vahlen, Munich 2020.

Krause, R., *Arbeitsrecht*, 4th edn, Nomos, Baden-Baden, 2020.

Selected Bibliography

Muckel, M., Ogorek, M. & Rixen, S., *Sozialrecht*, 5th edn, Verlag C.H. Beck, Munich, 2019.

Preis, U. & Temming, F., *Arbeitsrecht, Praxislehrbuch zum Individualarbeitsrecht*, 6nd edn, O. Schmidt-Verlag, Cologne, 2019.

Steinmeyer, H.-D., *Casebook Arbeitsrecht*, 2nd edn, Verlag C.H. Beck, Munich, 2000.

Waltermann, R., *Sozialrecht*, 13th edn, Verlag C.F. Müller, Heidelberg 2018.

Zöllner, W., Loritz, K.-G. & Hergenröder, C., *Arbeitsrecht*, 7th edn, Verlag C.H. Beck, Munich, 2015.

General Books for Introduction

Däubler, W., Hjort, J.-P., Schubert, M. & Wolmerath, M., *Arbeitsrecht*, Handkommentar, 4th edn, Nomos, Baden-Baden 2017.

Deinert, O., Heuschmid, J. & Zwanziger, B., *Handbuch Arbeitsrecht*, 10th edn, Bund-Verlag, Frankfurt am Main 2019.

Erfurter Kommentar zum Arbeitsrecht, ed. Müller-Glöge, R., Preis, U. & Schmidt, I., 20th edn, Verlag C.H. Beck, Munich 2020.

Münchener Handbuch zum Arbeitsrecht, ed. Richardi, R. & Wlotzke, O., vol. 1, *Individualarbeitsrecht I*, 4th edn, 2018; vol. 2, *Individualarbeitsrecht II*, 4th edn, 2018; vol. 3, *Kollektives Arbeitsrecht I*, 4th edn, 2019; vol. 4, *Kollektives Arbeitsrecht II*, 4th edn, 2019, Verlag C.H. Beck, Munich.

Schaub, G., *Arbeitsrechts-Handbuch*, 18th edn, Verlag C.H. Beck, Munich, 2019.

Weiss, M., *Collective Labour Law in Germany*, in Tomaszewskeiej, M. & Stelina, J. (ed.), Zbiorowe Prawo Pracy W XXI Wieku, Gdansk 2010, 332 et seq.

Weiss, M., *Labor Law*, in Zekoll, J. & Wagner, G. (eds), Introduction to German Law, 3rd ed., Wolters Kluwer 2019, 375 et seq.

Weiss, M., *Labour Law Reforms in Germany*, in Davulis T. (ed.), Labour Law Reforms in Eastern and Western Europe, Peter Lang, 2017, 83 et seq.

Weiss, M., *Selected Problems in Development of Labour Law in Germany in the 21st Century*, in Barancová, H. (ed.), Pracovné Právo 21. Storica, Plzen 2009, 79 et seq.

Weiss, M., *The Development of Industrial Relations from the Perspective of Labour Law*, in Artus I., et al. (eds), Developments in German Industrial Relations, Cambridge 2016, 221 et seq.

Weiss, M., *The Sources of German Labour Law*, in Gyulavári, T. & Menegatti, E. (ed.), The Sources of Labour Law, Kluwer 2020, 229 et seq.

Information Available on the World Wide Web

Federal Constitutional Court: www.bundesverfassungsgericht.de.
Federal Labour Court: www.bundesarbeitsgericht.de.
Federal Ministry of Labour and Social Affairs: www.bmas.de.
Federal Parliament: www.bundestag.de.
Federal Statistical Office: www.destatis.de.
German Confederation of Employers' Associations: www.arbeitgeber.de.
German Federation of Trade Unions: www.dgb.de.
Institute for Employment Research: www.iab.de.

Index

The numbers here refer to paragraph numbers.

Index

www.ingramcontent.com/pod-product-compliance
Lightning Source LLC
Chambersburg PA
CBHW071429230926
51846CB00001B/167
9789403524603